Praise for Cooking with Kids For Dummies:

"Cooking for millions of television viewers is a breeze compared to cooking for my two six-year-olds at home. I am thrilled that Kate Heyhoe has written a book just for me. *Cooking with Kids For Dummies* is more than a book filled with fun recipes. It offers nutritional tips and cooking techniques that are designed especially for those of us who have little ones around the kitchen. The family that cooks together stays together and with this book, we can do it with so much fun."
— Martin Yan, TV Host of *Yan Can Cook*

"Now let's face it squarely — I'm sitting here very close to my 65th birthday, having just helped my four-year-old granddaughter, Jessica, make stuffed eggs (stuffed eggs would not have been my first choice, but it was Christmas!). She did all of the measuring and squeezed the piping bag — not bad either! What fun it is to cook with a new generation and what a joy now to have a brilliant new book like this to use to be ultimately creative and to pass on a passion for life and its healthy pleasures to a child!"
— Graham Kerr, International Culinary Consultant

"Gathered from Kate Heyhoe's pioneering food sites on America Online and the Web, *Cooking with Kids For Dummies* reflects the voices of real parents and kids. This book contains more than recipes and cooking tips — it shows how to turn the simple acts of cooking, shopping, and dining together into household keywords for family togetherness."
— Steve Case, Chairman and CEO, America Online, Inc.

"Seize the moment — and a copy of this delightful cooking guide — and call the children to the kitchen to experience the joy of an often-neglected pleasure of family life — cooking food together."
— Marcel Desaulniers, Author of *Death by Chocolate Cookies* and *An Alphabet of Sweets*

" Kate Heyhoe is definitely no dummy when it comes to helping kids cook together. Read her book, grab your kid, and head for the kitchen — it's a smart move."
— Lora Brody, Author of *Kitchen Survival Guide*

"It is important to make cooking a part of kids' lives so that they can develop skills and an appreciation for good food. *Cooking with Kids For Dummies* brings kids into the kitchen and teaches them with not only great-tasting recipes, but cooking fundamentals such as how to hold a knife, measure ingredients, set a table, and survive in a supermarket. With families' busy schedules, this book is a wonderful sourcebook for family interaction."
— Emily Luchetti, President of Women Chefs and Restaurateurs and Executive Pastry Chef at Farallon restaurant, San Francisco

"Wow! Finally, someone with the insight to begin at the beginning with cooking! What better way to bring out the chef in a child than with the sights and sounds of the kitchen: whips in the bowl, blenders buzzing, and hands in the dough. A child side-by-side in the kitchen with his parent is a scrumptious combination. *Cooking with Kids For Dummies* is the perfect ingredient to convert master mess-makers to master chefs."
> — Chef John D. Folse, CEC, AAC, past President of the American Culinary Federation

""Like millions of moms, I want to prepare delicious, nutritious meals for my family, and after working all day in the restaurant, I also want to spend quality time with my sons. Cooking together is the natural solution. But in the kitchen, you need the proper tools to do the job well. *Cooking with Kids For Dummies* is just the tool to get you started."
> — Mary Sue Milliken, Co-host of Food Network's *Two Hot Tamales,* Co-owner of Border Grill (Santa Monica) and Ciudad (Los Angeles), Cookbook Author, TV Cooking Show Host

"If you don't have kids, you'll want to run and borrow some! The whole family will benefit when kids get involved in Kate Heyhoe's *Cooking with Kids For Dummies*, a course that includes nutritious food choices, food safety, meal planning, and enjoying meals together. Be prepared to have the fun of your life."
> — Robin Kline, MS, RD, CCP, President of the International Association of Culinary Professionals

"*Cooking with Kids For Dummies* is the kitchen cheerleader that all parents need! If you've ever wondered how to start your kids cooking safely and happily, here's the ticket. The recipes are hip and fun, and the tips alone are worth the price of admission."
> — Barbara Tropp, Author of *The Modern Art of Chinese Cooking* and *China Moon Cookbook,* Founder of Women Chefs and Restaurateurs

"Kate Heyhoe has written a book of brilliant recipes to cook with your kids, and also provides a veritable encyclopedia of kitchen lore to impart to novice cooks so that they will develop into thoughtful, tasteful, and above-all, safe cooks."
> — Nick Malgieri, Author of *How to Bake* and *Chocolate*

Cooking with Kids For Dummies creates fun and food for the family. Kate Heyhoe gives simple, practical tips on how to bring the family together for meal time magic."
> — Linda Gassenheimer, Award-Winning Author of *Dinner in Minutes — Memorable Meals for Busy Cooks* and *Vegetarian Dinner in Minutes,* and the syndicated column *Dinner in Minutes*

"In *Cooking with Kids For Dummies*, Kate Heyhoe takes your hand and leads you through the kitchen on a most delightful tour. The book is packed with easy-to-understand guidance and simple, tasty recipes that will delight kids of any age — that includes every inner child who never learned the secrets of the kitchen. It's a terrific resource for cooks of all ages."
> — Michele Anna Jordan, Author of *California Home Cooking*

 ™

References for the Rest of Us!™

BESTSELLING BOOK SERIES

Do you find that traditional reference books are overloaded with technical details and advice you'll never use? Do you postpone important life decisions because you just don't want to deal with them? Then our *...For Dummies®* business and general reference book series is for you.

...For Dummies business and general reference books are written for those frustrated and hard-working souls who know they aren't dumb, but find that the myriad of personal and business issues and the accompanying horror stories make them feel helpless. *...For Dummies* books use a lighthearted approach, a down-to-earth style, and even cartoons and humorous icons to dispel fears and build confidence. Lighthearted but not lightweight, these books are perfect survival guides to solve your everyday personal and business problems.

> *"More than a publishing phenomenon, 'Dummies' is a sign of the times."*
>
> — *The New York Times*

> *"...you won't go wrong buying them."*
>
> — *Walter Mossberg, Wall Street Journal, on IDG Books' ...For Dummies books*

> *"A world of detailed and authoritative information is packed into them..."*
>
> — *U.S. News and World Report*

Already, millions of satisfied readers agree. They have made *...For Dummies* the #1 introductory level computer book series and a best-selling business book series. They have written asking for more. So, if you're looking for the best and easiest way to learn about business and other general reference topics, look to *...For Dummies* to give you a helping hand.

IDG BOOKS WORLDWIDE

1/99

COOKING WITH KIDS FOR DUMMIES®

by Kate Heyhoe

Foreword by Mollie Katzen

IDG Books Worldwide, Inc.
An International Data Group Company

Foster City, CA ♦ Chicago, IL ♦ Indianapolis, IN ♦ New York, NY

Cooking with Kids For Dummies®

Published by
IDG Books Worldwide, Inc.
An International Data Group Company
919 E. Hillsdale Blvd.
Suite 400
Foster City, CA 94404
www.idgbooks.com (IDG Books Worldwide Web site)
www.dummies.com (Dummies Press Web site)

Library of Congress Catalog Card No.: 99-61120

ISBN: 0-7645-5097-7

Printed in the United States of America

10 9 8 7 6 5 4 3 2

1B/RV/QT/ZZ/IN

Distributed in the United States by IDG Books Worldwide, Inc.

Distributed by CDG Books Canada Inc. for Canada; by Transworld Publishers Limited in the United Kingdom; by IDG Norge Books for Norway; by IDG Sweden Books for Sweden; by Woodslane Pty. Ltd. for Australia; by Woodslane (NZ) Ltd. for New Zealand; by TransQuest Publishers Pte Ltd. for Singapore, Malaysia, Thailand, Indonesia, and Hong Kong; by ICG Muse, Inc. for Japan; by Norma Comunicaciones S.A. for Colombia; by Intersoft for South Africa; by Le Monde en Tique for France; by International Thomson Publishing for Germany, Austria and Switzerland; by Distribuidora Cuspide for Argentina; by Livraria Cultura for Brazil; by Ediciones ZETA S.C.R. Ltda. for Peru; by WS Computer Publishing Corporation, Inc., for the Philippines; by Contemporanea de Ediciones for Venezuela; by Express Computer Distributors for the Caribbean and West Indies; by Micronesia Media Distributor, Inc. for Micronesia; by Grupo Editorial Norma S.A. for Guatemala; by Chips Computadoras S.A. de C.V. for Mexico; by Editorial Norma de Panama S.A. for Panama; by American Bookshops for Finland. Authorized Sales Agent: Anthony Rudkin Associates for the Middle East and North Africa.

For general information on IDG Books Worldwide's books in the U.S., please call our Consumer Customer Service department at 800-762-2974. For reseller information, including discounts and premium sales, please call our Reseller Customer Service department at 800-434-3422.

For information on where to purchase IDG Books Worldwide's books outside the U.S., please contact our International Sales department at 317-596-5530 or fax 317-596-5692.

For consumer information on foreign language translations, please contact our Customer Service department at 1-800-434-3422, fax 317-596-5692, or e-mail rights@idgbooks.com.

For information on licensing foreign or domestic rights, please phone +1-650-655-3109.

For sales inquiries and special prices for bulk quantities, please contact our Sales department at 650-655-3200 or write to the address above.

For information on using IDG Books Worldwide's books in the classroom or for ordering examination copies, please contact our Educational Sales department at 800-434-2086 or fax 317-596-5499.

For press review copies, author interviews, or other publicity information, please contact our Public Relations department at 650-655-3000 or fax 650-655-3299.

For authorization to photocopy items for corporate, personal, or educational use, please contact Copyright Clearance Center, 222 Rosewood Drive, Danvers, MA 01923, or fax 978-750-4470.

About the Author

Known as "the Global Gourmet," Executive Editor **Kate Heyhoe** set high standards for food Web sites in 1994 by launching the very first food and cooking magazine online. The award-winning electronic Gourmet Guide (eGG) was voted the Number 1 food Web site by *USA Today,* and was consistently ranked among the top sites by television's Food Network (TVFN), *New York Times, Wall Street Journal,* and others. The eGG has since evolved into the even more popular Global Gourmet® Web site, where Kate continues as Executive Editor with her partner and publisher Thomas Way. Their company also produces two food sites on America Online, and has created a companion Web site to this book,  called Cooking with Kids. Traveling frequently as an industry consultant and lecturer, she is recognized within the cooking community as a culinary pioneer and by her readers as a warm, personable kitchen coach — their Global Gourmet who "brings you the world on a plate."

Kate Heyhoe's online sites include:

- ✔ Global Gourmet® (www.globalgourmet.com)
- ✔ Cooking with Kids (www.cookingwithkids.com)
- ✔ America Online editions of the eGG and Global Gourmet at keywords **eGG** and **GG**.

Dedication

To the Momster . . . Mama-Rama, Mother of All Mothers, Mamacita, Big Mama, Mommy Dearest . . . Mama Mia! Thanks for showing me how much good taste matters — in every part of life.

The author and her mother — in one of their more serious moments.

ABOUT IDG BOOKS WORLDWIDE

Welcome to the world of IDG Books Worldwide.

IDG Books Worldwide, Inc., is a subsidiary of International Data Group, the world's largest publisher of computer-related information and the leading global provider of information services on information technology. IDG was founded more than 30 years ago by Patrick J. McGovern and now employs more than 9,000 people worldwide. IDG publishes more than 290 computer publications in over 75 countries. More than 90 million people read one or more IDG publications each month.

Launched in 1990, IDG Books Worldwide is today the #1 publisher of best-selling computer books in the United States. We are proud to have received eight awards from the Computer Press Association in recognition of editorial excellence and three from Computer Currents' First Annual Readers' Choice Awards. Our best-selling ...*For Dummies*® series has more than 50 million copies in print with translations in 31 languages. IDG Books Worldwide, through a joint venture with IDG's Hi-Tech Beijing, became the first U.S. publisher to publish a computer book in the People's Republic of China. In record time, IDG Books Worldwide has become the first choice for millions of readers around the world who want to learn how to better manage their businesses.

Our mission is simple: Every one of our books is designed to bring extra value and skill-building instructions to the reader. Our books are written by experts who understand and care about our readers. The knowledge base of our editorial staff comes from years of experience in publishing, education, and journalism — experience we use to produce books to carry us into the new millennium. In short, we care about books, so we attract the best people. We devote special attention to details such as audience, interior design, use of icons, and illustrations. And because we use an efficient process of authoring, editing, and desktop publishing our books electronically, we can spend more time ensuring superior content and less time on the technicalities of making books.

You can count on our commitment to deliver high-quality books at competitive prices on topics you want to read about. At IDG Books Worldwide, we continue in the IDG tradition of delivering quality for more than 30 years. You'll find no better book on a subject than one from IDG Books Worldwide.

John Kilcullen
Chairman and CEO
IDG Books Worldwide, Inc.

Steven Berkowitz
President and Publisher
IDG Books Worldwide, Inc.

**Eighth Annual
Computer Press
Awards ≥1992**

**Ninth Annual
Computer Press
Awards ≥1993**

**Tenth Annual
Computer Press
Awards ≥1994**

**Eleventh Annual
Computer Press
Awards ≥1995**

IDG is the world's leading IT media, research and exposition company. Founded in 1964, IDG had 1997 revenues of $2.05 billion and has more than 9,000 employees worldwide. IDG offers the widest range of media options that reach IT buyers in 75 countries representing 95% of worldwide IT spending. IDG's diverse product and services portfolio spans six key areas including print publishing, online publishing, expositions and conferences, market research, education and training, and global marketing services. More than 90 million people read one or more of IDG's 290 magazines and newspapers, including IDG's leading global brands — Computerworld, PC World, Network World, Macworld and the Channel World family of publications. IDG Books Worldwide is one of the fastest-growing computer book publishers in the world, with more than 700 titles in 36 languages. The "...For Dummies®" series alone has more than 50 million copies in print. IDG offers online users the largest network of technology-specific Web sites around the world through IDG.net (http://www.idg.net), which comprises more than 225 targeted Web sites in 55 countries worldwide. International Data Corporation (IDC) is the world's largest provider of information technology data, analysis and consulting, with research centers in over 41 countries and more than 400 research analysts worldwide. IDG World Expo is a leading producer of more than 168 globally branded conferences and expositions in 35 countries including E3 (Electronic Entertainment Expo), Macworld Expo, ComNet, Windows World Expo, ICE (Internet Commerce Expo), Agenda, DEMO, and Spotlight. IDG's training subsidiary, ExecuTrain, is the world's largest computer training company, with more than 230 locations worldwide and 785 training courses. IDG Marketing Services helps industry-leading IT companies build international brand recognition by developing global integrated marketing programs via IDG's print, online and exposition products worldwide. Further information about the company can be found at www.idg.com.   1/24/99

Acknowledgments

I have been graced by many talented people in creating this book:

I fell head-over-heels in love with all the families who volunteered their wisdom, advice, and humor: Your stories touched me deeply. I wish I could have shared all of them here. Yours was the broth that held this stew together.

To the poster families, thanks for your words and snapshots: Your richly detailed slices of life added just the right amount of body to the pot. You gave our readers something to chew on!

To my Project Editor, Tere Drenth, who skimmed the fat and garnished with glee. Thanks for having an open mind and for correcting the seasonings — your diligence made this a far better book.

To Sarah Kennedy, who did the literary shopping, relentlessly bringing this project to life at IDG. Your hand was always in the pot. I hope it suits your tastes, wherever you are.

My appreciation to Kathy Welton, Holly McGuire, Kathie Schutte, Liz Kurtzman, and everyone at IDG Books Worldwide who helped serve up this grand bouillabaisse. To Jane Kirby for her sound nutritional and other advice, and to the recipe testers for their unflagging honesty. Too many cooks may spoil the broth, but it takes a mix of many fish to flavor the stew.

I'm grateful for having such a well-balanced family in my mom, Hank, De, and Sarah — how did *that* ever happen? I love you good.

A special word to all the staff at the electronic Gourmet Guide, Inc., and the Global Gourmet: Thanks for keeping us cooking with gas — and for stirring the pot every now and then. You're the best!

Thanks to my agent, Deborah Krasner, for persevering and to Lisa Ekus, whose support never waivers. Onward!

Big hugs and thanks to the generous and gifted Mollie Katzen, my mentor and leader — a true multi-media artist who seasons with love and cooks with passion.

Finally, I award medals of honor, patience, and action above and beyond the call of duty to Thomas Way. Thanks for eating, and eating, and eating, and eating . . . and *not* making funny faces. You give me nourishment and encouragement every second of every day.

Publisher's Acknowledgments

We're proud of this book; please register your comments through our IDG Books Worldwide Online Registration Form located at http://my2cents.dummies.com.

Some of the people who helped bring this book to market include the following:

Acquisitions and Editorial

Project Editor: Tere Drenth

Acquisitions Editor: Holly McGuire

General Reviewer: Jane Kirby,
Kirby & O'Brien Company

Recipe Tester: Cara Feeney Drenth

Associate Permissions Editor:
Carmen Krikorian

Editorial Manager: Mary C. Corder

Editorial Coordinator: Maureen Kelly

Illustrator: Elizabeth Kurtzman

Production

Project Coordinator: Regina Snyder

Layout and Graphics: Angela F. Hunckler,
Brent Savage, Kathie Schutte, Kate Snell

Proofreaders: Christine Pingleton,
Kelli Botta, Jennifer Mahern, Nancy Price,
Rebecca Senninger, Ethel M. Winslow

Indexer: Mary Mortensen

Special Help

Sarah Kennedy, Jonathan Malysiak,
Suzanne Thomas, Alison Walthal

General and Administrative

IDG Books Worldwide, Inc.: John Kilcullen, CEO; Steven Berkowitz, President and Publisher

IDG Books Technology Publishing: Brenda McLaughlin, Senior Vice President and Group Publisher

Dummies Technology Press and Dummies Editorial: Diane Graves Steele, Vice President and Associate Publisher; Mary Bednarek, Director of Acquisitions and Product Development; Kristin A. Cocks, Editorial Director

Dummies Trade Press: Kathleen A. Welton, Vice President and Publisher; Kevin Thornton, Acquisitions Manager

IDG Books Production for Dummies Press: Michael R. Britton, Vice President of Production and Creative Services; Cindy L. Phipps, Manager of Project Coordination, Production Proofreading, and Indexing; Kathie S. Schutte, Supervisor of Page Layout; Shelley Lea, Supervisor of Graphics and Design; Debbie J. Gates, Production Systems Specialist; Robert Springer, Supervisor of Proofreading; Debbie Stailey, Special Projects Coordinator; Tony Augsburger, Supervisor of Reprints and Bluelines

Dummies Packaging and Book Design: Patty Page, Manager, Promotions Marketing

♦

The publisher would like to give special thanks to Patrick J. McGovern,
without whom this book would not have been possible.

♦

Contents at a Glance

Cartoons at a Glance

By Rich Tennant

page 39

"I really wish you wouldn't wear that thing when you chop vegetables."

page 109

"Jane finally teach Boy how to cook. Before that, him just eat cheetah. Too much fast food not good."

page 7

page 351

"Don't blame us! The recipe clearly states, 'Add 4 tablespoons of sugar.'"

page 215

Fax: 978-546-7747 • E-mail: the5wave@tiac.net

Recipes at a Glance

Table of Contents

· ·

Foreword

*C*ooking with kids?

You mean spaghetti wars, right? Pancake batter wallpaper? Jello races? What do you think I am, a glutton for punishment?

I used to think this way, if I thought of cooking with kids at all. That was back when my son, who is now a teenager, was about three, and his preschool teacher introduced a cooking curriculum for the kids in the classroom. I was fascinated to learn that such young children could be so interested in cooking from the point of view of food itself and of *process* — and that the motivation for the kids was *NOT* merely to redecorate the room in the High Tomato Sauce motif.

With forays into homemade applesauce, blueberry pancakes, and pesto from basil that they grew themselves, the children in the class were developing a bona fide passion for food and cooking. When I started coming to the classroom to watch, and later to help teach the cooking, I learned that not only were the little angels totally focused and serious about what they were cooking, they also wanted very much to be as neat as possible and to like what they made. They were thrilled that the results of their efforts were "for real" and beamed with pride every time an adult took a taste of their creations.

In time, the kids began taking the recipes home to cook with their families. The enthusiasm was palpable — and contagious. Parents were as excited about the French toast as the kids were, but I think what they were *really* excited about was the opportunity to share the effort, and ultimately to create something of use and delight — together. I started cooking at home with my kids, too, and found that all those clichés about the bonding value of shared time at the dinner table were true for the cooking experience as well.

Yet, for a lot of us, it takes more than good intentions to find the courage to really cook with our kids at home. Beyond inspiration, we need instructions and guidelines to ensure that our adventures will be happy, fun, and productive. Here's where Kate Heyhoe steps in with this great book! In *Cooking with Kids For Dummies,* she is your exuberant, knowledgeable coach (not unlike a personal trainer, only less expensive and possibly even more energetic!). She'll take you by the hand, walk you through all the many particulars you need to get started, and help you keep the cooking experience on a positive track. And thanks for Kate's can-do attitude and good cheer, you'll be jolly and inspired all along the way.

This book does it all: It shows you how to shop with your kids, involve them in planning meals and getting adequate nutrition, set up a kid-friendly kitchen, and find ways to dine together. Even if you've never cooked before, the step-by-step cooking tutorial — designed for you and your kids — will make cooking a breeze. With dozens of recipes that are perfect for young chefs, you can't go wrong. Put yourself into Kate's experienced hands, and you'll become a superparent — in the kitchen with your kids — in no time flat.

I love this book, and believe me, I'm going to use it!

> — Mollie Katzen, Author of *Moosewood Cookbook*, the award-winning *Pretend Soup,* and the new children's cookbook, *Honest Pretzels.*

Introduction

• •

*G*reetings! I wrote this book for both you and your children — my goal is to get you side-by-side, into the kitchen and dining room, enjoying delicious and nutritious meals, snacks, and even sweet-to-eat treats that the whole family can pitch in and make together.

Sound challenging? It doesn't have to be. This book can help even the busiest parents find stress-free methods for bringing their kids into the kitchen regularly, jumping beyond the occasional rainy-day "let's make cookies" sessions. And because every family is different, this book is packed with a wide range of techniques, some of which are sure to work for your special brood.

In fact, many of the tips in this book come directly from several hundred families — families that may have some similarities to your own. These families discovered that by bringing their kids into the daily activities of cooking, dining, and shopping together, they actually improved their quality of life and became closer.

Busy parents, however, tell me that they face three very stubborn challenges:

- Fixing meals that are nutritious
- Creating time-saving meals
- Spending quality time with their kids

The good news is that families have come up with innovative ways to conquer these challenges — you can find many of these ideas in the pages ahead.

I adore the families that contributed to this book! They're warm, cuddly, happy, creative — and very, very real. Some of them I've known for years as part of my talented Web site staff at the Global Gourmet and at the electronic Gourmet Guide (eGG), the first food and cooking magazine ever created on the Internet. But many of the parents and children who contributed to this book are readers like yourselves. They've sent me e-mails over the course of two years, eagerly sharing their experiences, and looking for better ways to feed and spend time with their own loved ones.

About This Book

You may not realize it, but you're actually holding four books in one — what a bargain!

One book is for kids and kitchen novices (including some parents!) who want to walk through the basics in a cooking tutorial. Then, when you're ready to eat, children and parents can jump into cooking with a cookbook full of recipes to please the whole family — but the easy-to-follow instructions are specially written with kids in mind. In another book, parents can discover tried-and-true techniques for modern-day family management, including meal planning, shopping, and nutrition guides. And the final book is a collection of five poster families — everyone can enjoy meeting some of the contributing kids, moms, and dads in family profiles and photographs.

Conventions Used in This Book

While using this book, keep these few points in mind:

- Temperatures in these recipes are always based on the Fahrenheit scale. So, you can assume that when a recipe calls for an oven temperature of 350°, it means 350 degrees Fahrenheit, or 350°F.

- Preparation and cooking times at the beginning of each recipe are based on a single adult making the recipe. If kids are joining in, the recipe may take more or less time to make.

- If you're unfamiliar with a term or ingredient, flip to the cooking tutorial in Part III. You may also want to look it up in any basic cookbook or at the companion Web site to this book, www.cookingwithkids.com.

- The many contributors to this book e-mailed me from all over the world, but to respect their privacy, I've included only their first names and the towns where they live.

- Whenever a tip or message comes from one of the contributing families, you know it because it's either set off in quotes or comes with a "Good Advice icon" (browse ahead to the "Icons Used in This Book" section).

For more explanation of the conventions used in this book's recipes, read Chapter 16 before you begin cooking.

Foolish Assumptions

In creating recipes that kids can follow, I've had to give up a lot of assumptions that I normally make when writing for adults. However, try to keep these points in mind when cooking from this book:

✔ The recipes are broken into more steps than in most cookbooks — but that doesn't mean they take longer to make or are more complicated. On the contrary, I've tried to make the recipes simpler for kids to follow, by separating each action into its own step.

✔ Don't leave kids unattended in the kitchen. Always be there to supervise your children when they're cooking! The kitchen can be a dangerous place and your child's well-being comes first. Every recipe in this book assumes that you as a parent are right there next to your child, watching out for potential mishaps and coaching him or her along the way.

✔ Never assume that children know how to handle a knife or know when something is "safe" or "not safe." Chapter 8 covers the essential safety ground-rules — parents and kids should review these together.

✔ Never assume that because you've told your child something once, he or she remembers it. Sounds simple, but it helps to repeatedly remind kids of safety measures and other cooking tips.

✔ Follow your own common sense — you must decide what skills your kid is ready for. Even though general guidelines are outlined in this book, every child is different and your role as a parent is to set up guidelines that work specifically for your special child.

How This Book Is Organized

This book is organized into parts for parents, and parts for parents and kids.

The kid-friendly parts include the cooking tutorial (Part III) and the recipes (Part IV). The parts for parents have information of value to kids as well, but they're written in the hopes that parents will profit from these lessons and then pass them on to their kids in their own words and deeds. Parents can use their parts as family management guides, and for explaining nutrition, shopping, and meal planning to their children.

Part I: Cooking Together: The Wisdom of 400 Families

In this part, families explain the benefits of bringing kids into the kitchen, the value of family dining, and their tips for cooking together every day. Parents and children may enjoy looking at the pictures of other kids, moms, and dads who like to cook.

Part II: Putting the Meal Together — Together!

Cooking starts with meal planning and shopping. This part offers strategies for busy parents to put nutritious and tasty meals on the table, simultaneously involving their kids in quality time — without resorting to fast food, frozen dinners, or restaurant takeout. This part gives you creative tools and techniques for making yours a kid-friendly kitchen.

Part III: Cooking 101: A Handbook for Parents and Young Chefs

Kids and parents should read this section together. It contains all of the basics that a person needs to know before starting to cook, such as staying safe in the kitchen, chopping and knife skills, reading a recipe, measuring ingredients, cooking with all sorts of methods, operating small appliances, and setting the table.

Part IV: Recipes for the Whole Family

Hope you're hungry — this part is full of good things to eat! Kids get to start cooking in this part, with their parents' help and supervision, of course. Make these meals side-by-side, sharing in the tasks and the fun. Every child, from preschoolers to teens, can find ways to join in. The whole family will enjoy eating these dishes, which include breakfasts on the run, lunches on the go, holiday desserts, and a wide variety of both meaty and meatless dinners.

Part V: The Part of Tens

With so many recipes to choose from, it's hard to tell where to begin, so check out this part's chapters — they list the favorite recipes of teens, yummy snacks for preteens, and even recipes for preschoolers to make without using flame or fire. This part also lists the essential tools for your kid's own cookware kit.

Icons Used in This Book

I've put together several icons to alert you to the best ideas from parents, and to point out things that are particularly useful or creative:

When a golden opportunity for parents and kids to cook together comes along, you see this icon. It may highlight a kid-friendly recipe or a task that kids can do. As a parent, you still need to decide if your kid really is old enough or advanced enough to do this particular task. If not, you can include your child by performing the task yourself and explaining what you're doing. Sometimes, I don't expect a more advanced action to be a kid task and I don't include an icon, but if your kids are able to do it safely with your supervision, then by all means, let them!

This icon shows up whenever I suggest something that makes your life easier, saves money, or is just extra-handy.

This icon points out hot tips from real families, spoken in their own words. Hundreds of families share their experiences and advice. These tips may or may not work for your family, but at least you can see what approach others are taking, and may find something valuable for yourself and your own kids.

This icon pops up for tips that save time in the kitchen, at the store, or when cleaning up.

When you see this icon, you find a learning opportunity, just waiting for you to take advantage of it. It can be a quick math lesson, a chemical reaction, or a cultural tidbit. Kitchen discoveries make cooking fun! This icon also highlights opportunities to involve the entire family in something that's fun, educational, or interesting.

Attention! Look out! Be aware! This is a safety tip that means some part of the recipe or cooking process requires special attention or special handling. Be alert and cautious when you see this icon and make sure that a parent performs the task or is supervising very closely when a child is cooking.

A special note on emoticons: Internet e-mail has its own set of icons used to express emotions, known as *emoticons*. The e-mailed tips and letters from the contributing families often contain emoticons, which make more sense if you look at them by tilting your head to the left. There are dozens of emoticons in Internet parley, but here are the ones commonly found in this book:

- ✔ :)   Happy face
- ✔ ;)   Winking face
- ✔ :(Sad face
- ✔ <grin> Grin or laughing

Where to Go from Here

As the Cheshire Cat may say to Alice, deciding where to go from here depends on who you are and where you want to get to.

If you're eager to start cooking with your kids right now, speed to the back of the book and into The Part of Tens (Part V). It contains a list of the most popular recipes, organized by kids' age groups.

Older kids with some experience in cooking may feel comfortable jumping straight into the recipes in Part IV. Kitchen novices may be more comfortable starting with some basic training, which you can find in Part III.

Parents can find inspiration in Part I, where other parents offer personal advice for bringing kids into the kitchen. Or, if you're more concerned about how to plan nutritious meals and cook efficiently, flip directly to Part II, which also reveals sane ways to shop with kids — and even make it a pleasurable and profitable experience!

As you browse through this book and begin cooking together, I invite you to share your own experiences at my newest Web site: cookingwithkids. com. As a companion Web site to this book, cookingwithkids.com is jam-packed with all of the recipes, tips, and advice that I couldn't include in this book — there just wasn't enough room! Also, for additional cooking resources, check out the Appendix at the back of this book — after your kids get hooked on cooking, they'll want to explore a whole world of other recipes and foods all on their own.

Part I
Cooking Together: The Wisdom of 400 Families

The 5th Wave   By Rich Tennant

"Jane finally teach Boy how to cook.
Before that, him just eat cheetah.
Too much fast food not good."

In this part . . .

Today's families need help. Eating well is a balancing act. Time is always in short supply. Weeknight recipes can get boring, and parents yearn to serve their kids tasty, nutritious food — not fatty, artery-clogging junk (even if it is temptingly quick). Then, you have another complication: How can you put a healthy, home-cooked meal on the table and still devote the time and attention to your kids that they deserve?

Through my own experiences and with contributions from over 400 families, this part offers real-life, practical tips for quick, healthy eating in a work-a-day world. You won't find complicated recipes for Beef Wellington or Baked Alaska, but you also won't have to rely on instant Ramen noodles or canned mushroom soup meals. Starting with the chapters in this part, you discover how your family can successfully improve your lifestyle and eating habits by bringing kids into the kitchen.

Chapter 1

The Challenges of Today's Busy Families

In This Chapter

▶ Cooking together for daily pleasure

▶ Discovering the benefits of cooking with kids

What does the richest person in the world make for dinner every night?
Reservations.

Kids have a natural attraction to cooking — starting with their first mud pie in the backyard — so coaching them in cooking, meal planning, and sound nutrition isn't as difficult as you may expect. You helped your kids with the first basics of life, such as potty training, crossing the street, and tying their shoes. Inviting them into the kitchen trains them in skills that are equally as important.

Cooking with kids doesn't have to be limited to cookies and holiday treats. In this chapter, parents offer tips and techniques for involving kids in the daily routine of making complete dinners, shopping for groceries, and planning balanced meals — tasks they'll one day have to do for themselves, without your help. Follow these tips to make cooking together not just productive, but stress-free, tasty, and fun — even for busy parents like you!

Why Cook with Your Kids?

Children love to create things — mud pies, sand castles, and crayoned drawings of unrecognizable images that you proudly mount on your refrigerator.

Kids also have a natural curiosity about cooking. Many kids, just like grown-ups, even enjoy watching cooking shows on television. While some children may not seem to care about cooking at all, in many cases they just need a nudge of encouragement or a helping hand to walk them through the basics.

Making cookies on an occasional Saturday afternoon can be a treat, but when kids cook with their families on a regular basis, wonderful things start to happen. Parents can see the following lifelong benefits for their children:

✔ Bonding with siblings and parents, sharing affection, and communicating with one another

✔ Practicing teamwork and taskwork

✔ Developing a sense of responsibility

✔ Experiencing other cultures and lands through foods

✔ Reinforcing family heritage and traditions

✔ Developing fundamental reading, math, and reasoning skills

✔ Increasing manual dexterity and physical coordination

✔ Improving organizational skills, like scheduling and planning

✔ Establishing sound nutritional habits

✔ Building a solid foundation of fundamental cooking skills

✔ Becoming independent of fast foods and convenience foods

✔ Experiencing the joys of giving and sharing

✔ Elevating self-esteem and taking pride in their work

✔ Creating projects with immediately tangible results and rewards

Cooking a main meal together is just a first step — eating it together makes a difference, too. In a *Reader's Digest* study, 60 percent of students who ate with their families at least four nights per week received higher test scores. In another study, students whose families regularly ate dinner together scored better on national achievement tests.

You Can Lead a Horse to Water . . .

. . . but you can't make him drink. Similarly, putting a fresh, nutritious meal on the table is hard enough, but getting kids to actually eat it is a horse of a different color. Furthermore, it seems that every day, another nutritional study contradicts one from the week before. (See Chapter 4 for more on nutritional information.)

The best ways to get kids to eat a balanced diet is to include them in every step of food preparation — from cooking the food to shopping for it and planning the meals. Here's how some parents, frustrated by nutritional information, have come to make practical sense of it. They share their own tips for getting kids — even picky eaters — to eat a balanced, tasty diet.

Family feeding habits

Families are like snowflakes or thumbprints — no two are exactly the same. Yet the cross-section of families contributing to this book reveal that many share similar challenges when trying to survive meals. Through my own personal experience and by writing this book, I've discovered that

☺ Taste, time, and nutrition are often more important than price when fixing a meal.

☺ Parents are willing to spend an average of 30 minutes during the week preparing dinner.

☺ Teenagers eat an average of five meals per day.

☺ Kids — even teenagers — say they actually enjoy dining with their families.

☺ Parents want to feed their kids healthier meals, and today's health-conscious kids often prefer healthy foods to junk foods.

☺ Students perform better when they're fed breakfast and nutritional snacks at intervals throughout the day.

☺ Not all kids are picky eaters — some actually love vegetables, fish, and even anchovies. On the other hand, some kids do go through finicky phases and will refuse almost everything.

☺ It takes about ten tastings before a picky eater accepts a new food.

✔ **Get kids involved and focused on healthy options.** "Give them choices — but choices stacked in your favor! I ask my daughter (four years old) if she wants corn or beans for dinner. My husband and I choose the main course, such as pasta, chicken, or beef, and let the kids choose the other parts. When we're shopping, I let my daughter choose what fruit she wants. I think that if she has a stake in the choosing, she'll want to eat it (at least it works most of the time)."
— Martha from Madison, Wisconsin

✔ **Enjoy all foods in moderation.** "Although we utilize some lowfat and nonfat products (like baked chips, cheeses, and breads), we try to keep fresh produce, fruits, and lean meat as the foundation of most of our meals. We try to avoid processed, convenience-type foods, but honestly, they are convenient and they do slip in occasionally. We eat less beef overall — but we really enjoy it more now whenever we have it."
— Kathleen from Nixa, Missouri

✔ **Have the kids help plan the menu.** "We make up a monthly menu plan with the kids. This helps them to understand what goes into planning a balanced diet. They know how much they need of every vitamin and essential food group each day — which is a lot more than most adults know — and are honestly thrilled to help out."
— Laura from Indio, California

✔ **Be creative with picky eaters.** "With kids, you have to try all kinds of things to find what they like and will eat. For instance, I have a picky eater. In order for her to eat any green veggies, I blend up steamed broccoli or spinach and put it into pasta sauce or spread it on home-made pizza dough, before putting on the sauce. She loves it."
— Christin from Phoenix, Arizona

Becoming a Kitchen Coach

Where do today's kids find out how to cook? When many parents were young, students were offered home economics classes that included everything from cutting up a chicken to meal planning and shopping on a budget. Today, schools have to battle just to get funding for the core curriculum, so electives like home ec are rarely offered.

The 4-H Club, scouting, and other groups include some cooking programs, and the Internet carries over 7,000 food-related Web sites. Some children prefer watching TV cooking shows to cartoons. But for the most part, if kids don't get cooking experience at home, they enter the world lacking skills as funda-mental to independent survival as reading, writing, and 'rithmetic.

Most parents tell me their own mothers, fathers, or grandparents showed them how to cook. But for other parents, their moms or dads intentionally kept them out of the kitchen, which forced them to struggle with cooking later in life.

Today, as a result of both types of experiences, these parents actively encour-age their own kids to join them in the kitchen. They also take them shopping and make a point of dining together. Here are some nuggets of wisdom on how parents can encourage their kids to cook:

✔ "Kids learn by experimenting. So, if they aren't given the opportunity to cook, they may hate cooking because they don't know how the finished product will taste. But with guidance from an experienced cook, they can love cooking. I never had a chance to cook with my mom; I learned to cook in a hurry when I moved away from home. My first dinner didn't turn out well — the rice was soggy, the meat salty — it wasn't a pleasing experience for the recipient of my dinner. The next day, I called my oldest sister and asked her to walk me through a quick dinner, and it came out perfect. I've been cooking ever since."
— Marilyn from Detroit, Michigan

✔ "I learned to cook by doing jobs with my parents in the kitchen. I'm not sure how else kids can learn, except by doing — following recipes, measuring ingredients, and making changes. By helping me in the kitchen, my kids understand portion sizes, fat content (and how to change it by using applesauce in baking and cooking sprays in pans), safe food handling and hygiene (we don't wash hands — we scrub!), finishing a job (you aren't done until the kitchen is ready to cook the next meal), and looking at the pieces of a job to do the whole job (setting the table is part of cooking, as much as chopping an onion is)."
— Amy from Springfield, Virginia

✔ "I didn't really cook anything until the third grade. I ate at a friend's house and it was her night to prepare dinner. The deal was that she had to plan a complete, well-balanced meal for under $20; cook it; and serve it. Any remainder from the $20 was hers to keep (this was 30 years ago). My job that night was to prepare the salad. Her parents gave me rave reviews and I've been hooked ever since."
— Teri from Marble Falls, Texas

✔ "I picked up the basics by pushing my way into my grandmother's kitchen. Today, my daughter is a great fan of television's Food Network, especially Chef Sarah Moulton. Many of the shows spend time introducing ideas just for kids. My daughter also likes to gather recipes from anywhere she finds them — then we do our own modifications to make them fit our tastes."
— Michele from Lexington, Kentucky

✔ "I learned to cook from my mother. Her family is from Macedonia, so the foods I made first were basically peasant foods, which continue to be my comfort foods with just a little updating. The kids in my family have been learning to cook primarily by being present in the kitchen during food preparation and also by helping in the garden. Seeing foods start from seeds, watching them grow, harvesting them, and then cooking them give the kids an appreciation for their meals and the quality of foods, as well as a science and economics lesson."
— Tina from Ponte Vedra Beach, Florida

Whether you're cooking, shopping, or dining with your kids, remember these keys to success:

✔ Keep it simple.

✔ Keep it fun.

✔ Be flexible.

One of the key staff members at the Global Gourmet, Lori Policastro, has a fierce passion for knowledge and family values. She home-schools her children, using the kitchen as an extension of her home classroom. Lori offers these wise words and practical guidelines for parents jumping into cooking with kids:

- **Talk, talk, talk.** Tell them everything you're doing and why. Teach them menu planning; thereby, proper nutrition will be incorporated.

- **Discuss nutrition.** Show children the food pyramid and how a meal should be balanced not only nutritionally, but with colors, textures, flavors, and calories.

- **Give them tasks.** Let children set the timers. Let them pour batter in the waffle iron. Let them put the bread in the toaster, butter the toast, and so on.

- **Be encouraging and proud of their efforts — big or little.** Make sure the guests or the rest of the family know how helpful your child has been, and be specific in your praise. A workman is always worthy of honor.

- **Keep an eye on them.** Never, ever leave small children alone in the kitchen when you're in the middle of cooking.

- **Give your child life skills.** Show your kids how to purchase fresh fruits and vegetables, why they should wash them, and how to store them. Also make sure they understand the proper temperatures for cooking raw meat or eggs, the rules of food safety, the dangers of salmonella, and guidelines for proper meat handling.

- **Teach more than just cooking.** You're teaching them math — averages, percents, fractions, whole numbers, graduation, sequencing, algebra, counting, subtracting, and more. You're teaching them other concepts as well — art, music, colors, order, logic, reasoning. You're teaching them how to be responsible, be counted on, be part of the team, follow orders, learn rules, clean up after themselves — and you're increasing their self-esteem.

Peace, Love, and Kitchen Harmony

Before you decide to bring your kids into the kitchen, make sure the time is right for both of you. Cooking with kids takes patience. Little hands take longer to do things; they need detailed explanations and constant reminders, and the mess — well, the early stages of cooking with kids can be slow, painful torture for the neat and tidy.

Stressed-out parents and cranky kids make poor cooking teams. If you're an eye-bulging, nerve-wrecked, emotionally-strained ogre who just spent two hours in traffic, give yourself a chance to decompress before inviting the kids into the kitchen. Likewise, a tired and hungry child (or one that's too revved up) may not want to participate in cooking — and that's okay. Ultimately, the only time that you and your kids should cook together is when you're both relaxed and able to enjoy it.

To make cooking together more relaxing, parents offer this advice:

✔ "One of the things we like is classical music when food is in prep — it seems to calm the kids down, even though they say they hate it. It does work. I've also introduced it into some of my classrooms, and (especially at lunch break) it seems to have a soothing effect on children."
— Maryann from Peabody, Massachusetts

✔ "We try to analyze the tasks before we start. Young children are very literal and need explicit instructions. Instead of saying 'You can stir it now,' try saying 'Take the metal whisk and put it in the batter in the bowl. Start to make a circle in the bowl with the whisk. This is how you stir.'"
— Jean from San Antonio, Texas

✔ "Take a little extra time. The purpose is to let your kids help, even if it gets a whole lot messier. An extra five minutes in the kitchen is a small price to pay for the self confidence and esteem that my kids get from helping me! Believe me, I have worn my share of raw eggs, milk, and flour, but I wouldn't trade those moments for the world."
— Shari from Moravia, New York

The younger the kids, the more the mess. Relax! It's part of the process. Remember what feeding her in her high chair was like? How you kept sponges and washcloths glued to your hands? The early stages of cooking lessons aren't much different. Try to laugh off the spills as you wipe them up. Besides, adults, too, are known to make a mess in the kitchen, even without their kids' help.

The cooking kid

I'm 13. I live with my mom and Benny, my stepdad. My brother Stephen lives with Daddy and Stacey, our stepmom. We all cook. My mom and I cook together all the time. I started cooking because I couldn't read very well — my mom had me read recipes to her while she did the cooking. Since then, I can read better and now I like to cook. (I just don't like to clean up.)

One day I want to be a famous chef. I'm writing a cookbook on my computer with our favorite recipes. I've entered some contests at the fair and want to enter the book there. So far, I haven't won first place. But I've been practicing and think I will win this year. I'm going to cater a banquet at the ballpark, and I'm trying to do stuff for 4H.

My mom and I cook lots of presents to give away. Sometimes I make up my own recipes. My brother likes baseball, so we make him baseball stuff. Benny likes fishing, so we make him fishing stuff. Mom likes crafts, so we make cakes that look like quilts. I like animal stuff, and I can make a cheese ball that looks like a cat.

Here are my tips for kids just starting to cook in the kitchen:

☺ Before starting the recipe, read through the recipe to make sure that you have all the ingredients.

☺ Set all the ingredients out on the counter in the order that you need to use them.

☺ Don't be afraid to experiment and make a mistake.

☺ Remember practice makes perfect.

☺ Enter cooking contests.

☺ Help with cooking *and* clean up. That way nobody has to do all the work or have all the fun.

— James, "The Cooking Kid"

Chapter 2

Real Kids, Real Life — Five Family Profiles

How can you tell if an elephant has been in your refrigerator?
Footprints in the cheesecake.

The five "poster families" in this chapter aren't models of perfection. These are real families that face the same challenges that you do — eating fast-food on occasion, using convenience products, and taking shortcuts just to keep up with their daily demands. But one thing they all have in common is the value they've found in bringing kids into the kitchen.

The Doonan Family of Fort Worth, Texas

Sarah Doonan, smart, silly, and soon-to-be-six, puts the Energizer bunny to shame. Bright and active, Sarah provides her parents, John and DeAnn Doonan, with their own in-house fitness program — it's a rigorous routine just to keep up with her.

Like other dual-income families who beat the day-care dilemma by arranging for one parent to work from home, Sarah's dad practices architecture from a home office, taking charge of Sarah by day and often drawing up his plans late into the evening, after Sarah goes to bed. Her mother DeAnn works out of the house in a typical 40-hour (or more) managerial job.

"Like most working families, a day in the life of the Doonans' is pretty hectic," says DeAnn. "It starts about 6:15 a.m. when I get up to feed the pets, let the dogs out, and get ready for work. Sarah gets up a little after 7:00 and has a bath, dresses, and has breakfast. John gets up about 7:30, has coffee, and gets ready for work in the home office."

DeAnn knows that children need a solid breakfast, even if parents don't have the time or the desire for a morning meal. "Sarah always has breakfast and is the only one in the family who has breakfast at home."

While Sarah eats, DeAnn saves money by making brown bag lunches for Sarah and herself. The lunches aren't fancy, but she balances their diets by using all the food groups.

John and Sarah, shown in Figure 2-1, spend quality time together in the afternoon. After he picks her up at school, he makes sure she has a nutritious snack to keep her going until dinner. DeAnn's and Sarah's best time together begins after mom comes home from work. "In order to spend more time with Sarah, I have her help me out in the kitchen. Her favorite activities are cracking eggs, pouring in ingredients, battering and dipping, mixing marinades, and so on. She also loves to wash fruit and vegetables. Under close supervision, she is allowed to stir a soup or sauce."

"But — and this is important — Sarah is never, ever left in the kitchen unattended when a meal is being prepared," agree both John and DeAnn.

What can young children safely do in the kitchen? "I can always find a task for Sarah, whether setting the table (see Figure 2-2), washing and prepping the green vegetable, buttering the bread, pouring the rice into the water, adding the salt or butter, or washing the fruit," DeAnn explains.

As Sarah enters her sixth year, DeAnn and John offer this advice to other parents of budding young chefs:

> ✔ Teaching Sarah to cook was easy. Children have a natural tendency to enjoy being in a place where they find a lot of activity, as well as being curious about what Mom or Dad are doing. Sarah started washing vegetables, snapping asparagus, tearing spinach, cleaning Brussels sprouts, and doing other tasks at around age two. From there, the next step was to let her begin to pour premeasured ingredients into bowls or large resealable bags for mixing.

> ✔ When starting out with Sarah, we had to read the recipe and find ways to break the tasks into small steps that allowed her to help.

Figure 2-1:
John Doonan supervises daughter Sarah as she cuts veggies for shish kebabs.

Figure 2-2:
Little Sarah and DeAnn pitch in together to set the table at Granny's house.

Sarah goes shopping

Some parents view shopping with kids as modern torture — but many others have discovered ways to make it a pleasurable and productive experience for both parents and children.

DeAnn turns what can be a difficult trip into a fun-filled adventure by involving Sarah in all aspects of shopping, using the time to increase their bonds together. Here's her advice:

☺ Grocery shopping is a lot of fun with a child age 3 to 5 — but earlier ages can be a little challenging. I allow about one hour for our weekly shopping trip.

☺ We go down each aisle. We discuss the types of fruit we're going to get for the week and how to tell if a fruit is ripe enough. Sarah loves to weigh the apples, oranges, plums, and other produce. A lot of times I throw in a few facts about where the fruit or vegetable comes from, how it's grown, or how it's picked.

☺ Grocery shopping and meal preparation times are the best times to talk about why we eat certain foods. A child's attention span is pretty short up to age 5, but I make a point to talk about why we eat green vegetables, lots of fruit, and a wide variety of foods.

☺ I also allow her a lot of choices. In the paper products aisle, Sarah picks out the paper towels (usually by the type of print that appears on the towel). She helps load the cart. She also decides what type of treat we get for the dogs.

✔ Kids have a relatively short, but intense, attention span. Sarah may work diligently in the kitchen doing certain tasks — but not usually for a whole recipe. Unless the recipe is really yummy or is one with a lot of action (peeling, measuring, shaking, or mixing) most kids will assist by performing certain small, specific tasks. Parents shouldn't be discouraged if halfway through the recipe, the child takes a break and doesn't return.

✔ Sarah has her own apron and an old chair to stand on. The chair works better than a stool because she can move around more. She's allowed to run the mixer, as long as I'm right there — although we've had our share of chocolate, flour, and batter splash on the cabinet!

✔ She doesn't have any special kids' cooking tools. We primarily use small, thick, round, wooden spoons; soup spoons; and when necessary, salad forks; because these are a better scale for Sarah's small hands.

✔ We usually let Sarah make or create her own recipes. We've worked with rose petals, sticks, leaves, chili powder, raisins, apples, peppercorns, dish detergent (when we needed a little color) — just to name a few. Even though the end result isn't edible, the process is the key. She's measuring, mixing, peeling, and performing other tasks. She's also using all of her senses to create and experiment. Sometimes she is focusing on texture, sometimes on color, sometimes on scent.

✔ We try to allow a little extra time for cleanup. Spills do occur, so I strongly recommend keeping a damp paper towel handy — ready and waiting at all times!

The Talamon and Bates Family of Los Angeles, California

At seven years old, Jordan Talamon can hardly be called shy. The "King of the World" — as his parents, Karen and Bruce, facetiously call him — has strong opinions about which foods he likes (almost everything) and the few that he doesn't (which include, of all things, sandwiches!). Jordan's mother, Karen Grigsby Bates, knows all too well the social magic of food and the importance of good manners: she's co-author of the first etiquette book for African Americans, *Basic Black: Home Training for Modern Times.* Imagine what standards young Jordan must have to live up to — especially at the dinner table!

The Talamon and Bates family, shown in Figure 2-3, share much in common with many young, dual-income professionals.

"We're a three-person family," explains Karen. "I'm a journalist-writer and avid amateur cook. My husband, Bruce Talamon, is a photographer who spends a lot of time on movie sets, shooting still photographs, but he also likes to cook, especially with Jordan. Jordan is in the first grade and shows a strong interest in cooking." (One of his heroes is TV chef Emeril Lagasse).

Jordan is already an active young chef. Here's what his parents have done to encourage his cooking passion and maintain safe boundaries, without remodeling their entire kitchen:

✔ Our old kitchen had a custom-built knife drawer and a magnetized wall bar for our favorite knives. Now, they're in a knife block on a window shelf, to keep knives away from little hands.

✔ When he handles knives, we watch him carefully and guide him. He does better with big ones (an 8" chef's knife with a good hilt or bolster — or whatever that thing between the blade and handle is called). We don't let him hold cartons of tinfoil, waxed-paper, or plastic wrap by himself, because the serrated edges can give a nasty cut. (See Chapter 8 for more on knives and knife safety.)

Figure 2-3:
Bruce,
Jordan, and
Karen take a
break at a
birthday
party.

© Paula Swinford

- ✔ We keep the Cuisinart food processor at counter-level, but it's no-where near a plug, and the blades are stored separately.

- ✔ Our kitchen counters seem abnormally high, but we take out a sturdy stepladder when Jordan helps, and that seems to work well. If we're working on an activity like stirring batter or kneading bread, we do it on the breakfast room table, which is a good height for him. He's been handling everyday spoons, spatulas, and such since he was a toddler, so we don't use kid-sized tools for him.

"Like a lot of people before they became parents, Bruce and I used to eat out a lot — alone and with friends. They weren't always fancy meals, but we ate them at odd or late hours, made decisions to go out at the last minute, and enjoyed a meal uninterrupted by anything other than the waiter coming by to see if we needed anything.

"Since the King of the World made his debut (meaning Jordan), much of our entertaining has centered around eating in and inviting friends or visitors to join us. We feed an assortment of starving artists on a regular basis — one photographer often calls ahead and says, semi-seriously, 'So what're you serving tonight? What time do you want me to come by?' Weekend brunches are frequent and casual. And we rotate holidays with a close group of friends and family, so while we know that we'll probably see each other on those big food days, the venue changes from year to year.

"Bruce's schedule is kind of all-or-nothing-at-all: If he's between movies, Bruce and Jordan enjoy making dinner together. We usually manage to sit down together and have a regular meal, with lots of chat about how everyone's day has gone, what the politics of the first grade are this week, and so on.

"But when Bruce works his typical 12- to 16-hour days on a movie set, I become, *de facto,* a single parent. Then Jordan and I may eat things that his vegetarian dad won't, like red meat in the form of lean steak stir-fried with broccoli and mushrooms."

Even though dining together as a family can be difficult, Karen uses her own time with Jordan to nurture their bonds and stimulate his inquisitive mind:

- I like to bend the rules and break up the routine. Sometimes we eat at the dining-room table, sometimes we picnic on the floor in the den (yes, in front of the television!) while we watch a video or something suitable for parent-child viewing.

- If Bruce is away on location, Jordan and I try to eat out once a weekend as a treat. If I left it up to him, it'd be something with fries every time. So, we balance those meals by eating kid-food on one outing and healthier, more adult food on the next. Sometimes we can compromise: Instead of Chicken McNuggets and fries, we may have flame-broiled chicken and oven-roasted potato wedges, and if I can make him eat it, salad at one of the 'healthy' fast-food chains.

- When Bruce and I grew up in the '50s, breakfast was eaten at breakfast, dinner at dinner time, and so on. Foodstuffs were pretty much relegated to specific times. Not now, though. Jordan loves leftover dinner for breakfast; he often asks for Spicy Rice (Jambalaya) washed down with milk (see Figure 2-4), or a piece of chicken with rice and broccoli and a little soy sauce for dipping. He's been known to eat spaghetti, chili, grilled cheese, or leftover grilled Japanese tuna before going off to school. Bruce and I are all for it. These foods are probably better for him than a bowl full of sugared carbohydrates anyway.

- At least one person in my family seems to think that dessert is his birthright, so we usually have dessert right after dinner — usually ice cream. The men's favorite is Ben and Jerry's Cherry Garcia: big bing cherries in vanilla ice cream, studded with chunks of dark chocolate. We eat a lot of poultry and fish and very little meat (Bruce eats none), so I'm hoping that the guys' 17 percent butterfat habit is offset by their relatively healthy diet elsewhere. I sometimes try to sneak in the lowfat frozen yogurt version of Cherry Garcia, but have been vehemently assured that it's not the same. So, when I think they're approaching butterfat overload, I just make 'em skip the ice cream or choose something else. Oreo's seem to be an acceptable consolation prize, though they're still too high in fat for my comfort — and of course lowfat Oreo's aren't the same.

Figure 2-4:
Jordan
enjoys a
favorite
breakfast:
chicken-chili
and rice.

©Karen Grigsby Bates

The Evers Family of Portland, Oregon

As a working mom, Connie Evers knows the challenges that today's families face in feeding balanced meals to their kids. A registered dietitian, Connie works from home as a child nutrition consultant and is the author of *Teaching Nutrition to Kids,* a book and activity guide for teachers. She also consults with parents personally, in lectures, and through her e-mailed newsletter and Web site (www.nutritionforkids.com).

An etiquette author's own rules of the table

Karen Grigsby Bates co-authored a book on modern etiquette, called *Basic Black: Home Training for Modern Times.* Here's how she trains her own young son, Jordan, in the ways of the table:

☺ Come with clean hands.

☺ Use your napkin — it's not placed there as a table decoration.

☺ Say a blessing, however brief. (Jordan's is very meal-specific: "God is great, God is good, and we thank Him for our [insert meal here…])

☺ Ask for things properly ("more milk, please?" instead of "more milk!")

☺ Unless you're eating something like fried chicken or French fries, use your fork, not your fingers.

☺ Elbows off the table, please.

☺ Thank the cook — especially if you're eating at someone else's home.

☺ Ask to be excused from the table, instead of just wandering off.

Husband and father Scott Evers, a high-school history teacher, also sees firsthand how teens today eat. With a 45-minute commute to and from Salem, Oregon, Scott may miss his own kids in the morning, but the family makes every effort to dine together most nights, working around soccer practice, Connie's or daughter Kelli's travels, and other events.

Connie and Scott paint this picture of their three different, dynamic children (shown with Scott in Figure 2-5), whose daily activities have them frequently in the kitchen, whipping up meals and snacks:

✔ Kelli (age 12) has been a competitive ice skater since age 6. She competes in Regional competitions, and is passionate and serious about her sport. Kelli's up and headed for the ice rink by 4:30 a.m., four days each week. A typical oldest child, she is a high achiever with a straight-A average. She's also very modest and kind, for which we're very grateful. Kelli is the pickiest eater of the three. She's particular about how her food is prepared, even down to the exact doneness of her toasted bagel. She loves cooked vegetables but only eats carrots and cauliflower raw. The only fruits she eats are grapes and apples. She prefers her foods plain, separate and easily recognizable — definitely no casseroles for this child!

✔ Sam, our middle child at age 8, is the 'spice' of our family. He's active, incredibly curious, and highly creative, although he can also be ornery and disruptive at times. Sam is a child that needs to have action in his life — he plays soccer, enjoys basketball, and is excited about starting youth football this fall. Sam finds cooking fun and loves to bake homemade muffins and make smoothies in the blender.

✔ Adam (age 6) is more quiet and introspective. He's sweet and sociable, but he also really enjoys playing alone at times. This is understandable, because we have a noisy, active family. Adam also enjoys sports and plays roller hockey. He most enjoys making cookies, especially lowfat ginger cookies. He also makes his own sandwiches at lunch time and likes to look at the Food Guide Pyramid on the refrigerator to make sure that his meal has something from every food group. He's an adventurous little eater who'll try almost anything.

Figure 2-5:
The Evers kids "ham" it up with their dad, Scott.

Connie shares her own expertise on what works — and what doesn't — when feeding her kids.

✔ Breakfast — of some kind — is non-negotiable in our household. The evidence is overwhelming that children perform and behave better when they have eaten a morning meal before going to school.

✔ The kids are understandably hungry when they arrive home from school. I heard a statistic that children eat about 35 percent of their calories in the hours between school dismissal and the evening meal!

✔ To preserve my own sanity, I try to have them agree on a set time when they all sit down and have their snacks. I discourage ongoing eating, and we have a 'two food-group' rule, meaning a snack that provides at least two food groups. Common snacks include cereal and milk, cheese and crackers, yogurt and fruit, bagels and juice, sandwiches, bean burritos, and leftovers. (Sam typically has another lunch when he comes home!) The children normally prepare their own snacks, often with Kelli's or Scott's help or my supervision.

✔ Officially, all the children take turns being the 'cook's helper.' They each have one night per week when they're assigned to assist me or Scott. Other than that, the boys often pitch in, because they really enjoy it.

✔ When they cook, they do everything from peeling potatoes to opening cans, microwaving vegetables, getting things out of the refrigerator for me, washing and tearing up lettuce, making melon balls, stirring, pouring, measuring — you name it. As long as they're under supervision, I allow them to help do most things. We really emphasize hand washing, sanitation, and safety with tools and hot surfaces.

✔ The initial hassle of training kids to cook is well worth the outcome. Indeed, having children 'help' can often be more work, mess, and confusion! But starting children in the kitchen at a young age helps them become self-sufficient and develop critical life skills. It also eases family stress as they get older and begin helping with those daily tasks of living. (In Figure 2-6, Sam shows off his dessert!)

✔ Their father, Scott, can especially see the importance of teaching kids life skills (such as cooking), because he grew up in a traditional family where his mother did virtually everything — and I do mean everything — on the domestic front. When he got on his own, he initially subsisted on hot dogs, fish sticks, and frozen pizzas!

✔ I think one of the key reasons that our children eat healthfully is that they have a say in the food selection, menu planning, and preparation. When a child helps to concoct a recipe, they know exactly what's in it. They don't have to wonder what's really in the 'mystery casserole' that's on the table.

✔ I think kids need to understand where food comes from, and growing their own is a great way to teach this. Our children enjoy growing their own small vegetable gardens in the summer. They marvel at how fresh and sweet everything tastes when it is homegrown.

Figure 2-6:
Sam and
Connie turn
homegrown
blueberries
into
blueberry
crisp.

Connie's tips for fast, healthy meals

Although Connie is an expert on child nutrition, she and Scott aren't purists about making dinners from scratch. As busy parents, they incorporate certain time-saving products to help prepare nutritious meals that everyone enjoys. Here, Connie explains her family's methods, along with other meal management tactics:

☺ Dinner time is my "low point" — that's when I'm glad to have help from my husband and kids in getting a nutritious, tasty meal on the table. Our meals are simple and quasi-home-cooked. We rely on some convenience foods, such as bottled spaghetti sauce (which we also use as pizza sauce); canned, baked beans; individually quick-frozen, skinless chicken breasts; garden burgers; and prepared sauces such as stir-fry, teriyaki, pesto, and barbecue.

☺ Our fast foods on rushed nights include pasta with a prepared sauce (Paul Newman's Bombolina is our favorite), cold sandwiches paired with a hot item like a cooked vegetable or baked beans, or soup (one of the heartier canned soups or homemade) served with crackers, cheese, and fruit.

☺ Now that the kids are getting older, we put more assembly-line, buffet-type foods out. For example, Scott or I set out all the fixings for burritos on the counter and the kids come through and choose what they want. We also do this with sandwich fixings or reheated leftovers (not their favorite, though).

☺ We eat lots of fruit, lightly steamed vegetables (my kids prefer these to salads), whole grain breads, 1% milk, lower fat varieties of cheese (mozzarella and reduced-fat cheddar are the most common), lean meat, lean chicken, fish, vegetarian meals (I don't eat meat at all), and lots of pasta!

☺ We have dessert of some sort nearly every night. I enjoy dessert and I don't believe in making these foods forbidden. I think dessert promotes moderation and moves people away from guilt and restrained eating.

☺ Dinner is our sit-down-together family meal, and other than Friday nights, we don't allow any television during meals. Mealtime isn't always peaceful — we have spills and fights and the normal family chaos — but we're together!

☺ After dinner, the kitchen is closed! For my own sanity, I don't allow non-stop grazing. The children aren't forced to clean their plates or take a certain number of bites at meals, but they also know that they can't just eat something else an hour after a meal. I try to adhere to Ellyn Satter's division of responsibility (parents are responsible for putting the food out, kids are responsible for eating it), although my husband sometimes lapses back into the clean-plate/wasted food scenario of his youth!

The Stouffer Family of Rochester, Michigan

Can you imagine a family of four kids and two parents all agreeing on the same foods to eat? I can't — and neither can the Stouffers, an active family of six from the Midwest. Still, they manage to find a level of harmony and balanced meals among their many mouths to feed.

After having their second child, Julie Stouffer left her nursing career to become a stay-at-home mom — a smart move, especially because the family would later add two more kids to the nest. Her husband, John, works as a manager of business systems for a Detroit company, and just completed his MBA by taking night classes.

"The past two years were difficult for the family," explains John. "I was either at class or studying in the evenings, and it upset the dinner schedules." Today, the family dines together nightly, even if they have to delay the dinner until everyone is home. Dinner is served around the family's schedule — not the other way around.

An overabundance of sports, clubs, arts, and other after-school events can be the biggest obstacle to family dining. For many families like the Stouffers, the nightly meal is their only opportunity to be together. But their bright, energetic kids are developing social agendas of their own — they may soon face tough decisions to cut back on these competing activities if the nightly family dinner hour is to survive.

Mike (age 14) plays sax in the band, is on the soccer team (soccer being a family passion), and earns money as a golf caddy. Sarah, at age 11, is moving ahead in her own saxophone and piano lessons, and babysits neighbor children several nights a week. Little Rachel at 6 plays soccer as aggressively as her older siblings, and 9-year-old Thomas likes to join his father in whatever he's doing. "Thomas," says John, "is the one child that will stick with Dad through a four-hour fix-it job — including climbing up on the roof." John and Julie encourage their kids to broaden their interests, but they also know that time shared together, in cooking and dining, is just as important. Figure 2-7 shows part of the family making Sunday breakfast.

✔ **Rachel, age 6:**

- "I always go shopping for food with Mom. A fun part of shopping is going to the Brach's candy pick-a-mix and getting the samples for a nickel. Free samples at the deli are also good to eat." Mom assigns Rachel shopping assignments like picking out a good bunch of bananas or matching the picture on the coupon until she finds the right item on the shelf. "We have to go through all the cereals and choose who likes what," explains Rachel.

- Even at 6, Rachel energetically assists in the kitchen, as shown in Figure 2-8. "Rachel likes to move a kitchen chair over to the counter and help with the cooking," explains her father. "She likes to mix muffins and Jello. She chops carrots for the salad and tosses the salad. She likes to tenderize the meat by stabbing it with a fork. She just learned how to make Mickey Mouse pancakes."

- On the topic of dinner time, Rachel faces the dilemma most common to any family's youngest child: "I like to eat dinner with the family. I get to talk to my family, but sometimes they don't let me say anything — even though I have my hand up."

Figure 2-7:
John shows Thomas, Rachel, and Sarah how to measure milk "eggsactly."

✓ **Thomas, age 9:**

- "Thomas enjoys cooking just a few things," says his dad. "Thomas likes to make his own fajita cheese wrap thingimajigger: a flour tortilla, cheese, salami, and pickles. Roll it up and microwave for one minute. Be careful, though — it's hot! He also makes nachos by using tortilla chips spread on a plate; sprinkling on cheese, black olives, and salsa; and microwaving for one minute."

- "When we eat together, he likes to hear what older brother Mike did with his friends during the day, likes to talk about things he learned on the Discovery Channel (especially animal facts), and likes to talk about sports and what he did at school that day."

- "Thomas is good about cleaning up the table after dinner, except that sometimes he piles too much on his plate and something goes flying off." Oops! Accidents happen, even with the best of intentions.

✓ **Sarah, age 12:**

- At 12 years, Sarah has already developed a sophisticated perspective on eating. "When I go shopping, I enjoy seeing all the different kinds of foods and asking about the foods I never had."

- Sarah offers her own tips for kids learning to cook. "Sometimes, you can have fun by making up your own recipes. I invented my own cookies. They turned out well, but they were a little dry and not sweet enough. It was fun to try. It helps to have made cookies from a recipe before, so that you kind of know what to use. I want to make my own soup or stew from scratch. To do that, I'll have to look at recipes from other soups and stews that I've had and put in different kinds of vegetables and noodles and things."

Figure 2-8:
Julie guides Rachel's hand as they cook together.

- Sarah recently took a class for decorating birthday cakes. "She enjoys it and is very good at it," says her father. "She comes up with some very creative decorations." Sarah's cooking tip: "When decorating cakes, get ideas from the birthday person and look at other cakes at the cake shop."

- "When we eat together, I like all the different topics that come up in our conversation. Sometimes my brothers and Dad tease me about being a slow eater. I think it is better to eat slowly because I can enjoy my food and still talk to my family."

✔ **Mike, age 14:**

- "Mike likes to make his own lunch food so that he can have it his way," says his dad. "He likes cooking hamburgers on the grill, making omelets, making beef with barley soup, and whipping up his special "super sandwich" — a massive concoction of three meats, tomato, lettuce, cheese, Miracle Whip, mustard, Italian dressing, hot pepper rings, and bread (see Figure 2-9). "You have to sample the food while you make the sandwich," advises Mike. "Be careful — this sandwich can get very messy! Oh, and share any leftovers with Dad," his father chimes in.

Figure 2-9:
Mike fuels
up with his
special
"super
sandwich"
while
Rachel
looks on.

- "Mike likes to go shopping with Julie so that he can convince her to buy some things that she normally wouldn't buy," Dad cleverly points out. "For example, candy, soda pop, and the cereals he likes (Cinnamon Toast Crunch or Frosted Flakes)." (For this same reason, many parents say that they actually save money and eat better by *not* taking their teenage kids to the market!)

- "What Mike likes about eating together is that we get to talk about what we did during the day and enjoy good food. What he dislikes is waiting for everyone to get done eating — he wants to get back to watching the Red Wings win the Stanley Cup," says John.

- Mike's cooking tip for other kids: "Cook hamburgers five minutes per side over hot coals but on medium heat. Don't pat the burgers."

With such a large family, Julie and John Stouffer have developed these tips for other parents starting to cook with kids:

✔ When helping kids learn how to cook, accept that they're going to get messy. Parents need to let the children do their own thing and learn through trial and error. Sometimes, letting the older kids show is the best thing to do — sometimes it's the worst — you just have to see what kind of mood everyone's in.

✔ The best time to let kids experiment with cooking is when the parent has lots of time. When the parent is under the gun to get a meal on the table (whether for a regular dinner or a special occasion), then the situation is too stressful and not as much fun for the kids or the parents.

On the menu: Weekend breakfast and cooking lesson

John makes a pancake breakfast on weekends, a Stouffer tradition, but he also uses this time to show kids some basic cooking skills they need to know. During one weekend breakfast session, John came up with these tips, which he shares for other parents and kids cooking together:

☺ When we made scrambled eggs, I tried to teach the kids all the little things that adults take for granted. For instance: Step 1 — how to crack an egg without getting a shell in the eggs. Step 2 — how to get the shell out if you fail Step #1. We go over why you should wait to add the milk to broken eggs until all of the eggs are broken. The answer: You have a hard time finding a shell when the mixture's all cloudy with milk.

☺ For kids, the way to crack an egg is to grip it firmly, with your hand wrapped around it almost completely. Then crack it HARD on the side of the bowl, letting the edge of your hand stop the motion. Sometimes, the kids try to stop by just tapping the egg on the side — many times — which causes the splintering.

☺ We tell the kids that the perfect amount of milk to add to scrambled eggs is 'half-of-a-half.' Find one half of an egg shell (one that is closest to exactly half) and fill it with milk half as many times as the number of eggs used. For instance, for ten eggs, fill a half shell five times with milk. You get perfect eggs every time, and the recipe is self-adjusting to the size and number of the eggs.

☺ Julie and I show the kids how to check if the griddle is hot enough for eggs or pancakes. At first, they said, 'touch it to find out if it's hot.' After correcting that answer, we told them about using drops of water: If the drops of water dance around the skillet, then it's ready — a far safer method.

☺ During the latest scrambled eggs/pancake cook-a-thon, we talked about eating things with raw eggs. Rachel wanted to taste the pancake batter that had two eggs in it. We told her she couldn't and talked about the risk of food poisoning from many uncooked foods.

✔ The easiest way to emphasize nutrition is to make the right choices during shopping. Avoid buying bacon, fried foods, high sodium foods, sugary treats, whole milk, and so on. When eating fast food, we have the kids share the fries and shakes — a small portion is sufficient.

The Rodriguez and Rudd Family of Miami, Florida

Enchiladas, egg rolls, blintzes, moussaka, and felafel — joy to the world and its wonderful foods! Traditional foods help people keep in touch with their cultures and family heritages. You can literally taste the melting pot of cross-cultural communities in the Japanese noodle shops of Peru, the Vietnamese spring rolls of Paris, the Italian pastas of Argentina, the Indian curries of England, and in the wide range of foods and cultures stretching across the United States and Canada.

As a part of this global melting pot, Rosa Rodriguez and her husband Leslie Rudd find that food helps reinforce their Cuban background to their daughters Victoria (age 7) and Catherine (age 3). But they also face the same challenges as families everywhere: How to put a tasty, nutritious meal on the table and still enjoy family time together as well.

Of course, if Victoria and Catherine had their way, these Cuban-American youngsters would eat pizza seven nights a week. While the kids get their way some of the time, Rosa and Leslie encourage the girls to eat a wide variety of foods, especially many dishes from their own heritage. For them, food is more than just the meal itself — it keeps them in touch with their family and their roots.

Rosa and Leslie keep cultural traditions alive for their kids. "Victoria is discovering our heritage," says Rosa. "We eat a lot of Cuban food — both mine and Leslie's mothers are great cooks. We also try to speak as much Spanish at home as possible, but the kids prefer to speak English.

"For example, Thanksgiving is sort of your typical Thanksgiving, but with a Cuban twist. We usually end up eating two Thanksgiving dinners — we join the Rodriguez side of the family for lunch and have dinner with Leslie's family. In between, we usually rest and take an Alka Seltzer!"

Catherine and Victoria may not realize it yet, but their Thanksgiving dinners barely resemble the typical spreads seen in the Norman Rockwell covers of the *Saturday Evening Post*. Next to the traditional mashed potatoes sit black beans and rice, and the turkey itself is cooked with the flavors of Cuba — lots of garlic and fresh juice from sour orange (a fruit that resembles a large orange, but is more tart like a lemon or lime). Besides the turkey, Rosa's mom adds another element of her heritage by serving a roast leg of pork, which is a common Cuban dish during holidays.

Restaurant dining survival

As do many working parents, Rosa and Leslie ease the load of constant cooking by going to restaurants, especially on weekends. "Usually, we go out to breakfast after Mass on Sundays — we really enjoy this time together."

Many parents would consider dining at a restaurant with a three- and six-year-old an event of unparalleled torture — for both themselves and other patrons. But not for Rosa and Leslie:

"We've been taking the kids to restaurants since they were babies, so they're well-behaved — we rarely have an unpleasant experience. Now that Victoria can read, she goes over the kid's menu with Catherine. And though she's just now three, Catherine's been feeding herself since she was about a year old, so she's independent and responsible at the table."

"We celebrate Noche Buena (Christmas Eve) with all of the typical Cuban foods, such as pork, black beans and rice, yuca — a root vegetable common in Cuban cooking — and other dishes. Leslie's brothers make Cuban coffee, and one friend always arrives with a fresh loaf of Cuban bread. The whole family gets together for this celebration — four generations of grandparents, parents, siblings, cousins, aunts, uncles, grand aunts, and anyone else who wants to come. We never set up a kids' table. In our culture, kids eat with everyone else, right next to their grandparents, aunts, or cousins. Eating together helps keep the bonds of the family strong, whether on weeknights or holidays."

Rosa involves her kids in cooking — it's their time to spend together each day: "I usually arrive home from work around 5:30. Leslie gets home a couple of hours later. I start dinner with the girls and they love to help. Having them help usually slows me down and can get frustrating at times, but they absolutely love it. I find that when my kids cook with me, they seem to eat better. They're more enthusiastic about eating and usually finish their meal. Also, they are proud of themselves — their dad always tells them what great chefs they are." (Figures 2-10 and 2-11 show the girls helping Rosa shop.)

"On days when Victoria has a lot of homework to do, she sits at the table and does her work while I cook and help her with her homework. Then, before dinner, Victoria helps set the table before her Dad comes home."

"I like to have the whole family eat together, even though that means that the girls are eating later than they should be (around 8:00 p.m.). We usually talk about our day, Victoria tells us about school and her playmates. It's basically the only time of day that we're all together. After dinner, Leslie is really good about cleaning the kitchen (see Figure 2-12) — by this time, I'm usually exhausted."

Figure 2-10: Rosa and the girls pick vegetables for a Cuban-style stew.

Figure 2-11: Victoria picks the perfect tomato.

Rosa accommodates her busy work and meal schedules by planning ahead. "I at least try to have an idea of what I'm cooking before I get home. I try to have the meat defrosting in the refrigerator. Certain foods take too long to cook during the week, so I start them the night before, if I have time. I don't eat in the morning, but the girls have something easy and simple that's also good for them — frozen pancakes, cereal and milk, or juice.

"I usually pack Victoria's lunch, because the school cafeteria lets the kids pick out whatever they want to eat, without any sort of supervision. If Victoria buys her lunch, she gets French fries, Twinkies, and all sorts of junk food — which is not only unhealthy, but is expensive — about $2.10 per day.

Figure 2-12:
After the family dines together, Leslie pitches in with kitchen cleanup.

"I try to pack and prepare as much as I can the night before (for example, mixing the tuna), but I actually make the sandwich in the morning. Some of Victoria's favorites are a chicken spread made with cream cheese, a little mayo, and canned chicken; tuna sandwiches, cherry tomatoes, cheese sticks, grapes, and carrots. I always send juice and usually a cookie for a snack. When Catherine begins preschool this fall, I'll also fix a lunch and snack for her."

A family's food chronicles

Leslie's Aunt Viviana Carballos (known as *Tia Viviana* in Spanish) plays a role in the family's appreciation of food and their heritage. Viviana is a food writer for the *Miami Herald* and other publications, who shares her cooking knowledge with audiences in both Spanish and English.

"We always enjoy reading Tia Viviana's articles in the newspaper," Rosa says, speaking for herself and Leslie. "Her articles are much more than just recipes — she writes about the family and the foods that are part of our heritage. She wrote a beautiful article about her mother, Abuela, that included some of Abuela's favorite recipes. When we visited Abuela at Tia Viviana's home on Mother's Day, Tia Viviana was cooking those very same dishes for her mother."

Tia Viviana also invites Victoria over to bake cookies, something they both seem to enjoy.

Part II:
Putting the Meal Together — Together!

In this part . . .

Think of the many things that you do every day to put a meal on the table — from meal planning to shopping, from cooking to serving the meal. In this part, I show you how to include your kids in these daily tasks — without going nuts.

I start out by sharing ideas for turning your kitchen into a haven for young chefs. Then, I present easy-to-follow nutrition guidelines and tips for feeding even the most finicky eaters. I also present proven strategies for efficient cooking and meal planning, including a full month of menus that use recipes from this book. Besides my tactical tips for gathering everyone to the dining table at one time, I also present fun ways to keep them there and to make the dinner hour entertaining, engaging, and educational for kids and parents alike.

Chapter 3

The Kid-Friendly Kitchen

Why do chicken coops have two doors?
Because if they had four doors, they'd be chicken sedans!

In this chapter, you can find ways to make your existing kitchen more kid-friendly. Start by reorganizing a few cabinets, putting tools that youngsters should use within easy reach, and perhaps adding a few of the kid-safe stools and tools discussed in these pages. But making yours a kid-friendly kitchen doesn't mean calling in a contractor to redesign it or investing in a whole new set of pint-sized cookware. After all, you probably grew up in a family kitchen that was made for adults, adapting as a child to working within that kitchen — with your help and guidance, your kids can happily do the same thing.

Giving Young Chefs Their Own Station

Restaurant chefs have their own tools and work space, and kids can, too. When children have their own kid-sized kitchen tools and a comfortable place to work, they rapidly grow more capable in the kitchen, making the cooking experience increasingly more pleasurable and satisfying.

Finding a place to store tools

Designate a place in the kitchen for your child's tools — measuring cups and spoons, potholders, and so on. A low shelf or drawer works best, or use a storage container that can be readily accessed. Young chefs must understand that this is their own special equipment — they can take care of it by washing, drying, and storing it away after each use.

Pint-size proportions

"For successful cooking with children, I make an effort to have equipment that is kid-sized. All too often, a large mixing bowl is way too large for little arms to hold and control, especially if the kids are standing on chairs or stools. I make an effort to keep the tools my kids use proportional to their sizes. That may mean that batches of dough have to be cut in half to be stirred, for example. That may also mean that it takes longer to prepare the food. But my theory is, if you're in a big rush to get the meal prepared, perhaps this is one the kids should not be involved with. I'm not wild about kids sitting on counters or standing on chairs to help in the kitchen. When my guys and I set out to cook, I bring their Little Tykes table into the kitchen. It's the proper height and gives them enough surface area for both tools and ingredients."

— Carol from Madison, Wisconsin

An oversized lunchbox, hardware tool box, or small cardboard file box makes a terrific portable container for storing a young chef's tools. Make sure the box is large and deep enough to hold everything, but not so large as to make it unwieldy (this depends on the size of the child). Use a large marker to personalize the container; for example, "Chef Sarah's Tools." For a list of the top ten items for a kid's kitchen kit, jump to Chapter 22.

Carving out a workstation

Being little people, kids need a workstation that meets their height. The ideal surface should come to a child's waist, giving her room to bend her arms comfortably. Look for a portable table of the correct height, or use one with adjustable legs. Children can also stand on step stools to reach your existing countertops — and youngsters will certainly need a stool when cooking at the stovetop. In all cases, make sure worktables and stools are stable and balanced, so that they don't accidentally tip over.

Neat ideas

☺ "When kids cook, sleeves are in the way. Aprons are okay, but I personally favor a big T-shirt on top of whatever the child is wearing (we use these for art also). Throw it in the washer afterwards.

☺ "Get appropriate oven mitts for the child's hands (or well insulated mittens.)

☺ "Step stools are usually not wide enough for my taste. I prefer a small bench for standing on. Also, a table with adjustable legs will grow with your family. These are also very useful at full height for buffet serving and at lower levels are super for projects and children's parties.

☺ "Buy a roll of butcher paper. It's heavy enough to work on and then you throw it away or use it for art. I tape it down with masking tape. I really am a nut about contamination and think that the paper solves most of the problems. Nothing soaks through."

— from Jean from San Antonio, Texas

Young Chefs, Climb Aboard the Kitchen Tour!

One of the best — and most interactive — ways to introduce your kids to the kitchen is to take them on a tour. Very young ones can't see what's in those drawers or high cabinets, and the kitchen may be a place of mystery. Kids need to know not only where to find each piece of equipment but what it does as well.

Demonstrating kitchen consideration

"In my opinion, to make a kitchen kid-friendly you must involve the kids. Making decisions about where they should stand, what they should use, what to plug in and unplug, without their input, alienates them. We discuss the plans ahead of time, and the boys understand who will do which task before we start. This keeps the arguments to a minimum and potential hazards or risks eliminated."

— Carol from Madison, Wisconsin

Be sure to include these stops on your kitchen tour:

- ✔ **The pantry and spice cabinet:** Show children where canned and dry goods are stored and what items you always keep on hand. After shopping together, kids can help store these items away and keep a running list for when it's time to buy more. Let kids smell or taste herbs and spices to become familiar with them.

- ✔ **Utensils:** Open up the drawers of everyday utensils like the ones in Figure 3-1. Let the kids pick them up and hold them, and demonstrate what each tool does. Explain to kids that they'll get a better chance to use these utensils when they cook. Reinforce that nonstick cookware is damaged by metal utensils and point out the proper nylon spatulas, wooden spoons, and other tools safe for nonstick surfaces.

  For easy access, put wooden spoons, spatulas, ladles, and other long-handled utensils in a pitcher or wide-mouth jar next to your stove. That way, they're instantly accessible whenever you or your kids need them.

- ✔ **Measuring cups and bowls:** Demonstrate equipment specifically used for making and measuring recipes, such as the dry and liquid measuring cups and nested mixing bowls in Figure 3-2.

Figure 3-1:
Everyday utensils that every young chef will use.

Everyday Utensils

liquid measure cup   dry measure cups   nesting mixing bowls

✔ **Measuring spoons:** Traditional measuring spoons come as separate
spoons in individual increments on a ring (see Figure 3-3).

The KitchenArt company makes an all-in-one measuring spoon that's
not only handier to use, but visually shows kids the relationship
between the various measurements (shown in Figure 3-3). The spoon
has an edge that slides to different increments. The teaspoon model
stops at $^1/_8$, $^1/_4$, $^1/_2$, $^3/_4$, and 1 teaspoon levels. The tablespoon model
slides to measures of 1, $1^1/_2$, 2, and $2^1/_2$ teaspoons, and 1 tablespoon
(which is equal to 3 teaspoons). And unlike other measuring spoons,
these lie flat, so that you can fill up the measuring compartment and
rest the spoon on the counter without spilling the contents. Ask for
them at cookware stores.

Whichever type of measuring spoon you use, you can save time and
be less messy by keeping two sets of each around when cooking —
one for dry ingredients and one for wet ingredients.

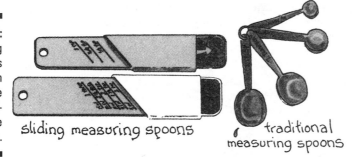

sliding measuring spoons   traditional measuring spoons

> ✔ **Cookware:** Show your kids where pots and pans are stored and what each is used for. For example, saucepans are used for boiling foods and making sauces, stock pots are great for making soup, and skillets brown foods fast on the stovetop — see Figure 3-4. Have the child pick up and feel the weight of each pan, and explain that the pan will weigh more when it contains food.

Figure 3-4:
Let kids lift pots and pans to feel their weight.

> ✔ **Refrigerator:** Look inside the refrigerator with new eyes. Show children that some jars say "Refrigerate after opening" and that meats and cheeses have expiration dates. Open the crisper and storage compartments to show which foods go in them and how to properly wrap and store them. Keep juices and snacks accessible to little kids by putting them on a lower shelf.

> ✔ **Range:** Demonstrate how the oven, broiler, and stovetop work. Turn each burner knob to low, medium, and high heats. Show how to turn the oven and broiler on and remind children to always make sure to turn off the stove when finished cooking. Make sure all kids know whether they're allowed to use the range and to always ask for a parent's permission to cook.

Splatter guards with their fine mesh screen, shown in Figure 3-5, are most often used when frying bacon, but they can make the stovetop safer for kids when any food pops or splatters. Put a cover or splatter guard on simmering tomato sauces, frying chicken, and boiling soups to prevent hot ingredients from jumping out of the pan and onto tender skin. You can also cover mustard seeds and other whole spices when toasting them in a skillet to keep them from jumping out. (Mustard seeds pop like crazy when they're heated!)

Figure 3-5:
Splatter guards protect kids from hot oil and sauces.

✔ **Food storage supplies:** Show kids where food storage containers are kept and where to find the foil, plastic wrap, resealable bags, paper bags, and paper towels.

✔ **Knives:** Help your kids understand how and when knives should be used. Chapters 8 and 11 discuss the essential rules of knife safety, basic types of knives, the age for kids to start using knives, and proper cutting techniques. Consult these chapters during your kitchen tour to match the right knife for your child's age with the tasks at hand.

Every young chef should know to cut, chop, and slice foods *only* on wooden or plastic cutting boards — not directly on countertops. Unlike countertops, cutting boards are specifically made to absorb the nicks and scratches made by a knife, and they're soft enough not to damage the knife's blade. During your kitchen tour and before cooking, set out a cutting board — a damp dishcloth underneath it will help keep it from slipping during cutting. Keep a variety of cutting boards in various sizes handy for the smallest to the largest job — they're a lot more affordable than replacing a damaged countertop!

Time-saving appliances

In your tour, include a stop at each kitchen appliance. Pretend you're doing a product demonstration in a department store, showing kids how handy each appliance can be.

✔ Before starting the tour, reinforce that children always need a parent's supervision and permission when working in the kitchen.

✔ Begin with the safest, most low-tech appliances, like a toaster, and move up to those requiring more supervision, like food processors.

✔ Because of their compact size, microwave ovens and toaster ovens can be easier for kids to use than the large ovens of your gas or electric range. Take a snack break during your kitchen tour and use the opportunity to make easy, nutritious snacks like English muffin pizzas, nachos, or baked apples in the microwave or toaster oven.

✔ Instruct children in the proper use — and caution them on the improper use — of kitchen appliances. For instance, show how to adjust a toaster's cooking setting and explain why you should never put any utensils, especially metal ones, into a toaster. Do this with each appliance.

✔ Note which appliances your child can use (in your company, of course) and which ones are off limits. Use colorful stickers to mark the kid-able areas and the non-kid zones. For young children, food processors and anything with sharp blades get an unhappy face, and simple equipment, like toasters, get a happy face. As a child ages and becomes more skilled, she can graduate to more complicated appliances, changing the sticker to mark her achievement.

> For a handy reference during your kitchen tour, flip to Chapter 14 on appliances. It includes safety tips and fun cooking ideas, as well as helpful hints on handy handheld blenders and mini-choppers (shown in Figure 3-6), blenders and food processors (see Figure 3-7), mixers, and microwave ovens.

Figure 3-6: School-age kids can start working with handheld blenders and mini-choppers.

Figure 3-7: Blenders and food processors help older kids make shakes, soups, sauces, and more.

Favorite gadgets and gizmos for kids

With a little imagination, small kitchen tools can perform many tasks beyond their obvious function. Some can even replace knives for young, inexperienced hands to use.

During your kitchen tour and when you cook together, show kids how gadgets and utensils work. Peel a potato with a vegetable peeler and then let the kids try it. If a child has difficulty controlling the tool, place your hand around his, guiding him through the motion to help him get the feel of it.

You probably already have many of these inexpensive kitchen tools lurking in a drawer, just waiting for an eager pair of young hands to discover them:

✔ **Potato masher:** Like the model shown in Figure 3-8, potato mashers can mash and smash avocados, bananas, butter, beans, hard-cooked eggs, even whole canned tomatoes, and of course, cooked potatoes and sweet potatoes.

✔ **Ice cube tray:** With their many compartments, ice cube trays offer small children a world of fun. Little kids love to put everything from peas to pasta in the compartments — before actually eating them! Fruit juice ice cubes make refreshing summer treats, and parents can use ice-cube trays to freeze single-use portions of tomato paste and chicken broth.

✔ **Cookie-cutter:** Cutters that are similar to the varieties in Figure 3-9 bring immediate sparkle to a meal. Kids can cut sandwiches, biscuits, lunch meats, and cheese slices into fanciful shapes. Even picky eaters are more readily tempted to try cookie-cutter-shaped foods.

Make cookie-cutter-shaped croutons for soups and salads, as shown in Figure 3-9. Cut out lightly buttered bread, then slowly toast in a pan or low oven, until dry and crispy.

Figure 3-8: Little kids know instantly how to smash with a potato masher.

potato masher

yikes!

Figure 3-9: Cookie-cutters make eating fun — even for picky eaters.

✔ **Ice cream scoop:** An ice cream scoop, shown in Figure 3-10, goes beyond ice cream to scoop out consistent portions of cookie and biscuit dough, muffin batter, pancakes, meatballs, cooked rice, and cottage cheese. Cookware stores sell scoops in sizes ranging from 1 to 3 ounces.

Amazing, non-melting, kid-safe spatulas

Not only did technology put a man on the moon, but it solved the problem of melting rubber spatulas — a common accidental hazard when cooking with kids. Made from medical grade silicon rather than rubber, this type of spatula is flexible but won't melt or stain. Several companies make them, but my favorites are the ones by Le Creuset, which come in bright, happy colors and six different sizes. Their most versatile product, their "spoon spatulas," work (as the name implies) like a wooden spoon and spatula combined — perfect for stirring and scraping — and their stay-cool material keeps tender lips from being burned while tasting. Prices range from $4 to $12.

✔ **Jars:** Jars with screw-top lids give very young kids a chance to really shake things up. Simply put in the ingredients, shake vigorously, and instantly mix salad dressings, dips, batters, or marinades — easily, with no mess! Store leftovers in the same jar, to shake and pour again. As shown in Figure 3-11, some brands of bottled pasta sauce and canning jars even show measurement levels on the side.

✔ **Resealable bags:** Plastic resealable bags in various sizes have multiple uses, especially for younger children. Use them as easy, no-mess containers for mixing batters, squeezing decorative icing or melted chocolate designs on desserts, marinating, or freezing slushy ices, like the Watermelon Ice in Chapter 21. Kids can decorate Spider Web Brownies for Halloween by using melted peanut butter chips and a resealable bag, also shown in Chapter 21.

Figure 3-10: An ice cream scoop helps kids measure consistent portions.

ice cream scoop

Figure 3-11: Kids can mix, shake, and pour salad dressings in a screw-top jar.

✔ **Salad spinner:** This simple device, shown in Figure 3-12, offers children a kitchen task that's safe and easy enough even for preschoolers. To rinse and dry lettuce and other greens, place the spinner in the sink, fill the compartment about $1/3$ full, rinse well under running water, and then cover and spin. Don't fill the spinner too full or the water won't have enough room to escape. Spin the salad in batches if you need to. Kids can also dry shredded potatoes in a salad spinner.

✔ **Whisk or whip:** Whisks, also known as whips, come in many sizes, including ones shorter than five inches that fit small hands perfectly (see Figure 3-13). Use whisks to blend small amounts of sauces and salad dressings, beat eggs, and complete other mixing tasks.

Figure 3-12:
Salad spinners are safe tools for the youngest chefs.

Figure 3-13:
Wire whisks in small sizes fit little hands.

✔ **Egg slicer:** An egg slicer, shown in Figure 3-14, goes beyond hard boiled eggs to slice soft cheeses (like goat cheese or mozzarella), mushrooms, pitted olives, and even celery (by pushing the celery stalk through the wires).

✔ **Pastry blender:** Pastry blenders cut butter into flour properly for baking, as in the Cobblers for Gobblers recipe in Chapter 21, but kids can also chop hard-boiled eggs for egg salad and mash avocados or bananas using pastry blenders (messy but effective!). Make Green Eggs and Hamwiches (found in Chapter 17) with a pastry blender like the one in Figure 3-15.

Figure 3-14:
The versatile egg slicer slices more than just eggs — without cutting fingers!

Figure 3-15:
Pastry blenders also can mash avocados and eggs for egg salad.

✔ **Dough and bowl scrapers:** Dough scrapers and bowl scrapers, shown in Figure 3-16, work better than hands to move chopped vegetables from a cutting board to a pan or bowl. Inexpensive plastic bowl scrapers are flexible with a straight and a rounded edge, while metal dough scrapers cost a few cents more and are rigid for scraping and cutting dough on pastry boards. You can find out more about using dough scrapers in Chapter 9.

✔ **Mortar and pestle:** A mortar and pestle were used long before electrical appliances for grinding whole spices, sesame seeds, chiles, garlic, and herbs into seasoning blends or pastes. Even very young children can safely work a mortar and pestle, shown in Figure 3-17.

Figure 3-16:
Dough and bowl scrapers scoop chopped veggies off cutting boards better than little hands.

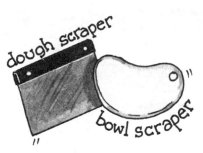

Figure 3-17:
Young hands can safely grind herbs, crush seeds, and mash garlic with a mortar and pestle.

✔ **Tongs:** Tongs come in many sizes, including small ones for small hands (see Figure 3-18). They keep fingers from being burned, offer more control than a fork, and pick up foods without piercing them. Use tongs to turn meats, mix salads, serve string beans, and keep fingers clean!

Figure 3-18:
Tongs pick up foods better than a fork and even come in kid-sizes.

✔ **Melon baller:** A melon baller, shown in Figure 3-19, can scoop seeds out of cucumbers and membranes out of bell peppers. Use a melon baller to drop exact measures of cookie dough in the Lacy Angels with Dirty Faces recipe (see Chapter 21).

Figure 3-19:
A melon baller can scrape like a knife, but without the super-sharp edge.

melon ballers

✔ **Safety scissors:** Safety scissors from your child's school supplies have endless uses in the kitchen. For children too young to use a knife, kid-size safety scissors, like those in Figure 3-20, can snip herbs, cut soft cheese slices, lunch meats, dried fruit, and sun-dried tomatoes — and can even open those impossible "easy open" plastic packages. Find them with either sharp or blunt tips wherever school supplies are sold.

To snip fresh herbs into small bits, place them in a shallow glass or cup, and then snip inside with safety scissors.

Figure 3-20:
Young kids can snip herbs, cut soft foods, and open plastic packages with safety scissors.

snip
snip

Safety Can really works — no sharp edges!

When I saw the Safety Can can opener advertised on TV, I was skeptical, but find that it really lives up to its claim. The opener uncrimps the lid from the can without cutting, so you don't end up with exposed, sharp edges. And because the opener's cutting edge never comes in contact with the food, it can't transport illness-causing bacteria (a common problem with traditional openers if they aren't washed after each use). The Safety Can takes getting used to, but if you're concerned about little fingers being cut by razor-sharp can lids and want to practice food safety measures, this is a worthwhile investment. Cookware catalogs, discount stores, and TV ads sell them as a set with the Safety-Jar easy jar opener for around $20.

- **Veggie peeler:** A vegetable peeler (also called a *swivel peeler*) shown in Figure 3-21, safely shaves peels from fruits and vegetables more thinly than most knives. For kids, a *harp peeler,* the harp-shaped or T-shaped model (shown in Figure 3-21), is easy to control and doesn't have a pointed tip like a swivel peeler does.

- **Sandwich spreaders:** True to their name, sandwich spreaders spread mustard, tuna fish, and condiments easily. Some come with a short serrated or saw-toothed edge, handy for cutting sandwiches, bread crusts, and soft foods, as shown in Figure 3-22.

- **Grater:** Graters come in all shapes and sizes, but the inexpensive box-shaped one in Figure 3-23 covers most needs. Kids can shred cheese or grate fruit, vegetables, ginger, and citrus zest.

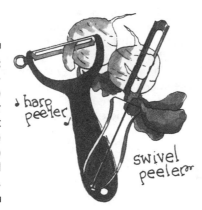

Figure 3-21:
A kid-friendly harp peeler works great without the pointed tip of a swivel peeler.

Figure 3-22:
Some sandwich spreaders have mildly serrated blades to cut soft foods.

Progressive International makes the Chop Top Box Grater shown in Figure 3-23, but similar models by other brands are available, including traditional Japanese versions. This type of grater has a clear plastic box to capture the grated foods, changeable grating blades, and a knuckle guard to protect fingers — making it especially kid-friendly. Look for them in cookware stores, mail-order catalogs, or for the Japanese models, in Japanese markets and hardware stores.

Figure 3-23:
Graters grate everything from ginger to cheese — but don't grate your knuckles!

✔ **Pizza cutter:** Pizza cutters (shown in Figure 3-24) come with plastic or metal blades and roll easily across soft foods like sliced bread, pie dough, tortillas, cheese, lunch meats, and dried fruits. Little fingers are less likely to fall underneath the blade as they would with a knife and a pizza cutter doesn't have a pointed tip. Kids especially like the rolling motion, so if parents pre-slice onions, garlic, and other vegetables, kids can further chop and mince them with a pizza cutter. Pizza cutters can also mince herbs and slice rolled up lettuce leaves into thin shreds or julienne.

Figure 3-24:
Pizza cutters let young kids slice, chop, and mince without a knife.

A really neat tip

To keep your work area dry and less messy, place a cutting board inside a lowsided pan, like a jelly roll, so that excess trimmings, spices, and spills fall into the pan. Place a damp towel under the cutting board or the pan to keep either one from slipping.

Chapter 4

Making Meals Delicious and Nutritious

What's the difference between boogers and broccoli? Kids don't eat broccoli.

Whether you're cooking with kids or racing solo to get food on the table, healthy meals can be challenging. In this chapter, I tell you which foods offer the biggest nutritional bangs for children and which ones to de-emphasize. Because nutritional information can be overwhelming, confusing, and contradictory, I've condensed a set of healthy common-sense guidelines that are easy to follow — including good news about snacks and fats.

What's the point, though, in cooking healthy meals if the kids don't eat them? In this chapter, I also show ways to make nutritious meals more appetizing by punching up flavors, colors, and textures. I outline easy techniques for making any recipe more healthful — and tasty enough to keep kids from feeding the family dog under the table.

Got a picky eater in the house? Families in this chapter share strategies for feeding finicky eaters while upping the vegetables, fruits, and vitamins in their diets.

Nutrition is a complex and changing subject, and this chapter focuses on basic guidelines for feeding children. For more information on the overall topic of nutrition, consult *Nutrition For Dummies* by Carol Rinzler (IDG Books Worldwide, Inc.). This book explains all of the essentials, including fat grams, calories, and cholesterol, in everyday words that are easily digestible.

Commonsense Nutrition for Kids

"I encourage anyone feeding my children to offer a wide variety of foods and to expect that on certain days, they'll scarcely eat at all. But not to worry — they make up for it the next day by eating twice as much. When I consistently offer a wide variety of healthy foods, they get the nutrients they need."
— Jeanne from St. Louis, Missouri

Children have a natural ability to listen to their body's food signals. They eat when they're hungry and don't eat when they aren't. One day your 5-year-old may barely eat a box of raisins, the next she'll chow down like a sumo wrestler.

How can you make sure your child is eating properly, without resorting to calculators and complex charts? By following commonsense practices:

- **Trust your children's instincts about their hunger.** Make enough food, but let kids decide how much they want to eat. Serve moderate portions and encourage them to ask for more when they want it. When a child isn't hungry, don't force her to eat. Respect her decisions.

- **Offer choices, but ones that are nutritionally appropriate for children.** Kids have different nutritional needs from adults — and parents' own fat, cholesterol, and fiber concerns aren't necessarily applicable to children. Dietitians caution parents against emphasizing diet foods with youngsters, because these foods can contribute to diet phobias. You don't want your kids to be fat, but you do want them to gain weight and grow. The "Focus on nutrient-dense foods" section, later in this chapter, offers more information on this topic.

- **Share the joy of eating by exposing children to new flavors, new foods, and various cooking methods.** Avoid routine ruts. The wider variety of foods a child enjoys, the more likely that she'll get all of the nutrients that she needs.

- **Never ban a favorite food.** Here's the rub: No whole food is inherently bad — not even fat, salt, or sugar — and no one should feel guilty about enjoying a treat from time to time. But all foods carry the potential for harm if they aren't balanced with other food groups. If the kids love hot, crispy, salty French fries, indulge them on an occasional basis, but reinforce that such special treats need to be balanced with healthier foods, and eaten in moderation, so that they can be enjoyed thoroughly, without guilt.

- ✔ **Give kids the opportunity to taste foods at their best.** This means buying fresh, seasonal, and whole foods. Today's busy parents often rely on convenience and packaged meals, but in the interests of good nutrition, balance these products with fresh, seasonal foods. Many packaged foods contain high levels of salt and unnecessary additives that offer no positive nutritional value.

- ✔ **Monitor nutrition over a period of time, not just in every meal.** Strive for a diet that is balanced over several days or a week. If one day's meals include high-fat foods, serve lower-fat foods the next day.

- ✔ **Empower children to make positive food choices.** Involve them in deciding what to cook and what to eat. Kids are more likely to eat a meal when they've been included in its planning and preparation.

- ✔ **Be an example.** Practice good eating habits. Explore new foods. Eat a balanced diet. Exercise regularly. Serve moderate portions. Try everything at least once, in front of your kids — then try it again. Eat foods you enjoy and enjoy the foods you eat.

Focus on nutrient-dense foods

Vitamins and minerals are nutrients that allow the body to use the protein, carbohydrates, and fat that you eat. The body can't manufacture these nutrients and instead gets them by ingesting plants and animals.

Kids who eat a balanced diet every day, with portions from each food group shown in the Food Guide Pyramid in Figure 4-1, get all the recommended daily allowances they need for vitamins and minerals. But few kids are pyramid-perfect. When planning meals for kids, focus on nutrient-dense foods.

Certain nutrients are especially important for children's growth:

- ✔ **Calcium:** Calcium makes bones and teeth strong — and the calcium kids eat now is meant to last a lifetime. Studies show that adequate levels of calcium ingested before the age of 20 keep bones strong, even into old age, especially when combined with exercise. But calcium intake for girls and young women today is usually insufficient and even boys aren't getting the recommended levels of calcium in their diets (see the sidebar "Calcium — good for girls"). Dairy products like milk, cheese, and yogurt are the best sources of calcium. Non-dairy foods rich in calcium include canned fish with bones (sardines), mustard greens, kale, tofu, beans, dried fruit, calcium-fortified orange juice, and broccoli. Vitamin D, which the body manufactures when exposed to the sun, aids in the absorption of calcium.

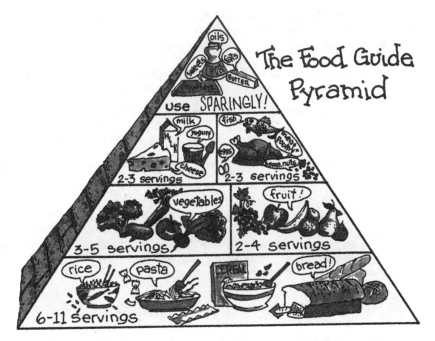

Figure 4-1:
The Food
Guide
Pyramid
illustrates
how to
balance
daily food
choices.

Even though the Food Guide Pyramid (refer to Figure 4-1) recommends two to three servings of dairy products a day, some nutritionists say that three to four servings better ensure adequate calcium for children, especially preschoolers. Boost the calcium, but not the fat in your cooking, by adding nonfat dry milk powder to milk or cream-based sauces, smoothies, desserts, or into fresh milk itself.

✔ **Vitamin C:** Also known as ascorbic acid, vitamin C is a powerful nutrient. It aids in healing, helps form the body's connective tissue, and improves the immune system. It's also an antioxidant, a substance that helps reduce damage caused by naturally-occurring and environmental toxins. Being a water-soluble nutrient, vitamin C isn't stored in the body and must be replenished daily. Kiwifruit is especially high in vitamin C. Other sources include citrus fruits, strawberries, tomatoes, bell peppers, papayas, cantaloupe, cabbage, potatoes, and raw, leafy vegetables — a colorful diet!

✔ **Iron:** Iron is an essential mineral that helps the blood carry oxygen to all the body's cells and strengthens the immune system. Iron is most commonly found lacking in infants, menstruating teenage girls, young women, and some vegetarians. Iron from meats, poultry, egg yolks, fish and especially liver is most readily absorbed by the body. Non-animal sources of iron may not be absorbed quite as well, but don't discount them — beans, peas, dark green vegetables, blackstrap molasses, dried fruit, and enriched cereals are all good sources of iron, as is iron-fortified cereal. Vitamin C helps the body absorb iron, so drinking orange juice while eating iron-rich foods is a good idea.

✔ **Vitamin A:** Another antioxidant, vitamin A promotes good vision, healthy growth, and a strong immune system. Being fat-soluble, vitamin A is stored in fat cells, so a certain amount of fat is needed in the diet to make vitamin A available to the body. When looking for good sources of vitamin A, think colorfully — orange, yellow, and red fruits and vegetables tend to be high in vitamin A. The best sources include carrots, sweet potatoes, winter squash, apricots, cantaloupes, spinach, and dark leafy greens.

✔ **Vitamin B complex:** Vitamin B complex reads like the back of a multi-vitamin supplement bottle and consists of thiamin, riboflavin, niacin, vitamin B6 (pyridoxine), folic acid, vitamin B12, pantothenic acid, and biotin — nutrients essential for energy metabolism. Being water-soluble, these nutrients aren't stored in the body and must be replenished daily. The good news is they can be obtained by eating a variety of foods. Following the Food Guide Pyramid (refer to Figure 4-1) and ingesting all the food groups is the best way to ensure adequate levels of vitamin B complex.

What counts as one serving?

The Food Guide Pyramid (refer to Figure 4-1) suggests the number of servings that everyone from age two on up should eat, but the recommendations aren't clear about the size of each serving, so the total number of servings per day can seem like a lot.

In the Food Guide Pyramid, the smaller of the two numbers of servings indicated by each food group (such as Fruit Group — 2 to 4 servings) is suggested for less-active women, older adults, and toddlers. The higher number of servings applies to teenage boys, active men, and older children, while teenage girls, active women, and less-active men fall somewhere in between.

But the size of the servings also counts, and this is where the Pyramid can be confusing. The recommended serving sizes within each food group vary from food to food and from adults to young children, as shown in Table 4-1. Be flexible — younger children may prefer smaller portions, and the energy needs among school-age kids can vary dramatically depending on growth rates, activity levels, and body sizes. For best results, use the Pyramid as a general guide for balancing all of the food groups in the diet, but adapt it to each person's unique appetite and caloric needs.

Table 4-1	Serving Sizes Recommendations by Age Groups	
Food Group	*Ages 4 and 5*	*Age 6 and Up*
Breads:		
Slice of bread	¹/₂ to 1	1
Cooked cereal, rice, pasta	¹/₃ cup	¹/₂ cup
Vegetables:		
Raw, leafy vegetables	¹/₄ cup	1 cup
Other cooked or chopped raw	¹/₄ to ¹/₂ cup	¹/₂ cup
Fruits:		
Medium fresh fruit	¹/₂ cup	1 whole
Chopped, cooked, or canned	¹/₂ cup	¹/₂ cup
Juice	¹/₂ cup	³/₄ cup
Dairy:		
Milk (any variety) or yogurt	³/₄ cup	1 cup
Cheese (hard)	1 to 1¹/₂ ounces	1¹/₂ ounces
Meats and proteins:		
Cooked meat, poultry, or fish	1¹/₂ ounces	2 to 3 ounces*
Cooked beans	¹/₄ to ¹/₃ cup	¹/₂ cup
Eggs	1¹/₂ to 2	1¹/₂ to 2
Peanut butter	1 to 2 tablespoons	2 tablespoons

*3 ounces is about the size of a deck of cards

The skinny on fat

The subject of nutrition seems more complicated every day — health recommendations seem to change with each new breakthrough and current research result. But no matter what formulas, plans, and pyramids are currently en vogue, the ultimate best diet is one that works for each individual. As dietitians and chefs alike recommend, "In matters of taste, consider health. In matters of health, consider taste. In all cases, consider the individual."

Faux food fake-outs

A lower-fat diet is definitely a healthy choice for anyone over the age of two, and parents who emphasize balanced nutrition, including limiting fat intake to 30 percent of calories, should be applauded. But cooking with lowfat and nonfat products has its pros and cons. I agree with Lynn from Medford, Oregon, who says: "Some lowfat and nonfat products are about as good as the packaging they come in. Others are very good. The quality depends on the product."

Nonfat cheeses may not add fat calories, but they don't really taste like cheese either. Lowfat salad dressings can be gummy and uninspiring, and nonfat sour cream doesn't taste like much of anything. I call these *faux foods,* because *faux* means "fake" in French. Many of the nonfat or lowfat products are frequently heavily doused in salt or sugar to replace the flavor lost by the fat. On the other hand, a few products, like certain breads, milk, and crackers, have cut the fat out naturally, without compromising on flavor or beefing up with additives, sweeteners, and salt.

I'm not advocating a diet high in fat, and I'm not slamming fat-altered products — there's nothing inherently wrong with them. Parents may want to enjoy these products in their own diets, but kids deserve a chance to taste the real thing.

I encourage you to introduce children to the tastes and textures of real foods — not faux foods. As kids' palates develop, flavors imprint themselves in memory. The taste of whole cheddar cheese on potatoes or freshly whipped cream on berries is unmatchable — you can serve these full-flavored ingredients in smaller amounts or less frequently, but at least your kids experience how wonderful the real thing tastes.

You can find strategies for healthy cooking — without faux foods — in Chapter 5 and in the recipes in Part IV.

Some nutritionists recommend a diet with no more than 30 percent of calories from fat, and no more than 10 percent from saturated fat (the kind that comes from animals and dairy products). Other research shows some cultures around the globe can eat diets of 35 to 40 percent fat without becoming fat or unhealthy. Many pediatricians balk at restricting the intake of nutrient-dense foods like milk, meats, and eggs for most children under five and all children under two, whose growing bodies require the higher levels of vitamins, protein, and minerals that foods with fat provide.

What can a parent do to make sense of conflicting recommendations? Use common sense and consider the individual. Instead of subscribing to claims made one headline at a time, look at reports substantiated by a whole body of evidence.

To keep fat in track, bust out of the following myths:

✔ **Myth: All fat is bad.**

Fact: Not all fats are created equal — fat in itself isn't a bad food. Without it, the body misses out on the fat-soluble vitamins A, D, E, and K. Fats that come from nuts, seeds, avocados, olives, certain types of fish, and many vegetables (unsaturated fats) actually bear healthful properties — nutritionists approve of them in the daily diet. But fats from animals and dairy products (saturated fats) can raise cholesterol to unhealthy levels, so eat them sparingly.

✔ **Myth: Cut out the fat and you won't get fat.**

Fact: Excess calories cause fat — regardless of the source of those calories. It's true that ounce for ounce, fatty foods contain more calories than do proteins or carbohydrates, but any food can make you fat if you don't burn up the calories. So even if you cut all fat out of your diet (not recommended because you need fat to transport fat-soluble vitamins), you can still become fat. Keep your children's and your own weight in check by increasing daily exercise and cutting back on total calories — reduce fat calories first, but don't eliminate them entirely.

✔ **Myth: Lowfat margarine is healthier than oil.**

Fact: Fats that are solid at room temperature, like margarine, lard, and butter, clog the arteries. These fats raise cholesterol levels and increase the risk of heart disease. Olive and canola oils actually lower cholesterol levels when used in place of other kinds of fat. Similarly, soft-tub margarine isn't as damaging as the more solid stick margarine or butter.

Don't be afraid to cook with fat, but choose your fats wisely, enjoy them sparingly, and balance foods containing both fats and nutrients within the overall diet.

Pacifying Picky Eaters

Are picky eaters born or made? Both. Kids go through stages. One week they hate asparagus. The next week, they adore it — and want nothing but asparagus at every meal, much to a parent's frustration. It's normal for kids to latch onto a favorite food and it's just as normal for kids' palates and tastes to change over time. Don't be too concerned when your child eats only one type of food one day — the next day she may compensate. Look for patterns over weeks and days, rather than meal by meal.

Calcium — good for girls

Growing boys need more calcium than adults do, but if you have a daughter, make an even greater effort to get extra calcium into her diet. The more calcium she has while she's young, the less likely she is to suffer from *osteoporosis*, a condition in which the bones become exceedingly fragile and brittle with age. While some men suffer from osteoporosis, women are especially prone to this disorder, which causes bones to break easily, even from a simple fall or tap. Asian women and women with tiny body frames have smaller bones, making them even more susceptible to bone loss. People who are lactose-intolerant and can't digest milk also have a greater need to ensure adequate calcium levels.

Help your daughters prevent osteoporosis — encourage them to build up calcium levels in the bones by ingesting plenty of calcium-rich foods. Girls and their mothers can help avoid osteoporosis together by walking, running, biking, and practicing other weight-bearing exercises regularly.

To give girls and boys more calcium, serve beans, whole grains, dark leafy green vegetables (broccoli, mustard greens, kale, and others), apricots, calcium-fortified orange juice, yogurt, lowfat milk, calcium-fortified soy milk, sardines with bones, canned salmon with bones, tofu, and blackstrap molasses. And avoid serving sodas with calcium-rich foods, because the phosphorus in soda interferes with calcium absorption.

Parents and siblings play a large role in what a child may choose — or refuse. Showing pleasure when eating certain foods instills positive reactions in kids. Force feeding results in negative ones. Peers can also influence what children like one day and hate the next. Jordan, Karen Grigsby Bates' son in Chapter 2, was crazy for tuna fish — until the day his new best friend said it was 'yucky.' "He secretly still loves the taste," she says. "He just won't eat it at school now."

Experts' tips on feeding kids

When feeding kids, parents are responsible for what foods to offer, when to offer them, and where to serve them. Kids are responsible for which foods they eat and how much. For parents trying to feed their kids balanced diets with sufficient nutrients, accommodating a finicky eater can be frustrating. And when kids don't eat what parents expect of them, too often a battle over food begins.

The following good advice, as suggested by child nutrition expert Ellyn Satter, makes so much sense that other nutritionists now wholeheartedly endorse it.

- **Never force a child to eat.** Enforcing the clean-plate rule creates negative associations with food. Let kids decide for themselves when they've had enough to eat.

- **Offer the child choices.** Allow her to determine the amount of food she needs to meet her hunger level. Let her eat what she wants and ask for more food or drink. Start with small portions and be willing to serve more when she asks for it.

- **Make a rule that the child must at least taste the food.** Expose children to new foods a little bit at a time. If she doesn't like the new item, praise her for trying it, respect her decision, and let her eat something else from the meal. As a safety net, include other dishes in the meal that you know she'll eat — bread and pasta are often good standbys.

- **Kids change their minds over time.** When a child doesn't like a food, reintroduce the food a few weeks later. It may take several attempts, but as kids' palates develop and with repeated exposure to the same food, kids do accept new tastes — although it can take as many as ten tries over time before a child accepts a new food and enjoys it.

- **Allow children their freedom of expression.** Food fads and food refusals are common. Kids often assert their developing personality and express themselves through their food likes and dislikes. If the overall diet is balanced over time, parents need not be concerned over a few food rejections.

- **Monitor your child's milk and juice consumption.** If a kid is picky at mealtime, she may be drinking too much milk or juice, filling up on these calories rather than ones from other food groups. Encourage her to drink water when she's thirsty, instead of drinking calorie-heavy beverages, and serve milk and juice as part of her scheduled snacks. Pour only a small amount to drink at one time.

- **De-emphasize desserts.** If you serve desserts, de-emphasize them by serving them with the meal. Avoid using desserts as bargaining chips for finishing a meal. Let kids know that the whole meal, including dessert, is part of a balanced diet. Strive for desserts that have nutritional value, such as pies made with fruit, or serve non-sweet desserts like fruit and cheese.

Parents' practical ways — managing picky eaters

"I never tell them to eat all of anything; instead I encourage them to eat until they're full. We always serve plenty of food and if green beans are ignored, I ask them to take five bites of the beans. I did this when they were younger — now their growing bodies send them to the table hungry and they eat everything."
— Pat from Medfield, Massachusetts

The parents I consulted became self-made experts in fighting the finicky food battle. Through years of trial and error, success and failure, and hit-and-miss tactics, parents have devised some practical — and innovative — tips for tackling picky eaters:

✔ **Sneak in veggies.**

"Give them what they like to a certain point, but sneak in the vegetables and other foods into their pasta sauces, casseroles, and so on. It really works!"
— Julie from Bloomington, Minnesota

✔ **Be inventive.**

"When my kids were toddlers, I had them convinced that frozen vegetables were a dessert item, just as yummy and delicious as a Popsicle, and easier to handle. They enjoyed it then, and now that they are 8 and 11, they still enjoy frozen vegetables with their dinners instead of cooked veggies. They defrost rather quickly and are actually very cold instead of frozen by the time they sit down to eat. I know this sounds really goofy, but it works!"
— Nancy from Wayne, New Jersey

✔ **Start kids with veggies before sweets.**

"I got my sons to like fruits and veggies when they were babies. Most new moms start their babies on the fruits first, but I started them on veggies first — I was told by my oldest son's doctor to do it this way so that they get use to the taste of veggies first rather than the taste of sweet fruits. After they had gone through the veggies, I started giving them fruit. I guess I just got lucky, because both of my kids prefer vegetables and fruits as snacks, instead of cakes and cookies."
— Lisa from University Park, Illinois

✔ **Tempt kids with dipping sauces.**

"My youngest son really didn't like to eat meat. I can season it to my heart's delight when I cook it and he still won't eat it. But I find that if I put some sort of sauce on his plate — steak sauce, ketchup, barbecue sauce, extra gravy, or whatever goes with that particular meat — he eats it. I guess he finds it fun to dip the meat in it. All I know is that it has stopped a lot of hassle trying to get him to eat his meat."
— Lisa from University Park, Illinois

✔ **Try unconventional presentations.**

"Toss salads with lots of veggies and meat mixed in and ranch dressing. Serve breakfast for dinner. Or, offer them buffet-style plates of fruit and veggies."
— Mary from Chandler, Arizona

✔ **Be patient.**

"When our children were young we had a wise pediatrician who said, 'When they get hungry, they will eat.' We never insisted on cleaned plates, never forced a child to eat something he didn't want, and balanced meals nutritiously. There were times I thought one may starve to death, or another would turn into a food he was bingeing on, but they always managed to even out sooner or later."
— Sunnye from Bartlesville, Oklahoma

Snack Facts — Grazing through the Day

Small meals make sense. Eating healthful snacks or mini-meals several times a day can provide more energy than three big meals — for adults and children alike. If you have self-reliant adolescents in the house, be sure to stock your kitchen with healthy snacks and quick meal fixings that can stand up against a teenager's relentless snack attacks, rather than the usual potato chips and cookies.

Grazing works best with a balanced variety of foods eaten in moderation. Mix and match the following healthy snacks to ensure samplings from all the food groups:

✔ **Bread group:** Pretzels, bagels, whole grain crackers, saltines, graham crackers, animal crackers, dry cereals, rice cakes, gingersnaps, tortillas (corn and flour), pita bread, whole grain breads or rolls, rice crackers, and popcorn.

✔ **Vegetable group:** Baby carrots, celery, broccoli, cauliflower, cucumber slices, green beans, peas, zucchini, radishes, bell peppers. Serve any of these plain or with dip.

- ✔ **Fruit group:** Fresh fruits and dried fruits of all types.

- ✔ **Milk group:** Cheese slices, string cheese, cottage cheese, ricotta cheese, yogurt, frozen yogurt, milk, and sherbet.

- ✔ **Meat group:** Hard-cooked eggs, peanut butter, and lean deli meats such as ham, turkey, or chicken.

- ✔ **Nuts and seeds:** Toasted pumpkin or squash seeds, sunflower seeds, hazelnuts, almonds, pecans, walnuts, peanuts, pine nuts, and cashews.

- ✔ **Sweets:** Spiced applesauce, frozen raspberries, angel food cake, frozen yogurt, lowfat yogurt, smoothies, and pudding.

Kids need snacks

Young children need to *graze* — eat small amounts of food throughout the day. Three meals a day can't give their small stomachs enough food to fuel their growing bodies. And active teenagers, whose bodies are also undergoing rapid growth spurts, thrive on snacks, more so than do school-age youngsters. But there's a knack to snacks — these mini-meals should keep kids going, whatever their ages, without disrupting the appetite at main meals.

Work towards hunger management by letting appetites develop; that is, feed kids when they're truly hungry, but not famished. Kids need to experience that coming to the table with a moderate appetite is a prelude to enjoying a meal. Being hungry sparks an interest in eating and a greater willingness to try new foods — but being overly hungry results in eating too much food too quickly.

Follow these tips to make snacks a balanced part of your children's daily fare:

- ✔ Serve snacks at planned times to help regulate kids' appetites.

- ✔ Preschoolers need to eat every three to four hours. Fill in the gaps between meals with nutritious snacks selected from a combination of food groups, shown in the Food Guide Pyramid (refer to Figure 4-1).

- ✔ A day's snacks, lumped together, should total about one-fourth of the calories for the entire day. Think of a day's worth of snacks as one more average-size meal.

- ✔ Offer children two or three choices for their snacks, but only offer choices with nutritional value. Emphasize nutrient-dense snacks.

✔ Serve snacks in limited portions. Set out a handful of pretzels, rather than the whole bag.

✔ Allow 1^1/$_2$ to 2 hours between a snack and a meal to allow your child's appetite to develop. If a child is too ravenous at snack time — devouring a meals' worth of food instead of a snack-size portion — move the snack period up so she doesn't get so hungry. If the child isn't hungry at dinner, change the snack time or the snack amount.

✔ For snacks within a couple hours of mealtime, opt for lighter foods, like fruits and veggies. If the next meal will take longer than a few hours, select heartier snacks, like crackers with yogurt or milk.

Parents' practical ways — snacks and mini-meals

The snack savvy parents in this book prepare kid-friendly snacks regularly and share the following tips:

✔ **Fill up a fruit bowl.**

"For snacks on the go, I find that if I leave a big bowl of fruit on the counter where the kids can get it and don't have to look for it or ask for it, I end up filling it about three times a week. If they're late for school or sports, they grab an apple or a banana (or two) and eat it on the way."
— Karen from Southborough, Massachusetts

✔ **Cut up the fruit.**

"I keep a 'rotating fruit bowl' in the refrigerator and every Sunday I add new fruit. I find that everyone eats more fruit if it is cut up and prepared. I also pack fruit into lunches: if the fruit is ready in a serveable form, it is more readily eaten. I hate to get back unpeeled oranges in lunch bags."
— Fern from King George, Virginia

✔ **Serve morning snacks.**

"A child who isn't nourished has a lower level of concentration and happiness about him. As a teacher, I always provided a snack time about one or two hours into the morning for all the kids."
— Shea from Port Washington, New York

Shake, rattle, 'n' roll!

What you do is as important as what you eat, so instead of restricting a child's calories, encourage healthy eating habits and lots of exercise. The best way to maintain your own weight and stay healthy is to exercise regularly. Physical activity not only balances the calories you consume, but it also gives you more energy and improves the way your body functions. Keeping your weight in check reduces the risk of heart disease, stroke, certain cancers, and the most common form of diabetes.

Parents and kids can become more physically active together. Try to do 30 minutes of any of the following activities, several days per week.

☺ Shake your hands and move your feet, dance together to a rhythmic beat.

☺ Rattle your bones with a hop, skip, and jump in the yard.

☺ Roll away those sleepyhead blues with a brisk morning walk.

☺ Play a game of tag or basketball.

☺ Run in the park.

Expend more energy every day simply by walking more often, using stairs, parking far away from the supermarket or mall entrance, placing frequently used items on shelves that require you to stretch to reach them, and whipping cream or kneading bread dough by hand instead of by machine.

Producing Flavor-able Reactions

Healthful foods have gotten a bad rap. When it's nutritious and it's good for you, then it must not taste very good, right? Baloney! Lowfat turkey baloney, I say!

Giving meals a makeover

Anyone can cook healthy meals without compromising on flavor. Try the recipes in Part IV to get started, but use the same techniques with your own recipes to make them more nutritious — and still delicious.

Make your favorite meals more healthful by doing the following:

✔ **Change the recipe ingredients.** Substitute ingredients that are richer in nutrients or lower in fat. Instead of traditional meatloaf, add a can of pumpkin puree to the mix, like the Harvest Moon Meatloaf in Chapter 18. Your family won't detect the pumpkin in it, but they'll be eating a favorite meal that's richer in vitamin A and calcium, and lower in fat.

✔ **Change the cooking method.** Avoid deep-fat frying. Instead of french-fried potatoes and fried chicken, switch to oven-frying, like the 2-Bucket Batch of Oven-Fried Chicken (Chapter 18) and Everyday Oven Fries (Chapter 19). Or, broil or grill instead of fry — the fats melt away. Steam or microwave vegetables, instead of boiling them, to retain more nutrients (see the microwaved Minted Mini-Carrots in Chapter 19). Use a nonstick pan and sauté foods in a fraction of the oil, or use a nonstick cooking spray.

✔ **Create new combinations of foods.** Expand your cooking repertoire through an increased variety of foods mingled in new ways. Make salads of carrots, cranberries, and celery; pears and hazelnuts; or oranges and fennel. Fill sandwiches and tortillas with apples and cheese, spinach and ricotta, or roasted peppers and mushrooms. Bake buttermilk cornbread with cooked and chopped spinach, corn kernels, diced apples, or red and green peppers. Emphasize more fruits and vegetables in your combinations.

✔ **Switch to lower-fat proteins.** Emphasize poultry, lean pork, and non-meat proteins like beans and grains. Pick white meat over dark meat chicken and remove the skin from chicken before serving. The recipe for Ruby-Red Grapefruit Chicken in Chapter 18 is so flavorful, you won't even miss the skin — or the fat.

Cooking with charisma

Create tempting meals that appeal to all the senses — that's the key to making healthy foods a regular part of your diet. When a meal looks inviting, smells irresistible, and tastes great, your family will eagerly eat it and appreciate it.

Appetizing and nutritious meals don't require extra time, just a little creativity and well-applied tips like the following:

✔ **Sparkle with spice.** Cook with spices, herbs, and seasonings to create nonfat flavor bases. Toast spices to release their flavorful oils. Whenever possible, use fresh herbs instead of dried ones and add them toward the end of the cooking time. An extra pinch of a spice or herb in the last few minutes of cooking refreshes the flavors, especially when a dish has been simmering a long time. Experiment with unfamiliar spices by heating them in a bit of butter or oil, then tasting them on a cube of bread, to see what the flavor is like when they're cooked. The recipes for Mexican Fiesta Tacos in Chapter 18 and Irish Poppy Seed Soda Bread in Chapter 17 jazz up common ingredients just by using spices.

✔ **Pucker up.** Tart and tangy ingredients punch up flavors without fat. Zip up a dish with vinegar, lemon juice, mustard, fruit puree, green onions, capers, salsa, chiles, and citrus zest.

✔ **Cook with an accent.** Use foreign seasonings for international flair. Soy sauce adds flavor and helps meats brown better. Mix Lebanese pomegranate molasses with brown sugar for a tangy ham glaze. Rub skinless chicken breasts with Middle Eastern sumac powder for lemon-like tartness. Consult international cookbooks or the Global Gourmet Web site at www.globalgourmet.com for recipes that use these and other unusual ingredients.

✔ **Be a little saucy.** Spoon on, or dip into, healthy sauces — ones that are low in fat or rich in nutrients. Boost simple foods like chicken, vegetables, and chips with the Chimichurri Sauce or Jamaican Sunshine Salsa in Chapter 20.

✔ **Pinch with power.** Ramp up the taste of finished dishes and whole recipes with a pinch of nuts, cheeses, or flavored oils. A little goes a long way when using flavor-intense, nutritious foods like sesame oil, hazelnut, walnut, and extra virgin olive oils; Parmesan, romano, feta and goat cheeses; and toasted hazelnuts, pecans, walnuts, sesame seeds, sunflower seeds, and pumpkin seeds.

✔ **Dress for success.** Create full-flavor salad dressings from ingredients that are naturally low in fat. Use fruit juices, rice wine vinegar, balsamic vinegar, and other mild acids — you need less oil for balance. Thin out a high-fat creamy dressing with tangy lowfat buttermilk, or make the Home-on-the-Ranch Dressing in Chapter 20 and use it on salads or as a dip.

✔ **Paint a rainbow.** Pick colorful foods for visual appeal — and essential nutrients. Red, yellow, and orange fruits and vegetables are rich in vitamin A. Dark green leafy vegetables supply calcium, vitamin C, and a whole range of important nutrients. Cook these fruits and vegetables as side dishes, main courses, or as garnishes — cut them up raw for color, texture, and flavor accents. Fortify pastas, soups, casseroles, and salads with diced red bell pepper, grated carrots, yellow squash, or chopped spinach. Cook simple meals with bright fruits as in Sweet 'n' Sour Kiwi Shrimp (Chapter 18).

✔ **Eat like a rabbit.** Enjoy a wide assortment of vegetables — they're nutritious, naturally lowfat foods. Besides using brightly colored vegetables, emphasize cruciferous vegetables like cabbage, broccoli, kale, mustard greens, bok choy, cauliflower, turnips, and kohlrabi. These and other members of the cabbage family contain cancer-fighting nutrients, beta-carotene, fiber and vitamin C. For best flavor, eat these vegetables raw or cooked quickly, until just crisply tender. Because of their strong flavors, these vegetables taste best when eaten within a day of cooking.

✔ **Go with the grain.** Add a variety of flavor and texture by serving more grains. Increase energy-supplying carbohydrates, B vitamins, and iron by putting grains in the center of the plate — eat pastas, rice, barley, and whole-grain foods as main courses, and switch to whole-wheat bread, whole-grain cereal, bran flakes, and brown rice. Jazz grains up with vegetables, spices, and herbs, and if desired, small amounts of meat, fish, shellfish, cheese, and poultry. Try these good grain recipes in Chapter 19: Easy, Cheesy Polenta; Orange-Scented Couscous; and Perfectly Nice Rice.

✔ **Use your bean.** Be smart — eat beans as main courses or add spoonfuls to other dishes. Protein-rich beans and legumes like lentils and peas boost a meal's flavors, fiber, and nutrients when mixed into salads, soups, rice, pastas, and casseroles. For a winning strategy to cook up any kind of flavorful bean, check out the Basically Great (Dried) Beans recipe in Chapter 19.

✔ **Leave them breathless.** Because of their intense seasoning abilities, garlic and onion can be a cook's best friend for punching up flavor without fat. For variety of flavor and color, add red onions, green onions (scallions), chives, and shallots — all members of the garlic and onion family. Use them raw or, for a milder flavor, cook them until soft. Some evidence suggests that garlic and onion may also provide medicinal benefits.

✔ **Dance to a beat without any meat.** Make more meatless meals and use meat sparingly. Use meats as seasonings, adding small bits to perk up the flavor of a main-dish pasta or salad. Grilled, smoked, cured, and marinated meats are especially flavorful. When serving meat as an entree, serve 3-ounce portions (about the size of a deck of cards) for adults and teens, and smaller portions for younger children. Nutritionally, that's all the protein from meat that most people need. Eating less meat cuts back on unhealthy saturated fat, the kind that comes from animals and dairy products.

Chapter 5

Meal Planning

. . . .

In This Chapter

▶ Inviting kids to help plan meals

▶ Making meaty and meatless meals in one

▶ Creating jazzy meals — out of leftovers

▶ Taking boredom out of weekday meals

. . . .

Why did the cabbage beat the carrot in a race? Because it was a head.

*O*nly three things are certain in life: death, taxes, and the inescapable question "What's for dinner?"

Developing a weekly meal plan saves time, makes cooking more pleasurable, and gives you a happy, snappy answer to that ever-burning what's-for-dinner query. In this chapter, you find specific meal plans using the kid-friendly recipes in Part IV, but the handy strategies featured here go way beyond my recipes. These proven methods empower you to plan your own healthy, tasty meals that you can prepare in just 15 to 60 minutes — including ones that satisfy both vegetarians and meat-eaters alike. Also in this chapter, families share their own creative tips for making the most of meal planning by involving kids in the process, resulting in bonus lessons for the kids and happier eating for all.

Mapping Your Meals

Which comes first when planning meals: the recipe or the ingredients? Some people sit at their desks or computers, writing up specific menus, recipes, and shopping lists and plotting out meals for a week or even a month — before ever venturing to the market shelves. Others shop first, picking up fresh foods and timely specials, and then decide what to make. I find both methods have much to offer and work best when combined together — have an idea of what you plan to cook, but be flexible.

Planning meals has much in common with playing classic board games, like Risk or Clue, because both activities create strategic plans of action using logic, organization, and inventiveness — and they can both include the element of surprise.

Meal planning, like strategy games, can be challenging and fun. Whether you use a large calendar to plot out your meals one week or month in advance or prefer to cook on the fly, ask yourself the following questions to help organize menu priorities and set up your plan of attack.

- ✔ **Who's making the meals?** If it's you, can you expect help from your children or partner? Is the meal intended for teens to simply pop in the oven or microwave? Will school-age children make the meal as an after-school snack? Consider the level of cooking expertise needed when planning meals.

- ✔ **Who's eating the meals?** Are you feeding picky eaters, vegetarians, or a grandparent on a special diet? Will you cook the same meal for all or make adjustments for an individual? Planning meals to accommodate a range of diets can be tough. Jump to the "Vegetarians in Carnivorous Households" section in this chapter for ways to cook for multiple diets, and check out the tips for feeding picky eaters in Chapter 4.

- ✔ **What ingredients will you use?** What fresh foods are available? Check the newspaper's weekly food section (usually published on Wednesdays or Thursdays) for seasonal produce and advertised specials. Perhaps you'll plan to include leftovers or *morphed* meals, described later in this chapter. Keep a well-stocked pantry with ingredients for every circumstance, including non-perishable items like pastas and canned beans, and specialty foods like olives and roasted peppers for jazzing up simple meals.

- ✔ **When will the meals be eaten?** Must a meal be ready at a set time or can it wait until the family is assembled? If dinnertime may be delayed, plan a meal that won't dry out or overcook while waiting. For a preschooler's mid-morning snack, consider the type of food and portion size that won't disrupt his lunchtime appetite (see Chapter 4 for more on snacks).

- ✔ **Where will the meals be eaten?** Will a meal be served as a sit-down dinner with a full place setting or a casual barbecue with paper and plastic tableware? Are you preparing the meal as a handheld breakfast on the run, a tidy snack at school, or a brown-bag lunch on the go? Plan meals that can be easily eaten in each circumstance. Be sure to practice food safety tips in Chapter 8, especially for portable meals.

✔ **How long are you willing to spend cooking the meals?** Do the meals need to fall into a 15-minute plan or can you allow up to an hour? If kids are helping, will this mean more or less time to make the meals? If you have more free time on weekends, can you prepare foods then to save time later in the week? To make the most of your time in the kitchen, zip to the "Streamlining Strategies for Peak Performance" section, later in this chapter.

✔ **Why are you making the meals?** Understanding why you're making a meal helps set realistic expectations and priorities. Some foods, like breakfast bars, are eaten mainly for nourishment on the run, others are part of social events for enjoyment and to bring the family together. Sometimes a special dessert is often "special" because you crave it and will spend hours creating it. When you or your family indulges in an occasional high-calorie (but irresistible) treat, recognize the need to make lower-calorie meals that balance the diet over the week.

When planning meals, follow the Food Guide Pyramid (see Chapter 4) to balance your diet by incorporating all the different food groups in your menus and recipes.

Recruiting Kids for Beaucoups Benefits

Don't hoard all of the fun for yourself — involve the kids in meal planning. When kids contribute their ideas for weekly meals, it stimulates their creativity and offers them a chance for personal expression.

Meal planning means much more than just putting food on the table efficiently and nutritiously. It's an opportunity to benefit kids in ways that go beyond the food on the plate. When kids become active in meal planning, parents can see winning results like these:

✔ **Kids who help plan meals are more likely to eat foods they've selected. When given the freedom to express themselves, kids' healthy choices may surprise parents.**

"Involve kids who are old enough to help by talking over menus and preparing them together. You can teach by example, and eventually your kids will accept your standards of healthy eating. Kids today are quite nutrition conscious — that's a great motivator to your meal planning."
— Shea from Port Washington, New York

✔ **Asking children for their suggestions says they are important, boosts their self-esteem, and nurtures parent-child bonds.**

"We try to plan weekly menus while making out the grocery list. The kids love this, because it is their time to say what we are and aren't going to eat in the coming week and what was 'bad' and what was 'good' about last week's meals, especially if it was one of our 'experimental' weeks."
— Erin from Tennessee

✔ **Kids who take an interest in selecting the foods that they eat are more likely to join you in the kitchen so that you can cook together.**

"Kids like food that is simple, but tasty. The best situation is when they come up with the menu and you just help them make dinner."
— Christy from Woodstock, Georgia

✔ **Kids' meal suggestions relieve parents from constantly deciding what to eat. New views can transform boring routines into refreshing, innovative ideas.**

"When we get in a rut, I ask them to list the foods and recipes they like best. Then we plan menus from there. I expect my kids to eat what we have (no short-order cooking) unless it's a long-standing dislike. Then they only have to taste it."
— Susan from Early, Texas

✔ **By using the Food Guide Pyramid (flip to Chapter 4) to plan meals, children discover how to develop healthy nutrition habits. Encourage them to vary the groups they eat, and also to vary the foods within each group.**

"I have a Food Guide Pyramid posted on the fridge that the kids can look at all the time — for grains, fruits, veggies, proteins, and dairy, along with examples of each. They are in the habit of looking at it. I try to have these foods available at all times — cereals in the morning, with lots of fruits available for them to grab. They also make their own lunches with the Pyramid in mind."
— Charlene from Cleveland, Ohio

✔ **Planning meals over an extended time period enhances children's organizational skills. Kids see that many factors must come together to create meals.**

"I think it's important to teach the boys to plan for what they need. We spend time figuring out how much each person will eat so that we don't waste a lot of food. Kendal is particularly concerned with this as his teacher taught them about tigers early in the year. Tigers don't waste any of the food they catch and Kendal strives to be a tiger with every meal."
— Carol from Madison, Wisconsin

The game of lucky leftovers

"We have leftover night once a week at our house. On that night we give the children a menu of what we have left over and there is a price by each one. My husband becomes the waiter and I the cook. We give the children their play money and they order what they want from the menu. The children have a blast ordering from the menu and my fridge gets cleaned out. They also learn how to place an order and how to use money. It's fun!"

— Cindy from Little Rock, Arkansas

Snap! Crackle! Pop! Banishing Boredom

Which dinner makes your mouth water: a plate of roast chicken, baked potato, and creamed corn or a plate of roast chicken sprinkled with chives, oven-roasted red potato spears, and a salad of leafy spinach, diced red pepper, and fresh corn kernels?

Both dinners are simple meals and take about the same amount of time to prepare — but the second meal is designed to be more appetizing. On the second plate, the main course and side dishes all have deep and contrasting colors, and the textures include soft, chewy, crispy, and crunchy. The second meal also includes protein, complex carbohydrates, and a wide assortment of vegetables that complement the other dishes — the salad's tartness contrasts with the chicken's richness and the mildly flavored potatoes offset the intensity of the salad and chicken. Unlike the first dinner, the second meal has balance.

The best tasting recipes combine ingredients to complement each other, making the end result more than the sum of the parts. Successful meal planning does the same thing — it balances a combination of recipes into one harmonious meal that satisfies all the senses in its taste, color, aroma, and texture.

When selecting recipes for a meal, balance them nutritionally (as discussed in Chapter 4) and also strive to make the total meal balanced in these three ways:

✔ **Flavor:** Avoid serving a meal with all the same flavors in the foods. Your taste buds register sweet, sour, salty, and bitter. If you put too much of one flavor on the plate, it becomes overwhelming. To plan meals with flavors that contrast and complement each other:

- Prepare a single dish that has contrasting flavors in it, like the Sweet 'n' Sour Kiwi Shrimp recipe in Chapter 18.

- Serve the dish accompanied by a dish of opposite flavors. To offset the sharpness and intensity of the Sweet 'n' Sour Kiwi Shrimp in Chapter 18, serve it with the neutral taste of steamed white rice (like the Perfectly Nice Rice in Chapter 19).

- Prepare the dish, then add a complementary accent after it's done. Add chopped green onions to the top of the shrimp to accent the sweet and sour flavors and also add texture and color.

✔ **Texture:** Mix different food textures on one plate. To balance a soft food, serve it with a crispy one. To add crunch as a contrasting texture, try the following:

- Prepare a soft dish that has crunch built into the recipe, such as baking an au gratin casserole topped with toasted breadcrumbs, like the Butternut-Gouda Gratin in Chapter 19.

- Serve a smooth dish with a crunchy side dish, such as Easy, Cheesy Polenta in Chapter 19, accompanied by a crisp and colorful carrot, radish, and cucumber salad.

- Top off a dish with a quick, crunchy garnish, such as sprinkling nuts on top of ice cream or toasted sunflower seeds on top of rice.

✔ **Color:** Pick contrasting colors to make a dish more appetizing and attractive. As with textures, you can:

- Prepare a recipe that has contrasting colors within it, such as Spinach-Mango Technicolor Salad (Chapter 19).

- Serve the dish accompanied by one or more dishes of different color, such as serving Poached Pink Salmon (Chapter 18) with Peas and Shiitake Mushrooms (Chapter 19).

- Prepare the dish, then add a contrasting topping, such as sprinkling a broiled white fish fillet with diced red and green peppers.

Vegetarians in Carnivorous Households

Cooking healthy meals for family members of differing diets — without making two completely different dinners — can be difficult. Diabetes, allergies, being overweight or underweight, or food sensitivities may dictate special meals for some, but not all, family members.

Similarly, households with both vegetarians and non-vegetarians present a challenge when meal planning. School-age children and teenagers in particular frequently opt for meatless meals in an otherwise non-vegetarian household. Or, sometimes the family cook may personally commit to a vegetarian diet, but still serve all food groups to the rest of the family.

Some vegetarians avoid foods of all animal origins, while others allow eggs and dairy products in their diets. But when vegetarians cut meat from their diet, they're also cutting out dietary sources of iron, protein, and vitamin B12. To maintain a healthy diet, vegetarians need to get these nutrients from other sources, such as beans, tofu, and other soy-bean products like miso; eggs (if allowed); dark, leafy vegetables; and whole grains. Cheese adds calcium but should be eaten moderately because of its fat content. Vegetarians who don't consume any dairy products, especially teenagers, should take calcium supplements. To ensure vegetarians are getting the proper nutrients, especially as children, consult your physician or pediatrician, and check out the vegetarian resources in the Appendix.

I'm turning vegetarian, I'm turning vegetarian. . .I really think so

If you're not a vegetarian, you may one day decide to cut all meats out of your diet, for any number of reasons. Or, your mate or kids may object to eating any food that had a mother. Some people opt for vegetarianism simply because they feel better when they don't eat meat, or because they prefer the taste of vegetables, grains, and non-meat foods. Or, they may choose vegetarianism for moral reasons.

Even if you're not totally vegetarian, nutritionists recommend pushing proteins to the side of the plate and centering the meal on vegetables, grains, and non-meat foods. By emphasizing grains and produce, and serving meats less frequently, you can more easily offer meals suitable to vegetarians and committed meat-eaters alike.

Veggie vesting

Streamline the tasks you perform most frequently — cutting up vegetables — by chopping or slicing them in bigger batches but less often. You can save time if you do the following:

☺ **Precut your vegetables.** If a recipe calls for onion, chop up two or three onions at the same time and refrigerate the remainder in resealable bags for use in later recipes. Use a food processor to really speed things up. If you use sautéed onions often, make a large batch and store in recipe-size portions in the refrigerator or freezer.

☺ **Buy prepared, packaged vegetables in the produce section.** Peeled baby carrots, cleaned spinach, sectioned fruit, and coleslaw mixes save chopping time.

☺ **Rinse enough lettuce for use for two days.** This is a great kid task. Remove the leaves, rinse them thoroughly, and spin them in a salad spinner or roll them in a clean kitchen towel to dry. Place the towel in a plastic bag, leaving the end of the bag opened, and store in the refrigerator crisper. The leaves stay fresh and instantly-ready for salads or sandwiches.

☺ **Make salad dressing for the week.** A homemade vinaigrette takes minutes to prepare, whether you're making enough for one salad or five. A blender or handheld blender produces a thick, creamy dressing that won't separate. Store the dressing in a wide-mouth jar and let younger kids shake it up before use. School-age kids can make the dressing themselves.

☺ **Soak beans overnight so they cook in less time.** Alternatively, if you forget to soak, follow the quick-cooking tips in the the "Beanology 101" sidebar in Chapter 19.

To cook for both meat-eaters and non-meat-eaters, plan meals with these guidelines in mind:

✔ **Select the side dishes first.** Most side dishes, such as soups, salads, breads, pastas, and vegetables, are typically made without meat. Prepare extra portions of these meatless sides to feed vegetarians. Offer a variety of non-meat foods at meals.

✔ **Change the center of the plate.** Instead of making meat and protein the focus of the meal, put grains, vegetables, and pastas in the spotlight. Make these meatless dishes as satisfying and attractive as you would any entree. Gradually move meat into a side dish position, giving your family time to adjust.

✓ **Prepare favorite vegetarian foods in quantity, then freeze in individual portion sizes.** Thaw the portions in the refrigerator or microwave oven. Pastas, grains, beans, some casseroles, and breads freeze well and can be served plain or reheated with a fresh sauce.

✓ **Switch to true vegetarian staples in all your recipes.** Many products are made with some meat but don't have to be — and meat eaters won't miss a thing. Instead of cooking with chicken broth, use vegetable broth. Check product ingredient labels for meats and poultry, and opt for canned beans, soups, and frozen convenience foods that are completely meatless.

Universal meal-making

Vegetarians in carnivorous households shouldn't feel like alien beings — they deserve meals as special and wholesome as the rest of the family's. The key to cooking meaty and meatless meals begins by planning a simple, universal recipe adaptable to both meat eaters and vegetarians. Here's how it works:

1. **Pick a starting recipe — meatless or with some meat — that has flavors that everyone enjoys.**

2. **Prepare the same chopped vegetables, herbs, spices, and seasonings for two versions of the recipe — one meatless and one with meat.**

3. **Cook as much of the recipe as you can without meat, such as sautéing onions, making the sauce, or boiling pasta.**

4. **Complete the final cooking process using two pots or pans — one for the meatless meal and one for the vegetarian.**

To better illustrate the universal meal-making process, I've created two recipes that can be made into both meaty and meatless versions at the same time. Look in Chapter 18 at the recipes for Calabacitas Vegetarian or Turkey Tacos and Paprikash, Two Ways.

Streamlining Strategies for Peak Performance

To make the most of your time in the kitchen, keep meals simple, and avoid complicated cooking techniques. Simple meals don't have to be boring. They can range from excitingly new to comfortably familiar. Simple meals offer two advantages: they're usually quicker to prepare and it's easier to involve your children in making them. The real test of a streamlined meal is in the active time required to make it — quick-to-fix meals can easily be slow-cooked ones. A stew or roast may take hours to cook, but takes only a few minutes to put together.

Make the time you spend cooking with or for your kids more efficient by practicing these techniques:

- ✔ **Be a weekend warrior.** Use weekends to prepare weekday meals — fully or partially. See the "Marvelous, Morphable Meal Plans" section later in this chapter for practical tips on making food ahead of time.

- ✔ **Remember the big chill.** Freeze cooked recipes and some raw ingredients to extend your recipes without forcing the family to eat the same thing night after night.

- ✔ **Freeze cut-up fruits and whole berries.** Drop them in a blender with some juice, yogurt, or milk and blend up a healthy frozen smoothie. Or, puree berries as a quick topping for ice cream or pancakes.

- ✔ **Shop for shortcuts.** Buy time-saving foods that are fresh or freshly cooked. Whole roasted chickens from the deli counter can be made into tacos and burritos. Cruise through the salad bar for an instant side dish or sandwich greens. Buy bags of precut veggies.

- ✔ **List it.** Keep a running list of perishables, like produce and meats, that need to be eaten. As you freeze and thaw foods, keep a list of what's available in the freezer. Make a list of the pantry staples always on hand for quick meals. Kids are great at updating lists.

Don't throw away your shopping list. Keep it for the week and mark off the perishables as you use them. This saves time by not having to make another list, and it reminds you of those fresh produce items buried out of sight in the crisper. Grouping perishables together on the list makes them easier to read, shop for, and cross off.

- ✔ **Avoid trying new recipes when you're rushed.** Stick to something you can make by memory. The first time you make a recipe always takes longer until you become familiar with it. Make new recipes on weekends or when your time is flexible.

- ✔ **Plan recipes that use fast cooking methods, like sautéing, grilling, and steaming.** Take a look at Chapters 12 and 13 for instructions on these cooking techniques and recipe examples.

- ✔ **Make less labor-intensive meals by using slow cooking methods, such as simmering, baking, and roasting.** These methods may take more time to cook, but usually the labor is less and they don't require much hands-on attention. Chapter 13 explains these techniques and illustrates them with recipes found in Part IV.

- ✔ **Use time-saving appliances, such as food processors, handheld blenders, rice cookers, slow cookers, and microwave ovens.** Pressure cookers work wonders for making nutritious meals in minutes. Get tips on using these and other handy helpers in Chapter 14.

✔ **Develop 911 meals.** Create a repertoire of 15-minute favorites that can be made in any emergency. Try to avoid serving these fast meals every night, but keep them and their ingredients handy for super-quick meals when you really need them. (See the sidebar "911 meals to the rescue" for more tips.)

911 meals to the rescue

When you're dead tired, the pickings are slim, and your loving family looks at you with wide, hungry eyes, whatcha gonna do? Dial up these one-dish *911 meals* — they're ultra-quick, satisfyingly tasty, and you'll likely have all the ingredients on hand in your pantry or refrigerator. Improvise on the seasonings (garlic and onions perk up most everything), but start with key ingredients like these:

☺ Angel hair pasta tossed with olive oil, garlic, and cheese; canned clams, garlic, and parsley; or fresh or canned tomatoes, roasted red peppers, garlic, cheese, and olive oil.

☺ Tortillas filled with cooked beans, onions, and cheese; scrambled eggs and salsa; diced green chiles and refried beans; sautéed vegetables; leftover meats; or just about anything else.

☺ Tuna or salmon, canned and drained, mixed with noodles, chopped spinach, yogurt, or cheese and baked as a casserole. Or, serve with rice or couscous, capers, celery, carrots, green onions, olives, lemon juice, and olive oil as a grain-salad.

☺ Rolls, French bread, or sliced bread broiled with any combination of tomatoes, cheese, mushrooms, artichoke hearts, lunch meats, mustard, pickles, grated apples, onion, green onion, canned tuna, salmon, sardines, sprouts, lettuce, or sunflower seeds.

☺ Chicken broth, simmered to make a hearty soup with wonton skins, noodles, stuffed pasta, shredded cabbage or lettuce, carrots, ginger, shredded chicken, or dried mushrooms. You can also puree the broth with cooked, frozen potatoes and broccoli, top with cheese, and serve with toast.

☺ Omelets filled with olives, roasted red peppers, diced green chiles, cheese, cottage cheese, any vegetable, slivered lunch meats, cooked pasta, or cooked meats and poultry.

Parents' practical ways

See if these tips can streamline breakfasts, lunches, and dinners in your home:

☼ "My husband loves to make French toast, pancakes, and waffles on his off day, quick-freezing them on a cookie sheet, and then packaging them for the freezer. In the morning, the boys either pick a cereal and juice, or heat dad's French toast or pancakes in the microwave."

— Kimberly from Norwalk, Connecticut

☼ "Breakfast pizza is another favorite that we eat sometimes for dinner or breakfast — it freezes well. Using a pizza crust, homemade or store-bought, place picanté sauce on crust, scramble an egg and place on top of the pizza, crumble sausage onto pizza, and add cheddar cheese. (I usually cook my sausage in the microwave in the colander so that grease will drain — this takes only a few minutes.) Heat until the pizza is warmed through and the cheese melts. Freeze in slices and warm it in the microwave for quick on-the-go breakfasts."

— Berenda from Honolulu, Hawaii

☼ "Our most common family meal is a mixture of soup and sandwiches. We can each have a different kind of soup and sandwich and to speed things up, we all participate in the making of this meal. My 6-year-old sets the table, the 16-year-old pours drinks and helps my husband make the sandwiches, and I make the soups."

— Edith from Selden, New York

☼ "My son likes noodles and sauce. I cook pasta (like bow ties) and freeze it in sandwich bags. When he wants it, I open it, put a little water in it and microwave it for a minute. It's just like new."

— Jill from Bethesda, Maryland

Marvelous, Morphable Meal Plans

Morphing in motion pictures refers to the computer-generated process of gradually transforming one image into another, like when a man changes into a werewolf within a sequence of frames.

I don't suggest you turn meals into hairy werewolves, but you can prepare some foods one night and use them in completely different ways later in the week — a process distinct from reheating leftovers — which I call *meal morphing.* This isn't to condemn leftovers, because I recommend them in meal planning, when used judiciously. Certain foods, like cooked greens, don't hold up well for more than a day's refrigeration, unlike stews and tomato sauces that improve after a day or two.

Morphable meals focus on fundamental foods — a roast turkey, baked ham, steamed rice, plain pasta, or cooked beans. If made and stored without sauces or domineering seasonings (like curry powder), these foods can be rede-signed into fresh, new dishes of different flavors. Cook morphable meals in sufficient quantities on weekends or whenever you have some leisure time. Some morphable meals are ideal for freezing in small serving sizes, in resealable bags, then thawed in the microwave or refrigerator.

Freeze or refrigerate foods like these to make easy, morphable meals:

- **Cooked pasta, rice, barley, and other grains:** Serve these grains as the basis of a main course or as side dishes — they make excellent meal morphers when seasoned with bits of vegetables, meats, poultry, sea-food, or cheese. Freeze them in plastic freezer bags or sealed containers, or refrigerate them for up to five days. Thaw frozen portions in the refrigerator or microwave before using. To reheat these grains, micro-wave them covered until hot. You can also reheat pastas by dropping into boiling water for a minute or two, then draining.

- **Ends and bits of bread:** Make Easy Overnight Strata (Chapter 17), bread pudding, bread crumbs, or croutons.

- **Puree cooked veggies:** Add to soups and stocks or gravies for richer flavor and more nutrients.

- **Poach or pressure-cook a whole chicken:** Use the meat in salads, enchiladas, sandwiches, and casseroles. Use the broth in soups, sauces, or wherever chicken broth is called for.

- **Brown ground turkey or beef with onions and garlic:** Use as the base for tacos, spaghetti sauce, casseroles, and omelets. Freeze in resealable bags.

- **Grill and freeze veggies:** Add roasted, peeled peppers and grilled onions as seasonings to enchiladas, casseroles, soups, salsas, and vegetable dishes.

- **Prepare a roast:** Use roast turkey, beef, or pork in hash, tortillas, soups, salads, sandwiches, pastas, and casseroles.

A Month of Menus

Using the recipes in Part IV, I've developed meal plans based on my meal-morphing strategy, with emphasis on the following:

- ✔ **Convenience:** For quick, wholesome meals using whole, fresh foods.
- ✔ **Quantity:** For large families and meals that can be stretched.
- ✔ **Balance:** For meals that appeal — to the eye, the palate, and the body.

I include menus for every day of the week except Saturdays, because many families take a break from the usual dining routines on Saturdays — kids may eat at the mall, parents may dine out, or family members may eat different meals at different times. And because many families don't always have dessert, I leave that choice to you, although I do recommend simple, healthy foods, such as fresh fruit with a slice of cheese or toasted Gone Bananas Bread (see Chapter 17).

If you find planning meals for the week to be overwhelming, try this method: Using a calendar that you can write on, plug in the number of breakfasts, lunches, and dinners that you need each day. Indicate which are self-serve and which are hot, freshly cooked, or morphed from other meals. This process helps determine how many times a week you'll need to devote to serious cooking and times when meal-morphing and other shortcuts can fill in the gaps.

Use the recipes in Part IV and apply the techniques shown in these menus to your own meals, balancing nutrients, fats, and calories across a week's time, rather than just in a single dish or meal. Recipes that are marked with an asterisk (*) can be found in this book — check the index for page numbers. Other recipes are recipe suggestions, such as a simple salad to create on your own. You can also look in any basic cookbook for recipes that are similar to what I list.

The meal-morphing tips on certain days show you how to save time — but still have variety — throughout the week.

Week 1

Sunday

Make extra salmon, rice, asparagus, and mustard sauce for meal-morphing later in the week.

- ✔ Poached Pink Salmon*
- ✔ Perfectly Nice Rice,* green onion garnish
- ✔ Grainy Mustard Sauce*
- ✔ No Muss, No Fuss: Tender Sweet Asparagus*

Monday

Use the extra asparagus from Sunday for the soup; wash and store extra lettuce and celery for Tuesday's meal.

- ✔ Asparagus-Potato Soup* (substitute asparagus for broccoli in the Cold or Hot Broccoli Soup*)
- ✔ Lettuce, celery, and carrot salad

Tuesday

Use cold salmon and heated rice from Sunday and the reserved lettuce and celery from Monday.

- ✔ Salmon Teriyaki-Rice Bowls*

Wednesday

Use remaining Grainy Mustard Sauce for the potato salad. Make enough ranch dressing for Friday's salad.

- ✔ 2-Bucket Batch of Oven-Fried Chicken*
- ✔ Cold relish tray with veggies, olives, and Home-on-the-Ranch Dressing*
- ✔ 15-Minute Potato Salad*

Thursday

Marinate chicken for Friday's Grilled Ruby-Red Grapefruit Chicken.

- ✔ 5-Minute Mini-Chops*
- ✔ Everyday Oven Fries*
- ✔ Steamed broccoli

Friday

Use Wednesday's ranch dressing for salad, and cook chicken marinated from Thursday.

- ✔ Grilled Ruby-Red Grapefruit Chicken*
- ✔ Minty Mini-Carrots*
- ✔ Salad with Home-on-the-Ranch Dressing*
- ✔ Grilled garlic bread

Week 2

Sunday

Make enough turkey for meal-morphing; reserve extra frozen peas for Thursday's seafood salad.

- Self-Basting Lemon-Pepper Roast Turkey*
- Peas & Shiitake Mushrooms*
- Mash 'n' Smash Parsnip Potatoes*

Monday

- Easy, Cheesy Polenta*
- Tuscan Braised Green Beans & Tomatoes*

Tuesday

Morph Sunday's turkey into tacos.

- Calabacitas Vegetarian and Turkey Tacos*
- Cucumbers in Kiwi Vinaigrette*

Wednesday

Make Pizza-Pizza: Double-Dough; freeze half and make one loaf into focaccia.

- Crock Pot Pizza Soup*
- Pizza-Pizza: Double-Dough Focaccia*

Thursday

Use some of tonight's cucumber dressing to marinate Friday's chicken overnight. Use remaining frozen peas from Sunday.

- Surf's Up Seafood Salad* with Cool as Cucumber Dressing*
- Cornbread

Friday

Marinate chicken in Thursday's cucumber dressing. Toast a batch of hazelnuts* and freeze for upcoming meals.

- Grilled Velvet Chicken*
- Orange-Scented Couscous*
- Hazelnuts, celery, and blue cheese salad

Week 3

Sunday

Make extra beans and pork for meal-morphing. Cut and refrigerate extra mango.

- Tender Shredded Pork*
- Jamaican Sunshine Salsa*
- Basically Great (Dried) Beans*

Monday

Morph Sunday's pork into sandwiches. Add prepared mango to salad. Rinse and store extra spinach for Tuesday.

- Whistling Dixie Barbecue Sandwiches*
- Spinach-Mango Technicolor Salad*

Tuesday

Make the Tortelloni Toss variation using the spinach cleaned on Monday.

- Tortelloni Toss*
- Sliced tomatoes platter

Wednesday

Mix Sunday's beans into the Fun-dido. Slice enough peppers for Thursday's Paprikash.

- Frijole Fun-dido*
- Soft tortillas
- Chopped bell pepper, tomato, and lettuce for garnish

Thursday

- Paprikash, Two Ways*
- Egg noodles
- Watercress and radish salad

Friday

- Grilled Meatless Mushroom Burgers*
- Hummus*
- Vegetable sticks

Week 4

Sunday

Make extra or reserve some of tonight's chicken, broth, and rice for meal-morphing on Monday and Tuesday. Prepare extra toasted sesame seeds, and freeze for future uses.

- Succulent Chinese Chicken*
- Simple Stir-Fried Asparagus*
- Perfectly Nice Rice*
- Toasted Sesame Seeds*

Monday

Use the chicken from Sunday. Use the frozen, prepared hazelnuts from Week 3. Refrigerate remaining uncooked wonton skins and fresh napa cabbage for Tuesday.

- Napa Chicken Salad*
- Baked Wonton Crisps*

Tuesday

Morph this meal from Sunday's chicken and broth, Monday's fresh napa cabbage, the reserved wonton skins, and the prepared (frozen) sesame seeds.

- Hearty Wonton Soup*
- Carrots and cucumber in seasoned rice vinegar

Wednesday

- Yo Quiero Taco Shells*
- Mexican Fiesta Taco Mix*
- Lettuce, salsa, and other taco garnishes

Thursday

Make breadsticks from pizza dough; refrigerate remaining dough for Friday.

- Lazy, Crazy Lasagna*
- Pizza-Pizza: Double-Dough Breadsticks*
- Green salad

Friday

Use Thursday's remaining pizza dough or thaw dough made previously. Make enough Chimichurri Sauce for salads or grilled meats on the weekend.

- Capture the Flag Pizza*
- Veggie sticks with Chimichurri Sauce*

Chapter 6
Supermarket Survival

● ●

In This Chapter

▶ Training kids as shopping assistants

▶ Coping with youngsters at the market

▶ Schooling kids in shopping skills

▶ Stocking pantry essentials and specialty foods

● ●

What does a karate teacher take to the market? A chopping list.

Kids treat a supermarket as either a fun house or a little shop of horrors, depending on their temperament, age, mood, and their parents' attitudes. In this chapter, parents share successful strategies for shopping with children — without losing their wits — and tips for making the weekly shopping jaunt a pleasurable and rewarding experience.

My own shopping tips in this chapter help speed you through any store. I show how nutritional labels, shelf tags, and expiration dates make a difference in the quality of foods you purchase. My list of goodies to buy — pantry staples and specialty foods — helps you cook tastier meals more efficiently, eliminating extra trips to the store and punching up the flavors of the meals you create.

Kids and Shopping — Are You Nuts?

I confess — I love grocery shopping. I enjoy trying new products as they hit the shelves, I can pick out produce for hours, meat and poultry challenge my quest for a weekly bargain, and I constantly read labels to compare the costs per ounce or seek out the most nutritious product. But of course it's my job to know about foods and their costs.

Not everyone experiences grocery shopping as such happy-go-lucky recreation. For many people, grocery shopping is as appealing as a root canal (ouch!).

When I ask parents for their tips on shopping with children, I discover that parents who enjoy shopping in the first place find ways to make it equally pleasurable with their kids — or at least manageable. Those who already hate shopping tend to view trips with kids as a weekly evil — a recurring root canal, without anesthesia. Whether you love it or hate it, efficient grocery shopping demands organization, strategy, and an abundance of patience — especially when shopping with kids.

Kids' helping hands

Grocery shopping offers a treasure chest of opportunities to expand children's abilities. Even if taking kids to the market challenges parents' patience and pocketbooks, parents can transform shopping trips from painful drudgery to fun excursions by putting kids to work, involving kids with assigned tasks that stop the boredom. Savvy parents tell me that these tasks also help develop their children's fundamental math, reading, and reasoning skills. In the short-term, this on-the-job training may take a while, but after a few attempts, parents see long-term benefits and before long, find their kids to be a big, big help when shopping together.

As a junior shopping technician, your child can help out by doing the following:

✔ **Making the list:**

"My eight-year-old daughter is in charge of the list before we go. She writes the list while I tell her what we need. My five- and six-year-olds help check the inventory of toothpaste, soap, toilet paper, and so on. They also check the stock of cereal and pancake mix as well as count eggs to see how many are left. After we get to the store, my oldest crosses the items off the list as we get them. I'm in charge of the calculator — just to be sure we get the right total <grin>. I tell them how much we can spend and after we get everything on the list, if we have any money left, then they can each pick one treat for helping."
— Lisa from Clarksville, Tennessee

✔ **Gathering items on the list:**

"When I take kids along and I have a shopping list, I tear the list into as many sections as we are people and send everyone off with a cart."
— Marci from Gladwyne, Pennsylvania

"I used to lay out the ground rules before entering the store: 'I need your help today, so you're permitted to pick one box of cereal for yourself.' Or, I would have them help me find an item and give them tasks within the store. We still divide up the list when several of us shop. It makes it go faster and as they get older, they compare prices, work on math and learn about saving."
— Terri from Maple Plain, Minnesota

✔ **Matching coupons:**

"I usually use coupons, so I give some to my daughter and have her find the product. She loves to do this and she gets really excited when she finds it."
— Cherie from Monroe, Connecticut

"Give the kids a list of their own and let them read the labels. Also, show them how to use a coupon with each item — they get excited like you when coupons can save money, maybe enough money for a movie."
— Karen from Baker, Louisiana

"I let them clip the coupons we use, and then they can keep the money."
— Mary from Rapid City, South Dakota

✔ **Checking unit pricing and expiration dates:**

"My mom usually gives me part of the list and my job is to find the stuff on it and compare prices per ounce. She taught me how to read the tags on the shelf and what it means."
— Ronda from Bear River, Utah (age 13)

"I still go grocery shopping with my mom. She used to send me to pick out special foods for her. She showed me how to look at the date to see when the food goes bad. It was my job to check the dates on all of the milk, cheese, and yogurt."
— Lisa from Lansing, Illinois (age 17)

✔ **Selecting and weighing produce:**

"They love to use the scales in the produce section so this will occupy the guys while I finish the rest of the produce selections."
— Carol from Madison, Wisconsin

Comparing unit pricing for best buys

When comparing liquids, remember that:

☺ 16 fluid ounces = 1 pint

☺ 32 fluid ounces = 1 quart

When comparing solids by weight, as with cheeses, meats, cereals, and breads, note that:

☺ 16 dry ounces = 1 pound = 500 grams

☺ 8 dry ounces = 1/2 pound = 250 grams

When Jimmy goes gimme — parents' strategies for sane shopping

When I ask parents how to shop with kids and not go nuts, they tell me that they rely on a combination of tactics for smooth cruising, devising specific and unique ways to involve their children in the shopping process. Each parent's modus operandi was slightly different from the next, but these parents all had success in getting their kids — from toddlers to teens — to behave better when shopping.

✔ **Find a treat that the kids can eat.**

"When my children were little and I had to take them shopping with me, I found that if I let them pick out a treat right from the beginning, they would leave me alone the rest of the time. When they would ask for something else, I would say 'Sure, if you would rather have that instead of your first choice.' It made them have to decide for themselves what they wanted most. It was worth the small cost of a treat. After all, shopping isn't fun for them either!"
— Debbie from Sandy, Utah

"Make shopping a learning experience. Teach kids the history behind some of the foods and their origin, have them pick out a meal they would like to cook, and then have them shop for the ingredients. At the end of your trip, if they have been good, get them a treat. Even we adults usually buy something for ourselves that isn't good for us, but we want it anyway."
— Christina from Huntington Beach, California

✔ **Set up a snack allowance.**

"I let them both make a small list of things they want for their lunch or to snack on for the week, then tell them it's their responsibility to compare prices and get the best value for their money. Because they only have so much to spend, they learn to shop wisely, and have so far done well."
— Pamela from New Carlisle, Ohio

"Each child gets $2 to buy what they want. That's the limit — if they save their money they can purchase more goods."
— Erin from Seattle, Washington

✔ **Don't give in to demands and avoid sample tables.**

"I never give in to demands, like when my child sees a package of cookies and wants me to put it in the cart. If you give in once, you're doomed! I also avoid the sample tables — I just don't think encouraging kids to eat in a grocery store is a good idea, especially young children. They don't understand the difference between the samples that they can eat and the items in the cart that can't be opened."
— Karen from Pierre, South Dakota

✔ **Give kids a choice.**

"When I take my grandson shopping, I have to remind him, before we go in, what's expected of him. In case of a temper fit, we leave. But I always let him pick something that isn't on our list. I think it helps him to feel he has some control."
— Patricia from Lebanon, Tennessee

"When my children know they can pick one item off the shelf at the end of the trip, it prevents them from grabbing everything placed at a child's eye level. They can walk through the store and get ideas, and then at the end of the store they know their options. I put a price limit on items that can be picked. They also like being able to have some input as to what's bought. I always ask what they would prefer. I usually can only afford four different fruits a week so I ask each child to pick one and then I pick one. This also helps at snack time because then I always have something each one will eat — because they usually don't agree on anything!"
— Lisa from Clarksville, Tennessee

✔ **Shop at a good time.**

"I go early in the morning, while they're all still somewhat sleepy. After they start waking up, I give the boys coupons to look for and that makes them feel important. I keep a few expired ones handy for Sammy to chew on and play with. I also include the boys in deciding what we will cook the next week."
— Christine from Mansfield, Texas

"Do your shopping after a meal, not when the kids are hungry. Share the shopping list with them. If possible, when bringing them along, try not to let it be for a long shopping list. They can get very distracted and want to add many additional items to your list! I try to tell them we only have a certain amount of time and must get done quickly."
— Marisa from Essex Falls, New Jersey

✔ **Show kids that you appreciate them.**

"I always thank my boys when we get to the car for helping make what so many people see as a chore, a nice hour just for Mom and the boys."
— Carol from Madison, Wisconsin

Do the label lingo — how low can they go

Kids can pick out the most nutritious foods by comparing the Nutrition Facts labels found on most packaged foods. (See Figure 6-1.)

Serving size: This varies from package to package. Serving sizes don't always reflect the typical amount that an adult may eat. In some cases, the serving size may be a very small amount.

Calories: The calories contained in a single serving.

% daily values: The percentage of nutrients that one serving contributes to a 2,000-calorie diet. Parents or children may need more or less than 2,000 calories per day.

Nutrient amounts: The nutritional values of the most important, but not all, vitamins and other nutrients in the product.

Figure 6-1:
Nutrition labels help parents and kids make sound nutritional choices.

If you're trying to limit no more than 30 percent of your calories from fat, you can tell at a glance how a product fits into your daily fat allowance by comparing the "Calories from Fat" to the "Total Calories." If you're trying to increase the calcium or vitamin A in your children's diets, look for higher percentages of these nutrients. Your goal is to combine foods that total 100 hundred percent of vitamins A and C, calcium, and iron. (See Chapter 4 for more on eating nutritiously.)

With the growing interest in lowfat products, manufacturers' nutritional claims were zooming out of control — until the United States government stepped in a few years ago. Manufacturers must now use standard definitions for these terms:

- **Fat-free and 100% fat-free:** Less than one-half fat gram per serving.

- **Lowfat:** Three grams of fat or less per serving.

- **Reduced-fat:** At least twenty-five percent less fat when compared to similar foods.

- **Variable percent fat-free:** The product must be lowfat. The percentage is based on the amount of fat grams in 100 grams of food. If 100 grams of food contain 5 grams of fat, it can be labeled as "95% fat-free."

You won't find the expiration date on the nutrition label, but it's there on the package somewhere — or at least it should be. All fresh products are required to have expiration dates stamped on them so that consumers can tell for themselves just how long a product will remain fresh.

Always check the expiration date. Kids are especially helpful at checking the dates and monitoring quality control. Show them how to search the entire package for the date — sometimes the printed dates aren't where you would expect. If a date is prefaced by the words "Sell by," the product is good for another few days beyond that date. If it says "Use by," make sure you'll be eating it before that date passes. It may still be good for a day or two beyond, but you always want to avoid the risk of food poisoning.

Perking Up the Pantry

A well-stocked pantry is a cook's treasure chest — it prevents unnecessary shopping trips, extends the range of fresh foods, offers the cook emergency meals when fresh foods are out of stock entirely, and turns boring meals into deliciously exciting and exotic feasts. Besides kitchen cupboards and shelves, today's pantry includes the refrigerator and freezer, and in some cases, even the family garden.

Here are a few of the items that I keep on hand to perk up my pantry. Whenever I'm snowed in, or if I'm just too busy to shop, I can always throw together a great, wholesome meal using a few of these ingredients (and whatever else I may have on hand). Keep this as an idea list — you and your kids can probably think of lots more goodies to add.

To market, to market . . .

Take kids shopping in ethnic markets. Looking at all the unusual (and sometimes seemingly weird) ingredients is fun and fascinating. Field trips like these help expose children to the vast world around them, and sampling ethnic foods gives kids a tangible experience of other cultures.

Kids also love farmers' markets. Farmers are proud to share tastes of their produce, generally picked that day or the day before. Besides the standard vegetables, many farmers sell rare hybrids or unusual fruits and vegetables that aren't normally stocked in supermarkets. To find a farmers' market in your area, visit this USDA Web site at `www.ams.usda.gov/farmersmarkets/`. It lists location, days, and times of farmers' markets across the United States.

Freezer helpers:

- ✔ **Chicken pieces:** Individually Quick Frozen (IQF), often called *ice-glazed* (these can be baked without thawing, or thawed first).

- ✔ **Frozen, filled pastas:** Ravioli or tortellini. The frozen ones are a better buy than the ones in the refrigerator case, and they last longer.

- ✔ **Frozen fruit and vegetables:** Berries, peach slices (puree for instant dessert sauces), peas, broccoli, corn, green beans, shredded potatoes. Buy fresh lemons and limes and freeze whole; thaw to squeeze juice.

- ✔ **Nuts:** Buy fresh, shelled nuts in packages, then freeze in resealable freezer bags to last longer; if desired, toast and chop before freezing.

Canned and bottled helpers:

- ✔ **Beans:** Plain varieties, seasoned varieties, and refried pinto beans.

- ✔ **Broths:** Chicken, beef, and vegetable (preferably reduced salt).

- ✔ **Fruits and juices:** Tomato, grapefruit, orange, pineapple, peach. Buy 6-pack cans to use in desserts, sauces, and marinades.

- ✔ **Oils and vinegars:** Canola oil, extra-virgin olive oil, Asian sesame oil, walnut oil, or hazelnut oil. Red wine vinegar, rice and seasoned rice vinegar, balsamic vinegar, and cider vinegar.

- ✔ **Sauces and salsas:** Soy sauce, teriyaki sauce, barbecue sauce, red and green salsas, mild enchilada sauce, Dijon mustard, flavored mustards, whole-grain mustards, prepared horseradish.

- ✔ **Seafood:** Tuna, clams, salmon, crab, anchovies, sardines.

- ✔ **Vegetables:** Diced tomatoes (plain or herb-seasoned), corn (plain or fiesta style), diced roasted green chiles, roasted red bell peppers, artichoke hearts (marinated or canned in water), olives (whole, chopped, or sliced), capers, pickles (sweet and sour).

Dry helpers:

- ✔ **Crumbs for coatings:** Corn Flake Crumbs, seasoned bread crumbs.

- ✔ **Dried grains, pastas, and legumes:** White, brown, and wild rices; Arborio rice for risotto; couscous; pastas; beans and lentils.

- ✔ **Dried vegetables and fruits:** Sun-dried tomatoes packed dry or in oil; dried wild mushrooms (for breads, pizzas, sauces, pastas). Raisins, apples, cranberries, blueberries (for breads, pancakes, sauces).

Refrigerator helpers:

- ✔ **Dough and bread products:** Wonton skins, pre-made pie crusts, corn and flour tortillas, pre-made refrigerated pizza dough.

- ✔ **Dairy products:** Pre-shredded cheeses, Parmesan cheese, ricotta, cream cheese, feta cheese, plain yogurt.

- ✔ **Vegetables:** Pre-sliced mushrooms, washed spinach or other greens in bags, peeled baby carrots, fresh ginger for Asian and Indian dishes.

Chapter 7
Dining Together

What does a dog say before it serves dinner? Bone appetit.

Dining with children can represent the foundation — or the downfall — of civilization. In this chapter, I show you how to make the dinner table the cornerstone of family life instead of a battleground for bickering. Parents also share their tips for making dinner time the most important time of day, no matter what other conflicts may arise. To keep meal time lighthearted and stress-free, I list ways to make dining more entertaining that include conversation topics, ideas for theme nights, and simple (but challenging) word games guaranteed to bring the kids back to the table for more.

The Power of Positive Eating

Breakfasts may be self-serve and lunches may be eaten in separate places, but dinner time is time for families. By dining together, kids and parents share their days, communicate, and parents can set good examples for positive eating habits. It's also been shown that dining together helps kids scholastically. In one particular study, students whose families regularly ate dinner together scored better on national achievement tests.

Besides being an efficient way to feed many mouths, dining together produces valuable rewards that endure over time.

✔ **Dining together means eating balanced meals.** Families generally eat better and enjoy a wider variety of foods when a full meal is served.

✔ **Dining together creates food experiences that kids remember for life.** Favorite foods when you're young become comfort foods later in your life, bringing back good feelings and happy memories. Follow the parents' tips in this chapter to ensure that dinner time at your house produces positive experiences, instead of negative ones.

✔ **Coming together at the dinner table builds strong bonds between parents and children.** Parents and kids stay in touch and show that their lives are important to each other.

✔ **Family dining develops important characteristics in kids.** Lessons of respect, patience, and consideration for others creep in at dinner time. These lessons grow cleverly but covertly out of normal daily rituals, such as waiting for the family to assemble before eating, obeying parents' requests, following rules, practicing table manners, listening to others speak about what's important to them, enjoying the gift of home-cooked food, staying at the table until everyone is finished, complimenting the cook, and sharing in the preparation and cleanup of dinner.

Dinner Time Devotion

Sharing family meals together creates positive values and good communication, but it can take a minor act of Zeus to get everyone to the table at once. Extracurricular activities are the biggest conflict to family dining. Sports, music, clubs, and other after-school events may vary from day to day or even week to week. Similarly, many parents must occasionally work late, attend community meetings, or run errands that prevent them from eating at the dinner table with the rest of the brood.

No matter what obstacles come your way, make dining together a priority. Rather than foregoing events, schedule dinner time around them as best you can. Set up an understanding with the family that no one — parents and kids alike — can cancel out on their commitment to the family dinner, period.

Scheduling dinner time

To schedule dinners, make a chart of everyone's activities and when they occur each day. Find as many days of the week that offer a mutually convenient time for everyone to get home and dine together, including time for kids and parents to pitch in and make the meal.

When setting up the family dinner period, don't feel that it has to occur at the same time each day. Be flexible. If it happens on Mondays at 5:30 p.m., then on Tuesdays at 7:00 p.m. because Suzy has a basketball game, that's fine. Just set aside healthy snacks for the rest of the family until meal time, like a big bowl of fruit that kids can grab from as they rush out the door.

What to do on those nights when, no matter how hard you try, family members still end up scattered all over the place? One reader of the Global Gourmet, Karen McCarthy, is a caterer in Boston, and makes this great suggestion:

"For busy weeknights when we all tend to eat at different times due to sports and coaching schedules, I make what we call *the big sandwich*. I split a whole loaf of French bread and fill it with turkey breast, grilled vegetables, lettuce, tomatoes, and so on. (I try to make it lowfat and pack in as many veggies as I can.) The big sandwich is available to everyone to slice into at whatever time is convenient for them, and I know that everyone gets a balanced meal."

Don't make dinner time your only family meal time, though. Many families spend weekend breakfasts or brunches together, getting the whole family involved in cooking. Put a younger child in charge of mixing the pancake batter, and make an older one the flapjack flipper. Youngsters can scramble eggs and grate cheese, and everyone has fun customizing their omelets with an omelet bar of assorted chopped goodies (a handy way to use up leftovers, besides). To work off the meal together and extend the good feelings, follow it up with an outdoor activity or a neighborhood walk.

Parents' practical ways — family dining

When teaching children about manners, dish up the do's and don'ts with dignity. Speak comfortably, in an easygoing tone. Emphasize manners as positive behavior and avoid using them as weapons. If adults or a child's peers are guests at the table, try not to humiliate your child by admonishing him verbally. Often, a well-shot glance and a discussion later is the best way to remind kids of their manners.

Make dinner time relaxing — not stressful. Let each family member share something personal from their day and have fun together. If food or another topic becomes a source of friction, avoid talking about it at the dinner table. Change the subject to something more harmonious, like praising your child's latest clay creation. To preserve the table as a place for community, discuss conflicts at times other than the family dinner.

Parents' notions on the meaning of dining together range from lauding the benefits to reciting the rules. See if the following practical tips and observations can find an open chair at your house, to make dining with your family a pleasant and rewarding experience for all.

> ✔ **Make dining together a family tradition.**
>
>   "My extended family gets together every Thursday to eat dinner. My grandmother usually comes up with unusual things — not that we always like them — but the main thing is the togetherness. We used to do it on Sundays, but that got too difficult for everyone."
>   — Johana from Wichita Falls, Texas

✔ **Turn meal times and cooking times into positive memories.**

"Dinner time was our family time — that's when we shared our day's events and it was fun hearing what went on during the day from everyone. So, now I let the kids help peel the potatoes, stir the sauce, roll the meatballs, or toss the salad. Cooking now includes memories of my grandma, family, and most important, love."
— Nicholas from Union, New Jersey

✔ **Plan the meal to fit the schedule.**

"We eat dinner together every evening. Of course, during baseball/soccer/track season, we have difficulty having an organized dinner every evening, but even if we can only manage a quick sandwich or burger, we do it together. Dinner time is the best time for the four of us to discuss our days and share any special moments or problems. I feel that dining should be a pleasurable experience and what better way than to be with those you love the most."
— Pamela from Lanoka Harbor, New Jersey

✔ **Make talking the featured entertainment.**

"Dinner is for letting everyone know what's going on in our lives. We try to let everyone just say whatever is on our minds. Even if you've already eaten, you must at least sit down and tell everyone one thing that happened in your life that day. Usually everyone hangs out for a while."
— Corene from Kennewick, Washington

"Our youngest child borders on being hyperactive and it was physically impossible for him to sit through a whole meal — but he can get up, walk around, and then come back and sit with us. Or he sometimes has to stand by his chair to eat. It would have been a losing battle to get him to sit and be still, plus we'd all have been miserable. Our goal at meal times is to share, talk, and connect with each other so it was more important for us to keep the communication going then for everyone to sit quietly in their chairs."
— Terry from Nashville, Tennessee

✔ **Listen to others, show respect.**

"Everyone at the dinner table must take turns talking and be polite listeners. Sometimes I put a glass or ketchup bottle in front of one of them — as long as the bottle is there that person is the only one allowed to talk. I do this because sometimes the older ones monopolize the conversation. The kids must also wait to be excused and everyone must be finished before they can ask to be excused. I think if you don't expect the best from your kids, you won't get the best they have to offer."
— JMC

✔ **TV rules — or not.**

"My mom makes my brother and I set the table alternately every night. Also, we have to shake off our place mats. We're allowed to leave the radio or CD player on, but not the TV."
— Jessica from Edmond, Oklahoma

✔ **Adults set the examples.**

"Dinner time is a casual affair, except on the weekends when I love to invite the neighbors for dinner — especially in the summertime when I barbecue my heart out all summer long. My teenager gets aggravated at times and asks, 'Why do we always have to have company for dinner?' That's my cue to chill the grill and just enjoy cooking for my own family instead of the whole neighborhood."
— Yvonne from Fishkill, New York

✔ **Emphasize table manners at home as much as in public.**

"Manners are a real issue at my house lately. I wish I had started to be serious about table manners sooner instead of having the 'kids will be kids' attitude for too long. One of our rules: No disparaging remarks about the food."
— Brenda from Stockport, Ohio

"Just as we share the cooking and conversation, we share in the cleaning up. Dinner time is family time, and we talk about many things. But manners are a must — please and thank you, may I? and excuse me. My grandmother used to say that 'if you expect nothing you will always get it, and if you demand something you will never get it, but if you ask nicely you will get everything.'"
— Christina from Huntington Beach, California

✔ **Make dinner time special — play music and eat by candlelight.**

"On special occasions, or just because we want to, we eat by candlelight. It makes an ordinary meal special and more fun."
— DeAnn from Fort Worth, Texas

"We love food and wine (the kids don't drink the wine). We enjoy a bottle of wine almost every night with dinner, so the evening meal is an important one for us as a family — a time to talk, to taste, and to nourish the body and soul. Our children are developing a proper palate for all kinds of foods by sharing dinner time with my husband and myself."
— Claudia from Barrington, Illinois

✔ **Pitch in at dinner time.**

"Everyone takes turns setting and clearing. Whoever sets one night, clears the next. Everyone helps, including the 2-year-old, who puts the napkins on the table (in sort of a lump!)."
— JMC

"Everyone helps clean up and is in charge of cleaning up their own messes. When they forget they usually only need one reminder."
— Jenny from Tempe, Arizona

Table Topics for Fun and Profit

"We don't discuss heavy topics at meals. Usually the conversation is about what we've done, what our plans are — and lots of jokes."
— Jenny from Tempe, Arizona

Nightly conversation brings parents and children closer together and kids profit even more when the topics are both entertaining and educational. Stimulate your children's minds through such fun activities as word games, jokes, or theme nights, and remember to do the following:

- ✔ **Keep the atmosphere casual and stress-free.** You won't find winners or losers at dinner — you're dining together purely for enjoyment.

- ✔ **Give everyone a chance to speak.** Younger children can take longer to communicate ideas and may be drowned out by an older child. Make sure that everyone has enough time to express themselves.

- ✔ **Ask questions.** Follow the journalist's mantra: *who, what, when, where, why,* and *how.* Reporters use these questions to make sure that they cover a story thoroughly. Guiding kids with exploratory questions helps them address topics comprehensively, both at the dinner table and away from it.

To increase dinner time entertainment, try a few of the table games and topics described in the following sections.

Play the Name Game

To play the Name Game, ask everyone at the table to name a series of items, such as "Name ten fruits." You can name the items as a group or take turns as individuals. The first few names are usually easy to come by, but things can get tougher as you go along. Try the following to start and then create your own.

- ✔ Name ten spices, ten grains, or ten herbs.

- ✔ Name five vegetables that begin with the letter *R,* five that grow underground, or five that are orange in color.

- ✔ Name five countries that serve tortillas, grow rice, or use soy sauce.

Host a "Did You Know?" dinner

Once a week, challenge everyone to discover an interesting tidbit and share it. The night before your "Did You Know?" dinner, select a topic. You can draw topics out of a hat or let individuals take turns choosing topics. Each person must find something interesting about that topic to share at the "Did You Know?" dinner. Topics can be anything — plants, animals, space exploration, food, science, or geography. Encyclopedias, Web sites, libraries, textbooks, cookbooks, almanacs, and magazines are all are good sources of information. My own favorite morsels of food trivia include the following:

- ✔ Did you know . . . that Duncan Hines was a real person, not just a cake-mix brand? A popular Chicago restaurant critic, Duncan Hines agreed in 1950 to let a line of food products use his name. In 1951, Duncan Hines Cake Mix debuted, allowing consumers to make a white cake, yellow cake, or chocolate devil's food cake from one basic mix, simply by adding egg and water or cocoa. (Topic category: famous names in food.)

- ✔ Did you know . . . that the city of Tomatina, Spain, hosts an annual tomato fight — probably the world's largest food fight and certainly the messiest! Townspeople hurl more than 240,000 pounds of tomatoes at each other for two hours — together they clean up the mess. The streets are literally flooded with tomato juice, pulp, seeds, and skins — the slop is ankle deep and all over the walls. If you plan to attend, don't forget to duck and cover! (Topic category: Spain, tomatoes, or world festivals.)

- ✔ Did you know . . . that Santa Claus has a melon named for him? Also called a Christmas melon, the Santa Claus melon is so-named because it peaks in December. It has a green skin, similar to a watermelon, but its flesh is green and tastes somewhat like a honeydew melon. (Topic category: unusual fruits, melons, or Christmas foods.)

Hold international and heritage nights

"Once a week we have international night and read about other cultures, and I cook something from that ethnic group," says Sally of Tucson. An international theme night is an excellent way to expose kids to other cultures.

To hold an international theme night, make a meal from another country, talk about the culture and its customs, check a globe to see where it's located, and discuss how the geographical location may affect the foods of the area. Take a look at pictures of the people, monuments, and terrain.

Be sure to include your own family's heritage, with foods that your grandparents ate, stories about your family's roots, and pictures of your forebears.

Create theme dinners

A bit different from international nights, theme dinners focus on any topic of interest. For instance:

✔ **Pick a fictional character or fairy tale.** If your youngest child loves Winnie-the-Pooh, hold a Pooh Night — wear red and white striped T-shirts, cook honey-mustard chicken, and serve honey and fruit for dessert. Read your favorite Pooh passages from the A.A. Milne books.

✔ **Select a composer.** For the budding pianist, create a Beethoven night. Listen to Beethoven's concertos while dining, serve a German meal, and discuss what it may have been like for such a great composer to lose his hearing. Talk about other composers, artists, and events of the era.

✔ **Explore an Olympic sport.** If a child has an interest in swimming, for example, create an underwater night. Pretend that you're having a picnic at the beach — spread a blanket out on the lawn, wear bathing suits (this works best in summer), and eat seafood off the grill. Open the almanac and find the gold medal winners for different swimming events. Discuss the diet of Olympic athletes and the different countries that the athletes come from.

Jump-start creative conversations

Get the ball rolling with conversation starters. As Erin of Seattle says, "We talk about all sorts of things while we teach manners." Questions and topics work best when they encourage a person to relate something positive or personal. Parents can open up by revealing aspects of their own lives their kids can relate to — like who their favorite teacher was, the first time Dad ate an artichoke (prickly choke and all), and other BC *(before children)* events. To get everyone involved, initiate the conversation by asking questions like the following:

✔ Who are your favorite all-time heroes, teachers, athletes, or celebrities?

✔ If you could be an animal for a day, which one would you be?

✔ What's the most embarrassing (or funniest) moment you've had?

✔ What's the funniest thing you've seen this week?

✔ What did you dream about last night? (A good breakfast topic.)

✔ If you were going to the moon, what would you take?

✔ Who is the most interesting (or amazing) person you ever met?

✔ What country or place would you most like to visit? What would you take?

✔ If you could invite anyone to dinner — from present or past — who would it be?

✔ If you had a time machine, where in time would you travel back to? Where would you go forward in time?

Part III
Cooking 101: A Handbook for Parents and Young Chefs

The 5th Wave By Rich Tennant

"I really wish you wouldn't wear that thing when you chop vegetables."

In this part . . .

Welcome to the *Cooking with Kids For Dummies* book-within-a-book — a step-by-step tutorial on cooking basics. While most of the other parts in this book speak solely to you as parents, this part and Part IV (which includes recipes for the entire family) are written for both you and your child to use together.

As a parent, your job is to introduce your child to cooking, and this minibook gives you a structure to follow as you go along. I start off with the golden rules of kitchen safety, and then begin the cooking lessons. These lessons jump right into real cooking, covering all the basics, from slicing 'n dicing to cooking methods to the final presentation to — the best part of all — eating the meal.

But this handbook isn't all kid-stuff — it has something to offer all cooks, new or experienced. I include dozens of handy tips for faster, easier, and tastier cooking in this part — some of these tips are ones I've gathered over the years, and others are new and original ones shared by my very creative online readers.

Chapter 8

Getting Started: Safety Makes Sense

What's the worst thing about being an octopus?
Washing your hands before dinner.

*E*ven the greatest chefs of the world have rules for cooking, and every rule starts with safety. Without a doubt, safety is the most important part of this basic kitchen handbook, which is why I recommend that you review this chapter very thoroughly with your child before you begin your cooking lessons. In this chapter, you can find safety guidelines for each phase of cooking, from setting up to cleaning up.

I include more specific tips in the lessons on working with knives in Chapter 11, stovetops in Chapter 12, and ovens in Chapter 13. But as everyone knows — safety first!

Rules to remember

Safety in the kitchen applies to parents and children alike. Tear out the Cheat Sheet at the beginning of this book and post the Ten Kitchen Commandments on your refrigerator. Review these essential safety rules together, reading them out loud and referring to them whenever you need a refresher.

Discovering the Make-It-Safe Zones

Make-it-safe zones are areas where you and your kids should pay special attention to safety rules — these are active areas where mishaps often occur. In the following sections, I list the most critical zones and give tips for avoiding injuries.

Whenever you cook, always use dry, good-quality potholders or oven mitts.

The stovetop

Most cooking takes place on the stovetop, making this the most active make-it-safe zone in your kitchen. (Chapter 12 is chock-full of information on using the stovetop.) Foods on the stovetop usually cook quickly but require plenty of visual attention and physical involvement, as in stirring and frying.

- ✔ Turn pan and pot handles inward, away from the front of the stove, as shown in Figure 8-1, so they can't be accidentally brushed against and knocked off.

- ✔ When boiling water or other liquids, pay attention so they don't boil over. Never put your face or hands directly above a pot because the steam can burn you. Lift the lid off a hot pot or pan by raising the lid at the back side first, so steam pours out away from you (see Figure 8-1).

- ✔ Kids should never lift a hot pan or pot by themselves unless parents give them permission to do so. Parents, be absolutely certain that your child is old enough, strong enough, and skilled enough to handle hot pots and pans safely.

- ✔ If a pan starts to smoke, turn off the heat and use a potholder to remove the pan from the burner, placing it on a cold burner or hotpad. Don't add water to it.

- ✔ When frying and sautéing foods, be careful — hot oil splatters. Parents should do the cooking when vigorous frying oil is involved. Kids should only cook with small amounts of oil or other fat on low to medium heat to avoid grease splatters and injuries. Wear protective clothing (oven mitts, long sleeves, and aprons) to prevent hot oil from touching your skin or clothes.

- ✔ When frying or sautéing, keep the lid to the frying pan handy. If the food in the pan catches on fire, cover it with the pan lid to smother it or pour baking soda on it.

- ✔ Be sure to turn the burners off after you're done cooking. Burners that have been cooked on stay hot even after you turn them off, especially electric burners.

Figure 8-1:
Cook safely by turning handles inward and lifting lids away from you.

Turn your pot handles in !

Remove the BACK of the pot lid first! This allows the steam to escape.

The oven

The oven zone consists of two parts in one: the oven itself and the broiler, both of which can get scorchingly hot — which is, of course, exactly what they're meant to do. Here's how to avoid getting burned:

✔ Arrange oven racks to the desired level *before* heating the oven.

✔ Use dry, good-quality potholders or oven mitts that prevent the heat from penetrating. Some are too thin or made from ineffective materials and don't truly protect you from the heat. The best ones have a silvery surface, sometimes labeled as Flameguard, which looks like the dull side of aluminum foil, is flame retardant, and is liquid and grease resistant. Never use them when wet — wet potholders can burn fingers in a split-second.

✔ Young children should never take things in and out of the oven. Parents should do it for them until they are old enough to handle the weight of the items and can avoid burning themselves.

✔ Use care when opening and closing the oven door, so as not to catch clothing or fingers in it.

✔ Oven doors and the outsides of the range can become quite hot when baking. Be careful not to brush against them.

✔ Always make sure to turn the oven off after you're finished cooking. To remind yourself to turn off the oven, set a timer or leave the oven light on. When you turn off the kitchen lights, the glowing oven will remind you to turn it off.

For more information on using ovens, check out Chapter 13.

Small appliances

What would the modern kitchen be like without blenders, food processors, toasters, or microwave ovens? Probably much less efficient. But as handy as these time-savers are, they also require their own set of safety rules.

- Keep small appliances, except for the microwave oven, unplugged when not in use. When you're ready to use the appliance again, parents should plug them in, not children. Microwave ovens have heavy, sturdy cords that are meant to be left plugged in so that the clock continues to run. Microwave ovens also tend to be used frequently, so it makes more sense to keep them plugged in. For more microwave oven safety tips, jump to Chapter 14.

- Water and electricity can cause shocks. Never let any appliance sit in spilled liquids. Never use wet hands to plug in appliances or operate them. Never put a wet plug into an outlet.

- Never stick a fork, knife, or other metal object in a plugged-in toaster. If toast gets stuck, unplug the toaster before using a tool to remove it.

- Store the blades of food processors, mini choppers, and blenders safely away where children can't get to them. Seal the blades in heavy duty plastic containers and store on an upper shelf.

- Parents (not children) should insert the blades into the machines, remove the blades, and wash them. Food processor blades in particular are especially sharp and their curved design makes them more awkward to handle.

The sink

The sink is a fairly safe place, but it does require a few safety precautions.

- Make sure utensils haven't fallen down into the garbage disposal before turning the disposal on.

- Don't put your fingers into a garbage disposal when it is running. If something gets caught in the disposal, turn the garbage disposal off and let the blade come to a complete stop before retrieving the object.

- Don't add water to a very hot pot or pan — it can sizzle up and hurt you, and cold water in a hot pan can ruin and warp the pan. Let pans cool before placing them in water or adding soaking water to them.

- Use hot, soapy water when washing dishes to kill any bacteria.

- Never soak knives, food processor blades, or other sharp objects in soapy water. You could reach in and accidentally cut yourself.

> ✔ Avoid splashing water on the counter or floor; if you do, be sure to wipe it up immediately. Water is dangerous if it comes in contact with electrical appliances, and someone may slip on a wet floor. Keep towels handy.

You!

Everything else in a kitchen stays put — you're the one that's moving around, so take the following precautions:

> ✔ Keep long hair tied back. Hair can catch fire or get caught on things.

> ✔ Never wear loose or baggy clothing that can catch on things.

> ✔ Wear clean, protective clothing free of foods and bacteria that can contaminate foods. Cooking can be messy, so use an apron or wear a cooking T-shirt that you can afford to get dirty. Long sleeves protect your arms, especially when frying.

> ✔ Long oven mitts protect hands, wrists, and lower arms, especially from oven racks and when grilling outdoors. Make sure they are dry — wet ones won't protect you.

Cuts, Burns, and Scrapes: A First Aid Primer

"Ouch!" is one four-letter word that you never want to hear in the kitchen, but even the best trained chefs still cut themselves, scald their fingers, or burn their tongues.

Kitchen safety includes doing everything you possibly can to avoid injuries, but if something does happen, you want to be prepared. In this section, I outline handy kitchen safety equipment and some basic first aid procedures for common kitchen injuries; however, this information isn't meant to be a medical reference or a replacement for a doctor's advice. Keep in mind that anything more serious than a minor cut, scrape, or burn needs immediate, professional medical treatment, so children should know to immediately report any injury to a parent, no matter how minor it may seem.

Use the following simple safety equipment and first aid information to prevent and treat minor injuries:

> ✔ Keep a small fire extinguisher readily accessible in your kitchen. Hardware stores sell kitchen fire extinguishers for $10 to $20. Parents and kids should review the instructions together.

- ✔ If your kitchen or a nearby area isn't equipped with a smoke detector, be sure to install one! If you use a battery operated one, remember to change the batteries once a year.

- ✔ Keep a large box of baking soda handy by the stove. In case of a grease fire, you can pour the baking soda on the fire to smother it. Salt works, too. Never throw water on a grease fire.

- ✔ Make sure your family knows how to stop a person from choking, as shown in the sidebar "Doing the Heimlich," and how to stop, drop, and roll in case of fire. See the "Stop, drop, and roll" sidebar.

- ✔ Keep a list of emergency phone numbers posted by your kitchen phone or on your refrigerator. Include the Police, Fire Department, 911, Poison Control Center, the nearest emergency hospital and its address, and the directions for getting to your house. Also include any parents' work phone numbers and numbers of neighbors, teachers or other adults the children can call if needed.

- ✔ Keep a compact first aid kit with bandages and first aid cream in the kitchen for cuts and burns. Replace the contents as you use them. Keep a first aid manual available for quick reference. Also have ice and ice packs (or bags of frozen vegetables) handy.

- ✔ If you cut yourself, wash the area and your hands with soap and warm water. Apply gentle pressure to the cut with a clean cloth or gauze until the bleeding stops, which may take up to five minutes. Cleanse the cut with hydrogen peroxide, rubbing alcohol, or an antibiotic ointment and cover with an adhesive bandage. Change the bandage and clean the wound daily. (If the bleeding continues past five minutes, or if it is gushing or spurting, contact professional emergency help right away.)

- ✔ Keeping an adhesive bandage on your finger can be tough when you're working in the kitchen, because most bandages fall off in water. A few ultra-techno bandages, though, truly live up to their waterproof claims. I prefer a brand called Clean Seals — you can apply Clean Seals with one hand, and they adhere firmly to the skin, even in dishwater, to protect from lemon juice, salt, and other kitchen substances that aggravate open wounds.

- ✔ Treat only first-degree burns — the least severe type — at home. In first-degree burns, caused by direct contact with a hot object, exposure to steam, or an electrical shock, you'll usually see skin that is reddened, slightly swollen, and sometimes bearing small welts. (For more serious burns that are blistered or charred or that cover a large area, seek professional medical aid immediately.) Treat a first degree burn by immersing it in icy cold water until the pain stops. Don't apply ice directly or put oil or butter on the burn (grease conducts heat and makes the burn more painful). Dry the burned area and apply antibacterial burn ointment — aloe vera if available — and a loose bandage that allows for some air circulation.

Doing the Heimlich

1. **Stand behind the person and wrap your arms around his waist, as if you were hugging him.**

   You can also kneel, but standing is better.

2. **Make a fist, placing your thumb across the top of your wrapped fingers.**

3. **Place your fist with the thumb against the person's abdomen, just below the ribs.**

4. **With your other hand, grab the fist and push upward into the person's abdomen with quick, forceful thrusts.**

   Do this until the person starts to breathe again.

If you are the one choking and no one is there to help you, place your abdomen against a table or chair and force your body against the furniture so that it thrusts upward against your abdomen, as if someone were using his fist against it.

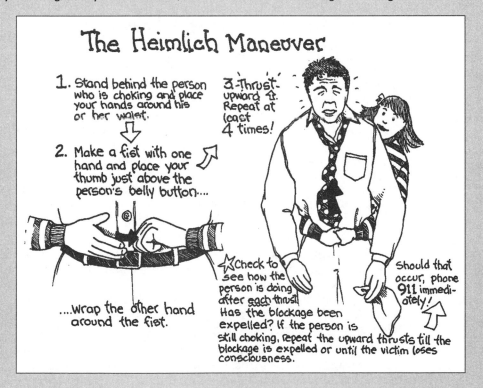

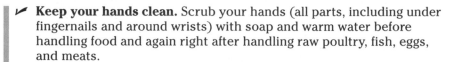

Stop, drop, and roll

If your clothes ever catch on fire, stop, drop, and roll, like this:

1. **STOP running.**

2. **DROP to the ground.**

3. **ROLL to extinguish the flames.**

> ✔ If you sprain a wrist or other joint, or if you bump your head, immediately apply an ice pack. To make an ice pack, fill a plastic zipper bag with ice cubes and water. Wrap the ice pack in a towel and apply it to the injured area. Or, use a bag of frozen vegetables.

Handling Food — the Safe Way

Everyday surfaces all contain microscopic organisms known as *bacteria*. You can't see them, but they're there, all around you — on your skin, in your mouth, and even in your foods. Some bacteria, such as the ones that turn milk into yogurt and cheese, are good for people, while other forms of bacteria can cause food poisoning. All people — but especially children, the elderly, and those with weakened immune systems — are affected by food poisoning, which can take hours or days to show up. Follow the food handling tips in this section to prevent food-borne illnesses.

> ✔ **Keep your hands clean.** Scrub your hands (all parts, including under fingernails and around wrists) with soap and warm water before handling food and again right after handling raw poultry, fish, eggs, and meats.

> ✔ **Be careful with chiles!** After working with chiles, always wash hands and work surfaces thoroughly to prevent the volatile oils from affecting other foods and utensils. Parents should never let kids cut up chiles or touch their children's skin until their own hands are clean of any chile oils. For the best protection, wear rubber or plastic gloves when cutting and seeding chiles.

> The fiery heat of a chile is most concentrated in the veins and seedpod, so scrape out the seeds, seedpod, and membranes to reduce the heat. Dairy products are the only sure-fire way to tame a chile's heat. If your lips, tongue, or mouth burns from a chile, take a spoonful of yogurt, eat some ice cream, or drink a glass of milk to put out the fire.

✔ **Rinse all vegetables and fruits before eating.** Organic vegetables are grown without pesticides, but other produce may retain pesticide residue. The Food and Drug Administration recommends washing all produce with tap water, and using a vegetable brush to lightly scrub the surfaces of sturdier produce, like potatoes and carrots, and discarding the outer leaves on heads of lettuce, cabbage, and other leafy greens. You can also wash the surfaces with plain soap to help remove the pesticides, rinsing well after use. Most commercial non-organic fruits and vegetables are also coated with a thin, edible wax to extend their shelf life and retain freshness.

The edible skins of fruits and vegetables bear a gold mine of nutrients just below their surface, so don't waste those peels. Instead, thoroughly wash thin-skinned fruits and veggies, like potatoes, carrots, apples, and peaches, and eat them raw or cook them with their skins on.

✔ **Use food by its use-by date.** Butcher departments date their meats, poultry, and seafood with the expected last date the food will still be good, printing it on the weighing label. Even if a date expires during home storage, a food product should be wholesome and of good quality for a reasonable period of time after the purchase date — if handled properly and kept at 40° or below. Refrigerate fresh poultry, ground meat, and deli meats for 1 to 2 days, fresh red meat for 3 to 5 days, and most perishable processed products for about 3 to 7 days.

✔ **When in doubt, throw it out!** If your instinct tells you that food is bad, toss it. Foods can develop an off odor, flavor, or appearance due to spoilage bacteria. If so, you won't want to use them.

✔ **Thaw meats safely.** Thawing meats at room temperature leads to uneven thawing: the outsides will thaw faster than the insides, which means that illness-causing bacteria can develop. Instead, use these three safe ways to thaw meats:

- In your refrigerator section, thawing slowly (overnight)

- On the defrost setting of your microwave, for foods you plan to use immediately

- In the sink, under cold running water or with cold water that you change every 20 minutes

✔ **Wash cutting boards.** Use hot, soapy water each time you wash your cutting board. Occasionally, scrub the cutting board with a solution of 2 teaspoons liquid chlorine bleach to a quart of water. Alternatively, you can run a plastic cutting board (and even sponges) through the dishwasher on its hottest setting.

✔ **Avoid *cross-contamination* (the transfer of harmful bacteria from one food to another).** During and after food preparation, make sure that you use hot, soapy water to clean all of the surfaces (cutting boards, knives, counters, and so on) that have been exposed to raw poultry, meats, eggs, shellfish, and fish. This includes your own hands.

✔ **Keep hot foods hot and cold foods cold.** Hot foods should be kept over 140°, and cold ones below 40°. The United States Department of Agriculture says cooked foods shouldn't sit at room temperature longer than two hours, but for safety's sake, I recommend no longer than one hour — even less time if the weather is warm. Store foods by wrapping tightly with as little air as possible and refrigerate or freeze.

✔ **Cook foods thoroughly.** Cook eggs until the yolk no longer runs when pricked with a fork. Use an instant-read thermometer (described in Chapter 3) to make sure red meat reaches an internal temperature of 160° and is no longer pink. Cook poultry breasts to 170° and dark meat to 180°. Cook pork to a minimum of 150°. Refer to the recipes in Part IV for more cooking techniques.

Tasting foods as you cook makes you a better cook — you need to taste a dish before you serve it to make sure that it's properly seasoned. But always taste with a clean spoon, one that hasn't been touched by yours or another person's mouth. Cook food sufficiently before tasting and never lick cake or other batters that contain raw eggs. Taste hot foods with a wooden spoon (metal spoons may burn you).

Put your hands on — not off! Hands are the most perfect tools ever made, and kids know that. Kids love to mush things up with their hands, to squeeze tomatoes, mix salads, and pat dough. Let them do it! They have fun, they get to feel the texture of foods, and they become more adept working in the kitchen. Just make sure that safe food handling becomes part of their normal routine. Remind kids to scrub their hands well both before and after working with foods and to never to put their fingers in their mouths when cooking.

Using Knives Safely — Kids, Too!

A good knife is the single most valuable kitchen tool, but like all tools, kids and parents alike must treat knives with respect. Cutting, slicing, dicing, and chopping may be the main events in preparing a meal, but even most adults aren't trained in using a knife properly or safely. Chapter 11 illustrates the correct way to hold a knife and how to perform basic cutting techniques, but first, parents need to determine if a child is ready to use a knife, and if so, what kind.

A chef's approach with her kids

Stephanie of Plattsburgh, New York, and her husband are both chefs. Here's how they taught their kids to use knives:

"We taught them to use knives at about 2 years of age, simply because they each started to grab them and we preferred they use them the right way, instead of hurting themselves or others. We started out with butter knives so they knew it was a real knife (unlike a plastic one which resembled a Play-Doh knife). We let them cut their sandwiches or a banana in half — you have to be prepared because they will want to cut everything up after this :)

"We taught our daughter how to use a real knife at age 4. We made sure that it was a sharp knife though, because in the restaurant business we see people hurt by misusing dull knives. We started with a chef's knife because her fingers couldn't get under the blade and we thought it would be safer. We showed her how to cut up veggies and fruit to start, then worked our way on to different knives, like bread knives and such, so she knew each knife had a use and none of them were for play.

"Finally, we got to a steak knife which actually can be the hardest to handle for a child (in my opinion). She is now 7 and has some difficulty cutting up a steak or a pork chop but she does well otherwise. As for our 2½-year-old son, he is already starting to learn on a chef's knife. Children learn by example, and we take care of our knives and use them properly; so far, our children do too."

No universal rules exist for when kids should begin using knives, but I'm an advocate of the policy that states: Teach your children to use knives in whatever manner you — and your child — feel most comfortable and confident. The decision of which knife your child should begin using isn't yours alone — you must make a judgment call for both of you.

- ✔ Set out several types of knives and let your child pick up and hold each one to see which is most comfortable, just as you would do if shopping for a knife for yourself. Then set out different pieces of soft food and let him try cutting each one.

- ✔ Keep in mind that the biggest danger in working with knives comes from blades that are too dull for the job. It doesn't matter what material the knife is made of, if the blade isn't sharp enough to cut cleanly and effortlessly, the knife is more likely to slip and cut the person using it.

An everyday starter knife

Besides my professional-quality knives, I have an inexpensive serrated, wavy-edged knife that I bought at the supermarket years ago. With its plastic handle, this knife is definitely not a German-made expensive forged-steel chef's knife, but I use it often. The serrated edge can chop onions or slice steak. It also fits my hand perfectly and is the ideal weight for my frame. If you want to train your young chef on a decent knife but aren't sure he's ready for the $100 professional-quality chef's knife, then look in the cookware section of your supermarket or in restaurant supply stores for decent knives that won't break your budget. The one I use cost only a few dollars and has a 5-inch blade, although many lengths and varieties exist.

✔ Likewise, a knife that's too heavy or too light can be hard to control. A chef's knife is heavy, which makes chopping easier, but the knife may be too heavy for small arms. On the other hand, a very lightweight or flimsy knife may be dangerous if you have to work too hard to make it cut. Pick the right knife for the right job — and the right size knife for the cook's big or little hand.

✔ Whichever knife-training approach you take, keep in mind that as the parent, you must closely supervise your child when he uses a knife. Knives can be dangerous, but when used properly, they are a cook's best friend. They shouldn't be feared (that would take the fun out of cooking), but should be treated with care and respect.

Every family and every child is different — what works for one family may not work for another. Each knife-teaching method has pros and cons and all must be weighed against the age and abilities of your particular child, keeping safety at the forefront:

✔ **The plastic serrated knife approach:** This approach recommends that very young children, such as preschoolers, start by using a sturdy plastic knife with serrated edges, the kind that you would take on a picnic. (Or, use a kid's pumpkin carving knife.) These knives fit small hands well. They aren't very sturdy or very sharp, but they're fine for foods like soft cheeses, mushrooms, or bananas. If used for tougher-skinned foods, a plastic knife may break, or worse, it may slip. Even though the knife's not metal, those serrated edges can still cut.

"I feel that a child can begin to use a knife around the age of four, depending on the child. I bought some great heavy-duty plastic knives at a party store. The child can use the knife in a sawing motion. Table knives also work well in the beginning. Cutting can be hard, so make sure it isn't frustrating for the child. It is hard to remember not to be judgmental if the pieces are cut in different sizes."
— Kimberly from Norwalk, Connecticut, a teacher and mother

✔ **The serrated dinner knife approach:** This approach suggests using a knife that's similar to the plastic knife, with serrated edges, but with a heavier weight. The serrated dinner knife can, depending on the age of the child, offer more stability and control, although smaller hands may find it too long and unwieldy. Use this knife for soft foods or ones that can be cut using a sawing motion, such as mushrooms, cooked chicken, cucumbers, apples, and cheese.

✔ **The paring or serrated kitchen knife approach:** This approach suggests using a paring knife, which is small and lightweight but has a pointed tip, which many experts think is too dangerous for pre-schoolers. However, a small serrated kitchen knife is more efficient and versatile than a serrated dinner knife because the edge is sharper and cuts more quickly through just about any type of food, and the handle is smaller. Most professional chefs like starting their kids off with a paring knife or serrated kitchen knife, because they feel that their children should learn to use and respect real knives from the start.

Shea, a recently retired teacher from Port Washington, New York, writes: "I always cooked with my students; children love to prepare and eat their creations! By third grade, kids could learn to cut things and to pare simple things. If they work with a dull knife, cutting foods is too difficult, so I believe in using a sharp one. (I compare it to sewing — they will prick themselves with the small, dull needle, but they'll only be successful using a real needle.) Kids using knives need a specific lesson and demonstration. Discuss the safety rules. After you have talked about the care they should use, kids are usually very cautious."

Issue your kids a Knife Safety Certificate

Catherine Pressler teaches knife-training to 8-year-olds in public schools in Reston, Virginia. While studying Ancient China, kids learn proper ways to handle a knife by cutting up vegetables for Chinese-style stir-fry.

"The children cut with real kitchen paring knives. I make sure the children understand that even though they are proud of their knife skills, their skill level is still confined to a small kitchen knife or paring knife," she explains.

After a child is trained, Catherine issues a Knife Safety Certificate that reads:

"This certifies that [child's name] has completed Beginner's Knife Training and is 'licensed' to use a small kitchen knife with adult supervision."

This laminated license, the size of a driver's license, has the student's school picture on it . The fact that it is, in the kids' minds, the next best thing to having a driver's license adds a great deal of value to the experience. The kids swell with pride and take even more care in the kitchen, vigilantly aware that their knife license is a very specia! honor indeed.

Chapter 9
Lesson 1 — Setting Up, Cleaning Up, and Cooking Together

When are cooks mean? When they beat the eggs and whip the cream.

The key to fun and successful cooking is getting organized. Just as every professional kitchen has procedures for the chefs and their assistants to follow, so too can your kitchen. In this lesson, parents and kids team up to create your own set of kitchen guidelines. Then, you begin the cooking process itself by organizing your ingredients and equipment, preparing the ingredients, and cleaning up as you go along. You also discover the secrets used by professional chefs to cook easily and quickly, no matter what recipe you're following. Practicing these kitchen habits every day makes cooking an efficient, creative, and pleasurable experience.

Step 1: Creating a Kitchen Code

A *kitchen code* is a list of ground rules and guidelines that will help everyone working in the kitchen avoid mishaps. Discussing and setting up a kitchen code involves the entire family in the cooking process and encourages kids to be more responsible. Ten kitchen commandments for safety, listed in the Cheat Sheet at the front of this book, lay the groundwork for your own code of the kitchen.

Adapt that code to childrens' aptitudes, ages, and abilities, setting up a list of agreed upon do's and don'ts. For example, if your older son Thomas is a big, strong quarterback on the varsity football team, then he can certainly lift a hot tray of cookies out of the oven (with an oven mitt, of course), but not so for little Mikey, who is much smaller (for now!). Or, perhaps young Arnette has been trained at preschool on how to cut up an apple using a real paring knife, and she does so quite safely. She may be allowed to use a real paring knife under parental supervision, but other kids without her training may be better off with a plastic knife.

Step 2: Setting Up the Kitchen

Think of the kitchen as a workplace. Kids have their desks as their workplaces at school, parents may have an office as a workplace. For a mechanic, the workplace is his garage, for a doctor, it's her examining room. A chemist uses a laboratory, and so on. Every workplace is used for very specific tasks, is equipped with its own unique tools, and is designed to make those tasks easier to perform.

Your kitchen workstations

How can you make your kitchen a better workplace for parents and kids? Follow these guidelines to set up a kitchen that is efficient and practical for everyone.

✔ **Stand up for yourself.** Set the work surface to the proper height. For most tasks, the ideal countertop height should hit slightly below a person's bent elbow. Unless your kitchen has been custom-designed, the counters are probably the standard 36-inches high, so shorter adults or teenagers may want a stool or low bench (like an aerobics bench) to stand on. Youngsters need a step stool or rubber-footed bench to reach standard countertops, or set up a child's work table that suits his or her height.

✔ **Break out of the crowd.** Make sure everyone has enough physical space to work comfortably — this means plenty of elbow room and surface for cutting boards. A cluttered workspace is dangerous and frustrating. Allow two to three feet of counter space per person.

✔ **Let there be light — and plenty of it.** Kitchen tasks require lots of detail, especially when cutting or chopping. In just a few minutes, you can install inexpensive under-the-cabinet fluorescent fixtures to illuminate the counter and cutting areas — they plug right into your existing wall outlets.

> ✔ **Go low for flow.** Put any utensils and tools that you want the kids to use in a lower drawer or cabinet, where they can easily get to them. This helps your children feel more independent, and you won't have to keep handing them things from upper shelves. Put their juices, snacks and favorite fruits on a low shelf in the refrigerator, too.

Take a look at Chapter 3 for more ideas on finding kids' kitchen tools, using alternatives to knives, and designing a kid-friendly kitchen.

Organize first: Getting your ducks in a row

Are you familiar with this scenario? You open a recipe and innocently jump head first into the first step in the recipe, instead of first setting out all the ingredients. Then, about midway through the recipe, you realize that you have to turn off the burner and chop some onions or celery, or toast some nuts before you can continue. At this point, the meat in the pan stops cooking and begins to cool. You then need to reheat the meat in order to get it hot enough to brown the onions and celery. So the meat cooks again, toughening up or drying out. These interruptions in the cooking process can cause the dish to taste all wrong.

To make cooking a pleasurable experience, take the time to get organized before turning on the flame. The process of preparing and assembling all of the ingredients and equipment right up to the point of cooking is known as *mise en place,* which is a French term (pronounced MEEZ-ahn-plahs) that literally means "everything in its place," or as I like to say, getting your ducks in a row. To get organized, line up your ingredients, measure your spices, chop your vegetables, precook any ingredients that require it, rinse and dry produce, or soak beans overnight.

When I know that everything I need for a recipe is ready and in its place, I relax and concentrate on the actual cooking, which helps me to become a better cook. And when I cook with kids, the cooking process goes much more smoothly if we take the time to get organized before we cook.

So, whenever you begin to cook, follow these techniques of mise en place:

> ✔ Read the recipe all the way through. If you need to complete any tasks in advance, such as soaking beans overnight to soften them or marinating meats to tenderize and flavor them, do those first.

> ✔ Set out the necessary mixing and cooking utensils, such as bowls, whisks, pots, pans, potholders and oven mitts, measuring spoons and cups, wooden spoons, timer, thermometer, and other equipment.

✔ Set out all your dry ingredients, including spices, herbs, grains, and condiments. To speed things up during cooking, pre-measure these ingredients into small dishes, making them instantly ready-to-add.

Small paper bathroom cups, like Dixie cups, make handy, disposable containers for setting aside small amounts of pre-measured spices, sugar, honey, and other liquid and dry ingredients. If you can safely reuse them, you can save money and trees.

✔ Remove any required ingredients from the refrigerator, setting out whatever you need for the recipe and returning what you don't need to the refrigerator.

✔ Wash and dry the vegetables and fruit you will be using.

✔ Peel, chop, mince, grate or cut up any vegetables, meats, cheeses, fresh herbs, and other ingredients as called for and set them aside in piles or in small cups.

✔ Put large piles of chopped, grated, or otherwise cut-up ingredients on plates (or disposable paper plates) and set aside. This leaves more room on your cutting board, keeps your workspace neat, and saves time cleaning up.

✔ Perform any tasks that require precooking, such as scalding milk, toasting nuts, or melting butter.

✔ Prepare whatever cold dishes you can in advance, such as salads.

✔ Wash up cutting boards, pots, pans, bowls, and utensils as you go along, before you begin cooking.

If you're making more than one recipe, combine whatever tasks you can for both recipes. If two recipes call for chopped onion, for instance, peel and chop the amount needed for both recipes at the same time, and then divvy up the portions as needed for each recipe.

Whenever parents or kids practice mise en place, they're doing the same thing that professional chefs do, including those you see on television and in restaurants. The mise en place habit gives kids the same type of organizational skills they can use in all parts of their lives, but "mise en place" sounds a lot more snappy than "learning organizational skills."

The mise en place method offers another very valuable benefit: time to take a break! After you finish the preparation work, you can relax for a few minutes. Get off those tired dogs and join the family for a play session. Have a refreshing beverage, listen to music, check e-mail, ask your family how their day was, tickle the dog, and pet the cat. Then, when you're refreshed, gather the troops and return to the kitchen for the final stages of cooking. (If taking a 15-minute break or longer, return raw meats, poultry, eggs or other easily-perishable food to the 'fridge until you're ready to cook.)

Step 3: Who Can Do What?

Deciding who gets to do what is one of the most enjoyable parts of cooking together. Cooking with others is a group effort and helps build cooperation and teamwork. Recipes offer plenty of tasks for kids — from rinsing lettuce to setting out equipment — and a child's abilities and kitchen experience, especially with younger kids, largely determines which tasks they can do. Parents can further encourage and involve their kids by asking them what tasks they enjoy and *want* to do.

When kids first begin cooking — especially younger children — recipes can take longer to prepare. But as kids grow and become more skilled in the kitchen, their helping hands can actually shave time off the preparation steps of recipes.

For best success when first cooking together, use recipes that are forgiving and flexible, like the ones in Part IV, that don't rely on super-precisely measured ingredients, don't use complicated procedures, and generally won't suffer if not served instantly.

How should you determine which tasks each person will do? Match up your children's abilities with the tasks at hand. Chapter 10 explains how to read a recipe, which is how you identify the exact tasks you'll need to follow.

Children often find it easier to focus on one type of task, such as using a grater (covered in Chapter 11), for a week at a time, so that they can see their own improvement every day. As a child masters each skill, he not only gains self-confidence, but his enthusiasm for cooking grows, as well.

Most kids can perform the following types of tasks:

Preschoolers' tasks

Preschoolers enjoy

- ✔ Stirring
- ✔ Mixing batters
- ✔ Simple measuring
- ✔ Rinsing and tearing up lettuce leaves
- ✔ Squeezing lemons
- ✔ Adding salt and pepper
- ✔ Shaping hamburgers and meatballs

Ages 6 through 8

Early school-age children can perform

- Light chopping
- Peeling onions and garlic
- Grating cheese
- Opening cans
- Washing vegetables
- Advanced measuring
- Kneading dough
- Breaking eggs
- Melting butter

Ages 8 to 12

This preteen group can help by

- Working small appliances like blenders, mini-choppers, juicers, and microwave ovens
- Moderate chopping
- Sautéing and pan-frying
- Steaming
- Broiling
- Boiling
- Baking

Ages 13 and up

This age group can complete just about any task that adults can (with appropriate supervision, of course!).

Parents, kids will let you know what tasks they prefer, and those tasks can indicate what level of skills they're ready to take on. If a kid finds something frustrating, then perhaps that skill is too advanced. They'll find their own way naturally. Just be sure to stick with them and supervise closely! For lessons on the more advanced cooking tasks, look in Chapters 11 through 14.

"Don't let children use anything that you will be upset about breaking. Things are only things, but children's feelings are truly fragile."
— Jean from San Antonio, Texas

Step 4: Cleaning Up

Every aspect of cooking is important — including cleaning up. It's a natural part of the cooking process — not a chore or punishment — and is as important as washing the vegetables, seasoning the food, and mixing the cookie dough. Whenever you cook, be prepared to clean up, as well.

Cleaning up is simple, especially of you practice these tips regularly:

- ✔ Clean as you go along. Use hot, soapy water to wash any dishes, pots, pans, cutting boards, and utensils you are finished using or are too dirty to use again. Cleaning as you go gives you more counter space and makes cooking safer and more enjoyable.

- ✔ To avoid cross-contamination, immediately wash up any cutting boards, utensils, and counters that come in contact with raw proteins, such as poultry, eggs, seafood, or meat. Be sure to wash your hands well, too. Use hot, soapy water. For extra cleaning protection, add 1 teaspoon bleach to a sink full of water.

- ✔ To clear the food off a cutting board, use a plastic or metal dough scraper, like the one shown in Chapter 3. It has a flat edge that slides easily under piles of chopped vegetables and its wide surface is perfect for carrying veggies to a bowl, a pan, or a garbage container. If you see your child scooping foods up with tiny hands, give her a metal or plastic dough scraper to make her job easier.

- ✔ Use clean dish towels. Dirty towels can spread germs. Keep a supply of clean towels available so that you always have one handy. Don't use pot holders or oven mitts to clean surfaces — they won't protect their hands if they get wet and dirty potholders spread bacteria.

- ✔ Don't use an old or smelly sponge. Smelly sponges indicate they are carrying bacteria, which may cause illness.

  To kill bacteria in a kitchen sponge, heat the damp sponge in a microwave oven on high in 10-second increments, until the sponge is almost dry and smells fine again. Or, place sponges in the dishwater and wash with hot water.

- ✔ Soak pots, pans, and dishes that have food baked on or stuck on them in hot, soapy water. This loosens the food and makes the dishes easier to clean. But don't place knives or sharp objects in standing dishwater. You or the next cook may stick her hands in the water and cut herself.

✔ Wash the can opener. The cutting edge of a can opener is one of the leading harbingers of bacteria and can cause food poisoning. Wash can openers after every use. See Chapter 3 for a can opener that works without coming in contact with food.

✔ Use the proper cleaning aids on nonstick pans and sensitive surfaces. Clean nonstick finishes with a soft sponge or nylon scrubber, never with steel wool or anything hard that can damage the finish.

✔ Keep countertops clear as you cook by putting away any items you no longer need, like spice bottles, utensils, vegetables, and so on.

✔ Keep paper towels handy. Tear off a few towels before you begin so they are available in case of a sudden mishap. Wipe up spills as they happen and make sure electrical appliances never sit in spilled water. Keep the floor dry, and clean up food spills immediately so that someone doesn't slip or track food to other rooms.

✔ Place measuring cups inside larger containers, like a pan or jelly roll sheet, so that anything that a child spills is contained. Place a paper towel or sheet of paper on the counter and let her measure spices over it. Pour spilled spices back into their respective jars.

✔ Use a spoon rest or saucer on the stove to hold spoons and spatulas as you're using them; this keeps the stove cleaner.

Parents, young hands may not be strong enough to wash pots and pans, but they can still wash small items like forks, spoons, and spatulas (but not knives). Fill a large bowl with soap and water and give them their own sponges. Be forewarned though: you and your kids may end up getting as wet as the sponge, but that's just part of it. Keep towels handy!

Keep your cutting area clean with a small paper or plastic bag on the counter. As you go along, put your vegetable trimmings and other debris in the bag. It keeps your counter clean and saves time moving back and forth to your main trash can (or the compost container). Plus, it keeps those wispy onion and garlic peels from floating to the floor as you move them. When the bag is full or when you're ready to begin cooking, just drop the bag in your kitchen trash can and voilà! — you have an instantly clean counter.

Rubber-backed bathroom or kitchen rugs help keep the kitchen floor clean. Place them in areas that get lots of use — by the sink, on the floor beneath the cutting board, or in front of the refrigerator. These rugs catch falling bits of debris and spills. When they get messy, simply shake them out or vacuum them. They're also machine washable and their rubber backing keeps them from slipping. As an added bonus, they make standing on them for long periods less taxing on your feet and legs, particularly the extra-thick varieties.

Chapter 10

Lesson 2 — Reading a Recipe and Measuring Ingredients

Why did the dragon spit out the clown? Because it tasted funny.

Marcella Hazan, a famous Italian cookbook author, once told me, "The first time you make one of the recipes from my books, it's my recipe. The next time you make it, you may decide to change the ingredients — then it becomes your recipe. But first, you need to make it my way to see how it should be done."

I agree with Marcella. A recipe is a precise formula for making a dish, written in such a way that any person in any place can re-create it. Changing the steps or ingredients of a recipe offers great opportunities to be creative, but first you have to know what you're doing. And you have to understand how to read a recipe before you can make it or adapt it. This chapter explains the language of cooking used in recipes, ways to measure ingredients as called for by recipes, and the best tips for following the steps within recipes.

If you get lost while trying to follow a recipe, stop and ask for directions. You can ask a parent or someone else who has cooking experience. Or, you can consult another cookbook and compare similar recipes. Finally, you can check out the Appendix of this book for more resources, including the Internet, your local library, and cooking classes.

Don't be discouraged, though, if a dish doesn't turn out right — it may not be your fault. Peoples' tastes differ, and the flavors used in the dish may not appeal to you. Sometimes, recipes are poorly written, assuming too much from the readers or not explaining the steps in enough detail. And occasionally, the recipe is accidentally printed with errors, such as missing steps or ingredients.

Step 1: Reading a Recipe

Why is it that most people can't set the time on their VCRs? Because the instruction manuals frequently make no logical sense, skip steps, or are not written with the average user in mind.

Recipes are also sets of instructions, but thankfully, good recipe writing follows specific rules. (I only wish that VCR makers had the same type of guidelines!) A well-written recipe always lists the ingredients in the order used, gives equivalents, and includes short but exact directions so that it can be easily re-created by anyone. Figure 10-1 shows a sample recipe.

A recipe is only an instructional guide. Using the following steps for reading a recipe, you can decide whether you're able (or even want to) make the recipe, and what ingredients and equipment you need.

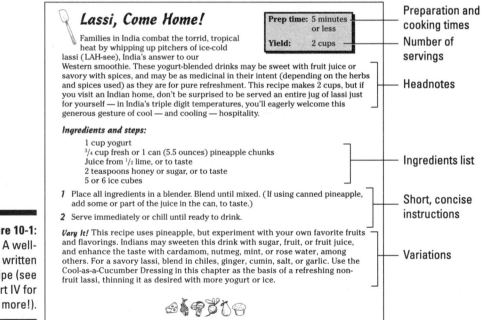

Figure 10-1: A well-written recipe (see Part IV for more!).

Lassi, Come Home!

Families in India combat the torrid, tropical heat by whipping up pitchers of ice-cold lassi (LAH-see), India's answer to our Western smoothie. These yogurt-blended drinks may be sweet with fruit juice or savory with spices, and may be as medicinal in their intent (depending on the herbs and spices used) as they are for pure refreshment. This recipe makes 2 cups, but if you visit an Indian home, don't be surprised to be served an entire jug of lassi just for yourself — in India's triple digit temperatures, you'll eagerly welcome this generous gesture of cool — and cooling — hospitality.

| Prep time: | 5 minutes or less |
| Yield: | 2 cups |

Ingredients and steps:

1 cup yogurt
³/₄ cup fresh or 1 can (5.5 ounces) pineapple chunks
Juice from ¹/₂ lime, or to taste
2 teaspoons honey or sugar, or to taste
5 or 6 ice cubes

1 Place all ingredients in a blender. Blend until mixed. (If using canned pineapple, add some or part of the juice in the can, to taste.)

2 Serve immediately or chill until ready to drink.

Vary It! This recipe uses pineapple, but experiment with your own favorite fruits and flavorings. Indians may sweeten this drink with sugar, fruit, or fruit juice, and enhance the taste with cardamom, nutmeg, mint, or rose water, among others. For a savory lassi, blend in chiles, ginger, cumin, salt, or garlic. Use the Cool-as-a-Cucumber Dressing in this chapter as the basis of a refreshing non-fruit lassi, thinning it as desired with more yogurt or ice.

Preparation and cooking times

Number of servings

Headnotes

Ingredients list

Short, concise instructions

Variations

1. **Read the recipe all the way through.**

   Then read it again. When cooking with others, read the recipe out loud so everyone knows what steps are involved. Recipe writers often include tips and hints about the recipe in the *headnotes* (or introduction), such as how the finished dish tastes or looks, special equipment or ingredients required, and serving suggestions.

2. **Check the number of servings (also called *yield*).**

   How many portions does the recipe make? Will this be enough for your meal? The yield is usually indicated at the beginning or end of a recipe and may be phrased as "Serves 6" or "Yield: 6 servings." In some cases, the yield is defined in units, as in a bread recipe that yields 1 loaf.

3. **Make sure that you have all the ingredients listed.**

   Do you have the ingredients in sufficient quantities? Do you have to do anything to these ingredients before using them — for example, a recipe may call for melted butter, sifted flour, or chopped garlic, and these items don't readily pop off the shelf in that form? Make a mental note when you need to do something to a raw ingredient to make it usable for the recipe.

4. **Look for recipes within recipes.**

   A recipe may cross-reference another recipe in the ingredients list by putting a chapter or page number next to it, as in: "Tangy Tartar Sauce (page 349)". Make sure that you have the ingredients for both the cross-referenced recipe and the main recipe. Look to see whether you need to make the cross-referenced recipe first, or if it's one of the main recipe's steps.

5. **Determine the hidden or "we think you know that" steps.**

   This includes washing vegetables and fruits, peeling the outer skin off onions and garlic, trimming green onions, and so on. Some recipes are very explicit and tell you to do these steps, but not all of them.

6. **Make sure you have the proper cookware and measuring tools.**

   Very few recipes include an equipment list, so when reading a recipe, make a note of the pots, pans, utensils, and other equipment that are mentioned in the steps or that you think you will need.

   - Does the recipe call for a nonstick pan? If so, the recipe may not turn out as well in a pan without a nonstick coating.

   - Does the recipe specify a size for equipment, such as an 8-inch square pan? If so, that size may be critical to the recipe and no other size will work. However, most recipes avoid exact pan sizes unless the size is critical to the recipe's outcome.

Reading through the entire recipe helps you see whether you can substitute one piece of equipment for another. When the recipe calls for such specific equipment, does it also tell you what to use instead? If not, and you don't have the equipment, you may want to skip that recipe and find a new one.

For most recipes, you need dry measuring cups, liquid measuring cups, measuring spoons, and in some cases, a kitchen scale. (See the "Wet versus dry ingredients" section and the "Weigh too much fun!" sidebar, later in this chapter.)

7. **Look for variations.**

Some recipes include variations, such as adding a different herb or vegetable, or substituting ingredients (say, using lemon juice for a salad dressing instead of vinegar). Simply follow the main recipe and adapt it in small ways as explained in the variations. By reading a recipe and looking at the suggested variations, you can figure out how to make it slightly different using your own original ideas.

8. **See whether you need to preheat the oven and, if so, when.**

A good recipe tells you when to preheat the oven, usually in Step 1. But some recipes bury this instruction way down in the recipe, using language like "Bake in a preheated 375° oven." If the recipe doesn't tell you to preheat the oven earlier in the instructions, your oven may be cold when you're ready to put your goodies in it. This isn't the best way to write a recipe, but it happens, so look out for it.

Step 2: Measuring Up, Out, and Down

To make recipes successfully, you need to know how to measure accurately. You also need to understand the language of measurements — the terms used and what they mean. The Cheat Sheet in the front of this book contains essential measurement information. Tear the Cheat Sheet out and keep it handy, taping it to the inside of a kitchen cupboard or posting it on your refrigerator, for quick reference whenever you need to know:

- **Abbreviations of recipe measurements:** Most cookbooks spell out the measurement units in full, but some publications abbreviate because of space limitations, and not all of these use the same abbreviations. The Cheat Sheet at the beginning of this book shows the abbreviations that are commonly used in recipes. Refer to it whenever a recipe abbreviation seems unclear.

- **Measurement equivalents:** Sometimes you need to adjust a recipe, such as when you're halving it or doubling the recipe yield. But you may have a hard time trying to halve a measurement like 2/3 cup or 1 tablespoon. When you need to adjust a recipe, use the Cheat Sheet to determine equivalent measurements.

✔ **Ingredient amounts to purchase:** Recipes should (but don't always) call for ingredients in the ways they're commonly sold, which can be quite confusing when you're doing the shopping. How many apples should you buy when the recipe calls for 3 cups sliced? When shopping, use the Cheat Sheet as a guide but keep in mind that you should still measure each ingredient when making the recipe.

Wet versus dry ingredients

Measuring spoons (shown in Chapter 3) can be used to measure both liquid and dry ingredients, so you can feel comfortable using the same set of measuring spoons for both flour and water, for example. When a recipe calls for ingredients larger than 3 tablespoons, you jump to using measuring cups.

Unlike measuring spoons, two different types of measuring cups are used in cooking — liquid measuring cups, shown in Figure 10-2, and dry measuring cups, shown in Figure 10-3. The dry ones usually come nested in sizes starting at $1/8$ or $1/4$ cup and continuing with $1/3$ cup, $1/2$ cup, and 1 cup. Liquid measuring cups are often see-through glass or plastic and have different levels of units — including cups, pints, and ounces — marked on them. As you build up your kitchen inventory, think about purchasing a 1-cup liquid measuring cup, a 2-cup version, and a 4-cup version.

Figure 10-2: Look through a see-through measuring cup to measure liquids.

Follow these tips when measuring wet and dry ingredients:

✔ To measure liquids, place the liquid measuring cup on a level counter and look through it to see how high the liquid comes. Don't hold the liquid measuring cup up in the air to read it, because you're likely to tip the cup slightly and not get a very accurate reading.

✔ To measure dry ingredients, place the empty dry measuring cup over a clean paper towel or waxed paper. Add the ingredient into the dry measuring cup by spoonfuls, adding a bit more than fills the cup. (Don't scoop the ingredient out with the cup — the measurement won't be accurate.) Level it off by scraping a ruler, knife or other flat-edged utensil over the top of the measuring cup, letting the excess spill onto the paper, as shown in Figure 10-3. If the dry ingredient is still clean, pour the excess back into its original container.

Figure 10-3:
Level-off ingredients in a dry measuring cup with a flat-edged utensil.

To easily spoon out flour and sugar, buy a couple of small scoops, and store one in each of your flour and sugar containers. Include a wooden tongue depressor or clean Popsicle stick for leveling.

✔ Measure some dry ingredients — brown sugar and softened butter or margarine — by packing them with the back of a spoon into the dry measuring cup or a measuring spoon.

✔ Never measure over the bowl or pot. Instead, measure all of your ingredients away from the cooking area; otherwise, you may spill the ingredients into the dish and end up adding too much.

✔ Measure grated or shredded cheese by lightly adding it to the measuring cup until level. Don't pack it down unless the recipe says to do so.

Clear as mud measurements

Some measurements are tricky and not very obvious, like *dash* or *rounded*. This section helps clear up the mystery of those tricky terms.

✔ How much is a *dash* or a *pinch*? When a recipe calls for a dash of cinnamon, for instance, it means from between $1/16$ teaspoon to $1/8$ teaspoon. For a dash, fill your $1/8$ teaspoon measure about half full and add that. A *pinch* of something is exactly that: a pinch between your thumb and forefinger. In some cases it also means the same thing as a dash and amounts to about $1/16$ of a teaspoon.

✔ A *rounded spoonful* calls for a spoonful that isn't leveled off and makes a little hill above the edge of the spoon. *Scant* means to fall just short of a specific measure.

Weigh too much fun!

Recipes sometimes list dry ingredients by weight (measured on a scale), instead of or next to a measurement by volume (measured in cups). A measurement by weight is more accurate, especially in baking. A cup of flour, for instance, may vary depending on how much the flour has settled or whether the air is humid. But a recipe that calls for 5½ ounces of flour is precise no matter how many cups it may fill. Volumes are affected by other conditions, but weight is constant.

A kitchen scale opens kids up to the world of weights and measures. Inexpensive kitchen scales start around $10. Scales with digital displays are more accurate than manual ones — the figure below shows both types. With a scale, kids can practice their measuring skills and record the equivalent weights and volumes of common ingredients to make shopping easier — such as how many pounds of carrots you need to make 1 cup diced carrots.

✔ Eggs range in size from small to jumbo, so read the recipe to see which size you need. When the recipe just says "an egg," use a large one.

✔ Measuring cut up ingredients — chopped, minced, or diced — can be confusing. Do you measure them before you cut them up or after? The answer depends on how the ingredient is written. Does the ingredient say *1 cup pecans, chopped* or *1 cup chopped pecans?* In the first instance of *1 cup pecans, chopped,* you pour the whole pecans into a dry measuring cup, then remove them and chop them up. In the second instance, *1 cup chopped pecans,* you chop the pecans first, then put them into the cup for measuring. The same applies to ingredients when called for as minced, diced, finely chopped, and grated, cuts that I explain in Chapter 11.

✔ Syrup and honey are difficult to measure because they stick to the measuring spoons and cups. Try this instead: Lightly coat the measuring spoon or cup with vegetable oil (use a spray or wipe it on), then pour in the syrup or honey. The sticky stuff won't stick — it slides right off.

✔ You use herbs in different quantities depending on whether they're fresh or dried. When a recipe calls for fresh herbs, by all means try to use them. Fresh herbs impart more of a vibrant taste, color, and texture to a recipe than do their dried counterparts. In some recipes, though, you can substitute dried herbs for fresh, and vice versa, but not in the same quantity.

Follow this guideline: To substitute dry herbs for fresh ones, use $1/3$ the amount called for. To substitute fresh herbs for dried ones, use three times the amount called for. So, when a recipe calls for 3 tablespoons fresh dillweed, you could substitute 1 tablespoon dried dillweed. Likewise, when a recipe calls for $1/2$ teaspoon dried oregano, use $1^1/2$ teaspoons of the fresh oregano instead.

When using dried herbs, measure the herbs, and then crush them with your fingers before adding, to release more of their flavors.

Double trouble

Doubling, tripling, and cutting recipes in half can be tricky, mainly because you won't find any hard-and-fast rules to follow.

You can usually double or halve most soups, casseroles, stews, sauces, vegetable dishes, and salads with success, but baked goods are not as simple.

I recommend not altering the yield of baking recipes. Baking is an extremely precise form of cooking and relies on the well-orchestrated interplay of heat, time, and ingredients. When you double a bread recipe, you double the kneading time, right? Well, no, because extensive kneading results in tougher dough. Similarly, adjusting the baking time and temperature is a tough call. For those times that you want twice as much of a baked good recipe, make the recipe as it's written — just make it twice!

When adjusting a recipe's yield, be careful with herbs, spices, and chile peppers — these ingredients are powerful and you rarely need to increase them in the same proportion as the other ingredients. For example, when you double the amount of chiles, your dish may end up way too hot. When doubling a recipe, you may wish to add an extra $1/3$ of the amount of herbs and spices at first, tasting as you go. Adding a small amount of most herbs and spices a few minutes before the end of cooking also refreshes the flavors and boosts them up a notch without making them too powerful.

Chapter 11

Lesson 3 — Cutting, Chopping, and Grating

● ●

In This Chapter

▶ Discovering all sorts of knives

▶ Finding out how to control a knife

▶ Cutting up in the kitchen

▶ Using graters and peelers

● ●

What did one knife say to the other knife? Look sharp!

A good set of knives saves you time and energy in the kitchen, so you may want to consider investing in quality knives that will last a lifetime and continue to stay sharp. (Remember that a sharp knife is a safe knife.) In this chapter, I delve into the key points in knife safety, and illustrate techniques for slicing, dicing, cutting, and chopping. I also explain other cutting tools of the kitchen, including graters and peelers that are especially useful for little hands. For more tips on safely introducing kids to knives, jump to Chapter 8.

Step 1: Getting Familiar with Knives

Not many recipes can be made without the use of a knife — which explains why most cooks consider a good quality, sharp knife to be their very best friend in the kitchen. Before starting to cook, you need to first know how to use a knife safely, the proper way to grip a knife, basic cutting techniques and finally, how to take care of your knives. Becoming nimble with knives makes you more efficient, and the act of cooking becomes not only speedier and easier but lots more fun.

Cutting-edge cautions

Because knives are sharp, you want to be extra careful and respect them as the most valuable tools of the kitchen. Get in the habit of following these rules:

- Never hold a knife by the blade — always hold it by the handle, pointing the knife tip away from you.

- Never point a knife at a person.

- Always walk with the knife pointing down at the floor, parallel to your leg and close to the body.

- Always use a knife on a cutting board — don't cut directly on a counter, plate, or metal. If the cutting board moves around on the counter when you're chopping or slicing, place three or four thin rubber bands or a damp towel underneath it to keep it from slipping.

- A falling knife has no handle. So, when a knife falls, don't try to catch it — you may cut your hand trying. Step aside (out of its path) and let it fall by itself to the floor.

- Always use the correct knife for the task.

- Always cut away from yourself.

- Don't try to cut with a dull knife — the knife may slip and you may end up cutting yourself.

- To wipe the blade clean, use a sponge, paper towel or kitchen towel — don't use your fingers.

- Always leave a knife in plain view. Don't cover it with a towel or other objects and don't submerge it in the sink.

When professional chefs are asked to name their favorite piece of kitchen equipment, almost all of them say that it's their knives — whether a cleaver or a 10-inch chef's knife. All sorts of knives exist for very specific jobs. Some of the most common knives include:

- **Chef's knife:** Also known as a French or a cook's knife, the chef's knife (shown in Figure 11-1) comes in lengths from 6 to 14 inches (measured along the cutting edge), with the 8-inch blade being the most popular for home use. The heavy, tapered blade makes this knife the single most versatile one in the kitchen. Use a chef's knife for slicing, dicing, chopping, and mincing everything from meats to herbs (try to avoid cutting bones with a chef's knife, however, or the blade will go dull very quickly).

- **Paring knife:** Looking like a miniature chef's knife (see Figure 11-2), the paring knife has a blade of 2 to 4 inches, useful for more detailed cutting, peeling, and trimming, especially on fruits and vegetables. This type of kitchen knife fits small hands well.

Figure 11-1:
Invest in a good quality chef's knife.

Figure 11-2:
A paring knife is good for small hands.

- **Utility knife:** A utility knife (shown in Figure 11-3) has a similar tapered blade that ranges in length from 5 to 8 inches — making it larger than a paring knife, but shorter and lighter than a chef's knife. A utility knife is an all-purpose knife that's handy for chopping, cutting, and slicing all types of ingredients, from produce and herbs to meats.

- **Boning knife:** Use a boning knife (shown in Figure 11-4) to efficiently separate flesh from bone, such as when you're boning a chicken. Unlike the gradually tapered edge of the chef's knife, the boning knife has a sharp tip that quickly rounds to a flat, narrow blade, making it easy for the knife to follow the contours of the bones. (When you don't have a boning knife available, you can get away with using a paring knife for boning. A paring knife's not as efficient for boning, but because it has a small blade you can use it in a pinch.)

Figure 11-3:
A utility knife looks like a small chef's knife.

Figure 11-4:
A boning knife bones chicken with ease.

✔ **Cleaver:** Cleavers, because of their heavy but well-balanced weight, swiftly cut through bones and cartilage, saving you wear and tear on your chef's knife. The rectangular-shaped blade has a 6- to 9-inch edge (see Figure 11-5). Chinese cooks use cleavers as their main kitchen knife, instead of a chef's knife, to cut all types of food (including vegetables), to tenderize meats by pounding with the cleaver's blunt edge, and to crush garlic with the cleaver's flat side.

Figure 11-5:
A cleaver can be used for all types of foods.

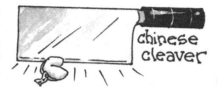

✔ **Slicer:** The thin, narrow, 10- to 14-inch blade of a slicer (see Figure 11-6) makes it handy for cutting cooked fish and meats into slim, even slices. Slicers come in many varieties, with thickness of the blades determined by the foods they are intended to cut — ham, salmon, roast beef, and even bread.

✔ **Bread knife:** The *serrated* — or wave-cut — edge of a bread knife enables it to saw through any bread easily, without mashing the loaf down. The long 10- to 12-inch blade of a bread knife (shown in Figure 11-7) can tackle even the largest of loaves.

Figure 11-6:
Slicers are made for thinly slicing salmon, roast beef, and other foods.

Figure 11-7:
Use a bread knife for slicing home-made loaves.

Best bargains on blades

I recommend investing in a good-quality knife — one that you'll use forever, that fits your hand well, and that has a blade that'll hold a sharp edge without frequent sharpening. When shopping for high quality knives, wait until they go on sale or buy them at bargain prices from mail order and online catalogs (as noted in the Appendix). I've seen good-quality three-piece knife sets (including a chef's knife, paring knife, and utility knife or serrated knife) for around $100. Many companies make affordable knives of good quality — I know that you won't be disappointed with such brands as Wüsthof-Trident, Sabatier, Henckels, or LamsonSharp.

When trying to decide which knives to start with, consider this: Most chefs say that they'd be happy with only a chef's knife and either a paring or a utility knife, and some add that a boning knife is important. I also think that a serrated knife, like a bread knife, is a worthwhile addition to any basic kitchen.

Step 2: Controlling a Knife

Whether you're an adult or a child, be sure to choose a knife that's not too heavy and fits your hand comfortably. Knives are weighted in order to make the chopping process easier — the weight of the knife bears down on the cutting edge so that you don't have to put much effort into chopping. When you hold the knife above a cutting board, it should feel solid and balanced, but a knife that stresses your wrist is too heavy. The handle shouldn't slip in your grip, and it shouldn't be so big that your fingers feel awkward wrapping around it.

After you select the proper knife for your hand, you simply have to grip, guide, and cut with the knife using the proper technique. The following sections show you how.

Gripping a knife

You can grip a knife in two ways — select the technique that's most comfortable for your hand and most efficient for the cutting job.

✔ **Handle grip:** When using the *handle grip,* shown in Figure 11-8, all four fingers wrap around and under the handle, with the thumb placed on the inside of the handle, opposite the knuckle of the index finger. Smaller hands may prefer this grip.

✔ **Blade grip:** Figure 11-9 shows the *blade grip,* which is easier for larger hands because it doesn't require all four fingers to fit under the handle. In this grip, you hold your index finger along the flat side of the blade, touching the *bolster* (the wider part where the blade and handle meet). The other fingers wrap under and around the handle and the thumb rests on the blade opposite the index finger.

Figure 11-8:
The handle grip works best for small hands.

Figure 11-9:
The blade grip is best for large hands.

Guiding a knife

When using a knife, one hand always needs to know what the other is doing. In fact, both hands should work in concert, whether you're left-handed or right-handed.

The hand not holding the knife is called the *guiding hand.* Use it to prevent food from slipping while you cut and to control the size of the cuts. But to avoid cutting your guiding hand, you need to place it in one of these positions:

- ✔ **Fingertips curled:** Curl the fingers of your guiding hand all the way under, so that the first joints rest on the item being cut, and the thumb and little finger are pulled back behind the other three fingers, as shown in Figure 11-10. The flat of the blade should rest against the knuckles. Rock the knife up and down, moving the hand to the side to guide the knife as you cut. This keeps your fingers safely away from the cutting edge.

- ✔ **Fingertips down:** Use your fingertips to hold the item being cut in place, as shown in Figure 11-11. Bend the fingers so that the knife blade rests against the knuckle, keeping the fingers out of the cutting line, but still guiding the knife.

Figure 11-10: Curl fingertips under, using your knuckles to guide the knife.

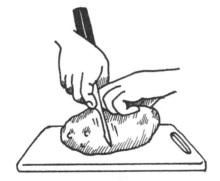

Figure 11-11: Hold fingertips down and use your knuckles to guide the knife.

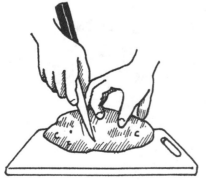

Cutting effortlessly

Always allow the sharpness of the blade to do the cutting. Forcing the knife is dangerous, because it may slip and cut you, so always use the proper knife for the job and make sure that the knife is sharp.

Chefs use two main cutting techniques for controlling their knives. In each instance, the knife pivots on a single point as you go along.

- **Rocking the knife on its tip.** In this method, the knife's *tip* stays on or close to the cutting board, while your wrist lifts the rest of the blade up and down. To make smooth, even cuts, place the knife at a 45 degree angle above the cutting board, just touching the food. Move the knife forward until the tip touches the cutting board, and then let the blade drop until it is horizontal on the board. To continue cutting, raise the handle, rolling the blade upward along the cutting board, just until the tip of the knife touches the board. Then rock your knife down again, using an even downward stroke, adjusting your guiding fingers as you cut through the food. Every few cuts, slide your guiding hand lengthwise down the food and continue slicing, rocking the knife on its tip. (See Figure 11-12.)

- **Raising the tip and lowering the blade.** Hold the knife so that the tip points slightly upward. Slice by drawing the knife back, down, and through the food, ending up with the knife horizontal. Your elbow should remain steady while your wrist pivots up and down, controlling the knife blade. Continue cutting as your guiding hand moves along the food. (See Figure 11-13.)

Rock the Knife on its Tip!

Angle knife, then move knife forward and down, horizontal to the cutting board.

Raise the handle of the blade up ⇧, pushing the tip to the board. Continue rocking the knife up and down as you guide the food under the blade

Rock the tip of the knife on the board!

Figure 11-12: Rock the knife on its tip to slice.

Raising the Tip and Lowering the Blade

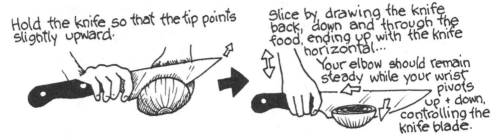

Figure 11-13:
Lower the blade by pivoting your wrist, not your elbow.

Hold the knife so that the tip points slightly upward.

Slice by drawing the knife back, down and through the food, ending up with the knife horizontal...

Your elbow should remain steady while your wrist pivots up + down, controlling the knife blade.

Step 3: Cutting Techniques — Practice Makes Perfect

In cooking, you use a knife to make a food smaller so it cooks more quickly. Cutting pieces of food into uniform sizes and shapes allows them to cook evenly and makes them look more appealing. The more you practice cutting, the easier it becomes.

Round foods, like carrots, tend to roll when you're trying to cut them. For safety's sake, first cut a flat edge or cut them lengthwise down the center, then place the flat edge on the cutting board and proceed with slicing, chopping, or cutting from there.

Slicing — basic and fancy

Slicing cuts food into thin, broad pieces — it may be the final cut or a step in producing other cuts. You can slice food by making straight cuts perpendicular to the food, or you can slice the food on the diagonal, which is frequently done in Asian cooking. (See Figure 11-14.) Some recipes call for special types of slicing, such as *julienne* or *chiffonade* cuts.

Julienne

You can cut foods into sticks by slicing them lengthwise. Potatoes, for instance, are cut into sticks to make French fries. Recipes may also tell you to *julienne* (joo-lee-EHN) vegetables, which means to cut them into matchstick-sized pieces about $1/8$-inch wide on all sides. Julienned vegetables are often used in Chinese stir-fries because they cook quickly and are all evenly sized. To julienne a carrot, follow these directions (and take a look at Figure 11-15):

Figure 11-14:
Slice straight across or at an angle.

Figure 11-15:
Julienne a carrot by stacking slices and cutting into matchstick-sized pieces.

1. **Slice a thin piece off the carrot's length so that it doesn't roll.**

2. **Laying the carrot flat, cut the carrot into 1- to 2-inch lengths.**

3. **Cut each piece lengthwise into $^1/_8$-inch-thick slices.**

4. **Stack the slices. Cut the slices into sticks, again $^1/_8$-inch thick, to end up with matchstick-sized pieces.**

Chiffonade

Similar to a julienne, a *chiffonade* (shihf-uh-NAHD) refers to thin strips or shreds of leafy vegetables, such as spinach, lettuce, sorrel, basil, and other leaves. Create a chiffonade, which means "made of rags" in French, by stacking several leaves on top of each other, then rolling them up tightly like a cigar, as shown in Figure 11-16. With your guiding hand, hold the roll tightly, then slice the roll into very thin lengths, $^1/_8$-inch wide or less. When shaken out of the roll, the cut pieces look light and airy. Use them — either raw, fried, or sautéed — to garnish a dish. (Part IV is chock full of recipes that can use a garnish made from a vegetable chiffonade.)

Figure 11-16:
Stack and
roll leaves,
then slice
into a
chiffonade.

Chopping and mincing

Chopping always begins with slicing. In fact, chopping is merely slicing a
food in one direction, then slicing it again in another. The width between the
slices determines the size of the cut pieces. Recipes use the following
specific names for the sizes of chopped foods, as shown in Figure 11-17:

- **Coarsely chopped:** Kids can get a good feel for using a knife by starting
  off with coarse chopping. This is the most fundamental form of cutting
  and follows the same movements as with slicing. Food should be cut in
  pieces of about the same size — $3/4$- to 1-inch lengths in all directions,
  so that the pieces all cook in the same amount of time — but, other
  than that, appearance and shape don't matter. For example, you can
  coarsely chop potatoes into chunks before boiling and mashing them,
  or you can coarsely chop celery into lengths to flavor a stock.

- **Cubed:** To cube meat, cheese, or other foods, cut them into pieces
  with square sides of $1/2$ inch.

- **Diced:** To dice generally means to cut a food into $1/4$- to $1/2$-inch sized
  cubes, but recipes usually specify the size using these terms as shown
  in Figure 11-17:

    - Large dice: $5/8$-inch cubes

    - Medium dice: $3/8$-inch cubes

    - Small dice: $1/4$-inch cubes

    - Finely diced: $1/8$-inch cubes or smaller pieces

- **Minced:** Mincing means the same thing as *finely diced* and refers to
  foods that are cut very small, but not necessarily of uniform shape,
  such as garlic, shallots, and herbs.

Preventing discoloration

Many foods discolor when cut, grated, or peeled, because the inner flesh is exposed to the oxygen in air. Acids, however, help slow this discoloration. To prevent discoloration of apples or artichokes, drop cut pieces in water with some lemon juice or vinegar added to it. Drop potato slices in water to prevent them from turning brown, and then dry them before use. To keep avocado flesh from browning, rub it with lemon juice.

Figure 11-17: Knife-cut veggies, shown in their actual sizes.

Mincing parsley

Mincing cuts food into even more finely-sized pieces than does regular chopping. Mincing parsley, shown in Figure 11-18, is a good way to practice your knife skills. Using a chef's knife or similar knife with a curved, non-serrated edge, hold the knife handle high with the tip resting on the cutting board above the parsley. Place your fingertips or the open palm of your guiding hand on top of the blade, on the spine, near the tip. Holding the tip down, chop the parsley by rocking the curved edge of the blade down and up again, repeating with more speed and pressure as you move the knife in a fan motion, left and right, over the parsley.

Mincing Parsley & Other Fresh Herbs

Figure 11-18: Practice your knife skills by mincing parsley.

1. Rinse and dry well

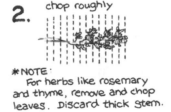

2. chop roughly

*NOTE: For herbs like rosemary and thyme, remove and chop leaves. Discard thick stem.

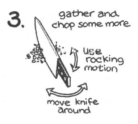

3. gather and chop some more

use rocking motion

move knife around

Chopping an onion

Chopping an onion uses the same movements as chopping other foods, but it starts with a few extra cuts to make such a large, round piece of food more manageable. Figure 11-19 shows the following steps to chopping an onion:

1. **Cut the onion in half lengthwise.**

2. **Place both halves cut side down on your cutting board.**

   Note that you have a *stem end* and a *root end*. The root end often has hair-like roots growing from it and is attached to a hard, tough section. The stem end usually tapers to a point and may have dried, papery edges.

3. **Cut the stem end off and discard it.**

   Don't cut the root end off — it helps hold the onion together as you cut.

4. **Peel the papery outer skin off and discard.**

5. **Holding your guiding hand on top of the onion, turn your knife sideways and make two or three slices, parallel to the cutting board, without cutting through the root end.**

6. **Using the tip of your chef's knife, cut parallel slices vertically through the onion, again without cutting through the root end.**

   Be sure to hold the onion securely with your guiding hand, curling your fingers under.

7. **Rotate the onion 45 degrees with your guiding hand and cut slices perpendicular to the second series of cuts.**

   The onion falls into pieces.

8. **Discard the root end.**

How to Mince an Onion

Figure 11-19:
Make even slices in three directions to chop an onion.

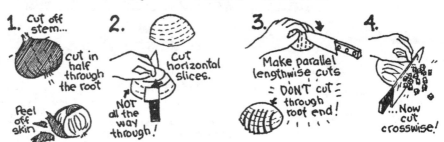

1. Cut off stem...
   cut in half through the root
   Peel off skin

2. Cut horizontal slices.
   NOT all the way through!

3. Make parallel lengthwise cuts = DON'T cut = through root end!

4. ...Now cut crosswise!

Chopping garlic

Garlic is one of the most often chopped foods in the kitchen. Garlic is grown as bulbs or heads, which are made up of many sections called *cloves*. When a recipe calls for a clove of garlic, be sure to use just a single section and not the whole head — unless you want to keep vampires away!

Figure 11-20 shows how to quickly remove the peel from one clove (or several cloves) of garlic:

1. **Place the clove on the cutting board.**

2. **Lay the flat of the knife blade on top of the clove.**

3. **Using your fist, quickly pound the flat of the blade once.**

   The force breaks open the papery peel, which you can easily remove with your fingers.

COOKING WITH KIDS

Kids can help peel garlic even without the use of a knife. Instead of whacking the knife's blade with your fist to crack the peel, use a flat bottomed can or jar. A spice jar works quite well.

Figure 11-20:
Wham!
Break the
garlic peel
and it slides
right off.

✔ To chop a peeled garlic clove, cut the clove lengthwise into thin slivers using the tip end of the knife. Keep the slivers together, and then cut them in the opposite direction.

✔ To mince garlic, press the side of the knife down on chopped pieces, moving the knife across the pieces to flatten them. Then, follow the instructions for mincing parsley (in the section called, oddly enough, "Mincing parsley"), rocking the knife to cut the garlic into fine pieces.

Step 4: Caring for Your Knives

As you probably guessed by now, knives are very powerful tools that need to be treated with respect, both when you're using them and when you're not. For tips on storing knives safely, check out the "Keeping sharp objects and knives safe, but accessible" sidebar.

Never place your good knives in the dishwasher. The banging around damages the edges and the heat can loosen the rivets. Also, never soak knives, as prolonged soaking may damage the handle or its construction. And never use your good knives to cut paper or twine — both dull the blade rapidly. Use scissors instead.

Keep a knife's blade sharp. Every time you use a knife, you're bending the edge, even though you can't see it. Use a long rod — called a *sharpening steel* — frequently to maintain the edge of chef's knives and other non-serrated blades. A sharpening steel, made of a harder metal than the knife, pushes the edge back into alignment and smoothes the blade. Some cooks use a steel every time they use their knives, but using a steel even once per week helps keep the blade sharp. Use a sharpening steel by drawing the knife blade at a 20 degree angle across the steel, working from heel to tip, as shown in Figure 11-21. Repeat several times on both sides.

How to Use a Sharpening Steel

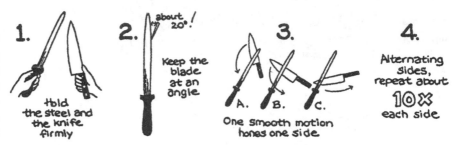

Figure 11-21:
Use a steel frequently to realign the knife's edge.

To sharpen a knife that's quite dull, speak to a salesperson in a cookware or cutlery store. He or she can either sharpen it for you, or you may want to invest in a sharpening stone (known as a *whetstone*) or in an electric knife sharpener — both grind the metal away to create a new edge. But with regular maintenance on a sharpening steel, a good quality knife will stay sharp for months or even years without the need to grind a new edge.

Knives with serrated or wavy edges shouldn't be used with a sharpening steel because it dulls their sharp, saw-like teeth. Consult a professional for sharpening these types of knives.

Sharpening knives is a task that takes practice and is best left to an adult until youngsters are old enough to understand the proper method and perform it with total control. Improperly-sharpened knives can make the knives dull and may damage the edges.

Step 5: Using Graters and Peelers

Graters and peelers are other essential kitchen tools. They do certain common tasks more efficiently than any knife can do, and they can be safer for younger children to use than knives.

Graters

All graters have at least one side that's dimpled with sharp points or holes to tear and shred food into small pieces. You can find tiny graters made specifically for nutmeg and little porcelain or metal ones designed to grate ginger. Every kitchen should stock a standard 4-sided metal or plastic grater, the kind used for grating and shredding cheeses, vegetables, and fruits, as shown in Chapter 3.

CAUTION!

Keeping sharp objects and knives safe, but accessible

To avoid accidental cuts, designate a special "sharp objects" drawer and keep tools with pointed tips or sharp edges in it — including scissors, peelers, and skewers. Kitchen knives can be easily damaged, though, when lumped loosely in a drawer, unless their blades are protected. You can protect both the knife blade and children's hands in one of these ways:

☺ **Knife sheath:** To protect loose knives inexpensively, slip a heavy plastic sheath over them. Knife sheaths range from $2 to $8 depending on size and can be found in cookware stores or knife catalogs.

☺ **In-drawer knife tray:** Many brands sell in-drawer knife trays of varying size and features, ranging from $15 to $40. Wüsthof-Trident makes a particularly compact knife tray that measures only 3$\frac{1}{2}$ inches wide, 16 inches long, and 1$\frac{1}{2}$ inches deep — it holds seven knives. It fits in most drawers, leaving room to spare for other tools.

☺ **Under-the-cabinet knife block:** Wüsthof-Trident also makes the Swinger — a knife block that mounts under a cabinet using three screws, swiveling under the cabinet for safe storage, and then swiveling out when you need to grab a knife. Magnets keep knives securely in place. It's just a tad over 2 inches deep, holds eight knives, and costs around $50.

☺ **Countertop knife block:** Heavy, wooden knife blocks rest on the counter, making them more accessible, which may not be a problem if children are old enough or know not to play with knives. Sold separately, knife blocks start at $40 and go upwards to $200. If you're thinking of buying a whole new set or starter set of knives, you can get good buys on sets complete with a knife block. They're frequently on sale in department stores and cookware catalogs, especially around the holidays.

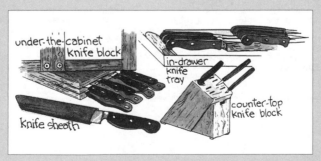

Say yes to zest!

Lemons, limes, oranges, and other citrus fruits can add tons of flavor to a dish (without adding extra liquid) through their finely grated or slivered rinds, known as *zest*. The zest comes from the outer skin of the fruit, which is packed with aromatic oils. When using zest, always make sure to use only the colored portion of the skin — the white part (called the *pith*) is bitter and will ruin the flavor of the dish.

When a recipe calls for both zest and fruit or juice, remove the zest first, before cutting the fruit open. You'll find it easier and less messy to remove the zest from a whole piece of fruit than from one that's been cut open.

You can remove zest with special kitchen tools (called *zesters* or *citrus strippers*), but a plain box grater works especially well for making zest. To grate the zest and easily remove it from the grater, cover the finest grating surface with a length of plastic wrap, as shown in the following figure. The grating surface pokes through the plastic but the plastic itself doesn't grate into the zest. Rub the citrus across the plastic-covered surface (remember to grate just the colored part, not the bitter white pith). When you think you've grated enough (it takes a lot of grating to make a little bit of zest), lift off the plastic and scrape the zest up with a flat edge, such as a dough scraper (shown in Chapter 3) or a knife. Use a measuring spoon to see if you've grated enough zest for the recipe.

Cover the finest surface of the grater with plastic wrap.
Rub the citrus across the plastic-covered surface... (JUST THE COLORED PART! NOT THE BITTER WHITE PITH)!

When you think you've grated enough, lift off the plastic and scrape up the zest with a flat edge.
Use a measuring spoon to see if you've grated enough.

For the kid-friendly kitchen, I highly recommend the Chop Top box grater, shown in Chapter 3. It comes with several interchangeable blades that grate, shred, julienne, and slice. The blades rest on a plastic box. The box catches the foods being grated, keeping the mess to a minimum. It also has a finger guard large enough to protect the entire hand as well as prevent knuckles from being grated — a common hazard with other graters. Cookware stores and catalogs carry it for around $15.

When using a grater without a finger guard, be careful not to grate your knuckles. When the piece of food starts to get small, discard it and start again with a larger piece.

Peelers

Vegetable peelers also come in different models (see Chapter 3). While you can use a knife to peel vegetables and fruits, peelers do the job more quickly and more thinly than a knife can.

A traditional swivel peeler has a sharp point for cutting out potato eyes and blemishes. The blade runs about 2 inches in length and the most kid-friendly ones have nonslip grips.

Personally, I not only prefer but adore the harp peeler. It doesn't have a pointed tip, which makes it safer for young kids to use. But I also prefer the way it handles. A harp peeler puts less stress on the wrist, moving more naturally up and down rather than laterally like the swivel peelers. They only cost a few dollars, so when the blade wears out, simply replace the peeler. Kids and parents alike may find the harp peelers much easier to use than traditional peelers.

Peelings, nothing more than peelings . . .

Why bother to peel a vegetable or fruit? In most cases you don't need to. A wealth of nutrients lies under the surface of most fruit and vegetable skin and is lost when you peel it away. As long as you wash produce well to remove dirt and any pesticide residue (or buy organic produce, which is pesticide-free), you'll enjoy a healthier meal by leaving the peels on potatoes, apples, pears, carrots, and many other types of produce.

Chapter 12

Lesson 4 — Stovetop Cooking: Boiling, Steaming, and Frying

Why did the cowboy take up cooking?
Because he liked being home on the range.

Whether you call it a range or a stove, that hunka, hunka, burnin' metal in your kitchen has two central cooking zones: the stovetop and the oven/broiler. This chapter introduces you to the basic cooking methods using the stovetop — from boiling to braising and stir-frying to deglazing. It includes references to recipes in Part IV that make use of each technique, with handy cooking tips that are helpful for even the most seasoned cooks.

The stovetop's four burners offer endless opportunities for quick and healthy home-cooked meals. The stovetop is also terrific for easy one-pot meals (like stews) that take a while to cook but need little attention after you get them started. Stovetop cooking includes over a dozen different cooking methods, using simple techniques that novice cooks can master easily.

Step 1: Equipment Review for Stovetop Cooking

The stovetop is one of the make-it-safe zones listed in Chapter 8. Review this section before beginning to cook.

Be prepared to cook on the stovetop using these tools:

- ✔ Saucepans for cooking sauces and other types of liquids.

- ✔ Frying pans for frying and sautéing — nonstick pans are especially handy. Nonstick cookware cuts down on the fat you need to use to keep food from sticking and, because food doesn't stick to the pan, is less frustrating for novices.

- ✔ Spatulas, wooden spoons, and other utensils, including ones safe for nonstick cookware. Include tongs for picking up food without piercing it.

- ✔ Large pots for soups and stews, and to boil water for pasta.

- ✔ Colander for draining pastas and boiled vegetables and to rinse produce. (See Figure 12-1.)

Figure 12-1:
Use a colander to drain pasta and rinse produce.

colander

- ✔ Steamer for steaming vegetables, fish, and poultry. Use a collapsible steamer or a steamer insert, as shown in Figure 12-2.

- ✔ An optional piece of equipment, a wok, is for stir-frying or steaming. As an alternative, you can also stir-fry in a heavy-duty frying pan and steam in a large pot with a steamer insert.

Figure 12-2:
Collapsible steamers and steamer inserts fit inside your pots.

steamer insert   collapsible steamer

Step 2: Hot 'n' Steamy Stovetop Cooking

Because stovetop cooking offers such versatile, yet simple, cooking methods, it's the best place for novices to begin cooking (and more experienced chefs to brush up). Get acquainted here with the various types of stovetop cooking methods — you can jump right in and practice each technique by making actual recipes found in Part IV.

Most stovetop cooking techniques use moist heat; that is, food cooks over or in hot water (or other liquid, like broth). Food cooked properly in moist heat tends to be moist and tender — not browned, dry, or crispy, as when fried (discussed in Step 3: "Sizzling on the Stovetop with Frying," later in this chapter). But don't overcook foods in moist heat: Vegetables will turn to mush, and meats and poultry dry out.

You can cook with moist heat in an enormous variety of ways. In the sections that follow, I explain different techniques for moist-heat cooking.

Boiling

At sea level, boiling occurs when you bring the temperature of water to 212°. Boiling produces large bubbles that rise to the surface in constant motion. The higher the heat, the more rapidly the liquid boils.

- ✔ A *rolling boil* occurs when very large bubbles vigorously appear.
- ✔ For a medium boil, lower the heat to make the bubbles smaller and more tame.

No liquid can ever become hotter than its boiling point, but you can change the boiling point itself by adding ingredients. Salt raises the boiling point, cooking foods at a higher temperature, while alcohol lowers it. Adding salt to boiling water before adding pasta (which lowers the water temperature) helps keep the water at a constant boil.

Pasta lovers, follow these tips when boiling pasta for recipes, like the Tortellone Toss in Chapter 18:

- ✔ Use lots of water for vegetables and pastas. Adding foods to boiling water brings down the temperature of the water. Starting off with more water means that you need less time to bring it back to the boiling point. Pasta also releases starch as it cooks. With too little water, the pasta ends up cooking in starch and becomes sticky and gummy.

✔ Use four quarts of water for every pound of pasta. Add 1¹/₂ teaspoons of salt when the water boils. This raises the temperature and seasons the pasta. Also, when you add the pasta, stir and put a lid on it — this brings the water back to a boil faster — but remove the lid when the water boils again. *Tip:* Pasta needs to cook in boiling water. Don't reduce the heat after adding the pasta, unless the pot looks like it will boil over.

✔ Before cooking pasta, use the same pot of boiling water to blanch vegetables for a sauce. The nutrients that leach into the water from the vegetables will help flavor the pasta, and you save time by not having to boil water twice and not having to wash another pan.

✔ Here's an Italian trick that will make your pasta taste better. Before draining pasta, reserve a cup of the cooking water. Adding a bit of the water to the pasta just before stirring in the sauce keeps the pasta from tasting dry. This also helps cut calories because you won't need so much of a fattening sauce to moisten the pasta, especially when using olive oil or butter sauces. Don't cook pasta with oil in the water, either — the oil coats the pasta, preventing it from absorbing the sauce.

Simmering, poaching, braising, and stewing

Foods cook more gently in simmering liquids than in boiling ones. When the temperature is just below the boiling point (around 185°), the liquid begins to *simmer* — tiny bubbles rise slowly to the surface, which quivers without bubbling up.

Poaching, braising, and stewing all involve simmering.

✔ *Poaching* a food (such as the Poached Pink Salmon in Chapter 18) calls for simmering it (completely submerged) in a liquid, usually water or stock. You can also poach eggs for breakfast by cracking them open and cooking them in a shallow pan of simmering water.

✔ *Braising* occurs when large pieces of meats, poultry, or vegetables (that have first been browned in hot fat) are tightly covered and cooked in a small amount of simmering liquid. Braising can be done on the stovetop or in the oven (discussed in Chapter 13).

✔ *Stewing* cooks foods similarly to braising, but uses more liquid than braising, though not as much as for a soup. Stewing cooks foods that are cut into chunks so the dish is done sooner than larger pieces that are braised. Chile con carne is one example of a type of stew.

Follow these tips when poaching, boiling, and simmering:

✔ Give more flavor to poached, boiled, or steamed foods by using a flavored liquid, such as a stock or broth. You can also add seasonings — herbs, onions, garlic, ginger, and lemon juice — before adding the food. Wine and liqueurs bring flavor to liquids as well (the alcohol evaporates during cooking, leaving just the flavor).

Try your hand at poaching with Succulent Chinese Chicken (see Chapter 18). In this recipe, a whole chicken simmers in water with ginger and green onions, gently poaching the bird, and then stands for an hour off the flame. The water becomes a delicate chicken broth, and the meat stays moist and tender.

✔ When boiling poultry or meats, skim off the brown scum that rises to the surface. It won't harm you but it clouds the liquid. The scum itself is merely blood that has solidified and lifts off easily with a spoon.

✔ Poach whole fruits, like pears, in wine or a fruit juice with a few cloves until just easily pierced by a fork. Serve at room temperature or chilled.

The following tips can help you braise better:

✔ When braising foods on the stovetop, use a heavy, thick-bottomed pot to better distribute the heat and keep the foods from scorching on the bottom. Cook the food slowly, over a low, steady heat.

✔ Vegetables release water when they're cooked, and braising catches these nutrient-rich juices and turns them into a natural sauce. For deeper flavor, cook aromatic vegetables, like carrots, celery, and onions, in some olive oil until lightly browned. Cover the vegetables and braise them alone or with other foods in a small amount of liquid.

You can try braising on the stovetop using a traditional Italian recipe, Tuscan Braised Green Beans (from Chapter 19), which braises green beans with tomatoes on a low, slow flame. The tomatoes themselves break down as they cook, adding to the braising liquid.

✔ Fish and poultry require very low flames and shorter cooking times when braising. Tougher pieces of meat, like pot roasts, take longer to cook.

✔ Occasionally stir stovetop braises and stews to prevent scorching the food in the bottom of the pot. (Unlike stovetop cooking, oven cooking surrounds the pot with heat, preventing the risk of scorching, as explained in Chapter 13.)

✔ Chapter 13 offers more tips that are useful for cooking braises and stews on the stovetop as well as in the oven.

Blanching and parboiling

To *blanch* a food, submerge it briefly in boiling water to either fully or partially cook it, and then remove it and place it in cold water to stop the cooking process. *Parboiling* is similar to blanching, but involves boiling food until it is only partially cooked. Denser vegetables, such as carrots and potatoes, may be parboiled before finishing their cooking by using another method, such as baking or frying. Unlike blanching, parboiled foods are generally not plunged into cold water after cooking.

- Blanch green vegetables like broccoli and spinach to lock in color and flavor. Skip to the "Keeping vegetables bright" sidebar, later in this chapter, for more tips on blanching.

- For blanching, cold tap water helps stop the cooking process, but a bowl of ice water works even better.

- To peel tomatoes or peaches, cut a small X in the skin at the bottom of the fruit, and then blanch for five to ten seconds in boiling water, just until you can easily lift the skin at the X and pull it away from the whole fruit.

- Parboil denser foods when cooking them with more tender ones. For instance, parboil carrot pieces before adding them to a stir-fry with bean sprouts, so that both ingredients complete cooking at the same time.

Steaming

When a liquid boils or simmers, some of it escapes into the air as steam. Surrounding foods in steam, by placing them over a boiling or simmering liquid (usually water), gently cooks them. Steaming retains more vitamins and nutrients than does boiling. As described in Chapter 14, microwave ovens are terrific for steaming vegetables, retaining even more nutrients than stovetop steaming does. Or, you can steam foods on the stovetop using a steamer insert — refer to Figure 12-2.

Follow these tips when steaming foods:

- Steam vegetables until crisply tender, that is, until they're just barely cooked through, are still crisp, have a little bit of bite to them, and aren't yet mushy or soft. Crispy, tender veggies taste delicious partly because they keep more of their nutrients when steamed.

- When steaming on the stovetop, keep the water level an inch or so below the steamer but don't let it dry out. Because microwave steaming cooks vegetables so quickly, and because the vegetables themselves give off water, you need to add only 1 or 2 tablespoons of water (or none at all, if it's a tender vegetable like asparagus) when micowave steaming.

✔ Steaming brings out the wonderfully delicate flavor of vegetables, fish, and poultry. Some people prefer this mild taste, others find it bland. To jazz up the flavor of steamed foods, serve them with tangy dipping sauces, like those in Chapter 20. Or, cook them on a bed of fresh herbs or steamed over a flavored stock. The flavorful juices of the steamed food fall to the bottom of the pot — you can reduce or thicken them into a sauce or add them to a soup or stew.

Double-boiling

Certain foods are too delicate to cook by steaming or boiling directly — custards, fragile sauces, and melted chocolate are best made using a double-boiler. A *double-boiler,* shown in Figure 12-3, consists of an upper pot that sits partially inside a bottom pot. The bottom pot holds boiling or simmering water, which gently heats the food in the top pot. The top pot never actually touches the hot water; instead, it sits above it. To keep egg-based sauces from curdling when cooking, use a double-boiler. You can also set a heatproof bowl on top of a regular pot to create the same effect as a double-boiler.

Figure 12-3: A double-boiler gently heats delicate foods.

double-boiler

Step 3: Sizzling on the Stovetop with Frying

Frying is another type of stovetop cooking, but it uses fats, such as oil, butter, margarine, shortening, or bacon grease, instead of water. Recipes may simply use the term *frying* whenever foods cook in hot fat, or they may use more specific terms to describe particular types of frying methods. In the following sections, I describe frying techniques that cook with fat.

Fat is a highly efficient heat conductor and serves two purposes: To create a hot layer of fluid that transfers the heat to uneven surfaces of the food and to prevent foods from sticking to the pan. The amount of fat and the temperature that you use produce very different results.

Recipes often use the term *fry* instead of one of the more specific methods described in this section. When a recipe simply says to fry a food, follow the recipe's directions for the amount of fat, temperature, and cooking time.

Frying — especially deep-fat frying — can cause hot oil or other fat to splatter out of the pan and burn tender skin. Keep a safe distance away from the pan and make frying safer by following these safety tips:

✔ Protect arms and hands with sleeves and long oven mits.

✔ Before frying, use a paper towel to dry any moisture on the food surface — moisture causes hot oil to splatter even more vigorously. For breaded foods, shake off any excess flour or breading before adding it to hot oil.

✔ Lower foods gently into hot oil using tongs so the oil doesn't splash.

✔ Never let young children fry, and start older ones with frying recipes that use just a little oil until they get the hang of it. Shorter kids should stand on a step-stool so their faces are high above the frying pan.

✔ To reduce the mess and keep you and your kitchen assistants from getting burned, use a *splatter guard,* shown in Chapter 3, to keep the oil from popping everywhere, especially when frying bacon.

Sautéing, pan-frying, and shallow-frying

These terms are all variations of the same technique — cooking in a small amount of fat, usually with a high heat. They are some of the quickest methods of cooking. By using very little oil in these methods, you can make healthy meals that also save time.

✔ *Sauté* (saw-TAY) uses the least amount of fat, as little as a thin film to coat the pan.

When cooking at high heat, use an oil that can withstand high temperatures. When oils get too hot they begin to smoke, producing bad-tasting, harmful toxins. Heat oils just until they start to ripple, before they reach their smoke point. Oils with high smoke points include canola, corn, peanut, soybean, sunflower, and safflower oils.

✔ *Pan-fry* and *shallow-fry* usually mean the same thing and use slightly more fat — not enough to submerge the food but more than a thin film.

To practice sautéing, make the Peas and Shiitake Mushrooms recipe in Chapter 19, in which you sauté green onions and sliced mushrooms in butter, then mix in cooked peas. The mushrooms release their own liquid which helps season the dish.

Keeping vegetables bright

Keep your vegetables bright with any of the following methods:

☺ Blanching vegetables for just a few seconds brightens the color of veggies by breaking up and dispersing the oxygen between the cells, allowing more of the natural color of the vegetables to shine through. To blanch vegetables, dump them into a bowl of ice water as soon as they're done to stop the cooking process and set the color, a technique known as *shocking* them.

☺ Longer cooking produces a different effect. As green vegetables cook, their cells release acids into the water. When these acids come into contact with the vegetable's lovely green chlorophyll, the vegetable turns brown. To keep the green color when boiling, use lots of water (so that the acids are diluted) and leave the pot uncovered (so that the acids can escape). Don't cook the vegetables longer than seven minutes, as this is about how long it takes before they start to discolor. When cooking broccoli or other thick vegetables, cut them into pieces that are small enough to cook in under seven minutes.

☺ Steaming keeps vegetables greener and retains more water-soluble vitamins and minerals than boiling does. The acids are much less concentrated in the steam (even with a covered lid) than in boiling water.

☺ Stir-frying also minimizes discoloration. The food pieces are small and cook fast, and the uncovered pan allows acids to escape into the air.

You can practice pan-frying by making the 5-Minute Mini-Chops in Chapter 18. These wafer-thin pork chops cook fast, making them ideal meats for pan-frying. After marinating the chops in soy sauce and lemon juice, you quickly fry the chops in a small amount of oil. Before serving, make a sauce from the pan drippings by deglazing the pan with the marinade (explained in the "Caramelizing and deglazing" section, later in this chapter).

Sauté and pan-fry more successfully by following these tips:

✔ Make sure the food is dry — moisture splatters and prevents the food from browning properly.

✔ Cut the food into uniformly sized pieces, so they cook evenly in the same amount of time. They don't always have to be small pieces, but they should be similar in size, thickness, and shape.

✔ Add foods to a pan that's hot, heated with a small amount of oil or other fat in it (the fat helps conduct the heat). A pan that's cold won't cook the foods properly.

✔ When sautéing, heat the pan on high, then add enough oil or fat to coat the bottom of the pan and continue heating until the oil just barely begins to smoke. Quickly add the food in a single layer, without crowding it. Adjust the heat so that the food takes only a few minutes or less to cook on each side. For larger pieces, like boneless chicken breasts, turn them after each side has cooked. With foods that you cut up into small pieces, toss or stir them periodically but not constantly. You want to develop some color on all sides and this won't happen if you turn or stir the food too soon.

✔ As meats and vegetables cook, especially mushrooms and onions, they give off liquid that you can use alone or with other liquids to make into a sauce, as described in the section on caramelizing and deglazing.

✔ You can coat foods before pan-frying with a batter or breading to seal the juices in and keep the oil from penetrating the food. The oil should come about $1/3$ up the depth of the food. It should be hot enough to make breadcrumbs or flour sizzle but the oil shouldn't start smoking. When the oil is too hot, the outer coating of the food burns before the inside cooks through.

✔ When pan-frying large pieces of food, like chicken breasts, use tongs so as not to pierce the food and release the juices. Always turn or flip the food *away* from you to prevent hot oil from splashing toward you.

Stir-frying

To *stir-fry* is to move small pieces of food around quickly and constantly in a pan with a small amount of oil on very high heat. Stir-frying is usually done in a *wok* (see Figure 12-4), but you can also use a large skillet. Most (but not all) stir-fried dishes start by having you sear the food in hot oil on high heat until almost cooked through. Then, you add a small amount of liquid and cover the pan with a lid for a minute or so. In some recipes, you finish the dish by stirring in a mixture of cornstarch and water (or broth) and bringing the mixture to a boil to thicken the sauce right before serving. To get acquainted with stir-frying, try the Simple Stir-Fried Asparagus recipe in Chapter 19.

French jumping beans

Sauté is a French word meaning "to jump" and originated because chefs would deftly, with the flick of a wrist, jerk the pan forward and up, tossing the foods into the air (making them jump) and catching them in the pan again. This food-flying method is quicker than stirring with a wooden spoon, but unless you're a trained chef, don't try this at home! If you do decide to give it a shot, practice by tossing dried beans in an unheated pan — and be prepared to sweep up the ones that fall!

Figure 12-4:
Use a Chinese wok for stir-frying, or use a large frying pan.

Follow these tips when stir-frying:

✔ Stir-frying requires foods to be cut into small, uniformly shaped pieces so that they cook very fast and all finish cooking at about the same time. Move the food by lifting and tossing. Woks come with their own utensils for this (refer to Figure 12-4), or you can use a wide heatproof spatula.

✔ Place the pre-cut, pre-measured ingredients in small dishes and line them up in order of use. Stir-frying cooks food so quickly that you need to have everything ready to add instantly without interrupting the cooking process.

✔ Be careful when cooking garlic, especially on high heat. When it cooks too fast and starts to brown, it turns bitter. When stir-frying, cook garlic in the hot oil for just a few seconds before adding the other ingredients to keep it from cooking so quickly.

✔ When stir-frying, be sure to use the proper heat. The food releases its valuable juices when the heat is too low. When the heat's too high, the food burns on the outside but is raw on the inside. Gauging the proper temperature comes more easily with experience and practice.

✔ When cooking large amounts of meat or poultry, stir-fry them in two batches. With too much meat in the pan, the foods release liquid and begin to steam instead of fry.

Dry-fry

This is essentially the same as pan-frying but without the fat, making it a good technique for those on lowfat diets.

Follow these handy tips when dry-frying:

✔ Nuts, seeds, and spices all have more flavor when lightly toasted. Cook them on a very low flame, stirring every few seconds. Be careful not to burn them — their high oil content retains heat and they continue to cook even after the flame is turned off. Try the toasted sesame seeds recipe in Chapter 18.

✔ Toasted nuts and seeds can add fat and calories to a dish, but they're also rich in protein, fiber, vitamins, and minerals. Save time by dry-frying them in batches and freezing them in zipper bags. Serve them in moderation to add crunch and heightened flavor to other dishes, or use nuts and seeds as a garnish.

✔ Nonstick pans allow you to dry-fry foods without oil or with just a light coating of vegetable cooking spray. Don't try to dry-fry lean cuts in a regular pan — the food sticks to the pan and doesn't cook properly.

✔ Make croutons without adding fat by dry-frying them. Cube day-old bread and toss with dried herbs, then cook slowly in a large, dry pan until toasted and crunchy.

Browning and searing

To *brown* a food is to cook it in a small amount of fat on high or medium heat until the outside is a golden brown color on all surfaces, but the interior is still moist. *Searing* is another term for browning meats, poultry, and fish quickly on very high heat, to seal in the juices (it may or may not require added fat in the pan). Browning and searing produce good color and a rich flavor.

To brown or sear, cook foods in a very hot pan on the stove, in the oven, or under the broiler, and follow these tpis:

✔ Don't keep turning the food that you want to brown or sear. Let it cook on one side until the right color is reached before turning. (See the "Carmelizing and deglazing" section for more tips.)

✔ When browning or searing, don't crowd the pan with too much food. Leave some space between the food pieces so the heat can surround them. Adding too much food at one time rapidly drops the temperature of the pan and its oil, so foods cook slowly instead of browning.

Nonstick cooking sprays made from vegetable oil are convenient for lightly coating a pan to prevent foods from sticking, but use them with care. Never spray them at an open flame, into a barbecue grill, or directly at a heat source, as the stream of liquid can catch fire and travel back to the can. Remove pots and pans from the heat before spraying them. Non-aerosol sprays (found in your grocer's dairy section) use pump nozzles instead of pressure, so they're safer for kids.

Deep-fat frying

In this method, foods are completely submerged in hot fat (usually oil or animal fats such as lard) until they are cooked through and are crisp. Deep-fat fried foods, such as fried chicken or shrimp tempura, are often coated in a batter before they're fried.

In this book, I avoid giving recipes for deep-fat frying because it's too dangerous for youngsters, but you can find such recipes in any general cookbook.

Caramelizing and deglazing

Caramelizing — how sweet it is! *Caramelizing* doesn't mean making candy-covered apples, but it does involve sugar — natural sugars in vegetables and meats cook until they turn brown and deepen in flavor. Caramelizing is an important technique because it makes food taste so good!

✔ You need a high, dry heat to caramelize, and using an oil or other fat helps reach the desired temperature (moist heat, such as steam, won't work). You can do this by sautéing and frying, and the techniques of roasting, broiling, and grilling (discussed in Chapter 13).

> ✔ The key to caramelizing foods is to let the surface area cook uninter-
> rupted until it begins to brown. Don't keep lifting the food and moving
> it around — the sugars will never get hot enough or concentrated
> enough to caramelize.

Deglazing, another way to punch up flavors, involves two simple steps: First
you fry, and then you add liquid. Frying, sautéing, and roasting leave
luscious little browned bits of caramelized food and tasty juices in the pan.

To deglaze, remove the meat or main food from the pan. Then stir a liquid
(broth, wine, water, or other fluid) into the pan to dissolve those bits of
intensely concentrated flavor. Simmer until the liquid reduces to make a
natural sauce. Also, lightly dusting chicken, meats, fish, and large vegetable
pieces with flour before frying helps them brown better and thickens the
sauce when deglazed.

Chapter 13

Lesson 5 — In the Oven: Baking, Roasting, Broiling, and Grilling

. . . .

In This Chapter

▶ Discovering tips for using the oven

▶ Roasting a variety of foods

▶ Baking cakes, pies, and pastries

▶ Braising and stewing foods of all sorts

▶ Cooking in the broiler and on the grill

. . . .

Why couldn't the sesame seed leave the gambling casino?
Because it was on a roll!

Got a burnin' desire to start baking? Time for a red-hot trip to the oven, where baking is just one method of oven cookery. The oven actually consists of two parts — the oven itself and the broiler — and this lesson introduces you to these two cooking areas. Because grilling is a close cousin to broiling (using the same cooking process but different equipment), I also discuss the basics of grilling in this lesson. Throughout this chapter, I include references to several recipes in Part IV that require roasting, broiling, grilling, and baking and give you tips on how to prepare each recipe quickly and successfully.

Step 1: Equipment Review for Ovens and Broilers

To become acquainted with the oven, review its parts, shown in Figure 13-1 before beginning to cook.

Before you begin using the oven, be sure to go over the information on make-it-safe zones for ovens in Chapter 8.

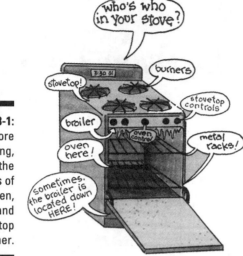

Figure 13-1:
Before
cooking,
review the
parts of
the oven,
broiler, and
stovetop
together.

Don't forget to have everyone in the family locate the oven mitts and try them on for size. After you turn the oven on, you never want to touch a metal rack, pot, or sheet of cookies without putting on a mitt or using a potholder.

You probably already own most of the following kitchen equipment. Take a look to see how each piece can be used for cooking in the oven or broiler. If you find some handy pieces here that you don't already own, you may want to add them to your kitchen cookware. See Figure 13-2 for examples of all of these pieces of equipment.

- **Baking sheet:** This versatile pan has low sides, and can be used for baking pizza, meat loaf, cookies, chicken pieces, and roasting vegetables and other foods that need to be surrounded by direct heat. Try to have at least two baking sheets on hand, especially when baking batches of cookies. For a description of the differences between baking sheets and similar pans, take a look at Chapter 16.

- **Baking dish** and **baking pan:** These two terms can be used interchangeably, but when a recipe calls for a baking dish, it generally means one made from glass or enamel-coated metal. A baking pan is made from uncoated metal, like aluminum or stainless steel. It's good to have an assortment of sizes. I recommend a rectangular glass baking dish (13 x 9 x 2-inch or 12 x 7 $\frac{1}{2}$ x 2-inch), and one or two smaller sizes, for cooking lasagna, winter squash, casseroles, small roasts and more. Also, an 8- or 9-inch square pan is useful for brownies and baked goods.

To see if your pan is the right size for a recipe, always measure from the inside edges of the pan's rim.

Figure 13-2:
You need a variety of equipment for baking, roasting, and broiling.

- **Casserole dish:** A casserole dish, sometimes called a *casserole,* is a more elegant type of baking dish that has a tight-fitting lid and handles, and is designed for cooking in and serving from the same container. (Actually, the word *casserole* refers to both the baking container and the food inside.) Most are round or oval, are deep, and are made from glass or metal, often with enamel coating. Shapes and materials may vary, though. Nonmetal ones are great for microwave cooking. Sizes vary, but a 2-to 2^1/$_2$-quart model is handy for most recipes. If you don't have a casserole, substitute a baking dish and cover tightly with foil.

- **Dutch oven:** A large, heavy pot with a tight-fitting lid, usually made from cast-iron or enamel-coated cast iron. Use a Dutch oven for braising and stewing. You can cook with a Dutch oven in the oven or on the stovetop, unlike most glass casserole dishes. For braising and stewing, use a Dutch oven on top of the stove to brown foods and then go directly into the oven, using just one pot.

- **Pie pan:** Pie pans come in glass, porcelain, or metal. Any of these are fine materials, but when using a glass pie pan, reduce the oven temperature by 25° to prevent the crust from overcooking.

- **Cake pan:** Also called round baking pans, 8- or 9-inch round cake pans (both 2 inches deep) aren't essential unless you like round cakes. You can also bake cornbread or other batter breads in a cake pan.

- **Muffin pan** or **muffin tin:** If you enjoy muffins, you need a muffin pan. A standard-size pan holds 12 muffins, each 2^1/$_2$ inches in diameter. If you want to get fancy, you can buy specialty pans to make very large or very small muffins.

- **Loaf pan:** A standard-size loaf pan measures 9 x 5 x 3 inches, but many recipes are written for one or two 8^1/$_2$-x 4^1/$_2$-x 2-inch pans. I recommend metal pans, but glass ones work fine too.

✔ **Roasting pan and rack:** A metal rack that fits inside a roasting pan keeps meat from stewing in its own juices — see Figure 13-3. Roasting pans come in various sizes. If your family cooks large roasts or turkeys, go with a pan that's at least 17 x 11 inches.

✔ **Broiling pan and rack:** To broil, you need a broiling pan (shown in Figure 13-3) with shallow sides and a low rack to keep chicken, steaks, vegetables, and other foods from cooking in their own juices or fats.

✔ **Rolling pin:** Use a rolling pin for making smooth pie crusts and for rolling out pizza crusts. See Figure 13-4.

✔ **Tongs:** Use tongs (see Figure 13-4) instead of a fork to pick up and turn food. This keeps you from piercing meats and letting their juices escape.

✔ **Bulb baster:** A bulb baster, shown in Figure 13-4, is a handy tool for basting, keeping meats moist when roasting or broiling. You can also use a brush-like baster or a spoon.

✔ **Instant-read** or **ovenproof meat thermometer:** Either of these two types of thermometers, shown in Figure 13-5, will work. See the "Taking the guesswork out of cooking" sidebar, later in this chapter, for information on inserting thermometers into food.

Figure 13-3:
Metal racks in roasting and broiling pans raise foods above liquids.

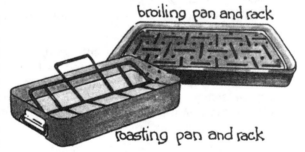

broiling pan and rack

roasting pan and rack

Figure 13-4:
A rolling pin, bulb baster, and tongs make baking, roasting, and broiling easier.

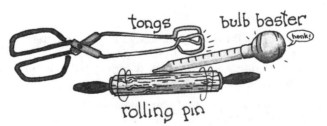

tongs   bulb baster   honk!

rolling pin

You can use any of the following types of meat thermometers:

- An *ovenproof thermometer* that remains in the food during cooking. The thermometer temperature scale is attached to a probe that you stick inside the food. Open the oven door or look through the oven window to check the thermometer when you think the food is close to being done. (These cost around $10.)

  Some brands, such as Polder, have a long probe that inserts into the food while it cooks and has a digital read-out (attached by a long wire) that sits outside the oven. When using this type, you don't need to open the oven door to monitor the temperature of the food. It also has a timer and an alarm that beeps when the desired temperature or cooking time is reached, so you don't have to check the food as often as other thermometers. (Cost is around $25.)

- An *instant-read thermometer* isn't intended to go into the food while it cooks. You simply insert this slender, compact type of thermometer into the food for a few seconds, read the temperature, and remove the thermometer from the food before returning it to the oven or when the food is cooked through. These thermometers come as digital models (around $30) or with dials (about $10).

I find that having both the instant-read thermometer and the Polder-style thermometer with the long probe covers all of my cooking needs.

Figure 13-5:
Use any of these thermometers to ensure that foods are fully cooked.

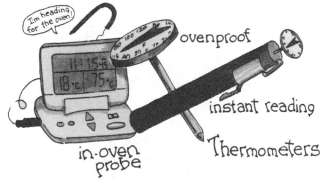

Step 2: Discovering Oven and Broiling Cooking Methods

Have you ever roasted a cake? You may not call it that, but roasting and baking are the same technique — surrounding food with dry heat to cook it. Although different from roasting and baking, broiling and grilling are similar to each other in technique — they cook by direct heat from a single source. You can also braise and stew foods in the oven by adding liquids to them. See Chapter 12 for the lowdown on braising and stewing on the stovetop — the process is the same in the oven, but the heat surrounds the pot rather than coming from below.

Roasting

Roasting and baking cooking methods actually do the same thing — they cook foods in a closed environment (the oven) by surrounding them with hot, dry air. The outside of the food browns, creating a deep flavor, while the natural juices or liquids inside steam to cook the interior.

Roasting is a term that generally refers to cooking meats, poultry, and vegetables. *Baking* usually refers to breads, pastries, and cakes (discussed in the following section), but you can find exceptions, such as "baked ham" and "baked potatoes."

Taking the guesswork out of cooking

Using a meat thermometer shouldn't be a "sometimes" thing — you can wind up with food that's not cooked enough (and contains bacteria) or is overcooked and tough. Instead, use a meat thermometer every time you prepare poultry, roasts, ham, casseroles with meats or egg in them, meat loaves, and egg dishes.

To test a food's temperature, carefully place the probe of the thermometer into the appropriate sections of your food:

☺ **Poultry:** For a whole bird, insert the meat thermometer into the inner thigh area near the breast but not touching the bone. For poultry pieces, insert the probe in the thickest part. Thermometers, though, don't do a good job with thin pieces like boneless breasts, so check for doneness by cutting into them and cook until the juices run clear.

☺ **Beef, pork, lamb, veal, or ham roasts, steaks, or chops:** Insert the thermometer into the center of the thickest part, away from bone, fat, and gristle.

☺ **Ground beef, turkey, or pork:** Place the thermometer in the thickest area of ground meat dishes, such as the center of a meatloaf. Insert the thermometer sideways in thin patties.

☺ **Casseroles and egg dishes:** Insert the thermometer into the thickest portion (the center).

For the best success when roasting meats, poultry, or vegetables, keep these tips in mind:

- ✔ Roasted vegetables get their intense taste from dry heat that causes some of their moisture to evaporate and concentrates their flavors. Long roasting or roasting at a high temperature causes the vegetables to *caramelize,* producing a sweet, brown exterior. (Chapter 12 discusses the caramelization process.) To see what roasting does to butternut squash, try the recipe for Gouda-Butternut Squash Gratin in Chapter 19.

- ✔ Root vegetables, such as potatoes, onions, carrots, sweet potatoes, and turnips, roast more quickly when they're cut into 1-inch pieces. Toss root vegetables with a small amount of oil and some herbs, then roast at 400° for about 25 minutes, stirring one time after about 12 minutes.

- ✔ Roasted meats and vegetables turn out best when they're cooked in a heavy pan with low sides, allowing the heat to surround the food more effectively.

- ✔ When roasting meats, poultry, and vegetables, cook them in the oven without a cover — this browns the food on the outside and keeps it moist inside. Place meats and poultry on a roasting rack, a metal stand that raises the food off the bottom of the pan, to prevent them from stewing in their own juices and to allow heat to circulate from below.

- ✔ To make a natural roasting rack, place the meat or bird on a bed of chopped vegetables, such as onions, potatoes, carrots, or celery. The vegetables elevate the meat and also absorb the meat's flavors, which makes a tasty side dish for the meal. Or, layer whole, trimmed carrots and celery stalks in the pan and set the meat on top.

- ✔ Let roasted meats and poultry stand for 15 to 20 minutes before carving. The interior continues to cook as it stands and the juices are reabsorbed into the meat. To keep the food warm, tent it with foil while it stands.

- ✔ Many factors can affect the time it takes to roast meat or poultry. Use your recipe as a guide, but for accuracy, test the temperature of the roast using a meat thermometer. Start checking the roast earlier than called for in the recipe — about three-quarters of the way through the suggested cooking time — to see whether or not the roast is done. It may be cooking faster or slower than the recipe indicates.

- ✔ Baste large pieces of meat or poultry with their own juices, a marinade, or a sauce to keep them from drying out as they cook. Use a basting brush or a bulb baster (refer to Figure 13-4) to coat the food with the liquid every 15 to 20 minutes, but avoid basting more frequently than that — the liquid can accumulate and steam the meat. The recipe for Self-Basting Lemon-Pepper Roast Turkey in Chapter 18 uses cheesecloth to keep the meat moist without much basting.

✔ Boneless roasts and poultry pieces are more convenient for you to carve, but bones add flavor to roasts. Bones also conduct heat, making the roast cook more quickly than boneless roasts do.

Baking

Desserts, cookies, pies, and breads bake differently than do meats, so keep these points in mind:

✔ Grease and flour a pan (when the recipe calls for it), to keep baked goods from sticking to the pan. (See Figure 13-6.) Lightly coat the inside of the pan with nonstick vegetable spray, or rub it with butter or vegetable oil, and then place a tablespoon or so of flour in the pan, moving the pan around and shaking it to coat the greased surfaces with the flour. Pour out any excess flour. Set the prepared pan aside until you're ready to fill it.

✔ Unless otherwise specified, most recipes are written with metal pans in mind. When using glass pans, reduce the oven heat by about 25 degrees — glass conducts and retains heat better than metal.

✔ When you put a baking pan in the oven, set the pan on the center rack. When you're baking more than one item at a time, leave plenty of room between the pans for air to circulate. When placing pans on two racks, stagger the pans, as shown in Figure 13-7, so that they're not sitting directly above each other.

✔ To cook food evenly, rotate your baking pan halfway through the cooking cycle by turning it 180 degrees. Ovens have hot spots, and the air in the front of the oven may circulate differently than the air in the back of the oven.

Figure 13-6:
Grease and flour a pan to keep batter or bread from sticking to it.

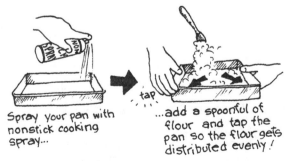

Spray your pan with nonstick cooking spray...

...add a spoonful of flour and tap the pan so the flour gets distributed evenly!

Figure 13-7:
Stagger two pans in the oven so the air can circulate freely around both.

Braising and stewing

You can braise and stew foods in the oven just as you do on the stovetop. When braising and stewing, you brown meats, poultry, or vegetables in hot fat then tightly cover the food and cook it in a small amount of simmering liquid. On the stovetop, the heat comes from below the pot, but when you cook the food in the oven, heat surrounds it on all sides. Stewing uses more liquid than braising, but both methods cook foods slowly. Some recipes use the stewing technique but aren't called stews — such as fricasees, ragouts, goulash, and chili con carne. Check out the tips for stovetop braising and stewing in Chapter 12 — they also apply to oven braising and stewing.

When braising and stewing in the oven, follow these suggestions:

✔ Before braising, brown roasts and large pieces of food in fat over high heat on the stovetop (flip to Chapter 12 for tips on browning and stovetop cooking). You can brown and braise or stew a food in the same pot if you use a Dutch oven (explained in "Step 1: Equipment Review for Ovens and Broilers," earlier in this chapter). Or, brown food in a skillet and then transfer it to an oven-proof pot with a tight-fitting lid.

✔ Some recipes call for coating meat or poultry with flour before browning. The flour helps the browning process and adds body to the braising or stewing liquid as it cooks.

✔ For braising, add enough liquid to come one-third to one-half way up the food being cooked. For stewing, completely cover the food in liquid. Liquid can be stock, vegetable juice, wine, or water (or a combination). After cooking, serve this liquid as part of the finished dish.

✔ For braises and stews, bring the liquid to a boil on the stovetop, then reduce the heat to very low and cover. Finish cooking in the oven or on the stovetop. The oven cooks more gently and evenly than the stovetop, and foods don't scorch.

✔ Flavor braises and stews by cooking vegetables in them. Carrots, celery, onion, garlic, and tomatoes add lots of flavor, but you can add any vegetable of choice.

✔ Braising cooks most foods whole or cut into large pieces, such as roasts, onions, and carrots. Stews use foods that are cut up into smaller pieces — meats are typically cut into 1-inch cubes, and vegetables are diced.

✔ Both braises and stews cook using low heat over a long period of time, but because the food in stews is cut into smaller pieces, cook stews for less time than braises.

✔ Add herbs, spices, and seasonings at the beginning of the cooking process to allow the flavors to blend. If desired, add a pinch of herbs in the last few minutes of cooking — this refreshes and highlights the slow-cooked flavors.

Broiling

In *broiling,* the heat source comes from directly above the food, without any obstruction (such as a pan or cover) between the flame and the food. The food cooks close to the heat, usually 1 to 4 inches, and the heat source itself is extremely hot. To broil, place the food on a rack in a shallow broiling pan (the rack raises the food and keeps the food from stewing in its own juices). Broil one side of the food first, then turn the food over with a pair of tongs and broil the other side.

Use the following broiling tips to take advantage of this fast-cooking technique:

✔ Line your broiling pan with foil for easy cleanup, and then set the broiling rack above it. Preheat both the broiling pan and rack to keep food from sticking to them.

✔ The thicker the food, the farther away it should be from the broiler. Some recipes specify how far to broil the food from the heat. Before turning on the heat, measure the distance from the flame to the food surface, not to the bottom of the pan.

✔ Keep the thickness of the meats and poultry that you broil between $3/4$- and $1^1/2$-inches thick. Thinner pieces dry out before browning, while thicker pieces don't cook sufficiently inside.

- ✔ Broil chicken pieces skin side down. After they become brown, turn the pieces with tongs to keep from piercing the chicken. Broil skin side up until browned and cooked through, being careful not to burn the skin.

- ✔ Trim excess fat from meats and remove skin from chicken to reduce the risk of grease flare-ups and to lower the fat content.

- ✔ Remove fat from the pan as it is released from the poultry or meat — the fat splatters under the broiler's heat and can start a grease fire. Pour the grease off, use a bulb baster (refer to Figure 13-4) to suck the grease up, or place a piece of bread in the pan to soak up the oil.

Grilling

Grilling is similar to broiling in that the food cooks from a single heat source, but in grilling, the heat source comes from beneath the food — the food sits on a rack directly above the heat. Grilling produces even higher heat than broiling, so the food usually sits a little farther — 3 to 5 inches — from the heat source. As with broiling, you grill food on one side before turning it over and grilling the other side.

You can grill outdoors using charcoal, hardwoods, or gas heat. During colder months, you can grill indoors on a stovetop that's equipped with a grilling rack or on an electric grill. Most recipes that call for grilling can also be cooked by broiling, as described in the previous section.

Grilling can be a mystical process at first, but it's really a simple form of cooking that can be mastered with practice. The heat is more difficult to regulate than stovetop and oven cooking, and cooking times vary depending on the air temperature, the type of fuel used, and the efficiency of the grill itself, which is why cooking times for grilled foods are always approximate. For complete tips on outdoor grilling, check out *Grilling For Dummies* by Marie Rama and John Mariani (IDG Books Worldwide, Inc.) — it gives you everything you need to know about grilling tools, fuels, and techniques.

Before firing up the grill, pay attention to these handy tips:

- ✔ Unlike the thick protective doors of kitchen ovens, hot grills and grill covers can burn little fingers instantly. Keep young children a safe distance from hot grills. Parents should take charge of setting up the grill and starting the fire. Teenagers can help turn foods with long tongs and metal spatulas, protecting their hands with long oven mitts, while parents supervise.

✔ Grilling is too dangerous for young children, but they can help make "campfire" packets for parents to place on the grill. Let them seal diced potatoes, mixed vegetables, boneless chicken breasts, or seafood in foil with herbs, seasonings, and a small amount of oil. Place the packets on the grill and cook until the food is tender when pierced with a fork (pierce straight through the top of the foil packet to test).

✔ Before heating the grill, brush the grid with vegetable oil or give it a spritz of nonstick cooking spray to keep foods from sticking. Don't oil the grid after it's hot, but if you forget to oil it before heating, lightly coat the food's surface with nonstick spray to prevent sticking.

✔ Marinades boost the flavor of grilled foods and help tenderize tough cuts. Marinate foods in glass containers, or for easy mixing and clean-up, in resealable bags (kids love to squish the marinade around!). Avoid metal containers, which can react badly with the acids in marinades. Give marinating and grilling a stab with the Grilled Velvet Chicken and Ruby-Red Grapefruit Chicken recipes in Chapter 18.

✔ To perk up the flavors of vegetables, coat them with oil and grill over high heat — you can marinate them before grilling, too. Skewering mixed vegetable pieces like tomatoes, zucchini, and onion on the same skewer looks pretty, but these foods all cook at different rates, so you're better off skewering each type of veggie on a different skewer.

✔ Baste foods with marinades or sauces as they cook to keep them from drying out and to add extra flavor. Cookware and hardware stores sell long-handled basting brushes that are specially made for grilling.

✔ If you plan to use a basting sauce or marinade as a dressing for your grilled dish, boil the sauce or marinade for 3 to 5 minutes before serving it. The boiling kills any bacteria that may be transmitted from the raw foods. Also, boiling the sauce before basting kills bacteria that may remain uncooked when basted on the food in the last few minutes of grilling.

✔ Sugar sauces burn. When using barbecue sauces that contain sugar or tomato sauce as a major ingredient, wait until the last few minutes to coat the meat. When you baste too early, the sauce burns before the interior of the meat cooks sufficiently.

✔ Partially cook thick pieces of meat by parboiling (described in Chapter 12) before grilling — this helps ensure that the interior cooks thoroughly without overcooking or burning the exterior.

Recommended minimum internal cooking temperatures

The U.S. Department of Agriculture (USDA) recommends foods reach the following minimum internal temperatures, as measured by a meat thermometer:

Fresh ground beef, veal, lamb, pork	160°
Beef, veal, or lamb roasts, steaks, and chops	
Medium rare	145°
Medium	160°
Well done	170°
Fresh pork roasts, steaks, and chops	
Medium	160°
Well done	170°
Ham	
Uncooked	160°
Pre-cooked, to reheat	140°
Poultry	
Ground	165°
Whole birds	180°
Breasts and roasts	170°
Thighs and wings	Cook until juices run clear
Stuffing (cooked alone or in bird)	165°
Egg dishes and casseroles	160°

Note: Allow roasts and thick cuts to stand for about 15 minutes after removal from the oven, to reabsorb the juices. During this time, the internal temperature continues to raise in these foods by about 10 degrees. Adjust cooking times with this in mind, to prevent overcooking roasts and thick cuts.

When cooking in the oven, broiler, or on the grill, try these tips:

✔ **Start the heat before you add the food.**

- Heat your oven for 15 to 30 minutes or until the oven reaches the desired temperature.

- Heat the broiler for at least 15 minutes or until intensely hot.

✔ **Don't crowd the food.** When baking, roasting, broiling, or grilling, allow plenty of space between foods or between pans for the heat to circulate.

Chapter 14

Lesson 6 — Small Appliances, Pressure Cookers, and Microwaves

- -

In This Chapter

▶ Discovering small appliances — blenders, food processors, choppers, mixers, and slow cookers

▶ Pressure cooking for fast, nutritious dinners

▶ Becoming a microwave oven expert

- -

Why didn't the toaster get married? He was afraid to pop the question.

Beat it, zap it, heat it, chop it, whir it, mix it, stir it, fix it! Small kitchen appliances — blenders, food processors, choppers, mixers, slow cookers, pressure cookers, and microwave ovens — can save you time, help you retain nutrients and use less fat, and allow you to expand your recipe repertoire.

In this lesson, you discover ways to cook more quickly, healthily, and easily by using these small appliances. I also include plenty of safety tips, so that you can update your kitchen code to include small appliances. (See Chapter 9 for more information on using a kitchen code.)

Read the manufacturers' manuals for safety tips and instructions on operating, washing, and assembling each appliance. Follow these additional tips when using small appliances:

✔ Take extra care when blending or pureeing hot foods, such as soup or sauces, with a blender, food processor, or other appliance. Parents can pour hot foods into and out of appliance containers, letting kids punch the buttons and hold the lid with an oven mitt to protect their hands.

✔ Children should never handle the blades of blenders, food processors, and other chopping appliances. Parents should be the only ones to assemble, dismantle, and wash the chopping parts.

✔ Never put any utensil in a blender or food processor container while the motor is running.

✔ Always let the blade come to a complete stop before opening the lid of an appliance.

✔ Use a wooden or hard nylon spatula to scrape down the sides of a blender or a food processor — these types of spatulas won't catch on the blades. Avoid using flexible rubber spatulas — the rubber can catch on the blades of the appliance.

✔ With the exception of slow cookers, bread machines, and rice cookers — all of which are made to shut off automatically — never leave a small appliance running unattended.

✔ To clean an appliance, unplug it before wiping down the base unit with a damp cloth, and never submerge it in water.

✔ Never soak the blades of an appliance in soapy water where they can't be seen, because the next person washing dishes may cut himself.

✔ Appliances that whir and chop, such as blenders and food processors, can be more easily cleaned by adding a small amount of soapy water to the container, and then blending or processing the soapy mixture for a few seconds. After that, stuck-on food should come off easily.

Get five-a-day the easy way: Whenever you cook, imagine ways to add even more fruits and vegetables to a dish simply by chopping or pureeing them using blenders, handheld blenders, mini-choppers, and food processors. Sneak vegetables into pastas, stews, beans, meatloaf, omelets, sauces, and salsas. Mix pureed vegetables, such as broccoli or carrots, into mashed potatoes or soups. Throw a cupful of chopped apples into pancake batter or a salad. Go wild!

Step 1: Using a Countertop Blender

A *countertop blender* (shown in Figure 14-1) can chop, mince, blend, and puree. The spinning blade at the bottom of the blender's container whips air into liquid mixtures — terrific for milkshakes, crushed ice drinks, and frothy beverages. (Unfortunately, the tall, narrow container prevents a blender from whipping enough air into egg whites or whipping cream, a task better left to a mixer.) Chefs love them because they process sauces into a finer, smoother texture than does a food processor. You can also turn bread into breadcrumbs, grind spices and coffee, and puree vegetables for baby food. However, mashed potatoes made in a blender (or food processor) turn gummy. Some models offer optional 1-cup containers ideal for salad dressings and smaller amounts of food.

Figure 14-1:
A blender
chops,
liquefies,
and purees
very
smoothly.

blender

Countertop blenders are relatively kid-friendly. The chopping blade is located at the bottom of the tall container, making it more difficult for young hands to reach. Also, a child can remove the container from the base and pour out the contents without the blade falling out (as is the danger with a food processor).

Blender containers may be made of glass, metal, or plastic, depending on the model. Glass containers are heaviest, so make sure children are strong enough before allowing them to handle glass containers. For young children, plastic containers work best, because they're lightweight but durable (though they will scratch over time, especially if cleaned in the dishwasher). Metal containers look stylish, but you can't see through them, making them less practical.

When blending hot foods, make sure the cover is tightly sealed, and then hold it in place with a kitchen towel. Start blending on low, and then work up to higher speeds.

Use these countertop blender ideas for healthier, easier, and quicker cooking:

✔ **Make natural sauces without adding fat or cream.** Blend broth or stock with cooked vegetables (such as carrots, parsnips, or broccoli) to make a deliciously-thick sauce that's full of nutrients and low in fat.

✔ **Rescue a lumpy gravy.** Pour the gravy in a blender and process until smooth.

✔ **Fix egg- or cheese-based sauces that accidentally curdle or separate.** Pour the mixture into the blender and give it a whir until it's smooth again.

✔ **Make fresh-fruit drinks and smoothies in a blender.** For a fast, lowfat breakfast or after-school snack that's full of vitamins and can be eaten on the run, make the recipe for Lassi, Come Home! (an Indian yogurt drink) in Chapter 20.

- **Mix frozen juice concentrate while it's still frozen.** Blend until liquefied with a portion of the water called for, and then add the remaining water.

- **Grind spices and coffee beans and chop fresh herbs.** A long-handled, clean artist's paintbrush helps brush out every bit of finely ground ingredients.

- **Make additive-free, homemade peanut butter or other nut butters.** To make peanut butter, blend roasted, unsalted peanuts with a few drops of peanut oil until spreadable, adding as much or as little salt, sugar, honey or other sweetener as you wish. You can also make the butter as creamy or crunchy as you want. For a lighter spread, blend in fresh apples, berries or bananas to sweeten the butter, add nutrients, and cut down on the fat.

Step 2: Handling a Handheld Blender

If I had room to plug in only one appliance, it would be a *handheld blender,* shown in Figure 14-2. A handheld blender is handy, easy to operate, washes up in a jiff, is compact, and can even be wall-mounted, saving valuable counterspace. Think of the handheld blender (sometimes called an *immersion blender*) as you would a countertop blender — it chops, mixes, purees, blends, and whips, but does all of that more conveniently — at least for small quantities of food and ones that aren't too tough. Handheld blenders have a rotary blade on the end of a wand-shaped handle. You simply immerse the blade into a pot, bowl, or tall glass to process, puree, or whip.

Handheld blenders come with a plastic cylindrical container known as a *chopper bowl* (though it looks more like a cup) that you can use to chop small quantities of food — just put the chopping blade and foods to be chopped into the container and let 'er rip. Sure, I use my handheld blender for its convenient blending capabilities, but more often for its mini-chopping assets. In fact, for some foods like salad dressings and chopped garlic, I prefer using a handheld blender to my mini-chopper or food processor — largely because it cleans up so quickly.

I use a Braun handheld blender, but other brands also work well. You can find most basic models for around $15 on sale. For convenience, look for ones with attachments that are dishwasher safe. Standard attachments include the chopping bowl and blade, and a blending container known as a *beaker.* Some models come with a whisk for beating eggs, and other attachments.

I find that handheld blenders are safer for kids to use than other chopping appliances. The chopping blade that fits into the container is blunt tipped and less likely to accidentally harm little hands than the razor-sharp, pointed tips of mini and standard food processors, which I discuss in "Step 3: Discovering the Food Processor and the Mini-Chopper."

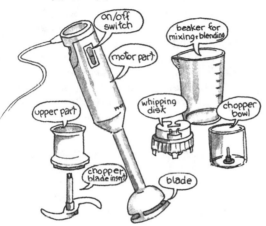

handheld blender

on/off switch

beaker for mixing+blending

motor part

upper part

whipping disk

chopper bowl

chopper blade insert

blade

Figure 14-2:
The handheld blender is the handiest of all small appliances.

For parents and kids to use a handheld blender successfully, follow these precautions:

- ✔ Don't overtax the motor of the handheld blender — it's made for small jobs or substances that aren't too fibrous or dense. (I once burned the motor out trying to chop a 1-inch chunk of ginger. Another appliance sacrificed in the name of cooking research!)

- ✔ Never operate a handheld blender without making sure that the blade is firmly inserted in the chopping container.

- ✔ Always keep little hands away from the blade end of the wand. If you mount your handheld blender on the wall, be sure that the wand sits in the beaker, a standard plastic accessory cup used for blending up smoothies and mixing liquids, to keep its blade away from fingers and hands.

- ✔ Handheld blenders can be a lot of fun, but can also be messy when working with liquids and kids. If you don't turn the handheld blender off before removing it from liquids, your kitchen will look like an ad for whirled peas. Similarly, if the depth of the liquid is too low, the mixing blade will splatter. Make sure the mixing blade is totally immersed. Move it slowly up and down for best results, and use a deep bowl or pot.

The following tips can help you use a handheld blender for healthier, faster, and easier cooking:

✔ **Make fresh, healthy salad dressings and marinades.** Drop in one clove of garlic, some fresh herbs, and a little oil and vinegar or lemon juice and the whole thing is completely mixed in 3 to 5 seconds. Make a lower-fat salad dressing in a few seconds by blending a smaller amount of oil with ingredients that are tart but less acidic than wine vinegar or lemon juice — see the Kiwi Vinaigrette in Chapter 20.

✔ **Thicken soups naturally and quickly.** Immerse the blender directly into the pot and puree cooked vegetables or beans for a thicker, richer soup without adding fattening cream. This saves time because you don't have to decant the food into another container, as you would with a countertop blender, and you also have less to wash. Try making the Basically Great (Dried) Beans recipe in Chapter 19 and when the beans are cooked (and you've removed any bones), plunge in the handheld blender and process some of the beans. Stir the pot to make a thick bean soup.

✔ **Grind spices.** You can grind whole spices, such as cardamom and cumin seeds, in seconds, but they won't end up as powdery as in an electric coffee mill or blender. Still, spices ground in a handheld blender are perfectly suitable for many dishes, and freshly-ground spices release much more flavor than pre-ground ones.

✔ **Chop fresh herbs.** Ever try to chop tough, needle-like herbs such as rosemary? The handheld blender does it neatly and effortlessly and is terrific for chopping more delicate herbs, like fresh parsley and cilantro, too. Try making the Chimichurri Sauce in Chapter 20 with a handheld blender.

✔ **Chop garlic.** Peel the cloves, drop them in the chopping cup, and pulse. If you want, add heart-healthy olive oil and keep the mixture on hand for basting chicken, roasting vegetables, making garlic bread, or creating an instant flavoring.

✔ **Make baby food in small quantities.** The fresher the food, the more nutrients it contains, so home-made baby food is about as nutritious as food will ever be. Steam fresh vegetables on the stovetop or in your microwave (for even more nutrients than boiling), and then puree the veggies with the handheld blender. Baby will smile.

✔ **Make smoothies and milk shakes.** Put soft fruit, juice, and milk or yogurt in a tall, wide glass or in the mixing container, then immerse the blender wand and puree away. Yum! An instant, healthy treat.

Step 3: Discovering the Food Processor and the Mini-Chopper

Unlike handheld blenders, a *food processor* (shown in Figure 14-3) can easily tackle large quantities of food and dense foods that are difficult to chop. The various blades and attachments of food processors make them versatile machines that can grate cheese, slice potatoes thinly, puree vegetables, mince onions, mix and knead bread dough, and chop solid foods. But food processors don't whip air into eggs or cream very well, and they make mashed potatoes turn to glue. Full-size processors can also be cumbersome to wash — they take up counter space and all of the pieces that come with food processors hog the dishrack space when drying. In response, the *mini-chopper,* shown in Figure 14-4, was invented. I cover both of these appliances in this section.

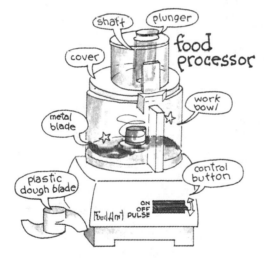

Figure 14-3: Use the food processor to chop tough foods, mix bread dough, and shred large quantities of food.

Food processors start at about $150 (on sale) and generally come with a metal blade that resembles a lethal ninja fighting tool (and is just as effective!), some slicing and shredding disks, and a plastic dough blade. You can also pick up optional equipment, such as slicing disks, extra work bowls, padded exterior covers, and even different size engines. Most of today's cookbooks assume that the reader has a food processor available and call for it as a standard kitchen tool in their recipes.

Figure 14-4:
Use a mini-chopper to chop small amounts of ingredients, make salad dressings, and mince herbs.

Even kids can operate these versatile machines by pushing one of two buttons: an *on* button that turns the blade continuously, and a *pulse* button that spins the blade only when the button is held down with your finger. (Parents should supervise their kids with any appliance, and only parents should handle the blades.) When the blade spins continuously to chop and blend ingredients, it's referred to in recipes as *processing*. Chopping by pressing the pulse button in short bursts is known as *pulsing*.

At around $30, mini-choppers cost far less than their big brothers and chop, mince, and puree in much smaller quantities. This can be more efficient for recipes that call for small amounts, as in $1/2$ cup chopped onion or 2 tablespoons chopped parsley. Mini-choppers have a base *footprint* (that's the amount of counter space it takes up) of about 5 square inches and they have only three or four small washable parts. (By comparison, food processors usually have five or six large parts.)

Follow these tips when using a food processor or mini-chopper:

- Cut foods into approximately 1-inch pieces before processing in a full size machine, and $1/2$-inch pieces for a mini processor. They'll chop more evenly.

- If you can't chop a food with a knife, don't put the food in the processor or mini-chopper. It will damage the blade.

- When using food processors, use only the *plunger* that comes with the machine. Never insert a wooden spoon or other tool that could drop in and ruin the machine.

- Don't fill the work bowl with liquids higher than the *shaft* — this prevents leaking.

- Hold the top of the closed *work bowl* steady with one hand. Sometimes hard or large objects cause the machine to shake and walk across the counter.

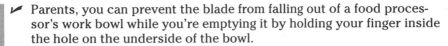

✔ Parents, you can prevent the blade from falling out of a food processor's work bowl while you're emptying it by holding your finger inside the hole on the underside of the bowl.

✔ Children should not remove the work bowl from the machine. The disk could fall out and hurt them. Instead, parents should remove the blade from a work bowl before letting a child scrape the ingredients out with a spatula.

✔ Place paper towels on the counter for catching drips from the *work bowl cover.*

✔ To keep the inside of the cover clean even while processing, place a length of plastic wrap over the work bowl opening before placing the lid back on. This way you keep the food from touching the inside of the lid and can skip washing it. Of course, this only works if you place the food in the bowl first and don't plan to use the *feed tube.*

How can the food processor be used for healthier, faster, or easier cooking? Try these suggestions:

✔ **Mix and knead bread dough — including pizza dough.** Make Pizza-Pizza: Double-Dough in Chapter 17 using a food processor. Freeze a batch, and then thaw for use anytime. No kid — or adult — will ever turn down fresh-baked pizza.

✔ **Prepare all of your pizza toppings in the same work bowl.** Start by cutting cheese into chunks and processing it with the metal blade into small bits. Remove the cheese and set aside. Repeat the process with the remaining ingredients (like pitted olives, peppers, onion, or garlic), pulsing the blade for each until they're just the right size — if you process too long, you'll puree them. Look in Chapter 18 for the Capture the Flag Pizza recipe.

✔ **Chop onions in large quantities, and then freeze or refrigerate.** If you cook with lots of onions, chop up a batch (using the metal blade), seal the onions tightly in resealable bags (squeezing out the air first), and freeze or refrigerate. Later, use only as much as you need. Fresh cut onions have more flavor and nutrients, but if you need to save time, this helps.

✔ **Make additive-free home-made peanut butter or other nut butters.** See the tip for making home-made peanut butter in the section on blenders in "Step 2: Handling a Handheld Blender," but use a food processor instead of a blender.

✔ **Chop nuts for cooking by adding flour or sugar.** This helps keep the nuts from overprocessing into nut butter. Process a $1/2$-cup of pecans or hazelnuts with 1 to 2 tablespoons of flour and use it as a coating for fish or chicken to add flavor and texture.

✔ **Make cookie and bread crumbs for crusts and toppings.** Break the cookies or bread into pieces into the work bowl and process until you reach the desired consistency.

✔ **Slice a summer vegetable salad in one work bowl.** Use the slicing disk, feed each vegetable through the *tube* using the plunger. Remove each vegetable after slicing and set aside, and then continue with another vegetable. Start with green onions and continue with radishes, celery, cucumbers, carrots, zucchini, green beans, or whatever is fresh. Then just dress, toss, and serve.

✔ **Make a concentrated mushroom flavoring to season chicken, vegetables, and soups.** Finely chop $1/2$ pound of mushrooms with 1 clove garlic in the food processor, then sauté the mixture in 3 tablespoons olive oil or butter until the liquid released by the mushrooms evaporates and the mixture is moist, but not soggy. Add a spoonful or two to sauces, soups, and other recipes to perk up the flavors. Use it fresh or freeze the flavoring in recipe-size portions.

Step 4: Utilizing Mixers

Mixers come in two models — a *hand mixer* (shown in Figure 14-5) and a *stand mixer* (shown in Figure 14-6). Both are used for adding lots of air to mixtures and for combining ingredients, but because one is portable and the other is stationary, they differ in their versatility.

Make sure the beaters of both hand and stand mixers come to a full stop before you raise them out of the mixture — otherwise you'll have a new, but sticky, splatter pattern in your kitchen.

Figure 14-5:
Hand mixers are handy: They're portable and compact.

Stand Mixer

motor head

flat beater

speed control lever

wire whip

bowl

dough hook

Figure 14-6:
Heavy
stand
mixers
remain on
the counter
to tackle
tougher
jobs.

Hand (or portable) mixer

Hand mixers are always portable, and models range from simple ones with three speeds and one set of beating blades to those with as many as nine speeds and additional dough hooks and whip attachments. Hand mixers are compact, making them great for small kitchens — you can even mount some models under a counter or on a wall.

Hand mixers are best used for mixing cake and pancake batters, whipping egg whites or cream, and making frostings. Some models, but not all, are sturdy enough to handle stiff cookie dough — but check the manufacturer's instructions before trying this.

Unlike the stand mixer that holds the beaters up for you, the hand mixer requires you to hold the unit in the air as the beaters whirl. This is a good way to build up your biceps (though not nearly as strenuous as beating egg whites by hand until stiff — the ultimate aerobic workout!). Look for models that feel comfortable in your grip, and are light enough for you to hold up for several minutes at a time.

Keep in mind that any task that a hand mixer does, a stand mixer can also do, but the reverse doesn't apply, because hand mixers are less powerful than their larger brothers. Follow these tips when using hand mixers:

✔ Be careful that the electrical cord doesn't get caught in the beaters, knock countertop items over, or come close to any heat sources or hot metal.

✔ When resting the mixer on its base, let the beaters hang over the bowl so they can drip into it and not on the counter. Place paper towels or wax paper over the counter work area to catch splatters or drips.

✔ To keep your mixing bowl from spinning or moving while using a hand-held mixer, set the bowl on a damp, folded cloth.

✔ Whip egg whites effortlessly for souffles, meringues, and angel food cake. Check for these recipes in any basic cookbook.

✔ Whip yogurt or whipping cream into a fluffy mixture to spoon into soups or dollop onto fruit and desserts.

✔ Cream butter and sugar together. Try the Lacy Angels with Dirty Faces recipe in Chapter 21.

Stand mixer

You may not need a stand mixer, but many cooks say they can't live without them. Cooks who make lots of pastries, breads, and baked goods — recipes that need lots of stirring, churning, and big bowls — use their stand mixers daily, probably much more often than their food processors.

A stand mixer mixes healthy, homemade bread dough with very little effort. Every week, I make breads with organic whole-grain flour and fresh vegetables. It takes only a few minutes of actual labor — simply add the ingredients to the bowl and then let the machine mix and knead the dough automatically for the required time. Let the dough rise as required, shape and bake. Easy! (Automatic bread makers mix, knead, and even bake the dough, but as an appliance, they're not as versatile as a stand mixer.)

Stand mixers start at about $200 (on sale) and now come with as much optional equipment as a new car! KitchenAid is by far the leading brand — this powerful workhorse, which comes in various models, offers attachments that do everything a food processor does and more. Besides the standard beating paddle, wire whip, and dough hook that come with the machine, you can get attachments that grate, shred, juice, make sausage, churn out pasta, and even open cans.

Even without the attachments, the basic stand mixer is a wondrous machine. It's powerful enough to handle all types of doughs, and (unlike a hand mixer) it holds the beaters over the bowl so that your arm doesn't get tired. The following is a list of what stand mixers, with standard equipment, do best:

✔ **Make bread dough.** Many bread recipes now offer directions for making and kneading the dough using a stand mixer, as well as for making the dough by hand.

✔ **Whip air into mixtures, as for egg whites or whipping cream.** Beaten egg whites and whipped cream are usually sweetened for dessert recipes, but try beating whipped cream without any sweetener for an airy topping for potatoes and steamed vegetables. Flavor it with salt and chives or other minced herbs, or whip in horseradish and serve it with roast beef.

✔ **Mix ingredients completely.** Stand mixers make smooth batters (see the Carrot 'n' Spice Cupcakes recipe in Chapter 21) that are lighter and fluffier than if made by hand.

Step 5: Simmering with a Slow Cooker

A *slow cooker* (see Figure 14-7), also known as a *crock pot,* can save you time and money. You can throw all the ingredients into one pot, plug it in, walk away, and let the food cook low and slow for hours — without ever worrying about burning the food inside.

Because slow cooking doesn't use a live flame and doesn't require sensitive timing, this technique is a safe way to involve youngsters in the kitchen. They can help prepare and add the ingredients to the pot. The exterior of the pot stays fairly cool, but make sure that little fingers stay away from the heating base.

Figure 14-7:
Slow cookers cook all day without burning foods.

slow cooker

Many working parents prepare the fixings in a crock pot and refrigerate them overnight. The next day, while the parents are at work, older kids can then start the crock pot cooking when they get home from school, helping to make a hot meal for the family.

Crock pot cooking has a decidedly dedicated following. One of the eGG's staff writers, Kathleen Michael, along with Jean, a Montessori School teacher from San Antonio, are crazy for crock pots. Kathleen owns several crock pots, ranging in size from 1-quart (perfect for dips and sauces) to a 6-quart model that's perfect for big families. And Jean loves them so much she's written a mini-book on them, which she e-mails to teachers and parents who ask for her recipes. "These recipes are saving my sanity," she writes. "You can cook while you sleep if you want to. I sometimes make meatballs overnight and in the morning put the pot in the fridge. Lunch can be meatball grinders, dinner can be pasta and meatballs with Parmesan cheese."

As dedicated crock pot lovers, Kathleen and Jean share these tips for using slow cookers:

- ✔ Long, slow cooking is not suitable for all dishes, but soups, beans, and stews are naturals for crock pot cooking. (Try Jean's recipe for Crock Pot Pizza Soup in Chapter 19.) Whole chickens and inexpensive, tough cuts of meat, such as brisket and chuck roasts, also turn out terrific when slow cooked. You can make vegetable casseroles, taco fillings, pork chops, pasta dishes, roasts, potatoes, shrimp, Spanish rice, and even desserts.

- ✔ All slow cookers aren't created equal. Kathleen prefers models made by Rival, which heat from both bottom and side with a crockery insert (which is not always removable). Slow cookers that heat from the bottom don't produce the same results. Jean prefers one with a Corning Ware casserole as the crock — it goes in the pot, on the stove, in the microwave, and in the fridge.

- ✔ Always lift pot lids, including slow cooker lids, away from you or anyone else to prevent steam burns.

- ✔ Because liquids remain in the crock pot, the cooking liquid is always a bit watery. Skim off any fat that may rise to the surface, then complete the sauce or gravy in a saucepan on the stove top, simmering it and adding flour or cornstarch as needed to thicken.

- ✔ Broil or brown meats before adding them to the slow cooker — this creates more flavor and removes excess fat.

- ✔ Put whole chickens, chicken pieces, chicken breasts, and whole roasts in the crock pot while they're frozen and they'll cook up perfectly when you slow cook them all day. The meat holds up better this way and isn't overcooked. (But you can't brown these foods first when frozen, unless you brown them before freezing.)

- ✔ Leave the food alone. The main advantage of slow cooking is to set and forget. You don't need to tend the pot. Don't hesitate to leave your home while your crock pot is on, just make sure that it isn't touching the walls or other appliances.

✔ Stirring isn't required for the great majority of crock pot recipes, though some may require basting. Keep the pot covered — leave the lid on. Every time the crock pot is uncovered, you lose half the cooking time. If for some reason you must open the pot, do all your ingredient additions at the same time to minimize heat loss.

✔ You generally have two temperature settings — low and high. Low is 200° and high is 300°. Most books tell you that one hour on high equals two hours on low, but cooking on low gives you much better results. Meat will be much more tender and juicy when cooked on low than on high. On high, you're cooking at a fast simmer, so the meat will be tougher. For best results, plan ahead and cook on low.

✔ Vegetables intended for the crock pot should be cut into bite-size pieces, not only for convenience in eating, but for better cooking too. Surprisingly, vegetables can take longer to cook than meat in crock pots.

✔ When the weather is cold and damp outside, warm your family up with a simmering, hot beverage — the crock pot keeps it at the perfect sipping temperature.

✔ Keep dips and other party appetizers (such as meatballs) at the right temperature and consistency for several hours in a crock pot.

✔ Use slow cookers on low heat to keep breads and rolls warm without drying out.

Step 6: Figuring Out the Pressure Cooker

Think of a *pressure cooker* (shown in Figure 14-8) as an appliance without the cord. Because it uses moist heat, it's like a slow cooker — only super fast. After the pot is heated enough to build up pressure, you can cook a tender, juicy whole chicken in just 15 minutes! Risotto as good as any in Italy cooks in just 7 minutes — without constant stirring. Pinto beans cook without presoaking in about 25 minutes, or in less than 10 minutes if you soak them overnight. Green vegetables not only cook quickly, they retain more of their vivid color. And on hot summer days, the pressure cooker cooks fast enough to keep the kitchen cool.

By quick-cooking foods in a closed container with very little water, pressure cookers retain more vitamins and minerals. Many vegetables that are rich in healthful antioxidants can be tough and may take a long time to cook. But put winter squashes, legumes, carrots, and root vegetables — even grains and meats — in a pressure cooker and zoom! — dinner is served. And because you retain more of the nutrients, the foods actually taste better, with brighter, more intensified flavors, than when cooked conventionally.

Figure 14-8: Pressure cookers retain more nutrients and make meals in minutes.

Pressure cookers are especially ideal for big families because they cook large quantities so fast. Invest in a good quality one, with a thick bottom for even heat distribution. I use a Kuhn Rikon Duromatic Pressure Cooker, which runs around $150, though other quality brands exist.

Children should never release the lid of a pressure cooker; leave this to the parents. You can use one of two ways to lower the pressure in a pressure cooker (pressure cooker recipes specify which method works best for the recipe). One is the *natural release method,* in which you turn off the flame and let the pressure cooker sit until the pressure has subsided on its own. The other is the *quick release method,* where you hold the edge of the pot under cold running water, cooling the temperature quickly and lowering the pressure.

If you own a pressure cooker, try making the Greek Skinny Chicken in Chapter 18, and be sure to follow these tips when using a pressure cooker:

✔ Don't wear a helmet. Good quality pressure cookers today are safe and don't explode like the ones of earlier eras. Just be sure to follow the manufacturer's instructions.

Don't pressure cookers explode?

They used to. Today's pressure cookers come with double back-up safety vents and locking lids that can't be removed until the pressure subsides, making them noncombustible. Before buying a pressure cooker, be sure to check out its safety and convenience features. Look for pressure cookers with excess-pressure release valves, a lockable lid, heat-resistant handles, and a rubber gasket around the lid, which expands when heated and prevents the lid from being removed until the pressure subsides.

✔ Pressure cookers create steam that escapes through a vent in the top. For safety reasons, parents can do the actual cooking and release of the pressure cooker lid, but children can still assist by putting the ingredients in the pot before cooking. Always lift a lid away from you to avoid steam burns.

✔ Pressure cookers are incredibly easy and uncomplicated. You can easily adapt recipes that rely on boiling, steaming, or braising, because all you're doing is cooking food faster while retaining more moisture and nutrients. Consult the manufacturer's instructions or a pressure cooker cookbook for more guidelines.

✔ Practice a few times with simple recipes. You may need to get a feel for how long dishes take to get up to either low or high pressure then you want to determine how much to lower the flame to maintain that pressure evenly. Kids can help monitor the pressure gauge and tell you when the flame needs to be adjusted. They can also set the timer when the correct pressure is reached.

✔ Set the timer only after the pressure cooker reaches the desired high or low pressure. Most of the recipes that I've made take from 5 to 20 minutes to cook after the pressure levels out — just enough time to whip together a fresh salad as a side dish.

Step 7: Mastering the Microwave Oven

Do people really cook with microwave ovens — or do they just use them for defrosting and reheating? A few cookbooks show how to adapt conventional cooking to the microwave, but in some recipes, the quality and end results are sorely lacking. If you figure out a microwave recipe that works well from scratch, then that's terrific! But don't let the microwave save you time at the expense of taste.

In some instances, a microwave oven really can make food tastier and healthier. The microwave does a bang-up job of steaming vegetables and fish by retaining more of the nutrients and color. It's a terrific time-saver for defrosting and reheating, and it's also good for finishing cuts (like roasted turkey or chicken pieces) that aren't completely cooked through inside. You may find that you can speed up certain recipe steps, such as melting butter or chocolate. You can also cook with less mess in a microwave oven, using microwave-safe dishes and measuring cups, which leaves fewer dishes to wash up.

Microwave ovens cook so differently from other appliances that they have their own unique set of safety rules to follow:

- ✔ **Don't put metal of any kind in a microwave.** Metal causes the electronic beams to bounce rather than penetrate. If you use metal (including metal twist-ties) inside a microwave, sparks can result that can cause a fire or an electrical short. Some newer models allow small amounts of aluminum foil, but you should do so only if the manufacturer's instructions say it's okay.

- ✔ **Don't put Styrofoam and disposable take-out containers in a microwave.** As the food gets hot, the container will melt into the food. Don't reuse disposable frozen dinner dishes either, because they're not meant to withstand frequent reheating.

- ✔ **Heat food in containers like glass and microwave-safe ceramic.** Not all ceramic dishes are microwavable — if they heat up before the food does, don't use them. Avoid containers with gold or silver designs, too.

- ✔ **Cover dishes to avoid splattering.** Plastic wrap can be used as a covering, but the jury's still out on its safety — the wrap can melt from the heat of the food and may give off unhealthy but invisible *polymers* — things you don't want to ingest. Instead, use a glass cover or place a plate on top. Make sure that the cover sits slightly ajar to allow some steam to escape. If you do plan to use plastic wrap because of its convenience, look for boxes labeled 'microwave safe' and avoid letting the plastic come in contact with the top of the food during cooking. To let steam escape, cover the container tightly with a sheet of plastic wrap, and then poke holes in the top with a fork.

- ✔ **Microwaved containers can become hot.** Always remove them from the oven with potholders or oven mitts. Remove covers with care, lifting them away from you to avoid steam burns.

- ✔ **Be careful with temperature settings.** Settings range from high to low but even when recipes specify the setting, the times may vary due to different oven wattages. Check the dish often. Microwaves are great for cooking foods fast, but if you're not careful, they can cook them too fast. In a matter of seconds, that wonderful specialty you prepare can be ruined by overcooking.

- ✔ **Never cook eggs in their shells.** They'll explode.

Microwave ovens perform impeccably well at certain tasks. Here's what microwave ovens do best:

- ✔ **Reheat leftovers.** Cover leftovers and either stir them periodically or rearrange the pieces occasionally. Cooked poultry, meats, and fish retain more of their moisture if you cover them with lettuce leaves.

- ✔ **Jump start a left-over casserole.** Warm it up on the microwave and then finish it off in a preheated oven — this brings the crispy topping back better than the microwave.

Microwave magic

How does microwave cooking work? Invisible electrons heat food by causing water molecules to rub against each other. These electrons penetrate inside the food, causing friction which heats from the inside out — a very different process from conventional cooking, which penetrates with heat from the outside in.

Microwave ovens aren't good for browning or roasting meats or for baking breads and pastries. Eggs cooked in the microwave turn rubbery.

Microwave cooking can also cook foods unevenly, leaving hot and cool pockets. To make sure that foods are evenly heated throughout, periodically stir or rearrange foods once or twice during the microwaving process.

- **Defrost frozen foods.** You can thaw chicken pieces and other frozen foods safely in a microwave (see Chapter 8 for more chicken handling tips). Be sure to remove any plastic wrap or Styrofoam before defrosting.

- **Steam vegetables, fish, and poultry.** Steaming foods retains more nutrients in a microwave because the foods cook so fast. Many foods that contain a lot of moisture don't need extra water when microwave steaming. Vegetables like asparagus and spinach, as well as small pieces of chicken, give off enough liquid to steam themselves. Broccoli and carrots cook best with a small amount of liquid.

- **Bake potatoes.** Potatoes baked in the microwave retain more of the nutrients than with conventional baking. Bake on high for 6 to 8 minutes. Half-way through, turn them and poke holes in them to allow steam to escape.

  For skillet home fries, cook the potatoes in the microwave as you would baked potatoes, but leave them slightly firm. When they're cool enough to handle, chop them up and fry them on the stovetop.

- **Soften cream cheese on low and soften brown sugar on high.** Add a slice of apple to hardened brown sugar and cover while cooking to make the sugar soft and crumbly again.

- **Melt butter.** Fats and butter tend to explode if cooked too high or too long. Cover the dish and cook on low or medium, checking every 10 to 20 seconds as the butter begins to melt.

- **Melt chocolate.** Cut into pieces or use chips. Heat uncovered on medium for 2 to 3 minutes until soft, then stir until smooth and liquid.

- **Liquefy crystallized honey and syrup in their glass jars.** Remove the metal lids before heating on high, checking every 10 to 15 seconds. Don't try this with plastic containers.

- ✓ **Warm lemons, limes, and oranges on high for 15 to 45 seconds.** You'll get more juice out of them.

- ✓ **Poach or bake fruit.** Cook pears in cranberry juice for a rosy snack or dessert, or bake apples with maple syrup for a hot breakfast.

- ✓ **Steam tortillas in your microwave in seconds.** Lightly dampen one side of up to six corn or flour tortillas with water and stack them on a microwavable plate. Invert another plate on top, slightly ajar, to let steam escape. Cook on high for 1 to 2 minutes, until soft and steamy. You may want to rearrange the tortillas, placing the inner ones on the outside and vice versa, and then cook again for a few seconds so that they steam more evenly. The plates also keep the tortillas warm for serving.

- ✓ **Help bread dough rise.** Place a cup of water in the microwave and cook on high until the water boils. Then place covered bread dough in the warm, steamy microwave to rise.

TIP

Frozen lemon-aid — freezing fresh citrus fruits

Don't rely on bottled lemon juice — it never tastes really fresh. Instead, keep fresh lemon and lime juice on hand by freezing whole lemons and limes. Just toss the whole fruit into the freezer. When you need juice, simply thaw in the microwave for 1 minute or so. Your cooking will taste so much better.

Chapter 15

Lesson 7 — Setting the Table and Presenting the Meal

What did the tablecloth say to the table? Don't move — I've got you covered.

Finally, it's time to eat! In this lesson, you set the table, serve the food, and dig in — sharing a delicious, home-cooked meal together. When the meal is over, this lesson tells you how to put everything safely away (including the leftovers) and clean up, making the kitchen ready for your next meal together.

This lesson shows you how to arrange a place setting and explains the type of tableware and serving equipment that you can use every day or for special occasions. I introduce you to garnishing — simple ways to make the meal more attractive. And if you cook enough food to be enjoyed again later, this chapter gives you tips on the best way to store and reheat leftovers for another day.

Step 1: Setting the Table

Setting the table is like getting dressed. Some days require fancy attire, and other days are more casual. Placemats, tablecloths, and napkins make up a table's wardrobe. They help set the mood of the meal, which can range from informal to elegant. Other parts of the table setting — the type of flatware or silverware, plates or fine China, glassware, or centerpieces that you choose to put out — also contribute to the dining atmosphere.

When setting the table, think about the mood you want to create. Even young children can find many creative opportunities in setting a table, from picking out the placemats to folding the napkins. And by setting the table, kids discover the various uses for salad forks, dessert spoons, and other specialized utensils that they may encounter at restaurants or in other dining situations.

Arranging the place settings

For most dinners at home, you use simple table settings — just a fork, knife, and spoon. But at holidays, for formal dinners, or at restaurants, you can add special utensils, plates, and glasses with very specific uses.

For informal family dining or special occasions at home, you may want to use some or all of the following items for each place setting, as shown in Figure 15-1 and Figure 15-2:

A Simple Table Setting

Figure 15-1:
Arrange a simple setting for everyday dinners.

✔ **Placemats** or **tablecloth:** Your family may use placemats or a tablecloth, or both. Placemats and tablecloths aren't necessary, but they can help protect your table, and can add warmth and color to the table setting.

✔ **Napkins:** Place a folded napkin on the left side of each plate with the fork on top of or next to it, or place it directly in the middle of the dinner plate (a clean plate without food on it). Unfold and place the napkin on your lap when you're seated at the table. When you need to leave the table, set the napkin on the seat of your chair until you return.

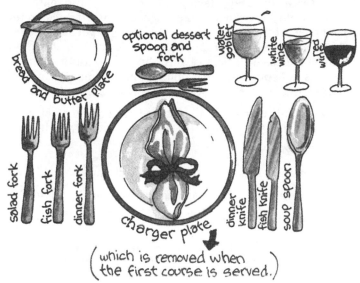

A Place Setting with the Works!

bread and butter plate · optional dessert spoon and fork · water goblet · white wine · red wine · salad fork · fish fork · dinner fork · charger plate · dinner knife · fish knife · soup spoon

(which is removed when the first course is served.)

Figure 15-2:
Put out all or some of these items for a formal table setting.

Paper napkins are fine for weeknight dinners at home, but cloth napkins add elegance to a meal. Don't be shy about using cloth napkins for *all* your meals. Cloth napkins can make the meal seem more special and they're more ecologically sound because they don't waste paper. You can reuse a cloth napkin that's only lightly soiled — in fact, napkin rings were originally invented to keep slightly-used napkins tidy between meals.

✔ **Plates:** Use *dinner plates,* large plates of about 12 inches in diameter, for the main course. Smaller plates of about 6 inches across are sometimes set out for salads *(salad plates)*, and even smaller plates are often used for holding bread and butter (known as *bread plates*). Place the dinner plate in the center of the place setting. You may also want to set a salad plate immediately to the left of the dinner plate and a bread plate at the eleven o'clock position. When you serve salad or soup as a separate course before the main meal, place the salad or soup bowl directly on top of the dinner plate.

Set out the *dessert plates* (a salad plate or a bread plate that's used for dessert) after you clear away the dishes from the main meal.

✔ **Flatware:** *Flatware* is another term for silverware and refers to knives, forks, and spoons that are used for eating at the table, as opposed to the types that are made especially for cooking the meal.

When setting the table, put out all of the flatware that you need for the entire meal. Place the dinner fork on the left side of the plate. The knife (with sharp edge facing inward, toward the plate) and spoon go on the right side. When you use a salad fork, it goes on the far left — to the left of the dinner fork. A soup spoon goes on the very far right. When you use a dessert spoon and fork, they go above the plate — place the dessert fork closest to the plate with tines on the right and the dessert spoon above it pointing in the opposite direction. For more formal occasions, set a butter knife across the bread plate.

✔ **Glasses** and **cups:** Place all glasses in the one o'clock area of the place setting, arranging them in the following order from left to right:

- Water glass

- Beverage glass (for iced tea or lemonade)

- Wine glass or champagne glass (often called a *flute*)

- Cup and saucer (for a hot beverage like coffee or tea)

When you're finished dining, lay your utensils next to each other, across your plate. This signals to the host or waitstaff that you're done.

Using serving utensils and centerpieces

Attractive serving bowls and festive centerpieces can make the dining experience more enjoyable and add a special touch to the meal, even on weeknights. (I bring out my whale-shaped wooden salad spoons whenever we have a "whale" of a salad!)

Consider the following practical and decorative tips when setting the table:

✔ Set out a large serving spoon, serving fork, tongs, or other utensil for each dish. If the serving utensils don't rest easily in the dish, set out a spoon rest or small plate to hold them.

✔ Put salt and pepper shakers on the table.

✔ Set hot casseroles or pots on hotpads or *trivets* (short metal stands) to protect your table surface. Woven mats, potholders, and ceramic tiles also work.

✔ Wrap hot bread or rolls in a towel to keep them warm, and serve them in a bread basket or bowl.

✔ When using a centerpiece or candles, make sure they're low enough for everyone to see over. Or, position them so they can't obstruct anyone's line of vision.

Only parents and older kids should light candles. Place candles and their holders on a protective surface (like a plate or mat), to keep dripping wax from damaging the table or tablecloth.

Garnishing with gusto

Turn meals into feasts for the eyes by adding a *garnish* — an edible decoration that can be as basic as a sprig of parsley or as complicated as a carved vegetable. For simple garnishes in seconds, try these techniques:

☼ **Dusting:** Lightly powder a dish with finely ground spices or flavorings. To dust a dessert with cocoa powder, use a shaker top or tap the powder through a sieve while holding it over the dessert.

☼ **Sprinkling:** Casually sprinkle on small bits of colorful food, such as chopped nuts; finely diced, julienned, or grated vegetables, fruits, or cheese; or minced herbs. (Chapter 11 shows how to make these types of cuts.)

☼ **Drizzling:** Using a squeeze bottle, drizzle a thin stream of a thick liquid randomly over a dish and onto the plate itself. Drizzle melted chocolate or pureed raspberries on cheesecake or red chile sauce on chicken.

Be creative with centerpieces. Set the clay animal that a child makes at school on a colorful placemat. Go for a walk together and gather some greenery for kids to arrange in a bowl or vase. Together, select natural items, like a simple bowl of mixed nuts, a potted herb, or a basket of squash.

Step 2: Wrapping Up the Meal

Every good meal comes with a price — such as clearing the table, storing leftovers and cleaning the kitchen. But now that everyone's so well fed and happy, they should be eager to jump in and help! Right?

Work out a fair system by deciding in advance who will do each after-dinner task — even if it means drawing straws! Some families clean up the meal together; others assign the tasks to specific family members. And reassigning or rotating the tasks every now and then prevents routine chores from becoming painful drudgery.

To set and clear the table more quickly, use an inexpensive tray to carry several items at once. Pick a tray that children can handle easily, one that's not too heavy when full, with a lip on the edge to keep items from sliding off.

As soon as possible after the meal, refrigerate or freeze the leftovers. Seal them tightly, and keep these tips in mind:

✔ Oxygen causes freezer burn, which discolors food and makes it taste stale. Double-wrapping helps keep oxygen out.

✔ Use plastic wrap and containers that are specifically made for freezing — not all materials are moisture-proof or vapor-proof.

✔ Double wrap food before freezing it to further protect it from the air.

✔ Resealable freezer bags take up much less space than hard containers. You can even store soups and stocks in them. Suck the air out of a resealable bag with a straw, then seal completely. Kids love to do this and are especially good at it!

✔ Liquids expand when frozen. Leave an inch or half-inch of space at top of the container when freezing liquids.

✔ Chill foods before freezing — they'll freeze faster and taste fresher.

✔ Label containers with the contents and date, using a marker or grease pencil (found at office supply stores).

Hopefully, you embrace the practice of cleaning up as you go (see Chapter 9), so that you only have to wash a few items — dinner dishes, pots and pans, and any serving ware. Only pots and pans that are labeled "dishwasher safe" can be washed in dishwashers; otherwise you should wash pots and pans by hand. Soak pots with stuck-on food in hot soapy water for several hours or overnight.

Be sure to clean the tabletop and counters and to wipe up any spilled food from the stove (make sure it's cooled off first). After the dishes and cook-ware are dry, unload them from the dishwasher or drying rack and return them to their cabinets and drawers, making them ready for your next wonderful meal together!

Part IV
Recipes for the Whole Family

The 5th Wave   By Rich Tennant

"Don't blame us! The recipe clearly states, 'Add 4 tablespoons of sugar.'"

In this part . . .

*I*t's time to eat — or at least to jump right into cooking. Every member of the family, from preschooler to grandparents (or as many cooks and assistants as your kitchen can hold) can pitch in with the recipes in this part.

These recipes are fun and flavorful — and certainly not complicated. Even the main courses are easy as pie. In this part, you can find dishes for every occasion, including meals from morning to night, holiday treats, snacks, and a few thirst quenchers. As tasty as they are, these recipes are all quick-to-fix, with minimal mess and loads of nutritional benefits. And, they all use only readily available ingredients. What else could a busy family want from a meal?

Kids and novices can ease into cooking with basic step-by-step instructions, and parents can use this part to break out of boring recipe ruts when that age-old "What's for dinner?" question arises. Look also for special tidbits about other lands, the foods of the earth, and cooking tips along the way — all great ways to explore the world through food.

Chapter 16

About These Recipes

In This Chapter

▶ Whipping up kid-friendly recipes

▶ Getting the best results with everyday ingredients

▶ Making a month of balanced meals

What do you get when you cross an avocado, a duck, and a food processor? Quackamole.

The recipes in this book are designed to coach you through cooking. They may look long, but that's because each step is clearly identified, so that novice cooks can easily follow along. Despite their terrific taste, these mouth-watering recipes are simple and flexible enough for parents and kids to make together, without fear of failure or frustration. Most recipes take less than 30 minutes of hands-on preparation time, although some require longer cooking time. Use these recipes to spur your own creative juices — with a bit of practice, you can devise your own original recipes for the whole family to enjoy.

Before You Begin

As you prepare the recipes in this part, keep the following in mind:

✔ These recipes are intended to involve all family members. For safety's sake, always make them with an adult around.

✔ All of these recipes are simple to make, and every recipe has steps in it that can include kids from preschool on up. Use children's ages and abilities to determine exactly what tasks they can do. Parents, encourage kids to join in, while you supervise or assist.

✔ These recipes are somewhat flexible, allowing for a certain margin of error or inaccuracy. Don't panic if you think you've messed up a recipe — it will likely taste fine, and if not, throw it out and try again.

Eating wine and spirits

Is it safe for kids to cook with wine or eat meals made with more potent alcoholic beverages, known as *spirits*? Made properly, foods cooked with alcohol are perfectly safe to serve youngsters. The dish should be cooked long enough, usually several minutes, for the alcohol itself to evaporate, leaving only harmless trace residues and the concentrated flavor of the wine or beverage used. Cooking with wine, beer, sherry, and spirits can greatly enhance the taste of some dishes, acting as a flavor conductor to heighten the taste of all the ingredients.

Certain religions or lifestyles suggest that people not use alcohol, though, so some families never cook with it. If you think your dinner guests may abstain from alcohol in any form, even in cooking, ask them before planning the meal. If for any reason you prefer not to cook with alcohol, you can usually substitute nonalcoholic wine, broth, water, or grape juice with a splash of lemon juice.

Don't buy so-called "cooking wine" — it's made from inferior wine that's laced with salt or additives. Cook only with wine that's suitable for drinking.

- ✔ Parents and kids alike should follow the Ten Kitchen Commandments in the Cheat Sheet at the front of this book and safety tips in Chapter 8.

- ✔ Chapters 8 through 15 describe basic cooking techniques and terms. Refer to them whenever you're unsure about a term or technique.

- ✔ Pay attention to the recipe's introduction, or *headnotes* and to the *sidebars* (the shaded boxes of text) in the recipe chapters. You can discover cooking tips, food tidbits, and information about other cultures, which open up all sorts of windows to the world through cooking.

- ✔ The recipes in this book use the Fahrenheit temperature scale, in which water freezes at 32° and boils at 212°. The United States uses the Fahrenheit scale, but many other countries use the Celsius (or Centigrade) scale, in which water freezes at 0° degrees and boils at 100°. If you need to convert Fahrenheit temperatures to Celsius, subtract 32 from the Fahrenheit degree, multiply by 5, and divide by 9.

- ✔ For more cooking fun, visit www.cookingwithkids.com.

No-flame, no-fire recipes

Certain recipes in this book can be made entirely without heat, preventing tender fingers from accidentally burning. (The recipes may require the use of a knife or appliance, though, so parents still need to pay attention and use caution.) Look for recipes marked "no-flame, no-fire" to avoid stovetop, oven, or even microwave cooking. Chapter 23 lists ten of them to get you started.

Kid-Friendlier Recipes

The recipes in this book look different from other recipes, because they're written with kids and novices in mind. Pay attention to these kid-friendly features in the recipes:

✔ **Skill level:** None of the recipes in this book are complicated, but some are more basic than others. Symbols indicate the minimal level of skill that the recipe requires, but don't forget that parents need to supervise whenever kids cook.

• **Easy:** Anyone can make this recipe! These easy recipes have very few steps and ingredients, and they whip up in a jiff, so even fidgety preschoolers can make them with a parent's helping hand. School-age children will find these recipes a breeze!

• **Moderate:** Almost everyone will find this recipe easy to make. You don't need much cooking experience, but you should be old enough to read the recipe and perform measuring and chopping tasks. Most school-age kids can make these recipes. Younger kids can perform many of the tasks, but a parent will need to help with the actual cooking and chopping. Most of the recipes in this book fall into the moderate category.

• **More challenging:** These recipes aren't complicated, but you need some amount of cooking experience to make them. In some cases, an adult or teenager may need to perform most of the cooking tasks (like lifting a turkey), while younger kids can assist with easier recipe tasks (like measuring). Only a few of the recipes in this book are considered "more challenging."

✔ **Recipe steps:** Recipe steps may seem long, but they're just explained in more detail. Most cookbooks streamline a recipe, condensing several steps into one description. They list ingredients according to the way they'll be added to the dish, such as "$^1/_2$ cup chopped onion" — but without telling you to actually chop the onion. Without making the recipes too cumbersome, I try as much as possible to list every ingredient in its store-bought form and explain all the steps needed to prepare it as part of the actual recipe instructions.

✔ **Do this first:** In some cases, when the ingredients you purchase vary in size (for example, a bunch of parsley), I list the ingredient the way it looks after it's been prepared, saying "^{1}/$_4$ cup chopped parsley," instead of 5 sprigs or ^{1}/$_4$ bunch. The "Do this first" area of the recipes identifies tasks to be done before jumping into the recipe, saying in this example, "Do this first: Chop enough parsley to make ^{1}/$_4$ cup." Other ingredients that need advance preparation, such as cooked chicken for chicken salad, are also listed in the "Do this first" area.

✔ **Prep time:** Use preparation times as approximate guides. The "Prep time" feature is based on one adult working alone — extra hands may increase or decrease the time. Time starts when you walk into the kitchen and turn on the lights, but I do assume the ingredients are reasonably accessible — if you have to excavate your spice cabinet just to find the basil, add more time.

✔ **Cook time:** Use cooking times as approximate guides. All cooking times may vary depending on the pans used, the oven's temperature accuracy, the thickness of a food, a fruit's ripeness, or the size of the vegetable. Follow the guidelines given in each recipe to determine doneness, instead of relying on exact times.

For these recipes as universal as possible, they were tested on both gas and electric ranges, and (where appropriate) an 850-watt microwave oven with cooking carousel (a less powerful microwave requires slightly longer cooking times). To be consistent with most home cooks, only the top-selling brands of cookware and appliances were used, including KitchenAid, Braun, and Chantal cookware (I love their stay-cool handles), and other commonly available brands.

✔ **Yield:** Consider the yield to be a portion guide — the yield indicated for each recipe reflects the number of average-size servings a recipe makes, not necessarily the number of people it feeds. Appetites may drastically vary from one person to the next, and a preschooler will likely eat less than the average serving while teens may go back for second (or third!) helpings.

✔ **Special equipment:** You probably already have every piece of equipment that you need for the recipes in this part, including a microwave oven. Some recipes call for a small appliance, such as a handheld blender, blender, mini-chopper, or food processor. In almost all cases, you can substitute a sharp knife and a cutting board and still make the recipes successfully. Flip to Chapters 3 and 22 for kid-friendly kitchen tools that can come in handy.

✔ **Ingredients:** Be flexible with ingredients. Don't avoid a recipe because you lack one ingredient — think of a similar ingredient to substitute, such as chicken rather than pork. If a recipe contains an ingredient that you don't like or isn't available, try to come up with an acceptable alternative and make the recipe with that ingredient instead.

✔ **Vary It!:** Look at the Vary It! sections after some recipes, for bonus recipe ideas. The changes that I suggest may be minor, such as substituting other seasonings, or may explain how to make an entirely different dish from the same basic recipe.

✔ **Serving Suggestion:** Look for these tips on ways to create an entire meal or present a dish with flair!

✔ **Meal Morphing:** When a recipe makes a dish that can be saved in part and then transformed into an entirely new tasting dish, I call this *meal morphing.* Meal morphing saves time without making the family eat exactly the same dish more than once. Check out Chapter 5 for meal morphing techniques and menu plans.

Baking sheet, cookie sheet, and jelly roll pan

What's the difference between a baking sheet, sheet pan, jelly roll pan, and cookie sheet? These terms are often used interchangeably in recipes, because the pans themselves are similar, though not exactly the same.

I prefer the more generic term of *baking sheet*. When you see the words *baking sheet* in this book, you basically need to use a large, flat metal pan with low sides, from $\frac{1}{2}$- to 1-inch deep, such as the jelly roll pan shown in the following figure — it measures 17 x 11 inches with 1-inch sides. (In most cases, you can substitute pans of similar dimensions.)

Cookies, though, bake better on pans with low or no sides, so you can use a jelly roll pan, or preferably, an actual cookie sheet. A *cookie sheet* has a very low lip on two opposite sides, mainly for easier handling, while the other sides are open for more even heating (see the following figure). Because the sides of a cookie sheet are open or very low, never use it to cook anything with juices that can run over the edges.

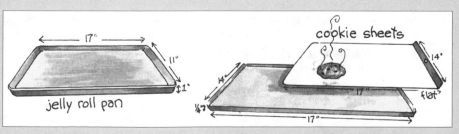

Assumptions about Ingredients

The recipes in Chapters 17 through 21 always use certain common ingredients in the same way. For best results, follow these guidelines when preparing ingredients from these recipes:

✓ **Peel onions and garlic first.** Because you almost always need to peel the papery skins off of onions and garlic before you use them, peel them before chopping (unless the recipe mentions otherwise).

✓ **Trim and use most of the green onion.** Before using a green onion, trim off the root end and discard. The recipes in this book use all of the green section of a green onion — not just the white part — or as much as is fresh and usable. Green onions are also known as *scallions*.

✓ **Use fresh, frozen, or canned vegetables and fruit.** Fresh tastes best, but if fresh isn't available, substitute a frozen or canned version. Many of the recipes in Chapters 17 through 21 specify canned or frozen products because of their ready availability, but you can always substitute the fresh version. Get your fruits and veggies any way you can!

✓ **Don't peel most fresh vegetables and fruits.** Don't peel potatoes, carrots, apples, or other produce unless the recipe tells you to — a treasure chest of the nutrients lie in or just under the skin.

✓ **Wash all fresh fruits and vegetables.** Rinse fruits and vegetables well, just before use (some foods, like berries, deteriorate if rinsed too far in advance). Scrub the skins of sturdier produce and remove and discard the outer leaves of leafy vegetables. Dry the produce before using. See Chapter 8 for tips on rinsing vegetables, and whenever possible, use organic vegetables to avoid pesticides.

✓ **Keep nonstick vegetable spray handy.** The recipes in this book frequently call for convenient nonstick vegetable sprays. If you don't have the spray handy, substitute a light coating of vegetable or olive oil, brushed on or wiped on with clean hands or with a paper towel.

✓ **Use low-salt varieties.** These recipes are intended to be made with lower salt versions of canned broth, vegetables, and tomato products, usually found on the shelf next to their full-salt counterparts. If you use salted versions, cut back on the salt in the recipes.

✓ **Choose your fat content.** Preferences vary on nonfat, lowfat, and whole dairy products and mayonnaise. These recipes work fine with most lowfat versions, but most nonfat products (except for nonfat yogurt) are too far away from their natural counterparts to taste good.

✓ **Use large eggs.** The recipes in this book assume that you'll use large eggs whenever eggs are called for.

✓ **Two halves make a whole chicken breast.** A chicken has one breast, which is sold in two pieces, known as *chicken breast halves* or *split-breasts*. The ingredient lists in these recipes use the term chicken breast half when referring to the triangle-shaped breast pieces that you often find at the market.

Chapter 17

Breakfasts, Brown Bags, and Breads

- -

In This Chapter

▶ Making balanced breakfasts for home, work, and school

▶ Dishing up luscious lunches on the go

▶ Baking basic breads and pizza dough

- -

Why did the man stare at the can of orange juice?
Because it said "Concentrate."

You can take breakfasts beyond cereal and milk — the recipes in this chapter offer ideas for wholesome fast food that's packed with fruit, grains, and nuts to give your family a nutritious head start on the day. Little ones can take pride in making many of the packable lunches by themselves, and these lunches taste so great that the rest of the family will want them too. In this chapter, you can also find healthy home-style breads that are foolproof enough for youngsters or parents to make, including everyone's favorite dough — pizza!

Never eat batters that contain raw eggs, or lick the batter from bowls or utensils. Remember that the uncooked bacteria in raw meats, poultry, fish, and eggs can be harmful, so cook foods thoroughly before eating them. Use hot, soapy water to clean hands, cutting boards, knives, and counters to avoid cross-contamination. Check out the safety tips described in Chapter 8.

Rise 'n' Shine Breakfasts

Jump start little sleepyheads with a healthy, hot meal that they can help make themselves. Kids and parents alike need breakfast for peak performance — it's the most important meal of the day! You can also enjoy the nutrition-packed meals in this section for brunch, lunch, or even for a break-the-routine dinner that may tempt even finicky eaters.

Bake 'n' Take Breakfast Muffins

Prep time:	3 minutes, plus 10 minutes to heat oven
Cook time:	8 minutes
Yield:	1 muffin sandwich

Fond of Egg McMuffins? If so, you can make this tasty home-made version in less time than it takes you to cruise the morning drive-thru window. These muffins are a neat and quick way to make a hot, healthy breakfast — you can even customize the flavors and ingredients to suit your tastes and nutritional preferences. For an entire family on the go, prepare the muffins assembly-line style, wrap them in foil, and leave them by the door as your family races off to work or school. Young eaters may find that half a muffin sandwich is plenty, while older kids, teens, and adults will likely want a whole one.

Do this first:

- Position a rack in the upper third of the oven. Start heating the oven — to 450° — at least 10 minutes before assembling the muffins, so that the oven is fully hot when you're ready to cook.

- Measure 2 tablespoons pre-shredded cheddar cheese (or shred enough cheese to make 2 tablespoons).

Ingredients and steps:

1 English muffin, preferably multi-grain or whole wheat
$^1/_8$ teaspoon dried herb of your choice (chervil, thyme, dill, basic, or parsley)
1 egg
2 tablespoons shredded cheddar cheese
Dash of salt
Dash of pepper

1 While the oven is heating, line a baking sheet with foil. Lightly spray the foil with non-stick cooking spray.

2 Open the English muffin and place the two halves on the foil, with the insides facing up.

3 In a small bowl, crumble the herbs between your fingers to release their flavor. Add the egg, cheese, salt, and pepper and beat with a fork until blended (about 10 seconds).

4 Carefully pour the egg mixture onto each half of the English muffin, keeping as much of the mixture from spilling over the sides as possible. Let the mixture soak into the muffin for a second or two before adding more to the muffin. (Don't worry if some of the egg mixture runs over the sides of the muffin — it will still taste fine.)

5 Bake for about 8 minutes, until the mixture is no longer runny and the cheese is melted. (Set a timer for 8 minutes when you put the muffins in the oven. Make sure the timer is within earshot while you get ready for work or school.)

6 Lift the muffin halves off the foil with a spatula. If you're eating at a table, let the muffin halves rest for several minutes until cool enough to eat (watch it — they're hot!) and serve the muffin open-faced. For a meal that you can take with you, place the two halves together to make a sandwich and wrap in the same foil used for baking. To keep the heat in longer, wrap in heavy-duty foil, and then in a cloth napkin to help retain the heat.

Vary It! Use this basic recipe as a starting point to add the seasonings and ingredients that you prefer — including those little bits of leftovers lurking in the fridge! Add salsa, chili powder, and ground cumin to make the muffin Mexican; use green onions to add zest; and add crumbled, cooked Italian sausage to give a Mediterranean flavor (try a lowfat turkey sausage). For a more savory taste, warm a slice of Canadian bacon on the foil as the muffins bake, and then place the bacon between the two muffin halves.

This meal packs protein, carbohydrates, and calcium, and adds notable amounts of iron and vitamin A. It gets about 36 percent of its calories from fat, but adding cooked vegetables or beans to the egg mixture brings down the overall fat content and increases nutrients. Cooked peas, mashed beans, and chopped spinach (squeezed dry) work well. Some vegetables and cooked meats, such as ham, give off water as they bake, so they require longer cooking times.

If you're watching your cholesterol intake, use an egg substitute instead of a whole egg. Whole-grain and multi-grain muffins provide more nutrients and fiber than do white or sourdough muffins.

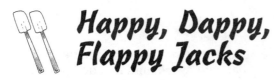

Happy, Dappy, Flappy Jacks

Prep time:	10 minutes
Cook time:	25 minutes
Yield:	4 to 6 servings

Pancakes (also called *flapjacks*) make a happy meal anytime of day — you can even prepare the batter the night before. Fresh fruit and cornmeal add a crispy texture, enhanced by the flavor of real maple syrup. For savory lunch, brunch, or dinner pancakes, see the variations listed after the recipe.

Do this first:

✔ Squeeze 2 tablespoons lemon juice from 1 lemon.

✔ Melt 2 tablespoons butter in a saucepan, or microwave covered on low heat, checking every 30 seconds until melted. Be careful not to microwave too long or the butter will overheat and splatter.

Ingredients and steps:

2 small pears or 1 large Granny Smith apple
2 tablespoons lemon juice
2 eggs
1$^1/_2$ cups nonfat, lowfat, or regular milk
1 cup all-purpose flour
1 cup cornmeal
2 teaspoons baking powder
1 teaspoon salt
1 tablespoon sugar (optional)
2 tablespoons melted butter
Maple syrup to taste

1 Core and cut the pears or apple into $^1/_2$-inch dice. Place the fruit in a small bowl and toss with lemon juice to prevent the cut pieces from turning brown.

2 In a medium mixing bowl, beat the eggs and milk together with the fork just until blended.

3 In a small mixing bowl, mix together the flour, cornmeal, baking powder, salt, and sugar (if using).

4 Using a rubber spatula, stir the dry ingredients into the bowl of wet ingredients until just moistened. Stir in the melted butter and one cup of the chopped fruit until all ingredients are evenly moist (small lumps are okay). Don't beat the batter — that makes pancakes tough. (For thinner pancakes, add a spoonful or two more milk.)

5 At this point, you can cover and refrigerate the mixture and the reserved fruit, if desired.

6 When you're ready to make the pancakes, lightly coat the cooking surface of a griddle or skillet with nonstick spray. Heat the griddle or skillet over medium heat until a few drops of water sizzle and dance across the surface. Use a ladle or measuring cup to pour $\frac{1}{2}$ cup (to make small pancakes) to 1 cup (for a large pancake) of the batter onto the griddle.

7 Cook pancakes until small bubbles open up all over the surface and the bottom of the pancake is brown, about 2 to 3 minutes. If the first pancake is too brown, lower the heat. Use a heatproof spatula to flip the pancake. If the pancake starts to break as you pick it up, it's not thoroughly cooked; cook it a few more seconds.

8 Cook pancakes until golden brown on the other side, about 30 seconds. Remove pancakes to a plate and invert a colander over them to keep warm. Repeat with remaining batter until all pancakes are made.

9 Serve the pancakes sprinkled with the reserved chopped fruit and maple syrup.

Vary It! For a different type of meal, make savory pancakes by adding herbs, ham, broccoli, spinach, or mushrooms and topping with sour cream, cheese, ricotta, salsa, or a light sauce. The French make thin pancakes (called *crepes,* pronounced KREHPS), and fill them with sausages for a breakfast dish or fruit and jam for dessert. To make thinner pancakes similar to crepes, add more milk to the recipe.

The first pancake usually ends up as a sacrifice — it may be over- or undercooked until you've adjusted the heat properly. It likely tastes fine, but may not be picture-perfect. Serve it underneath another pancake, or eat it as a snack as you go.

Make the pancake batter the night before and then cover and refrigerate for use the next morning. Save additional time by cooking pancakes in two skillets simultaneously.

All ages can help, from young ones measuring and stirring to older ones cooking and turning the flapjacks.

Peanut Butter French Toast Sandwiches

Prep time:	5 minutes
Cook time:	7 minutes
Yield:	4 sandwiches

Calling all peanut butter lovers! This one's for you. You simply put two slices of bread together with a lightly sweetened peanut butter filling, then dip into egg and grill. Stephanie Zonis, whose "I Love Chocolate" column appears at globalgourmet.com, created this recipe. She likes to use cinnamon-raisin bread, but you can use whatever bread you have. Serve with any variety of jam or jelly, or my favorite, no-sugar-added fruit preserves.

Ingredients and steps:

> 7 tablespoons confectioners' sugar (or to taste)
> $1/3$ cup peanut butter, smooth or chunky
> 5 teaspoons hot water
> 8 slices bread, each about $1/2$-inch thick
> 2 eggs or $1/2$ cup liquid egg substitute
> 2 tablespoons milk
> Nonstick vegetable spray, butter, or margarine
> Jam or jelly of your choice (for serving), slightly warmed if desired

1 In small bowl, combine confectioners' sugar, peanut butter, and water. With a spoon, stir until well-blended (mixture will be thin initially, but will thicken slightly).

2 Spread peanut butter mixture as evenly as possible on one side of each slice of bread, using it all.

3 Sandwich the two bread slices together, peanut butter sides in, and press gently to compact. Repeat to make 4 sandwiches.

4 In small, flat-bottomed bowl large enough to hold a sandwich, combine eggs and milk; beat well with fork to mix.

5 If your griddle isn't nonstick, melt a small amount of butter or margarine in it to coat the pan surface, or coat with nonstick spray. Heat the griddle (or skillet) over medium heat.

6 Dip both sides of each sandwich into the egg mixture, then place on the griddle.

7 Cook 2 to 3 minutes over medium heat, until golden brown on bottom.

8 Flip the sandwiches over with a spatula; continue cooking several more minutes until the second side is golden brown.

9 Remove from griddle. Serve hot with jam or jelly on the side.

Vary It! Omit the confectioners' sugar for a less sweet filling — except for natural peanut butter, most commercial brands already contain added sugar. Or, for a decorative presentation, dust the cooked sandwiches lightly with confectioners' sugar through a sieve. You can also serve with maple or other syrup instead of jam or jelly. Use multi-grain bread with seeds and nuts to bring out the flavor of the peanuts.

 # Easy Overnight Strata

Prep time:	15 minutes, plus refrigeration overnight
Cook time:	45 minutes
Yield:	6 servings

This basic breakfast, brunch, or lunch dish just loves variations — and busy mornings! Spend five minutes the night before and then simply pop it in the oven the next day. Preschoolers get a kick out of cookie-cutting and tearing the bread. Squeezing the liquid out of the spinach ranks right up there with making mud pies.

Stratas, meaning layers, are excellent dishes for using up leftover odds and ends and work even better with day-old or slightly stale bread. The more flavorful and hearty the bread, the better the strata tastes. To feed a large crowd, double the ingredients and use a 13- x 9-inch baking dish (add an extra 10 to 15 minutes to cook).

Do this first:

✔ Shred enough cheese to make $3/4$ cup (or use pre-shredded cheese).

Ingredients and steps:

1 package (10 ounces) frozen chopped spinach
6 slices multi-grain or whole wheat bread
2 green onions
3 cherry tomatoes (optional)
4 eggs
$1^1/2$ cups lowfat milk or buttermilk
1 tablespoon Dijon mustard, regular or coarse-grain
$1/8$ teaspoon dried tarragon
$1/4$ teaspoon salt, or to taste
$3/4$ cup shredded cheese, such as sharp cheddar, feta, or Swiss (or use a mixture)

The night before:

1 Defrost the spinach in the microwave according to manufacturer's instructions.

2 Lightly coat an 11- x 7-inch baking dish or equivalent casserole with nonstick spray.

3 While the spinach thaws, cut out the bread centers using a cookie cutter. Set the cut-outs aside. Tear the remaining pieces into small scraps.

4 Chop the green onions. Slice the tomatoes in half. Set these ingredients aside separately.

5 In a mixing bowl, combine the eggs, milk, mustard, tarragon (crushing the leaves), and salt until blended.

6 When the spinach has thawed, place it in a sieve in the sink. With clean hands, squeeze the liquid out of the spinach until it is very dry.

7 Place the torn bread scraps in a single layer in the bottom of the dish. Top with a layer of spinach and green onions. Sprinkle on the cheese. Arrange the bread cut-outs on top.

8 Pour the egg mixture evenly over the entire casserole. Top each cut-out with a cherry tomato half, cut side facing down.

9 Cover and refrigerate overnight.

To bake the strata the next day:

1 Remove the strata from the refrigerator and uncover.

2 Heat the oven to 350°.

3 Bake 45 minutes, or until slightly puffy and a knife inserted in the center comes out clean. Let stand 5 minutes before serving. To serve, cut into 6 sections, each with a bread cut-out and tomato half.

Vary It! Just about anything goes in a strata. Try bell peppers, olives, sautéed mushrooms, green chiles, ham, turkey, cooked ground beef or turkey, cheeses, herbs, and seasonings.

Take advantage of today's wonderfully varied, rustic breads — their dense texture and hearty grains make great stratas. These breads are often sold in the day-old section of the grocery or bread store because of their short shelf life. Cube and freeze them for stratas, stuffings, and bread puddings.

Tasty tips for better brown bags

Brighten an otherwise ordinary day by turning your brown bag into a mail bag. Pack a personal note, picture, cartoon, or joke, and add variety to lunch with special treats like these:

- **Add crunch for lunch.** Mix up an unusual variety of chips in plastic bags — try tasty bean chips, vegetable chips, and bagel chips. Add nuts or sunflower seeds to salads, soups, and even sandwiches for crunch appeal. Try toasted, spiced pecans instead of potato chips.

- **Get your five-a-day.** Pack fresh relishes and salsas. Try grilled corn and diced red and green peppers; black olives, tomatoes and grated cheese; or red onion, oranges, and cilantro. Pack some hummus dip and celery sticks, grate vegetables into a salad, or roll raw veggies in lime juice and mild chili powder. Be inventive!

- **Stop the sog.** Bag moist vegetables, such as tomatoes, separately for adding to a sandwich, and pack individual condiment packets (ketchup, salsa, mustard, and so on) like those found in fast-food outlets. The result? No more mushy bread.

- **Cook silly pasta salads.** Specialty and gourmet shops now carry all sorts of fun pasta shapes like basketballs, sailboats, and Christmas trees. Make pasta salads using those silly shapes — everyone will love them.

- **Make cookie cutter sandwiches.** Use cookie cutters to cut bread slices into fanciful shapes — bats and cats for Halloween, bunnies for Easter, or stars any time of year. Pack a few extra to share with friends, too!

Lively Lunches

Lunchtime at home can be very exciting — you have a world of options at your fingertips, from open-faced broiled sandwiches to stovetop pastas and soups. But making mouth-watering, portable meals for school or work can be more challenging. Break up the usual routine with crunchy sandwiches and other ideas that I suggest in this section. You also want to make sure that you make healthy lunches that travel well.

Follow these guidelines to maintain a healthy lunchbox:

> ✔ **Clean up with moist-wipes.** Pre-moistened wipes can clean messy hands gently, before and after eating. Kids can keep a box in a desk or locker. You can also buy them in individual packets.
>
> ✔ **Wash your lunchbox.** Bacteria can grow anywhere, so clean lunch boxes or bags out regularly.
>
> ✔ **Jump-start your thermos.** Get the thermos up to temperature by prefilling with iced or boiling water. Food stays the proper temperature longer, making it tastier and safer to eat. Remember to keep hot foods hot and cold foods cold to avoid food-borne illnesses.
>
> ✔ **Pack juicy ice-boxes.** Freeze individual juice containers and then pack them with sandwiches to keep them cold as the juice boxes thaw.

To save your family lots of time, form a lunch-pool with four other families. On one day of the week, one family makes lunch for all. Most people find it easier to make five of the same lunches one day per week than to make five different ones every morning. A lunch pool also adds variety — just make sure you all share similar tastes in food!

Hazelnut-Apple-Cheese Pockets

Prep time:	5 to 10 minutes
Yield:	4 pita sandwich halves

This nutty, nutritious sandwich travels well for lunches and picnics because it uses ingredients that don't spoil quickly. Even the youngest of young chefs can help make this sandwich, but adults may need to chop the apple and toast the nuts and seeds. To toast and skin the hazelnuts ahead of time, see the "Toasting, skinning, and crushing hazelnuts" sidebar or substitute bits of pecans, walnuts, or cashews instead.

Do this first:

✔ Toast and crush hazelnuts into small bits (see the "Toasting, skinning, and crushing hazelnuts" sidebar, later in this chapter).

✔ Shred $\frac{1}{2}$ cup cheddar cheese, or use pre-shredded cheese.

✔ For the most flavor, toast and bruise $\frac{1}{2}$ teaspoon caraway seeds (see the "Toasting seeds and spices" sidebar, later in this chapter). Or use untoasted caraway seeds.

Ingredients and steps:

1 medium Granny Smith or other tart apple
$\frac{1}{2}$ cup crushed, toasted hazelnuts
$\frac{1}{4}$ cup plain yogurt
$\frac{1}{2}$ cup shredded cheddar cheese
2 teaspoons spicy brown mustard, or mustard of preference

$^1/_2$ teaspoon toasted caraway seeds
2 pita breads
Lettuce leaves, as desired

1 Core and coarsely chop the apple into small bits, about $^1/_4$- to $^1/_2$-inch in size. Place in medium mixing bowl.

2 Stir in the crushed hazelnuts and yogurt.

3 Stir in the cheese, mustard, and caraway seeds.

4 Cut each pita in half and fill each pocket with the apple mixture and a piece of lettuce.

Vary It! Try the following variations:

- ✔ For a sweeter taste, use honey-mustard.

- ✔ Serve the spread on rye bread to enhance the caraway flavor.

- ✔ Try different cheeses.

- ✔ Replace the caraway seed with toasted cumin or fennel seed.

- ✔ Serve the mixture as a salad, on shredded lettuce.

Meal Morphing: To meal-morph the main ingredients into a differently seasoned salad, triple the amounts of apple, yogurt and hazelnuts. After Step 2 in this recipe, reserve $^2/_3$ of the mixture and use it in the Yogurt-Waldorf Salad in Chapter 19.

Toasting, skinning, and crushing hazelnuts

Hazelnuts, also known as *filberts,* are sweet and flavorful with a thin, brown skin that must be removed before using them in salads, sauces, desserts, and other recipes. If you can't find already-skinned hazelnuts, remove the skin yourself by spreading the hazelnuts on a baking sheet in a single layer. Bake in a 275° oven for 20 to 30 minutes, until the skin cracks all over and begins to flake off.

At this point, kids can be a big help by rubbing the nuts in an old, clean towel — the skins slip off easily (do this outdoors for easy cleanup). Don't be concerned if some of the skin stays on — it adds a pleasant contrasting color and flavor. To crush hazelnuts into smaller pieces, place them in a plastic bag and smash them with the side of a can or rolling pin. After skinning, store the prepared hazelnuts in a zipper bag in the freezer. Look for hazelnuts in bulk at whole food stores and some farmers' markets.

Toasting seeds and spices

Toasting spices such as whole caraway, fennel, cardamom, and cumin seeds brings out their flavorful oils. To do this, try the following:

☺ Toast the seeds in a small, dry skillet on medium heat, shaking the pan often, until the seeds release their aroma and darken slightly (this can take from a few seconds to three minutes — different spices release their oils at different times).

Be careful not to burn the seeds, which gives them a bitter taste. If they taste bitter, discard them and start again.

☺ To further draw out the toasted flavor, bruise or crush the seeds on a cutting board with a rolling pin, or in a mortar and pestle, as shown in Chapter 3. To grind them to a fine powder, use a clean electric coffee bean grinder or mortar and pestle.

Green Eggs and Hamwiches

Prep time:	5 minutes
Yield:	2 sandwiches

If parents hard-cook the eggs and cut open the avocado, even the youngest chef can make these silly (but tasty) cookie-cutter sandwiches, inspired by Dr. Seuss. An egg slicer, shown in Chapter 3, prevents little hands from needing a knife.

Do this first:

✔ Hard-cook 2 eggs (see the "Perfect hard-cooked eggs" sidebar, later in this chapter).

✔ Cut 1 ripe avocado in half and cut out or scrape out the flesh.

Ingredients and steps:

   2 hard-cooked eggs
   $^1/_2$ ripe avocado (flesh only)
   2 teaspoons mayonnaise
   Salt and pepper to taste
   2 thin slices ham
   4 slices bread, preferably whole wheat or multi-grain

Perfect hard-cooked eggs

To hard-cook eggs, gently place several eggs in a single layer in a saucepan. Cover with enough cold water to come one inch above the eggs. Bring to a boil on high heat. When the water boils, cover the eggs and turn off the heat. Set the timer for 15 minutes. Remove the cover and, using a slotted spoon, place the eggs in a colander in the sink and run cold water over them until they're cool to the touch. Peel immediately for best results or chill until ready to use.

1 Peel the eggs.

2 Place one egg in the egg slicer and lower the top, slicing through it. (Or, break up the eggs into small pieces with a knife or pastry blender.)

3 Raise the top and turn the egg on its side. Lower the top, slicing the egg into finer pieces.

4 Dump the sliced egg into a small mixing bowl.

5 Repeat Steps 2 through 4 with the other egg.

6 Add the avocado and mayonnaise to the bowl.

7 Using a fork, mash the ingredients together into a chunky paste. Taste and add salt and pepper as desired.

8 Spread the bread and ham slices out on the cutting board. Cut the centers out with your favorite cookie cutter.

9 Make the sandwiches by placing a ham cut-out on a bread cut-out, then spread on some egg salad. Top with a bread cut-out.

If the bread is soft enough and the cookie cutter sharp enough, you can assemble the sandwich first and then cut it with the cookie-cutter — some multi-grain breads can be too dense for this.

Bountiful, Beautiful Breads

Who can resist the dreamy aroma of fresh bread baking in the oven? Using these simple — but oh-so-yummy — recipes, every child can experience the joy of making bread from scratch. You can make some breads with yeast, knead them, and then let them rise, but other breads can be made without the need to knead and go straight from the bowl to the oven to bake. The recipes in this section include both types of bread and are an easy, mouth-watering training ground for basic bread baking.

Gone Bananas Bread

Prep time:	15 minutes
Cook time:	1 hour (plus 30 minutes to cool)
Yield:	One 9- x 5-inch loaf

Crunchy nuts, tart cranberries, and sweet molasses make this moist banana bread a tasty treat for breakfast, lunch, or snacks. Kids love mashing the bananas and mixing the batter — older kids can pour the batter into the pan. Parents or teenagers (not young children) should put the bread in and out of the oven.

Do this first:

✔ Ripen two bananas until very soft, with black spots on the skins.

✔ Peel and mash the bananas in a large mixing bowl (the same one you'll use for the wet ingredients) with a fork or wooden spoon.

✔ If using whole, shelled walnuts, chop them into small pieces. (Younger children can place them in a plastic bag and crush them into small bits with a rolling pin or side of a can.) Measure enough walnut pieces to make $1/2$ cup.

✔ Separate 1 egg; keep the white and reserve the yolk for another use.

Ingredients and steps:

Dry ingredients:

$1^{1}/_{3}$ cups all-purpose flour
$^{2}/_{3}$ cup whole wheat flour
$^{1}/_{2}$ cup chopped walnuts
2 teaspoons baking powder
$^{1}/_{2}$ teaspoon baking soda
$^{1}/_{2}$ teaspoon salt
$^{1}/_{4}$ teaspoon allspice
$^{1}/_{4}$ cup dried cranberries

Wet ingredients:

> 1 cup mashed bananas (about 2 ripe)
> $^3/_4$ cup lowfat (1%) milk
> $^1/_2$ cup molasses
> 1 egg
> 1 egg white
> 3 tablespoons canola or vegetable oil
> 1 teaspoon vanilla extract

1 Heat oven to 350°.

2 Grease and flour a 9-x 5-inch loaf pan. (See Chapter 13 for instructions.)

3 Stir together the dry ingredients in a small mixing bowl.

4 In a separate, large bowl, mix the wet ingredients together.

5 Add the dry ingredients to the wet ingredients and stir just until moistened (batter will be lumpy). Pour the batter into the pan.

6 Bake 1 hour or until a toothpick inserted in the bread comes out clean. Let bread cool in pan on a rack for 15 minutes. Turn bread out of pan onto rack and let cool about 30 minutes before slicing.

Vary It! Try using different dried fruit and nuts, such as blueberries and pecans. For a different taste, replace the allspice with cinnamon or nutmeg. For a lighter flavor, use honey instead of molasses.

Getting a rise out of yeast

Active dry yeast may look like a simple powder, but it's really a living organism — one that's asleep and waiting to be fed. Wake the yeast up with water that's warm to the touch but not hot. For accuracy, use an instant-read thermometer to test the temperature — water between 110° and 115° works best. Yeast will sleep through cooler water and water that's too hot kills it.

After the yeast dissolves in the water, it should bubble and start to froth within 5 minutes; adding sugar or honey to the water feeds the yeast and makes it more active, bubbling up with carbon dioxide gas. If the mixture does not develop a foamy top, throw it out and start again — the water was either the wrong temperature or the yeast was old.

Pizza-Pizza: Double-Dough Recipe

Prep time:	15 minutes
Rise time:	45 to 60 minutes
Bake time:	10 minutes
Yield:	Two 15- to 16-inch pizzas

By using this recipe, you can make ready-to-roll pizza dough in just over an hour. You need an active yeast, a warm place for rising, and some sturdy young hands to knead the dough (a food processor or stand mixer can speed the kneading up, too). This recipe makes enough dough for two large pizzas. Freeze extra dough to make easy pizzas on another day.

Ingredients and steps:

    1 cup warm water (see the "Getting a rise out of yeast" sidebar)
    1 tablespoon honey or sugar
    2 teaspoons quick-rising yeast (1 envelope or $^1/_4$ ounce)
    3 cups all-purpose flour, plus extra for kneading
    1 teaspoon salt
    1 tablespoon olive oil, plus extra for the bowl

1 Measure the warm water; test with an instant-read thermometer to make sure the temperature is between 110° and 115°. Stir in the honey or sugar and the yeast. Let mixture sit for 5 minutes until bubbly.

To mix the dough with a food processor:

2a Using the plastic dough blade, add 3 cups of flour and the salt to the bowl. Pulse 2 or 3 times to mix. With the machine running, pour the yeast mixture and olive oil through the feed tube until ingredients form a ball. Feel the dough. If it's sticky, process in more flour a tablespoon at a time. If it's dry and mealy, process with single tablespoons of warm water until smooth. Lightly flour a board or kneading surface and knead the dough for 2 minutes or until smooth and elastic. See Figure 17-1.

To mix the dough by hand:

2b Pour $1^1/_2$ cups flour into a large mixing bowl. Add the yeast mixture and mix well. Stir in the salt and olive oil. Gradually add the remaining flour, stopping when the mixture is smooth, but not too dry. If you add all of the flour and the dough is still sticky, mix in more flour by single tablespoons. Transfer the dough to a lightly floured surface and knead until smooth and elastic, about 10 to 15 minutes, as shown in Figure 17-1. Stop when the dough has a slight sheen and springs back when you poke it. (Keep in mind that too much kneading produces a tough crust and too little kneading makes the dough too dense.)

Figure 17-1:
Knead
dough by
pushing
down,
folding, and
rotating ¼
turn.

3 Rising the dough: Rub a spoonful of olive oil inside a large bowl. Roll the dough into a ball and place in the bowl, turning to coat with oil. Cover with a damp towel or plastic wrap and leave in a warm place to rise until doubled in bulk, about one hour. Poke the dough with two fingers — if an indentation remains, it has doubled in bulk. Punch the dough down with your fist and roll it into a ball, ready for shaping. You can refrigerate the dough up to 36 hours before using it by punching it down and rolling it into a ball each time it doubles in size. You may also wrap it well and freeze it. (*Tip:* If you're baking the pizza immediately after it rises, read the baking instructions in Step 5 — you want to start heating your oven 30 minutes before the pizza is done rising.)

4 Shaping the dough: Divide the dough into two balls. Shape each ball by gently stretching or pulling with your hands or by flattening with a rolling pin, or a combination of both. Build the edges slightly thicker than the center. Place the shaped dough on a lightly greased pizza pan or baking sheet. Top with your favorite fixings.

5 Baking the dough: Pizzas need high heat to make good, crispy crusts. Start heating your oven at least 30 minutes before baking the pizza. Bake according to the specific pizza recipe you're using, or for 10 to 15 minutes at 500°.

To speed up the dough's rising, set the covered dough bowl in a sink with enough hot tap water to come halfway up the outside of the bowl. Drape a towel over the sink (without letting it fall in the water) to hold in the steam. The dough will rise quickly and be ready to shape in as little as 45 minutes, but the flavor will be slightly less developed.

When measuring flour, lightly add it spoonful-by-spoonful into a dry measuring cup, then level it off with a knife or ruler — don't pack it down or you'll have too much.

As long as you have all the ingredients and equipment out, make two separate batches of this dough at the same time. You can make one right after the other, or make a double batch using the same amount of yeast. If tripling the recipe, double the yeast. Allow an extra ten minutes of preparation time to double this recipe. (Most baking recipes are tricky to double or triple, but this one works fine if you follow the instructions.)

To save time, make extra pizza dough and freeze it. After the dough rises, roll it into a ball and lightly oil the outside. Wrap tightly in plastic wrap, wrap again with aluminum foil, and seal air-tight in a freezer bag. To thaw, remove the wrappings and thaw overnight in a covered, greased bowl in the refrigerator. Bring to room temperature and shape as desired. You don't have to let it rise again, but if you're not making the pizza immediately, it's okay to let it rise before shaping.

Pazzo for pizza dough

In Italy, to go crazy for something is to be *pazzo* (PAHTS-oh). To go pazzo with pizza dough, you can:

☼ Make *focaccia* (foh-CAH-chee-ah), an Italian flatbread, by pressing pizza dough that already risen one time onto a baking sheet rubbed with olive oil, covering the dough, and letting it rise again until doubled, about one hour. With clean fingertips, dimple the surface all over and sprinkle coarse salt, herbs, and olive oil on top. Bake at 425° for about 20 minutes, then cut into squares.

☼ Roll dough into thick or thin breadsticks, brush with olive oil, and bake at 450° until crispy.

☼ Stuff a big sock — a calzone. *Calzone* (kal-ZOH-nay) means "big sock" in Italian and looks like a large turnover. To make four calzones from one batch of pizza dough, shape the dough into four circles, top half of each circle with your favorite pizza toppings, fold the other half over, and seal the edges. Cut a 1-inch slit in the top for steam to escape. Bake at 450° for 25 to 30 minutes.

☼ Partially bake pizza crusts, then freeze them, ready to top and cook. Prebake at 350° for 5 to 10 minutes, until the dough begins to stiffen and turn color. Seal well and freeze. Top the crusts and bake while still frozen. (This is a great time-saver for a kids' pizza party!)

☼ Vary the crust by replacing $1/3$ all-purpose flour with whole wheat flour or cornmeal. Add flavor to pizza dough by mixing in herbs, garlic, and onions.

Irish Poppy Seed Soda Bread

Prep time:	10 minutes
Bake time:	35 minutes
Cool time:	30 minutes
Yield:	2 loaves

I've heard that in Ireland, you can find as many recipes for soda bread as cooks to make it. Traditionally cooked in a three-legged iron pot over a fire, soda bread is unusual in that it uses baking soda and buttermilk as leavening, instead of yeast, and requires no rising time. This lightly sweetened version mixes whole wheat and white flours with crunchy poppy seeds and a hint of orange. Children have an easy time making this recipe and they get to eat the fruits of their labor in just over an hour.

Do this first:

✔ Grate 2 teaspoons zest from 1 orange, as shown in Chapter 11.

✔ Lightly flour a cutting board or other surface for kneading the dough.

Ingredients and steps:

$2^1/_2$ cups whole wheat flour
$1^1/_2$ cups all-purpose flour, preferably unbleached
2 teaspoons salt
1 teaspoon baking soda
$3/_4$ teaspoon baking powder
2 tablespoons poppy seeds
2 teaspoons orange zest
$1/_2$ cup honey
$1^1/_2$ cups buttermilk

1 Heat the oven to 375°. Coat a baking sheet with nonstick spray.

2 Combine the whole wheat and all-purpose flours, salt, baking soda, baking powder, and poppy seeds in a large bowl. Stir to mix them.

3 Using clean fingers, sprinkle in the zest a bit at a time to prevent clumping together. Stir to mix.

4 Stir the honey and buttermilk into the mixture until just absorbed.

5 Pour the loose, soft dough mixture onto a lightly floured surface (don't worry if some of the flour is still dry, pour it onto the work surface as well). Dough will be sticky (what fun!). Knead the mixture until all ingredients come together as an evenly moist dough, about 3 minutes.

6 Shape the dough into two smooth, even, round loaves. Place the loaves on the baking sheet.

When working with dough, flour your hands and the kneading surface lightly to keep the dough from sticking. This dough is exceptionally sticky, so expect your hands to be sticky too, even with light flouring. Don't keep adding flour to your hands or the dough will end up with too much flour.

Parents should perform the following tasks for small children. Using a sharp knife, cut an X across the top of each loaf. Bake the loaves for 30 to 35 minutes, or until the tops sound hollow when tapped and the center point of the X gives slightly, but no longer feels soft. Let stand 30 minutes before slicing.

Vary It! Try adding ¹/₂ cup raisins or using lemon zest instead of orange zest.

As a perfect example of naturally deep-flavored, lowfat cooking, this Irish Poppy Seed Soda Bread gets less than 7 percent of its calories from fat. Because of its hint of sweetness, this loaf makes excellent cream cheese and apple sandwiches. Round out a dinner salad with a few warm slices, or toast it for breakfast with all-fruit preserves.

Chapter 18

Main Dishes — with Meat and Without

In This Chapter

▶ Cooking up fast 'n' easy main courses

▶ Morphing leftovers into excitingly different dishes

▶ Feeding vegetarians and meat-eaters in the same meal

What did the cannibal order for take-out?
Pizza, with everyone on it.

Making the main dish doesn't have to eat up your time. For most of the recipes in this chapter, the actual preparation — chopping, washing, and measuring — takes less than 30 minutes. Some dishes take longer, but usually the extra time is for unattended cooking or for an occasional stir or baste. When parents and kids team together, they can usually make these recipes even more quickly.

In keeping with nutritionists' recommendations to reduce protein in your diet and increase vegetables and grains, serve the meat-based main courses in this chapter with ample side dishes of steamed vegetables, salads, rice, pasta, or other grains. Many of the recipes give you a head start by building nutritious amounts of vegetables and grains into the main dish. Vegetarian meals in this chapter offer meat-eaters and vegetarians flavorful, quick-to-fix meatless recipes, and some recipes meld both meat and meatless options into one preparation, effortlessly feeding both types of diners at one time.

A few of these main-dish recipes incorporate meal-morphing plans, in which one night's leftovers become a radically different and delicious meal later in the week. Use these as jumping-off points to create your own original meal-morphs. Chapter 5 has more meal morphing tips and menu plans.

You'll also find that the soups, pastas, salads, and polenta recipes in Chapter 19 make excellent main course dishes, as well. Round them out with bread or vegetables for a complete, easy, and satisfying meal in minutes.

Remember to wash hands, cutting boards, and utensils after working with raw meat, poultry, fish, and eggs. Also, cook these foods thoroughly before eating. Avoid cross-contamination and follow the safety tips in Chapter 8.

Chicken and Turkey

Poultry is to a cook what a blank canvas is to a painter. These recipes show how well chicken and turkey, with their own naturally mild flavor, can taste entirely different depending on the seasonings and cooking methods used.

2-Bucket Batch of Oven-Fried Chicken

Prep time:	15 minutes
Cook time:	20 minutes for boneless breasts; 45 to 60 minutes for bone-in
Yield:	12 to 16 pieces of chicken

This recipe uses two baking sheets to cook over five pounds of chicken pieces in about 1 hour — enough for a family of quintuplets — or an average family's meal plus handy leftovers. For three pounds of chicken, use half of the ingredients and bake at the same temperature. Kids can be a huge help by dipping the chicken in the coating and arranging the pieces on the baking sheets for parents to put into the oven.

Ingredients and steps:

1½ cups Corn Flake Crumbs
1 teaspoon granulated garlic
1 teaspoon paprika
½ teaspoon dried herbs (thyme, oregano, basil, or a combination)
½ teaspoon salt
½ cup buttermilk
5 to 6 pounds mixed chicken pieces, with or without skin

1 Position two oven racks evenly spaced so that air can circulate. Heat oven to 375°. Line two baking sheets with foil and coat with nonstick spray.

2 Add crumbs, garlic, paprika, dried herbs (crushed), and salt to a small paper bag (you can use a plastic bag, but I find paper easier to control). Shake well.

3 Gently shake out a single layer (about 1/4-inch thick) of crumbs from the bag into a medium baking dish. Shake the dish to distribute the crumbs evenly.

4 Pour buttermilk into large mixing bowl. Add 4 or 5 pieces of chicken and stir with a mixing spoon to coat the chicken completely with buttermilk.

5 Using tongs, place as many pieces of chicken as will fit without crowding on the layer of crumbs (4 to 6 pieces). Be sure to let any excess buttermilk drip back into the bowl before you add the chicken to the crumbs.

6 Gently shake enough crumbs out of the bag to coat the tops of the pieces. Use a dry spoon to scoop up crumbs that are already in the pan, so as to coat the sides of the pieces.

7 Using another dry set of tongs or a fork, pick the crumb-coated pieces up and arrange them top side up on a baking sheet, with at least 1 inch in between each piece.

8 Shake the bottom of the crumb dish gently to redistribute the crumbs into a single layer. If necessary, add more crumbs.

9 Repeat Steps 4 through 8 until all of the chicken is coated and arranged on the baking sheets. If the bag runs out of crumbs, pour excess crumbs from the dish back into the bag. When all of the pieces are coated, discard excess crumbs (don't re-use for food safety reasons.)

10 Bake 20 minutes for boneless, skinless breasts; bake 45 to 60 minutes for pieces with bone, or until juices run clear. (Larger pieces and dark meat take the most time to cook.)

For more even cooking, swap the positions of the baking sheets halfway through cooking. For better browning, lightly spray the tops of the chicken with nonstick cooking spray.

Vary It! Vary this recipe in the following ways:

- Instead of buttermilk, dip the chicken in yogurt, milk, evaporated skimmed milk, or 2 egg whites beaten with 2 teaspoons water — whatever you have on hand.

- Instead of Corn Flake Crumbs (available in the flour aisle), try seasoned breadcrumbs or cracker crumbs. To make your own Corn Flake Crumbs, seal Corn Flakes in a plastic bag and finely crush them with a rolling pin — a favorite kid-task!

- Oven-fry pork chops the same way, cooking about 30 minutes or until just pale pink inside (155°).

- Experiment with different seasonings. Try Cajun spices, Italian-herb blend, chili powder and cumin, herbes de Provence.

Greek Skinny Chicken

Prep time:	20 minutes
Marinate time:	15 minutes
Cook time:	10 minutes after reaching high pressure; about 20 minutes total
Yield:	6 to 8 servings

A pressure cooker recipe

I love the ease of a whole chicken — and the thriftiness! Made in a pressure cooker, this chicken dish cooks in just 20 minutes and stays moist and tender — even without its skin. A terrific dish all year round, this zesty Greek chicken is especially good in summer, when it's far too hot to consider roasting a chicken in the oven.

Ingredients and steps:

2 stalks celery

2 carrots

1 pound unpeeled red, Idaho, Yukon Gold, or white potatoes (about 2 to 3 medium)

4 cloves garlic

1 lemon

1 tablespoon tomato paste

1 teaspoon dried basil

1 teaspoon dried oregano (preferably Greek oregano)

1 teaspoon paprika

1 teaspoon fruity olive oil (optional)

$^1/_2$ teaspoon dried thyme

$^1/_2$ teaspoon salt

1 whole ($3^1/_2$- to 4-pound) chicken

$^1/_2$ cup dry red or white wine

1 Trim the root ends off the celery and carrots. Cut the celery and carrots diagonally into 1-inch lengths. Place them in the bottom of the pressure cooker.

2 Cut the potatoes into quarters. Add them to the pressure cooker.

3 Peel the garlic and add it to the work bowl of a mini-chopper or handblender.

4 Cut the lemon in half and squeeze the juice into the work bowl. To catch the seeds, squeeze the juice over a strainer.

5 Add the tomato paste, basil, oregano, paprika, olive oil, thyme, and salt to the work bowl and blend until a coarse mixture is formed.

6 Holding the skin of the chicken with a paper towel to keep a firm grip, pull the skin off the chicken. You may need a knife in some spots to cut away large pieces of skin. (***Caution:*** Kids can pull the skin with their hands, but a parent should do any cutting — the chicken can be very slippery.) Don't worry about the little bit of skin on the wing tips — it's almost impossible to remove easily.

7 Rub the seasoning mixture all over the chicken, including the cavity, pouring any excess into the pot. Marinate for 15 minutes. Place the chicken in the cooker.

8 Add the wine, pouring it into the side of the pot, instead of over the chicken — you don't want to rinse the spice rub away.

9 Lock the pressure cooker lid in place and bring the pressure to high, which takes about 10 minutes. Cook for 10 more minutes, adjusting the heat as needed to keep it at high pressure. Kids can be a big help by monitoring the pressure indicator.

10 *Caution:* Only parents should remove the lid of a pressure cooker in this step. Place the pressure cooker in the sink. Follow the pressure cooker manufacturer's instructions for using the quick-release method of running water over the edge of the lid until the pressure subsides and the lid opens easily.

11 Remove the chicken and cut into serving pieces. Serve with the vegetables and juices.

Serving Suggestion: The chicken has an attractive rosy red hue from the marinade. For an even more attractive presentation, sprinkle with fresh chopped parsley and crumbled feta cheese and serve over wide, country-style egg noodles or other pasta.

 Grilled Velvet Chicken

Prep time:	2 to 12 minutes
Marinate time:	30 minutes, preferably longer
Cook time:	7 minutes
Yield:	4 servings

I discovered this dish quite by accident. While creating the recipes for this book, I found myself with a surplus of Cool-as-a-Cucumber Dressing (see the recipe in Chapter 20) — the dressing tastes so good that I hated to waste it. When a heat wave hit, I fled from the kitchen to the outdoor grill. Killing two birds with one cucumber, so to speak, I quickly thawed some ice-glazed boneless chicken breasts in the microwave, poked them several times with a fork to marinate them more quickly, and heavily doused them with the Cool-as-a-Cucumber Dressing before grilling. What a success! The chicken came out tasting smooth as velvet, with a subtle mouth-watering sweetness, faint hints of cucumber, and a lovely smokiness from the grill. It also couldn't be easier. My family calls this the best chicken that I've ever made. Of course, I told them, I'd planned it that way all the time.

Score 'n' pour

Lightly *score* (cut shallow slashes in) steaks and poultry breasts before pouring on a marinade. Scoring increases flavor, adds tasty browned edges, and helps uneven cuts cook more evenly.

As shown in the following figure, use a sharp, straight-edged knife to make parallel slices about ⅛-inch deep and about 1 inch apart in one direction. Rotate the pieces 45 degrees and do the same thing. You end up with angled criss-crosses in the meat or poultry. Do this on both sides of boneless steaks and breasts or on the meaty side of bone-in breasts.

The slashes help marinades penetrate deeper into the meat. In addition, boneless chicken and turkey breasts, which are usually thicker in the middle than on the sides, often dry out on the thin, outer areas before the centers are adequately cooked — scoring the thicker sections a little deeper than the rest of the breast allows the heat to penetrate the centers more rapidly, so they stay moister without overcooking the thin areas. As an added benefit, the scored edges become nicely browned and crisp at the corners when broiled, grilled, or pan-fried on high heat.

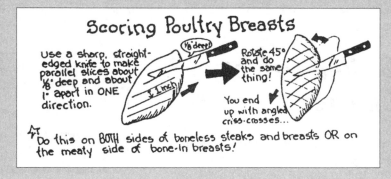

Ingredients and steps:

4 boneless, skinless chicken breast halves, shown in Figure 18-1
½ cup Cool-as-a-Cucumber Dressing (see Chapter 20)

1 Poke chicken pieces with fork about 7 to 10 times on each side.

2 Coat with Cool-as-a-Cucumber Dressing in a shallow dish or plastic bag and refrigerate from 30 minutes to overnight.

3   When ready to cook, lightly coat the grilling surface with vegetable oil. Heat the grill or broiler until very hot.

4   Grill or broil chicken pieces for a few minutes on each side, until the flesh is firm, not rubbery, and just barely pink inside, or until an instant-read thermometer registers 165°. Be careful not to overcook, or the chicken will dry out. Flip to Chapter 13 for tips on grilling and broiling.

Piercing the chicken pieces before marinating, a technique practiced in India, allows the dressing to penetrate better. Don't pierce the meat after it begins to cook though, or the juices run out and the meat becomes dry.

Figure 18-1:
The recipes in this book call for chicken breast halves.

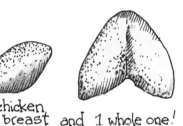

½ chicken breast   and   1 whole one!

 Harvest Moon Meatloaves

Prep time:	20 minutes
Cook time:	40 to 45 minutes
Yield:	4 meatloaves, approximately 8 servings

"Awesome!" That's what one reviewer said about this unusual but extraordinarily moist and flavorful meatloaf, which mixes ground turkey with, of all things, pumpkin. It may sound odd, but the pumpkin melds elegantly into the overall flavor of the meatloaf, mingling with tart cranberries and the warm flavors of allspice and fennel seed. No need to sauté any vegetables or do much chopping — it's just an easy 20 minutes or so of preparation, and cleanup is minimal. For the health conscious, the pumpkin contains no fat, delivers truckloads of beta-carotene and potassium, and contains a good amount of iron.

Little hands that like to squish and mush delight in mixing the meatloaf mixture, which is softer than most because of the pumpkin, but comes together in the end for an incredibly firm and tender meatloaf — one that captures the flavors of the autumn harvest in every bite.

Do this first:

✔ In a blender, food processor, or mini-chopper, process enough fresh breadcrumbs (preferably whole wheat or multi-grain) to measure 2 cups (tear the bread into pieces before processing). One average slice makes about $1/2$ cup fresh breadcrumbs.

Ingredients and steps:

2 green onions
$1^1/2$ pounds ground turkey
2 cups fresh breadcrumbs
1 can (15-ounces) solid-pack pumpkin
1 cup dried cranberries
3 eggs
$1^1/2$ teaspoons fennel seed
1 teaspoon ground allspice
1 teaspoon salt
$1/4$ teaspoon dried thyme
$1/4$ teaspoon fresh ground pepper
4 to 6 tablespoons ketchup (optional)

1 Heat oven to 400°. Line a baking sheet with foil and lightly coat with nonstick spray.

2 Trim and finely chop the green onions.

3 In a large mixing bowl, combine the green onions and the remaining ingredients, except the ketchup. Using clean hands, mix until all ingredients are blended. The mixture will be very moist and soft.

4 To shape 4 meatloaves, spoon $1/4$ of the mixture into an oblong loaf-like mounds in each quarter of the pan. Use a spoon or spatula to help shape the loaves.

5 If desired, drizzle or spread 1 tablespoon or so of ketchup on top of each loaf.

6 Bake 40 to 45 minutes, or until the mixture is firm to the touch. To make sure the meatloaves are cooked through, insert an instant-read meat thermometer through the side of the loaf (the loaves are too thin to insert it from top); the loaves should register at least 160°, but will be firmer but still moist at around 180°.

7 Let meatloaves stand for 5 minutes before slicing. Serve hot or at room temperature.

Serving Suggestion: Serve with buttered egg noodles in summer, or Mash 'n' Smash Parsnip Potatoes (see Chapter 19) in winter. Leftover meatloaves make incredibly addictive sandwiches!

Mexican Fiesta Taco or Burrito Mix

Prep time:	5 minutes
Cook time:	15 minutes
Yield:	4 cups taco filling, or enough for 12 to 16 tacos

Lightly seasoned, this tasty but mild mix satisfies delicate and sensitive taste buds; for a spicier flavor, simply increase the heat with extra ground chiles or add hot sauce. Mexican Fiesta corn, which includes red and green bell peppers, is readily available frozen or canned, making this an easy, instant, emergency meal, especially if you keep frozen ground turkey on hand. It comes together in 20 minutes and young children can safely help by measuring and stirring. Kids old enough to handle a knife and cook on the stovetop can make this meal themselves, with parental supervision.

Ingredients and steps:

2 cups frozen or 1 can (15.5 ounces) Mexican Fiesta corn
$^1/_2$ medium onion
1 tablespoon canola oil
$1^1/_2$ teaspoons ground cumin
$^3/_4$ teaspoon dried oregano
$^1/_2$ teaspoon paprika
$^1/_8$ teaspoon ground red chile (or chili powder)
$^3/_4$ pound ground turkey
$^1/_4$ teaspoon salt
1 lime

1 Drain and rinse canned corn; if using frozen corn, don't rinse or thaw.

2 Peel and chop onion.

3 Heat oil in skillet and cook onion on high until it begins to soften, about 1 to 2 minutes.

4 Stir in the corn, cumin, oregano, paprika, and ground red chile.

5 Spread mixture in single layer and cook on medium-high until lightly browned on the bottom, from 2 to 5 minutes depending on the cookware used.

6 Stir and cook in single layer until browned further, with little charred spots on the edges (from 1 to 3 minutes).

7 Spoon the corn mixture into a serving bowl and set aside.

8 Brown the ground turkey with salt on high in the same pan, breaking up the turkey until crumbly. Cook until the turkey is no longer pink, about 5 to 8 minutes.

9   Stir the corn mixture back into the pan.

10   Cut lime in half. Squeeze the lime's juice on top. Cook until heated through.

11   To serve, spoon taco mixture into the same serving bowl, and serve with your favorite taco fixings like shredded lettuce, cheese, salsa, tomatoes, or green onion. Scoop the mixture up with Yo Quiero Taco Shells in Chapter 20, or roll into soft flour or corn tortillas to make burritos.

Vary It! Turn this into Vegetarian Taco Mix by omitting the turkey and heating the corn mixture with a can of drained beans, such as black beans or pinto beans.

Ruby-Red Grapefruit Chicken

Prep time:	5 minutes
Marinate time:	30 minutes or overnight
Cook time:	6 to 16 minutes, depending on the breasts used
Yield:	4 to 6 servings

When I was a child, my mother made a scrumptious broiled chicken marinated in Lawry's Good Seasons Italian dressing (used as a dry powder) and Texas ruby-red grapefruit juice. The grapefruit juice tenderizes without being as harsh as lemon or as sweet as orange juice. I've replicated her marinade here, but use fresh ingredients instead of a mix and enjoy the taste even more.

Do this first:

✔ Squeeze ²/₃ cup grapefruit juice, if you're using fresh juice.

✔ Dice enough onion to make ¹/₄ cup.

✔ Peel and finely chop 3 cloves of garlic.

Ingredients and steps:

    4 to 6 chicken breast halves, with or without bone and skin

Marinade:
    ²/₃ cup fresh or 1 can (5.5 ounces) grapefruit juice
    ¹/₄ cup diced onion
    3 cloves garlic, finely chopped

> 1 tablespoon soy sauce
> 1 tablespoon red wine vinegar
> 1 teaspoon olive oil
> $^1/_2$ teaspoon Italian Seasoning (a dried herb mixture, not packaged dressing)
> $^1/_2$ teaspoon sugar

1 Score the chicken breast halves about $^1/_8$ inch deep, as shown in the "Score 'n' pour" sidebar, earlier in this chapter.

2 Mix together all marinade ingredients in shallow dish or plastic resealable bag.

3 Add chicken and coat thoroughly.

4 Cover the dish or seal the bag and refrigerate until ready to cook, from 30 minutes to 2 hours. If using bone-in breasts, marinate overnight or up to 2 days.

5 To cook, heat the broiler until very hot, about 20 minutes. For easy cleanup, line a broiling pan with foil, then place the broiling rack on top. Lightly coat the broiling rack with nonstick spray.

6 Broil the chicken until it's cooked through and just barely pink in the center, about 3 to 5 minutes per side for boneless, skinless breast halves and 6 to 8 minutes per side for bone-in pieces. (For tips on broiling, flip to Chapter 13.)

Vary It! You can also pan-fry the chicken (see Chapter 12) or grill it (discussed in Chapter 13).

Succulent Chinese Chicken

Prep time:	5 minutes
Cook time:	20 minutes, plus 1 hour to stand
Yield:	1 whole chicken, cooked

The Chinese method of poaching chicken leaves it far more tender and moist than the traditional Western technique. In both methods, the chicken is placed in a pot and covered with water. In the Western method, the chicken simmers until it's fully cooked and is then removed from the liquid. In the Chinese method, the chicken simmers until only partially cooked, then the flame is turned off and the chicken stays in the pot, where the hot liquid finishes cooking the chicken as it cools. Instead of drying out, the Chinese poached chicken meat stays delicate and moist, retaining more of the true chicken flavor.

This is the easiest whole chicken recipe you'll ever make! Young children may not be able to handle a whole chicken easily, but the recipe itself is as simple as one can get. Serve this chicken at room temperature, for example, shredded with dipping sauces, or use it in any recipe calling for cooked chicken meat. This recipe gives instructions for cooking a whole chicken, with additional tips for cooking chicken breasts. Plan ahead and morph the leftover broth and meat into a second meal, such as Hearty Wonton Soup or Napa Chicken Salad, both found in Chapter 19.

Ingredients and steps:

> 1 whole chicken, about 4 pounds
> 2 to 3 teaspoons salt (the larger the bird, the more salt is needed)
> 1^1/$_2$ inches fresh ginger
> 5 green onions
> 1 tablespoon dry sherry (optional)

1 Remove the giblet bag from the chicken and reserve for another use, such as stock, soup, or gravy.

2 Rub the chicken all over with the salt, including inside the cavity.

3 Place the chicken in a pot just large enough to hold it.

4 Cut the ginger into 6 slices, leaving the skin on.

5 Cut the green onions into 2-inch lengths.

6 Add the ginger slices, green onions, and sherry to the pot.

7 Fill the pot with enough water to just cover the chicken by ^{1}/$_2$ inch.

8 Bring the water to a boil on high heat.

9 Using a slotted spoon, skim away the brown foam that rises to the top and discard.

10 Cover the pot and reduce the heat. Simmer the chicken 20 minutes, but don't allow it to continue to boil — see Chapter 12 for an explanation of simmering and boiling.

11 Turn off the heat. Leave the chicken covered in the pot for 1 hour. Skim off the layer of fat that rises to the surface. Serve as desired.

You can eat the chicken right away, but by making it a day in advance, you'll be able to more easily remove the fat. Refrigerate the entire pot of chicken and broth. By the next day, the fat congeals; remove and discard it. Serve the chicken and broth as desired, removing the skin, ginger, and green onions before use.

Vary It! To poach boneless, skinless breasts, follow the recipe above, using 3 to 3^1/$_2$ pounds boneless, skinless chicken breasts, 1 inch of ginger cut in slices, and 4 green onions. Simmer for only 12 minutes and then let the chicken rest 1 hour in the broth.

Serving Suggestion: Add the moist, flavorful chicken meat to salads, soups, couscous, tacos, enchiladas, and sandwiches. Mix it with barbecue sauce and top it on a pizza. Shred the chicken and serve it plain or with dipping sauces. Use the broth as a soup or wherever chicken broth is called for.

Self-Basting Lemon-Pepper Roast Turkey

Prep time:	25 minutes
Cook time:	2 hours
Standing time:	15 minutes
Yield:	12 to 16 servings

Without the added trimmings of a huge Thanksgiving dinner, a simple roast turkey can take as little as two hours to cook and can feed a family of four for several meals — any time of year. This recipe makes cooking a whole turkey simple, by using cheesecloth, an absorbent, gauze-like material that's available in the cookware section of supermarkets. The cheesecloth is bathed in a lemon-oil mixture and placed on the breast to self-baste, keeping the breast meat moist without the cook's constant attention. (Most roast turkeys require basting every 15 minutes.) For best results, use a small 10- to 12-pound turkey, and allow the unstuffed turkey to roast for 10 to 12 minutes per pound. Jump to the end of the recipe for more cooking tips.

Caution: Only parents should lift the turkey in and out of the oven, but kids can help make the marinade, prepare the cheesecloth, and after the turkey is eaten, make a wish on the wishbone.

Do this first:

- Adjust oven rack to lower third of oven. Set oven heat to 350°.

- Cut enough cheesecloth to cover turkey breast in six layers when folded. (See the cheesecloth tip at the end of this recipe.)

- Tear off enough foil to cover the breast.

- If using fresh rosemary (an optional ingredient), pull off enough rosemary leaves from the woody stalk to make 2 tablespoons. Use only the needle-like leaves, not the tough, fibrous stalk.

- Grind enough pepper, using a pepper grinder, to make 1 tablespoon. (Use freshly ground pepper for the best flavor — after it's ground, pepper rapidly loses its punch.)

Ingredients and steps:

For self-basting:
1 lemon
$1/2$ cup mild flavored olive oil or canola oil or mix of both

For turkey seasoning rub:
3 cloves garlic
2 tablespoons poultry seasoning
2 teaspoons salt
1 tablespoon coarsely ground pepper
$1/2$ lemon
2 tablespoons mild flavored olive or canola oil, or mix of both
2 tablespoons fresh rosemary (optional)
1 (10- to 12-pound) turkey, fresh or thawed

1 Heat oven to 350°.

2 Prepare the basting ingredients by squeezing the juice of 1 lemon into a medium bowl. Add $1/2$ cup oil. Submerge the layers of cheesecloth in the mixture until completely saturated. Set aside.

3 Prepare the seasoning rub: Peel the garlic. Combine (in a mini-chopper or handheld blender) the peeled garlic, poultry seasoning, salt, pepper, juice of $1/2$ lemon, 2 tablespoons oil, and rosemary leaves. Blend until a smooth paste is formed. Reserve the squeezed lemon half for Step 7.

4 Prepare the turkey by first rinsing and drying the turkey. Remove and discard any fatty deposits from the neck cavity. Reserve giblets and neck for another use. If the legs are trussed together or pinned down, release them and discard any plastic or metal pins.

5 Place the turkey breast side down on a rack in a roasting pan. Fill the pan $1/4$-inch deep with water.

6 Using clean hands, rub the seasoning mixture all over the turkey, inside and out, flipping the turkey over so the breast points up.

7 Place the squeezed lemon half from Step 2 inside the cavity. (Even though the juice has been squeezed, the lemon half still flavors the cavity.)

8 Drape the oil-soaked cheesecloth lengths over the breast, one on top of the other, with the edges extending to, but not covering, the thighs. You will have some lemon-oil mixture left in the bowl; reserve it for basting after the cheesecloth is removed.

9 Shape a length of foil over the cheesecloth so it covers the breast but not the thighs.

10 If using an oven-proof thermometer (as described in Chapter 13), insert it in the thickest part of the thigh without touching the bone. (See Step 13 if using an instant-read thermometer.)

11 Place the roasting pan in the oven and set the timer for 1 hour, 45 minutes.

12 Remove the cheesecloth and foil covering after 1 hour. (***Caution:*** The cheesecloth will be hot — use tongs to remove.) Baste the turkey all over using the reserved lemon-oil mixture. (See soy sauce browning tip at the bottom of this recipe.)

13 Start checking for doneness after 1 hour, 45 minutes. If you're using an instant-read thermometer, insert it into the thickest part of the thigh (without touching the bone) and allow about 15 seconds for it to register the temperature. When either the oven-proof or instant-read thermometer registers between 170° and 175°, carefully remove the turkey from the oven and tent with foil to keep warm.

14 Let turkey stand for 15 minutes. The residual heat continues to cook the turkey to a safe temperature (180° in the thigh). The standing period also allows the juices to be reabsorbed into the flesh. After 15 minutes, the turkey is ready to carve and eat.

Follow these tasty turkey cooking tips when making this recipe:

✔ **Cheesecloth tips:** The thin, gauze-like cheesecloth sold in packages in the supermarket's cookware aisle usually comes already folded into three layers. For easier handling, cut two lengths of this prefolded cheesecloth, each one big enough to cover the breast. Soak both lengths in the oil mixture, place one length of cheesecloth over the breast, and add the other length on top of it. Gourmet stores sometimes sell thicker cheesecloth that looks more like cotton fabric then lacy gauze. When using thicker cheesecloth, use only three layers.

✔ **Don't truss:** The bird may look ungainly, but don't truss or tie the turkey's legs down. Keeping them free allows the heat to circulate, cooking the legs at a pace more akin to the breast, which cooks faster and dries out if it's overcooked.

✔ **Browning tips:** Soy sauce helps brown the outside of meats and poultry faster. Because cheesecloth covers the turkey breast during the first part of cooking, the breast stays moist, but doesn't brown much. For a browner skin, pour 2 tablespoons soy sauce over the breast after removing the cheesecloth.

Pork

Lean and flavorful, today's pork needs very little cooking time, making it a favorite for quick-to-fix meals like the ones in this section.

But because pork is now so lean, don't cook it beyond 160°; otherwise it will dry out. Perfectly cooked pork should have a slight pink blush in the center. Keep in mind that roasts and thick cuts continue to cook even after they're out of the oven, rising as much as 10° in temperature. To keep these large cuts from drying out, remove them when a thermometer reaches 150°, and let them stand for 15 minutes before serving.

Chinese "Barbecue" Pork

Prep time:	10 minutes or less
Marinate time:	2 hours or overnight, refrigerated
Cook time:	30 minutes
Yield:	10 servings

Dozens of cities around the globe now host neighborhoods known as Chinatown or Little Asia. *Char shu,* (CHAW-shoo) which is roasted pork strips glistening with a delicious dark, sweet, gooey glaze, hang from hooks in the restaurant windows of these areas. Also called barbecue pork on menus, the meat is chopped or sliced into fine pieces, then used in small amounts to flavor such dishes as fried rice, chow mein, and stir-fry. This homemade version is made from pork tenderloin, a cut so lean that it cooks quickly, but it can also dry out if overcooked. While not quite as gooey as the authentic version, these tenderloins still have the same flavor. Serve this pork the way the Chinese do — just a few, thin slices to accent a meal or to season other dishes.

One recipe tester loved this dish so much that she wrote: "This is a meal to serve guests — it presents beautifully and is better than anything you can get at a restaurant. Plus, you can prepare everything in advance and sit down with guests while it cooks." Kids can help prepare the marinade and squish the meat around in the sealed bag to mix, while parents take charge of the easy cooking and slicing.

You need a shallow pan with a rack for this recipe.

Ingredients and steps:

2 cloves garlic
1 inch fresh ginger
2 green onions
2 pounds pork tenderloins
$^1/_4$ cup soy sauce

3 tablespoons dry sherry
3 tablespoons brown sugar
$^1/_2$ teaspoon Chinese Five-Spice (optional — found in Asian products aisle)
4 tablespoons honey, divided

1 Peel and finely chop the garlic.

2 Finely chop the ginger (you can leave the peel on).

3 Trim and coarsely chop the green onions.

4 Cut the tenderloins to make approximately four 6-inch lengths.

5 In a plastic resealable bag or shallow pan, mix the garlic, ginger, green onions, soy sauce, sherry, brown sugar, Chinese Five-Spice, 1 tablespoon of the honey, and pork.

6 Seal the bag or cover the pan and marinate, refrigerated, 2 hours or overnight. Turn the bag over or mix the pieces up several times while marinating.

7 When ready to cook, heat oven to 450°.

8 Line a shallow pan with foil for easy cleanup, and then place a rack on top. Add enough water to the pan to come $^1/_4$ inch up the sides, but not enough to cover the rack.

9 Mix 3 tablespoons honey with 1 tablespoon of the marinade.

10 Place the pork pieces on the rack. Baste with the honey mixture.

11 Bake 30 minutes, basting every 10 minutes. Pork is done when it reaches 150° inside and the interior is just slightly pink. Let cool at least 15 minutes before serving.

12 To serve, slice thinly and serve at room temperature, or mix into other dishes as a seasoning.

Vary It! Adults may enjoy this as an appetizer accompanied by hot Chinese mustard (available in most supermarkets) and soy sauce; children may wish to eat it with plum sauce (available in the Asian aisle of most markets) or simply eat it plain. As a main course, slice pork thinly and serve only a few pieces per person.

Tenderloins can be pricey, but if they're used sparingly, they can stretch into several meals. Or, try a pork loin, which is also very lean and less expensive than tenderloin. Cut into 6-inch pieces about 2 to 3 inches in diameter and cook as above.

Never eat a marinade that has raw meat or fish soaking in it, unless you boil it for 3 minutes first. This marinade makes a wonderful sauce for rice and vegetables, but for food safety reasons, remember to boil it before serving.

Tender Shredded Pork

Prep time:	10 minutes
Cook time:	4 hours
Yield:	2 to 2¹/₂ pounds cooked pork meat, or 8 to 10 (4-ounce) servings

A slow cooker recipe

Keep the seasonings simple, and this easy, slow-cooker recipe can be your jumping-off point to endless morphable variations. Don't try making this with a very lean cut, like tenderloin — the meat will dry out. More marbled cuts like pork shoulder and butt stay moist and flavorful, but they add a lot of fat. For a lean cut that doesn't dry out too much, try a sirloin roast. Instead of maxing out your daily meat allotment, I recommend serving this pork as more of a seasoning in other dishes, or mixing it with lots of vegetables, as suggested in the variations after the recipe.

Older kids and parents can cut the pork into cubes, and younger children can lend helpful hands by seasoning the pork before cooking and then shredding the cooked, cooled pork with their clean fingers.

Ingredients and steps:

> 1¹/₂ teaspoons salt
> ¹/₂ teaspoon finely ground pepper
> 3¹/₂ to 4 pounds pork, such as sirloin roast

1 Mix salt and pepper in small bowl.

2 Trim excess fat from the pork and discard it. Cut the pork into large chunks (about 2 inches). Cut meat away from any bone, but don't discard the bone — it adds flavor.

3 Rub the pork chunks all over with salt and pepper.

4 Place the pork (and any bone) in a slow cooker and cook, covered, on low temperature, until tender, about 4 to 5 hours. (Leaner cuts take less time; fattier cuts take more.)

5 Let pork stand until cool enough to handle. Hand shred the pork or coarsely chop it with a knife. (Or, serve the pork in chunks without shredding.)

6 Mix the pork with some of the gravy and serve as a meaty main course. Or, for a lighter meal, stretch the pork by mixing a small amount of it with other ingredients, using it mostly as a seasoning.

If you use a fattier cut, cook the recipe and chill the dish overnight or until the fat rises to the top and solidifies (at least 3 hours). Then, remove the fat and reheat before serving.

Vary It! To make the most of this tasty cooked pork, add it to other dishes, as in these variations:

- Whistling Dixie Barbecue Sandwiches (a Southern favorite!): Heat 2 cups shredded pork with ½ cup barbecue sauce, 2 tablespoons vinegar, and 1 teaspoon mustard. Serve open-faced for neatness, or on buns for a messy meal. Makes 4 sandwiches.

- Mix the pork with cooked beans or sautéed vegetables (like corn, zucchini, carrot, lima beans, broccoli, or celery) and roll in tortillas. Serve with shredded lettuce and salsa.

- Use the meat in your favorite stir-fry recipe. Add pork to fried rice, chow mein, or stir-fried vegetables. If desired, toss the pork with soy sauce or teriyaki sauce before stir-frying.

- Add the pork to a spinach-mushroom omelet or scramble with eggs and salsa.

- Heat the pork with your favorite barbecue sauce and serve as a sandwich or topping on a Southwestern style pizza, with red onion and bell peppers.

5-Minute Mini-Chops

Prep time:	5 minutes (or less)
Marinate time:	15 minutes
Cook time:	5 minutes
Yield:	4 light main courses

Wafer-thin pork chops, often called breakfast chops, cook in less than 5 minutes. The chops themselves are only about ¼ inch thick, making them ideal for light eaters and folks limiting their meat consumption to the recommended three- or four-ounce portions. Kids old enough to cook food on the top of the stove can use these chops to experience how to *brown* foods (cooking the chops completely on one side before turning), as described in Chapter 12. These mini-chops are easy to handle using tongs, and you need only a tiny bit of oil, so you won't have much splattering.

A fresh, lemony, 15-minute marinade brightens the flavor considerably, and a bit of soy sauce helps the chops brown better.

Ingredients and steps:

1 lemon
3 tablespoons soy sauce (preferably Kikkoman)
¼ teaspoon crushed dried thyme
Freshly ground pepper to taste
4 to 6 wafer-thin pork chops
2 teaspoons canola oil

1 Cut the lemon in half. Squeeze 2 tablespoons lemon juice into a shallow dish large enough to hold the chops in a single layer. (Reserve remaining lemon juice for another use.)

2 Stir in the soy sauce, thyme, and pepper.

3 Add the pork chops and marinate about 15 minutes, turning halfway through.

4 To cook, heat 1 to 2 teaspoons canola oil in a nonstick skillet until hot. Let excess marinade drip off the chops, reserving the excess marinade for a sauce, then fry on high, about 2 minutes on each side. Don't overcook them or they'll become dry. Remove the chops from the pan.

5 For a fast, natural sauce, deglaze the pan by removing the pan from the heat and stirring in the reserved marinade along with about 2 to 3 tablespoons of water.

6 Return the pan to the stove and heat on high, stirring until the sauce thickens slightly, about 1 minute. Drizzle the sauce over the chops and eat!

Serving Suggestion: Serve with Simple Stir-Fried Asparagus and Perfectly Nice Rice (both recipes in Chapter 19).

Seafood

Good for the body and the brain, fish and shellfish deserve a regular spot on your weekly menu. Fast food never tasted so good!

 ## Crunchy Fish Kisses

Prep time:	10 minutes
Cook time:	10 to 15 minutes
Yield:	4 servings

Bake these crisp, Corn-Flake-Crumbs-coated fish pieces whole or in small bits, like bite-sized kisses. They're tastier and healthier than fried fish sticks, and except for using the oven, young chefs can easily prepare this recipe. Serve with Tangy Tartar Sauce in Chapter 20.

Do this first:

✔ Separate one egg, pouring the white into a shallow bowl. Cover and refrigerate yolk for another use.

Ingredients and steps:

$3/4$ to 1 cup Corn Flake Crumbs (use more crumbs for smaller fish pieces)

$1/2$ teaspoon granulated garlic

$^1/_8$ teaspoon salt
$^1/_8$ teaspoon black pepper
1 egg white, beaten
1 to 1$^1/_2$ pounds firm white fish fillets, like catfish or seabass

1 Place a rack in the upper third of the oven. Heat oven to 500°. Line a baking sheet with foil for easy cleanup. Lightly coat foil with nonstick vegetable spray.

2 In a shallow bowl or small pan, mix the Corn Flake Crumbs, granulated garlic, salt, and pepper and set aside.

3 Lightly beat the egg white in a shallow bowl.

4 If fillets are large and thick, cut them into bite-size pieces or strips about 2 x 3 inches. If the fillets are small and thin, use them whole.

5 Add all of the fish to the bowl of beaten egg white, tossing to coat. (Kids can use their clean hands to mix the fish in the egg white.) Piece by piece, roll the fish in crumb mixture to coat. Place fish in single layer on an ungreased, foil-lined baking sheet.

6 Bake 10 to 20 minutes, depending on the thickness of the fish, or until fish flakes and coating is crisp and brown. Serve with Tangy Tartar Sauce (see Chapter 20).

Poached Pink Salmon

Prep time:	10 minutes
Cook time:	8 to 10 minutes
Yield:	4 servings

Fresh pink salmon fillets and steaks from the Pacific Northwest and Alaska may seem expensive, but they often go on sale, and fish markets generally sell a whole or half salmon for less. Watch the newspaper food section for seasonal specials. Also, salmon's rich flavor, which comes in part from healthful omega-3 oils, tastes best in quick and simple preparations and in smaller servings. When you do find a good buy, make enough poached salmon to morph into other meals, such as the Salmon-Teriyaki Rice Bowl in this chapter. Kids old enough to cook on the stovetop can make this recipe with only a parent's supervision.

Ingredients and steps:

$1^1/_4$ pounds salmon fillets or steaks, about $^3/_4$-inch thick
4 or more cups water
1 cup dry white wine (or substitute more water)
2 tablespoons red or white wine vinegar
1 clove garlic
1 bay leaf
$^1/_2$ teaspoon salt
Parsley sprigs for garnish, optional

1 Place the salmon in a deep skillet and add just enough water to cover by $^1/_2$ inch. Remove the salmon to a plate and set aside, leaving the water in the skillet.

2 Peel and crush the garlic clove. Add the wine, vinegar, garlic, bay leaf, and salt to the pan. Bring this mixture to a boil, and then lower the heat and simmer for 5 minutes for the flavors to meld.

3 Using a slotted spoon or heatproof spatula, gently lower the salmon into the simmering liquid; the liquid should just cover the fish. Adjust the heat so that the surface of the liquid barely ripples and only a few bubbles rise to the surface.

4 Cook 8 to 10 minutes and then test for doneness with a fork. The flesh should be flaky, mostly opaque, and just barely translucent in the very center. For salmon steaks, the flesh should cling slightly to the bone. If it's not done, continue cooking, testing for doneness every minute or so.

5 Place the salmon on a plate and remove any skin. Cover and refrigerate until ready to serve. Garnish with parsley sprigs and serve with Grainy Mustard Sauce, found in Chapter 20.

If using an instant-read thermometer, the salmon should register 135°. However, with thinner pieces of food, some thermometers don't always register the temperature accurately. Poke the fish with a fork to test for doneness; if it flakes, the fish is sufficiently cooked. Some people prefer their fish, especially salmon, slightly translucent in the center.

Salmon-Teriyaki Rice Bowls

Prep time: 10 minutes, plus time to precook the rice and salmon

Cook time: 5 minutes

Yield: 4 servings

To serve this dish in just 15 minutes, morph this one-bowl meal out of leftovers from Perfectly Nice Rice (see Chapter 19) and the Poached Pink Salmon recipe in this chapter. Inspired by traditional Japanese rice bowls, this perfectly balanced dish tops steamed rice with delicate pink salmon and a slightly sweet teriyaki-style sauce, garnished with crisp, green shreds of lettuce, celery, and green onion. Young children can help flake the salmon, assemble the dish, and sprinkle the garnishes on the rice bowls.

Do this first:

✔ Set aside ¹/₂ pound leftover Poached Salmon, or prepare fresh.

✔ Reheat 2 cups cooked rice (see the recipe for Perfectly Nice Rice in Chapter 19), or prepare fresh.

✔ Prepare the sesame seeds, as described in the "Toasting sesame seeds" sidebar, later in this chapter.

Ingredients and steps:

¹/₂ pound cooked salmon
2 cups cooked rice (if necessary, reheat until warm)

Sauce:
One 2-inch piece fresh ginger
1 cup chicken broth
¹/₄ cup soy sauce, preferably low-sodium or Kikkoman Lite
¹/₄ cup honey
2 tablespoons dry sherry
¹/₂ teaspoon toasted sesame oil

Garnishes:
2 green onions
1 stalk celery
2 lettuce leaves
2 tablespoons toasted, crushed sesame seeds
Black pepper to taste

1 Set aside 2 cups warm, cooked rice; keep covered until ready to use.

2 Flake the salmon with a fork into bite-size pieces and set aside.

3 To make the sauce, cut the ginger diagonally into 4 or 5 slices to expose as much of the interior as possible.

4 Bring chicken broth, soy sauce, honey, sherry, ginger, and sesame oil to a boil in a saucepan. Boil until reduced by half, about 5 minutes.

5 To prepare the garnishes, thinly slice the green onions on the diagonal.

6 Thinly slice the celery on the diagonal.

7 Stack and roll the lettuce leaves and cut them into thin julienne strips.

8 To serve, fill four bowls equally with rice. Top rice with equal amounts of the lettuce, celery, and flaked salmon.

9 Spoon 4 tablespoons of the sauce on each bowl, or to taste. Leave the ginger in the remaining sauce or discard; don't serve the ginger slices.

10 Garnish with green onions and sesame seeds. Finish with fresh ground pepper on top.

Toasting sesame seeds

Like nuts and other seeds, sesame seeds have much more flavor when toasted. When I was a child, my mother took a few minutes every month to prepare a bowl of toasted sesame seeds, just like her mother had done when she was a girl. My favorite part as both a child and adult is sampling small spoonfuls of the warm, crushed sesame seeds. The slightly sweet, nutty sesame seeds explode with flavor and texture, and the inviting aroma fills the entire house.

To toast sesame seeds, heat a skillet over medium-low heat and add $\frac{1}{2}$ cup of white sesame seeds and $\frac{1}{4}$ teaspoon salt. Stir occasionally so that the seeds toast evenly. When the seeds begin to turn golden, but before they burn (about 3 to 5 minutes), remove them from the heat. Pour the warm seeds, in batches if necessary, into a mortar with pestle (shown in Chapter 3), crushing them to release their fragrant oil.

Keep the seeds in a closed jar, preferably in the freezer to prevent them from going rancid. Sprinkle them on vegetables, soups, fish, poultry, and meats, or on top of Asian noodles. Some Southeast Asians prepare sesame seeds by finely grinding the seeds almost to a powder, adding a bit of sugar to enhance the natural sweetness of the sesame. It makes an exquisite dipping condiment for crispy, fried springrolls, or for sprinkling on steamed vegetables.

Vary It! Be imaginative with this dish. Go with seasonal ingredients and your own taste preferences:

- ✔ Use other raw vegetables, cut into matchsticks, shredded or finely diced as shown in Chapter 11. Some ideas include cucumber, carrot, or napa cabbage.
- ✔ Substitute Chinese "Barbecue" Pork (found in this chapter), cooked shrimp, or cooked chicken for salmon.
- ✔ If you like your dishes hot, add a sprinkling of dried crushed red chiles.
- ✔ Serve pickled ginger on the side to accent the flavors.
- ✔ For vegetarians, substitute cooked broccoli, zucchini, carrot, tofu, or egg for the salmon; use vegetable broth instead of chicken broth.

Serving Suggestion: Serve with a crisp salad of cucumbers and carrot slices, tossed with seasoned rice vinegar.

Shrimp cocktail — class on a glass!

Rely on the convenience of your local seafood counter to prepare this favorite classic appetizer. Shrimp cocktail frequently headlines celebration menus like those found in Chapter 21, but there's no reason why you can't also enjoy it as a small main course for lunch or dinner, served with hearty side dishes of salad, bread, pasta, or soup. (Try it with Cold Cucumber Vichyssoise found in Chapter 19.) For four appetizers or small servings, you need:

- ☼ 1 pound cooked medium or large shrimp
- ☼ 1 jar cocktail sauce
- ☼ Assorted flavorings (optional)

Try to purchase cooked shrimp that still have the tails on, but any cooked shrimp will do. If still in their shells, peel the shells and leave the tail attached to act as a handle. Rinse the shrimp and set on a mound of ice in a bowl. Cover and refrigerate until ready to use.

Tip: Many varieties of premade cocktail sauce are available, but most can be enhanced with a few extra flavorings. Depending on your taste, add a bit of fresh lemon juice, horseradish, chopped onion, capers, Tabasco sauce, or other seasonings to brighten the flavor.

Serve the sauce in individual small cups or bowls, hanging the shrimp around the rim for dipping into it.

Sweet 'n' Sour Kiwi Shrimp

Prep time:	20 minutes
Cook time:	15 minutes
Yield:	4 servings

For this and other quick meals, keep peeled, cooked, frozen shrimp on hand. The fresh kiwi and colorful apricots (or nectarines) in this recipe add more color to the already pink shrimp, bathed in a citrusy sweet 'n' sour sauce. Light soy sauce, available in Asian markets, is paler in color than regular soy, making the sauce less dark, but you can substitute regular soy sauce. You can also make the sauce in advance and reheat it just before serving, adding an extra splash of vinegar to refresh the flavors. Children can practice their peeling skills and knife skills on the soft, easy-to-cut kiwi.

Do this first:

- Squeeze $1/4$ cup fresh lemon juice from 1 to 2 lemons.
- Peel and mince enough fresh ginger to make 1 tablespoon.
- Peel and mince 4 cloves garlic.

Ingredients and steps:

Shrimp and fruit:
> 2 kiwi
> 4 apricots or 2 nectarines
> 2 green onions, trimmed
> 1 pound peeled, cooked medium shrimp

Thickener:
> 2 tablespoons cornstarch
> $2/3$ cup water

Sauce:
> $3/4$ cup water
> $1/2$ cup distilled white vinegar
> $1/2$ cup sugar
> $1/4$ cup fresh lemon juice
> 1 tablespoon light soy sauce
> $1/2$ teaspoon sesame oil
> $1/4$ teaspoon white pepper
> $1/4$ teaspoon salt

1 tablespoon oil, preferably peanut or canola
4 cloves garlic, peeled and minced
1 tablespoon peeled and minced fresh ginger
6 to 10 cilantro sprigs for garnish (optional)

1 Peel and cut the kiwi in half lengthwise and cut across into $^1/_3$-inch slices.

2 Slice the apricots or nectarines lengthwise, into $^1/_3$-inch-wide wedges, removing the pits.

3 Slice the green onions diagonally into $^1/_2$-inch lengths. Set aside.

4 To prepare the thickener, in a small bowl or cup mix together the cornstarch and $^2/_3$ cup water as a thickener. Set aside.

5 To make the sauce, in medium bowl combine $^3/_4$ cup water, vinegar, sugar, lemon juice, soy sauce, sesame oil, white pepper, and salt.

6 In a medium saucepan, heat the oil over medium heat. Add the ginger and garlic. Stir-fry until softened, about 1 minute. (Don't let the garlic or ginger brown — they'll taste bitter.)

7 Stir the vinegar mixture into the pan, cooking and stirring until the sugar dissolves.

8 Stir the cornstarch mixture to blend it again and then add it to the sauce.

9 Reduce the heat and simmer until the sauce thickens, about 5 minutes. The sauce should be thick enough to coat the back of a spoon. Cover and set aside until ready to use, or continue with the next step if you're ready to eat. (Before serving, warm the sauce if it's not already hot.)

10 Stir the shrimp, kiwi slices, apricot or nectarine slices, and green onion into the warm sauce and turn off heat when heated through. Serve with steamed rice (see the recipe for Perfectly Nice Rice in Chapter 19) and garnish with cilantro sprigs.

Meatless Meals

Even meat-eaters will ask for second helpings of these tasty, meatless meals, and vegetarians will smile at every bite.

Frijole Fun-dido

Prep time:	5 minutes
Cook time:	3 minutes
Yield:	4 small servings

Fast, fabulous Frijole Fun-dido! As an easy meal or snack, Mexican families make queso fundido (KEH-soh fun-DEE-doh), which means "melted cheese." It's simply a tasty hunk of cheese, melted in an earthenware casserole in the oven, sometimes with green chiles, sausage, or onions. After it's bubbly, the cheese is served communally, for all to spoon into warm tortillas. It's delicious! — but not an everyday dish for those cutting back on fat.

This microwave version captures the same luscious fun and flavor in a more balanced dish, by baking creamy, seasoned pinto beans or frijoles (free-HO-lehs) with onion, bell pepper, and a dash of cumin under a layer of sharp cheese, and then topping it with fresh tomatoes. Kids and parents can microwave it in less than 5 minutes as a main meal or nutritious snack. This recipe makes 2 dinner servings or 4 snack servings.

Do this first:

- Shred enough sharp cheddar or Monterey Jack cheese to make 2 cups. Or, use pre-shredded cheese.

- Peel and cut 1 onion in half. Reserve ¹/₂ for another use. Finely chop the remaining half and set aside.

- Cut 1 bell pepper in half. Reserve ¹/₂ for another use. Chop the remaining half and set aside.

- Chop 1 whole tomato and set aside.

- Heat 4 corn or flour tortillas and keep warm (see Chapter 20).

Ingredients and steps:

¹/₂ onion, chopped
¹/₂ teaspoon ground cumin
1 teaspoon olive oil
1 can (15.5 ounces) seasoned pinto beans, preferably Ranch-style or Southwestern-style
2 cups shredded sharp cheddar or Monterey Jack cheese
¹/₂ bell pepper, chopped
1 whole tomato, chopped
4 corn or flour tortillas, warmed

1 In a microwave-safe casserole with lid, microwave the onion and cumin in olive oil on high until the onion softens, about 1 minute.

2 Stir in seasoned pinto beans (don't rinse the beans — you'll lose the seasonings).

3 Top with the cheese and bell pepper.

4 Microwave on high until the cheese melts, about 2 minutes.

5 Sprinkle with chopped tomato and serve with warm corn or flour tortillas. (Be careful, though, the container will be hot. Protect your hands with oven mitts or potholders.)

Serving Suggestion: To serve, let each person spoon the filling into a tortilla, adding some shredded lettuce, if desired. To add even more vegetables, cook the onion with corn kernels, diced zucchini, chopped celery, diced roasted green chiles, or with your favorite vegetable. Kick up the flavors, too, with some chili powder, hot pepper sauce, or salsa.

Grilled Meatless Mushroom Burgers

Prep time:	5 minutes, plus time for setting up condiments
Cook time:	8 minutes
Yield:	4 burgers

Even card-carrying carnivores enjoy burgers made with big, brown, meaty-tasting portabella mushrooms. Though it sounds exotic, the portabella mushroom is just an overgrown brown mushroom, with a flavor that increases dramatically as it grows in size. Most markets carry them either loose or packaged as caps. If parents take charge of grilling, kids can do the rest of the steps, including rinsing and preparing the hamburger condiments.

Ingredients and steps:

  2 cloves garlic
  2 tablespoons soy sauce
  2 tablespoons olive oil
  4 portabella mushroom caps, each about 4 to 5 inches in diameter
  4 hamburger buns or rolls

1 Peel and mince the garlic.

2 Combine garlic, soy sauce, and olive oil. Set aside.

3 Remove mushroom stems and reserve for another use. Wipe mushroom caps with a damp paper towel to remove any debris.

4 Place mushroom caps in a large shallow dish, feathery gills facing down. Rub or brush one-quarter of the marinade over the tops, coating the cap surface.

5 Flip the caps over and spoon the sauce on the gill side of the mushrooms, coating the edges as well. (You should have just enough sauce to drizzle on the underside, not enough to saturate.) Marinate at least 15 minutes or up to 2 hours.

6 Grill over medium heat, or broil (as described in Chapter 13), about 4 minutes on each side, or until softened, but not mushy.

7 Serve on hamburger buns or wheat rolls with your favorite hamburger condiments, or with a dab of the Hummus Sauce in Chapter 20.

Serving Suggestion: If desired, flip the mushrooms with their gills facing up and place a slice of cheese on them. Cover the grill and turn off the heat, letting the cheese melt (about a minute or so).

While cooking the mushrooms, you can also grill the bread. Toast hamburger buns or rolls indirectly, to the side of the heat. Watch them closely to make sure they don't burn.

Lazy, Crazy Lasagna

Prep time:	15 minutes
Cook time:	1 hour
Yield:	6 to 8 servings

You can make this lasagna without cooking the noodles first — a major time and energy saver — and you don't need to buy special, no-cook lasagna noodles to make it either. Use any brand of regular lasagna noodles without cooking them first. This sounds crazy, but it really works! The trick is to add plenty of sauce and to bake the dish tightly covered. This recipe uses the Twice-as-Red Tomato Sauce recipe (found in Chapter 20) or you can substitute 1 quart of your favorite tomato sauce. Kids can help prepare the filling and assemble the layers.

Do this first:

✔ Plan ahead by making 1 recipe of Twice-as-Red Tomato Sauce (see Chapter 20). If desired, make it at any time and freeze until ready to use; thaw overnight or in the microwave.

✔ Chop enough fresh basil to make 2 tablespoons, or use 2 teaspoons dried basil, crushed.

✔ To make the Twice as Red Tomato Sauce at the same time as the lasagna, start cooking the sauce first. While the sauce cooks, prepare the ricotta mixture and mozzarella for this recipe, and heat the oven. After the sauce and ricotta mixture are ready, assembling the dish goes quickly. Allow about 1 hour to prepare the sauce (mostly unattended) and another 5 minutes to assemble the lasagna before baking.

✔ Shred enough mozzarella cheese to make $1/2$ cup, or use pre-shredded.

Ingredients and steps:

1 large zucchini
1 container (15 ounces) lowfat or nonfat ricotta cheese
2 large eggs
$^1/_4$ cup grated Parmesan, plus extra for serving at table
2 tablespoons chopped fresh basil, or 2 teaspoons dried basil
1 recipe Twice-as-Red Tomato Sauce (see Chapter 20)
$^1/_2$ pound lasagna noodles, uncooked
$^1/_2$ cup shredded mozzarella cheese

1 Heat oven to 375°.

2 Using a grater, shred the zucchini, discarding the knobby stem. (Be careful not to grate your fingers.)

3 In a mixing bowl, stir together the zucchini, ricotta cheese, eggs, $^1/_4$ Parmesan cheese, and basil until blended.

4 To assemble the lasagna, spread $1^1/_2$ cups of sauce into a 13 x 9 x 2 inch pan.

5 Arrange $^1/_3$ of the uncooked lasagna noodles on top of the sauce, breaking the noodles to fit if necessary. (Don't worry about gaps: The noodles will expand during cooking.)

6 Layer half the ricotta mixture on the noodles.

7 Layer the remaining ingredients in the following order: half of the remaining noodles, half of the remaining sauce, all of the remaining ricotta mixture.

8 Complete the dish with a layer of noodles topped with the rest of sauce.

9 Sprinkle the mozzarella evenly on top of the sauce.

10 Cover tightly with foil and bake for 50 minutes. Let sit 5 minutes before removing the foil. Dust with Parmesan as desired before serving.

Capture the Flag Pizza

Prep time:	15 minutes
Cook time:	15 minutes
Yield:	1 15-inch pizza

With a red sauce on the bottom, and a white and green topping, this luscious pizza captures the colors of the Italian flag. It borrows Swiss cheese from Italy's northern neighbor, for a luscious, nutty taste that pairs perfectly with spinach, a vegetable that's rich in vitamins A and C. Kids of all ages can help make — and devour — this simply superb, crowd-pleasing pizza pie.

Do this first:

✔ Roll dough for one 15- to 16-inch pizza crust into a pizza pan or baking sheet. Use the Pizza-Pizza: Double-Dough recipe in Chapter 17 (it makes two crusts, but you only need one for this recipe), or use your favorite crust.

✔ Thaw a 10-ounce package frozen chopped spinach or cook 1 pound cleaned spinach leaves and chop. Squeeze the water from the spinach until it's very dry (reserve the squeezed liquid for a soup or sauce). Young children can do this by placing the cooled spinach in a sieve over a bowl and pressing on it with the back of a wooden spoon, a spatula, or with clean hands.

✔ Shred enough Swiss cheese to make 2 cups, or use pre-shredded cheese.

Ingredients and steps:

1 cup cooked, chopped spinach, squeezed dry
2 cups shredded Swiss cheese
Dash white pepper (optional)
2 cloves garlic
1 can (8 ounces) tomato sauce
1 prepared pizza crust, uncooked
$1/2$ teaspoon Italian seasoning (mixed dried herbs)
2 teaspoons olive oil
2 tablespoons grated Parmesan (optional)

1 Heat the oven to 450°.

2 Mix together the spinach, Swiss cheese, and a dash of white pepper in a bowl.

3 Peel and finely mince the cloves of garlic.

4 Spread the tomato sauce evenly over the crust.

5 Crush the Italian seasoning between your fingers and sprinkle over the sauce (a good task for little hands).

6 Arrange the spinach-cheese mixture on top of the sauce. Sprinkle on garlic.

7 Brush the edges of the crust with olive oil.

8 Bake until the crust is crisp and golden and the cheese melted, about 10 to 15 minutes. Let the pizza stand a few minutes before slicing. If desired, dust lightly with grated Parmesan. Serve hot.

Vary It! Add a few strips of thinly sliced ham or prosciutto, an Italian cured ham, under the cheese mixture. Instead of spinach, use cooked Swiss chard. Dot with sliced olives, chopped green or red onion, or chopped Roma tomatoes.

Tortelloni Toss

Prep time:	5 minutes
Cook time:	15 minutes
Yield:	4 servings as a main course, 6 to 8 as a side dish

This 20-minute, one-pot recipe calls for *tortelloni* (tohr-tl-OH-nee), which means "big hats" in Italian, because that's what these stuffed pastas resemble. Pick up two 8-ounce packages of fresh tortelloni (found in the refrigerator case) or a 1-pound package of frozen tortelloni. If you can't find the plump tortelloni, substitute its little brother, tortellini (tohr-tl-EE-nee) — smaller versions of the same pasta. Or, use stuffed ravioli, and even nonstuffed pasta, such as linguine or bow ties. Select any flavor of stuffing (cheese, meat, or mix) you prefer for this recipe.

Chard, sometimes referred to as Swiss chard, looks a bit like overgrown spinach, another green that's often substituted for chard. Rich in beta-carotene, chard has large, crinkly, green leaves with thick stalks and comes in two main varieties: one type has silvery white stalks, while the other has ruby red stalks. I prefer the more distinctive flavor of red chard for this recipe, but white-stalked chard, spinach, and other greens all taste great, too. (Be sure to rinse the chard well in a sinkful of cold water.)

The key to cooking chard is stripping the leaves from the stalks — you'll want to use both the leaves and the stalks, but the stalks take longer to cook, so you need to start them first. Equipped with safety scissors, a young child can easily cut the leafy parts from the stalks and even cut the stalks into small pieces, performing the most time consuming tasks of this recipe.

Ingredients and steps:

1 bunch Swiss chard, preferably red chard (about 12 to 16 ounces), washed
3 cloves garlic
1 pound fresh or frozen tortelloni
2 to 3 tablespoons extra virgin olive oil
$1/8$ teaspoon salt, or to taste
$1/4$ cup red wine vinegar
$1/4$ cup fresh basil (optional)
Grated Parmesan cheese for serving at table

1 Bring a large pot of salted water to a boil (about 4 quarts water and 2 teaspoons salt).

2 While the water comes to a boil, prepare the chard. Using a knife or safety scissors, trim the leafy parts away from the stalks. Tear the leafy sections into pieces about 2 inches in size. Place the leafy sections in a colander in the sink and rinse with water. (***Note:*** You need a colander to drain the cooked pasta. So if you have only one colander, remove the leafy sections to a bowl, allowing the water to cling to them.)

3 Cut the stalks across into $1/2$-inch wide pieces. Set aside.

4 Peel and chop the garlic.

5 When the water comes to a boil, gently cook the tortelloni according to manufacturer's instructions or until just cooked (about 9 minutes for most brands, but time may vary, especially if substituting a differently-shaped pasta).

6 Reserve one cup of the cooking water (carefully scoop it out with a ladle or a heat-proof measuring cup).

7 Drain the tortelloni in the colander.

8 In the same pot, heat the olive oil over medium heat. Stir in the garlic and cook until starting to soften but without browning, about 30 seconds.

9 Stir in the chard stalks and cook about 2 to 3 minutes. Add $1/3$ cup of reserved pasta water, cover and simmer until tender, about 2 minutes.

10 Stir in the chard leaves, salt, and another $1/3$ cup pasta water and simmer until the leaves have just wilted, about 1 to 2 minutes.

11 Stir in the red wine vinegar. Turn off the heat.

12 Toss the tortelloni with the chard sauce. If the mixture seems dry, drizzle on another spoonful of olive oil and a spoonful or more of pasta water.

13 If using fresh basil, chop it up. Serve pasta topped with basil and grated Parmesan.

Vary It! Substitute fresh spinach or other greens for the chard. Top with toasted pine nuts. Instead of extra virgin olive oil, use basil-flavored olive oil, available in most markets.

Meaty and Meatless Meal-Melds

For families with both vegetarian and meat-eating members, making meaty and meatless meals from the same basic dish saves time and energy. Use these vegetarian meal-melding recipes as guides for adapting your own family favorites.

Paprikash, Two Ways

Prep time:	7 minutes
Cook time:	30 minutes
Yield:	6 servings, when served on top of cooked egg noodles, rice, or couscous

The sweet Hungarian paprika in this dish makes it, well, sweet — not spicy. Paprika, made from red bell peppers, also comes in hotter varieties, so look for the cans or jars marked "sweet" on the label. This recipe shows how to cook two versions at the same time (one with chicken, one with mushrooms) for feeding a table of both meat-eaters and vegetarians.

Do this first:

✔ For the chicken version, slice 4 boneless, skinless breast halves into $^1/_4$- to $^1/_2$-inch- wide strips, cutting across the shortest side of each piece. Use half the amount if you're making the half-vegetarian, half-meat recipe.

✔ For the vegetarian version, clean and slice 1 pound of mushrooms, or buy pre-sliced mushrooms. They come in 6-ounce packages. Use two packages for a full vegetarian recipe or one package for a half-vegetarian recipe.

✔ If using a turnip for the vegetarian recipe, peel and slice it into thin strips, about $^1/_4$-inch thick. Use half of a turnip for a half-vegetarian recipe.

✔ Prepare egg noodles, rice, or couscous for serving with the Paprikash. Allow about $^1/_2$ to $^3/_4$ cup of each (cooked) per serving.

Ingredients and steps:

Paprikash sauce base:
>   1 medium onion
>   1 sweet red pepper
>   1 green bell pepper
>   1 tablespoon olive oil
>   3 tablespoons sweet Hungarian paprika
> $^3/_4$ teaspoon salt
> $^1/_2$ teaspoon marjoram, crushed
>   1 can (14.5 ounces) peeled, diced tomatoes
>   1 cup vegetable broth
> $^1/_4$ cup loosely packed fresh basil or parsley (optional)

To thicken the sauce:
>   3 teaspoons flour
> $^3/_4$ cup sour cream or plain yogurt (don't use nonfat versions)

Chicken version:
>   4 boneless, skinless chicken breast halves, sliced into $1/4$- to $1/2$-inch wide strips

Vegetarian version:
>   1 tablespoon olive oil
>   1 turnip, sliced $1/4$ -inch thick in bite size pieces
>   1 pound (approximately) sliced mushrooms

To make the paprikash base:

1   Cut the onion in half vertically. Remove and discard the skin, and cut off the bottom tip. Slice the onion across into very thin half-rings, discarding the onion top when you get to it. Set aside.

2   Cut the peppers in half lengthwise. Cut out the seeds and membranes and discard. Slice the peppers lengthwise into strips, between $1/4$- and $1/2$-inch wide.

3   Heat the oil in a large, heavy skillet over medium-high heat.

4   Mix in the onion, pepper strips, paprika, salt, and marjoram.

5   Cook, stirring occasionally, until the vegetables arc slightly limp, about 4 minutes.

6   Stir in the tomatoes and broth.

7   Bring the mixture to a boil. Cover, reduce heat, and simmer 10 minutes, stirring occasionally.

8   Julienne the basil or mince the parsley. Set aside.

9   Stir the flour into the sour cream or yogurt until well blended — the flour keeps the mixture from separating when cooked. (*Tip:* Don't use nonfat versions of sour cream or yogurt — they'll separate, even with flour added. Whole or reduced-fat versions work fine.) You'll be dividing this mixture evenly between the Vegetarian Paprikash and the Chicken Paprikash versions.

10   Remove half of the sauce from the pan and reserve it in a bowl for the vegetarian version. Continue with the following steps for the Vegetarian Paprikash and Chicken Paprikash.

Vegetarian Paprikash:

11   Heat 1 tablespoon oil in a separate skillet over medium-high heat. Sauté the turnip and mushrooms in the olive oil until the turnip starts to soften and the mushrooms give off their liquid.

12   Stir in the reserved bowl of paprikash sauce; cover and simmer over low heat for 10 minutes.

Chicken Paprikash:

13   While the Vegetarian Paprikash simmers, stir the chicken into the original pan of sauce. Cover and simmer over low heat, stirring occasionally, until just cooked through and tender, about 6 minutes.

To finish the Vegetarian and Chicken Paprikash recipes:

14 Stir half the sour cream (or yogurt) mixture into the Vegetarian Paprikash and half of it into the Chicken Paprikash. Cook just until heated through. Don't let the sauces boil. Serve both versions over egg noodles, rice, or couscous sprinkled with the reserved basil or parsley.

 Little ones can help by scraping the membranes from the peppers using a melon baller. They can also stir the flour into the sour cream and measure the ingredients. Older children can practice their knife skills.

Serving Suggestion: Serve the paprikash over egg noodles with a side of steamed green cabbage, a salad, or crisply steamed green beans.

Calabacitas Vegetarian or Turkey Tacos

Prep time:	5 minutes
Cook time:	15 minutes
Yield:	4 to 6 servings

Use two skillets to make a tasty taco mixture to feed both vegetarians and meat-eaters in the same meal. These tacos feature yellow squash and zucchini or *calabacitas* (cahl-ah-bah-SEE-tahs) as the main ingredients. The mixture is mildly seasoned so that even the most sensitive palates can enjoy it. Morph any leftover turkey from Self-Basting Lemon-Pepper Roast Turkey (found earlier in this chapter) for the meat-eaters, or substitute other cooked turkey or chicken.

Ingredients and steps:

1 medium onion
2 medium zucchini
2 medium yellow or crookneck squash
1 pound cooked turkey
1 tablespoon canola oil
$3/4$ teaspoon cumin
$1/4$ teaspoon salt

1 Peel and chop the onion.

2 Cut the zucchini into $^1/_2$-inch dice.

3 Cut the yellow squash into $^1/_2$-inch dice.

4 Cut the turkey into $^1/_2$-inch dice.

5 Heat oil in nonstick skillet on high. Stir in onion, zucchini, yellow squash, cumin, and salt. Leave vegetables in single layer and cook 2 minutes on high. Stir. Cook another 2 to 3 minutes until browned. Pour squash mixture into large bowl and set aside.

6 In same skillet, fry turkey in single layer on high 2 to 3 minutes. Stir. Fry another 2 to 3 minutes or until browned.

7 Mix turkey with half the squash mixture for the meat-eaters. Serve the vegetarians the remaining squash mixture.

Serving Suggestion: Serve with Faster-than-5 Black Bean Salsa (see Chapter 20), soft corn or flour tortillas, and crumbled feta or fresh Mexican cheese.

Vary It! For a full Vegetarian Taco recipe, omit the turkey and increase the squashes and onion by $^1/_3$ the amounts given above. For a full non-vegetarian recipe, combine the turkey with the full amount of cooked squash mixture. If desired, increase the turkey by $^1/_2$ pound.

This recipe shows how caramelization, the process of bringing out the natural sugars in foods, enriches the flavor of a dish. To develop a naturally deep, almost smoky taste, cook the ingredients on high heat in a single layer without stirring, then stir them and cook again until most of the pieces have dark brown edges. Flip to Chapter 12 for a more detailed description.

Measuring the marigolds

Keep a tape measure — the retractable kind used by carpenters — handy for kids in the kitchen. Recipes often specify the depth of a liquid in a pot, the distance between cookies on a baking sheet, or the size of a skillet. A measuring tape works better than a ruler because it slides compactly and can measure small distances as well as anything longer than 12 inches, such as a 13- x 9- inch baking dish. Tape measures can be addictive though — after they discover them, some kids start measuring everything!

Chapter 19
Sides, Soups, and Salads

In This Chapter

▶ Serving sumptuous salads as side dishes and main courses

▶ Cooking basic rice and beans

▶ Completing meals with summer and winter vegetables

▶ Cooling off and warming up with seasonal soups

How can you tell if a vegetable is really mad?
When it's steamed.

Get your five-a-day the side-dish way by serving lots and lots of vegetables with every meal. The recipes in this chapter highlight the choicest vegetables of every season, from spring asparagus to winter squash, as well as a refreshingly cold watermelon soup for summer and a comforting Crock Pot Pizza Soup for the busy back-to-school season. For satisfyingly filling foods, I turn the spotlight onto grains and legumes, including basic recipes that every cook can use and ideas for jazzing up plain rice and beans.

Side Dishes — Front and Center

You can round out a simple meal by using side dishes that capture the best of each season. Many of the recipes in this section are hearty enough to serve as a meatless main course, accompanied by an easy green salad and bread.

Basically Great (Dried) Beans

Prep time:	10 minutes
Cook time:	1 to 3 hours, depending on the beans and method used
Yield:	5 to 6 cups

Whether you're cooking red, black, white, or any other color of beans, of any other color, the real key to making great dried beans lies in the seasonings. Beans by themselves, cooked just in water, taste bland. But by adding some onion, garlic, bay leaves, and other seasonings, beans blooms with flavor. Use this basic bean recipe as a jumping off point for creating your own recipes. For some newfangled tips on cooking this ancient food, see the "Beanology 101" sidebar, later in this chapter.

This basic recipe works for any type of dried bean, except for lentils or split peas which cook quickly and don't need presoaking.

Ingredients and steps:

> 1 pound dried beans (any type except for lentils or split peas)
> 1 onion
> 3 cloves garlic
> 2 carrots
> 2 stalks celery
> 2 bay leaves
> 2 cans (14.5 ounces each) low-salt chicken broth (or vegetable stock)

1 Rinse the beans in a colander in the sink. Pick out any gravel or other debris.

2a Soaking method: Place the beans in a large pot. Fill the pot with water to cover by at least 4 inches. Soak the beans for at least 8 hours or overnight. When ready to cook, drain the beans in a colander in the sink. Return the beans to the pot. Continue with Step 3.

2b Nonsoaking method: After rinsing the beans, place them in a large pot. Continue with Step 3.

3 Peel and chop the onion. Add the onion to the beans. (Or, quarter the onion; see the tip later in this recipe.)

4 Peel and chop the garlic. Add the garlic to the beans.

5 Trim the carrots and cut into thirds. Add the carrots to the beans.

6 Trim the celery, but keep any leaves and add them to the beans (they contribute great flavor). Cut the celery stalks into thirds and add to the beans.

7 Add the bay leaf and chicken broth to the beans. Add enough water to cover the beans by 2 inches.

8 Bring the beans to a boil over high heat on a small burner. As soon as the liquid starts to boil, reduce the heat and simmer the beans slowly. Check the beans about 5 minutes after you reduce the heat — they should just be simmering. If they're boiling, reduce the heat. If the liquid is not simmering with small ripples, raise the heat slightly.

9 Check the beans as they cook to make sure that they remain covered with liquid. If the liquid level goes below the beans, add more water or chicken broth.

10 Cook the beans until they're tender, but not mushy. They shouldn't be crunchy, but they should have some body. Test the beans for doneness periodically to prevent overcooking. The actual cooking time depends on the variety of bean used, the age of the bean (older beans take longer to cook), and whether they were soaked. Most soaked beans take 1 to 2 hours to cook. Unsoaked beans take longer, from $1\frac{1}{2}$ to 3 hours.

11 Serve the beans plain, with some of the flavorful broth or "bean liquor," or adapt them to a favorite recipe.

Vary It! Pump up the flavor of beans by simmering them with dried or fresh herbs like thyme, basil, oregano, rosemary, parsley, or sage; ham hocks, salt pork, bacon, smoked turkey legs or wings; sweet peppers, hot chile peppers, or ground chiles; spices like cumin, fennel seed, and coriander; or aromatic seasonings like onion, garlic, carrot, celery, or fresh ginger (for an Asian flavor).

✔ Some people (especially kids) don't like to see bits of onion in their food. Instead of chopping the onion, cut the onion into quarters, leaving the root end to hold the pieces together. Cook as directed and remove the chunks of onion when the dish is finished cooking. You can also slide a toothpick in the quarters to help hold them together. Some cooks stick three whole cloves into the onion during cooking for flavor.

✔ To test the beans for doneness, blow on them. If the skin splits, they're just about done; at this point, taste them to see if they're cooked through.

✔ For better taste and texture, use cooked beans wherever canned beans are called for in this cookbook. Most 15-ounce cans of beans equal about $1\frac{3}{4}$ cups cooked beans. Cooked beans freeze well, so cook up a batch and freeze half of the beans for later.

Beanology 101

Beans cook more quickly when you soak them overnight or *quick-soak* them by covering the beans with water, bringing them to a boil, covering with a lid, turning off the heat, and letting them sit for 1 hour before cooking. But you can also cook beans without soaking them first — they just take about one-third more time to cook.

Los Angeles Times' food writer Russ Parsons has stirred up a potful of bean-cooking research to discover the following:

☺ **Unsoaked beans taste better!** It's true — compared to soaked beans, unsoaked beans have deeper flavor, better texture, and retain more of their color — instead of looking bleached out.

☺ **Salt doesn't toughen beans.** I've been salting beans or cooking them in canned chicken broth (which contains salt) for years — without them tasting tough. Flavoring beans while they cook requires less salt than flavoring them after they cook. Russ cooks 1 pound of beans with 1 teaspoon salt. Or, do as I do: Cook the beans in canned broth and omit the salt.

☺ **Eat beans more often to reduce the gaseous effects.** Beans cause gas because your body has difficulty digesting the sugars and fiber in the beans. But if you eat beans more frequently, the body adapts and more effectively digests the gas-causing substances in beans. And because beans are bursting with protein, carbohydrates, nutrients, fiber, and antioxidants, use your bean — and eat more beans!

Easy, Cheesy Polenta

Polenta, a Northern Italian cornmeal specialty that's often served with grilled sausages, ends up soft, creamy, and comforting, but usually requires constant stirring on the stovetop. This amazing, oven-baked version doesn't build up your biceps, because you stir it only twice, but it tastes just as good! This recipe was adapted from one by cookbook author and radio personality Michele

Prep time:	3 minutes
Cook time:	50 minutes, plus 5 minutes to stand
Yield:	2 to 3 main course servings, 4 to 6 as a side dish.

Anna Jordan, an expert on polenta, olive oil, tomatoes, mustard, and all things tasty. This recipe is especially well-suited to kids, who usually love cornmeal dishes. They can measure the ingredients and do what little stirring this dish requires, while parents take the dish in and out of the oven.

Do this first:

✔ Grate ¹/₂ cup Parmesan or Romano cheese, or use pre-grated cheese.

Ingredients and steps:

> 1 quart water
> 1 cup cornmeal
> 1 tablespoon olive oil
> 1 teaspoon salt
> ¹/₈ to ¹/₄ teaspoon white pepper
> ¹/₂ cup grated Parmesan or Romano cheese

1 Place a rack in the upper third of the oven. Heat the oven to 350°.

2 In a 2-quart baking dish, stir the water, cornmeal, olive oil, salt, and white pepper together.

3 Bake 40 minutes. (The mixture will look separated and watery but will come together in the end.)

4 Stir the cheese into the polenta. Bake 10 minutes. Remove from oven and let stand for 5 minutes before serving.

Vary It! After the first 40 minutes of cooking, stir in any of the following ingredients: sun dried tomatoes, fresh or dried herbs, chopped olives, green chiles. Other cheeses to use include feta cheese, cheddar, Monterey Jack, Swiss, goat cheese. Serve this dish during the winter as a hearty, warm breakfast that can substitute for oatmeal.

Melt grated cheddar cheese on top of the polenta for a dish that rivals a kid favorite, macaroni and cheese. It's just as comforting, tastes rich, is easier to make, and is lower in fat.

Don't try doubling this recipe — it won't cook properly. Instead, make two batches and cook them at the same time on the same rack.

Everyday Oven Fries

Prep time:	5 minutes
Cook time:	40 to 45 minutes, depending on the thickness of the "fries"
Yield:	4 small servings

French fries will always be near and dear to my heart — it's almost impossible to resist such hot and crispy treats. But these oven-fries are a strong rival to the deep-fried kind, and health-wise, they beat fat-laden French fries hands down. Hot out of the oven, these crispy-on-the-outside, soft-on-the-inside fries are good enough to enjoy every day of the week — without guilt. Youngsters old enough to control a sharp knife can make them with a parent's supervision, while little hands can smoosh the potato wedges around in the oil to coat.

Ingredients and steps:

    2 pounds Idaho potatoes
    2 to 3 tablespoons corn oil or other vegetable oil
    Salt and freshly ground pepper

1 Heat oven to 400°. Line a baking sheet with foil for easy cleanup.

2 Wash the potatoes well, but don't peel them. Pat dry.

3 Slice the potatoes into halves, then into quarters lengthwise. Placing your knife at the pointed edge of each quarter, carefully slice down into thin wedges, as shown in Figure 19-1. (The thinner the slice, the crispier the fry will be.) Even if this seems like a lot of potatoes, they shrink considerably during cooking.

4 Pour the oil into the center of the baking sheet. Using clean hands, push the potato wedges around in the oil, flipping as needed to coat on all sides.

5 Line the wedges up on their sides, as shown in Figure 19-1. Sprinkle the tops with salt to taste and plenty of fresh cracked pepper.

6 Bake about 45 minutes, depending on the thickness of the potatoes. Check the potatoes after 35 minutes to make sure they're not browning too much. Serve hot out of the oven as a side dish or snack.

Corn oil imparts a particular sweetness to the potatoes in this dish, although any vegetable oil will work.

Be sure to use a sharp knife to cut through the potatoes effortlessly. Dull knives can slip, risking an accidental cut. If children can't control a knife safely, parents should cut the potatoes and let the kids rub them in the oil and add salt and pepper.

Figure 19-1: Forget French fries — hot, crisp, oven-fried potatoes taste terrific!

Gouda-Butternut Squash Gratin

Gouda cheese, Holland's most popular cheese, enriches this roasted squash gratin with its buttery, nutlike taste. Parents should cut the squash, but youngsters can scrape out the seeds and mash the ingredients. Gouda (GOO-dah) cheese, sealed in red wax, is sold in most markets. If you can't find it, substitute Edam (EE-duhm), another red-waxed Dutch cheese, or sharp cheddar.

Prep time:	20 minutes
Cook time:	1$^1/_4$ to 1$^1/_2$ hours, mostly unattended
Yield:	6 to 8 side dish servings, or 4 main course servings

Do this first:

- Grate enough Gouda cheese to make 1$^1/_2$ cups (about 3$^1/_2$ ounces).
- Grate enough Parmesan cheese to make 1 tablespoon, or use pre-grated.

Ingredients and steps:

1 medium butternut squash, about 3$^1/_2$ pounds
Nonstick vegetable spray, preferably olive oil flavored
1$^1/_2$ cups grated Gouda cheese (about 3$^1/_2$ ounces)
$^1/_4$ teaspoon salt
$^1/_4$ teaspoon white pepper
Dash allspice
2 tablespoons seasoned dry breadcrumbs
1 tablespoon grated Parmesan cheese
1 teaspoon olive oil

1   Heat oven to 425°. Line a baking sheet with foil for easy cleanup. Lightly coat a large baking dish (such as a 13- x 9-inch or 11- x 7^1/$_2$-inch) with nonstick spray and set aside.

2   Using a chef's knife or other heavy, sharp knife or cleaver, cut the squash lengthwise into quarters. ***Caution:*** Only parents should perform this step.

3   Scrape out the seeds and discard them.

4   Place the squash pieces on the foil, flesh side up. Lightly coat with nonstick spray.

5   Roast 45 minutes, or until soft and a fork pierces the flesh easily. Remove the squash from the oven.

6   Reduce oven temperature to 400°.

7   When squash is cool enough to handle (about 10 minutes), scrape the flesh into a bowl. Mash in the Gouda, salt, pepper, and allspice.

8   Spread the squash mixture in a thin layer in the coated baking dish.

9   Evenly sprinkle the breadcrumbs and Parmesan on top. Drizzle with olive oil.

10 Bake until hot throughout, about 20 to 25 minutes. If the topping isn't browned and crisp, run the pan under the broiler for a few seconds, being careful not to burn the topping. Serve hot or at room temperature.

Mash 'n' Smash Parsnip Potatoes

Prep and cook time:	30 minutes
Yield:	4 to 6 servings

Call the little ones into the kitchen for this dish —
a pair of small hands and a potato masher are
essential to its success! Comforting potatoes blend with sweet, nutty parsnips and tart green apples for a rich tasting, but lowfat, twist on traditional mashed potatoes. Just one serving provides ^{1}/$_3$ the recommended daily value of vitamin C. This recipe pairs well with the Self-Basting Lemon-Pepper Roast Turkey in Chapter 19.

Yukon Gold potatoes, found in most markets, have a naturally buttery flavor, but you can use regular baking or russet potatoes as well.

Ingredients and steps:

^{1}/$_4$ pound parsnips (about 2 medium)
1 pound Yukon Gold or russet potatoes (about 3 medium potatoes)
1 cup water or low-salt chicken broth
1 large Granny Smith apple (about ^{1}/$_3$ pound)
2 teaspoons butter

$^1/_8$ teaspoon ground cardamom (optional)
$^1/_4$ teaspoon salt or to taste
Dash white pepper (or black pepper)
$^1/_3$ cup milk

1 Peel the parsnips but don't peel the potatoes (just scrub them well).

2 Coarsely cut the parsnips and potatoes into $^1/_2$ to $^3/_4$ inch chunks.

3 Place the parsnips and potatoes in a large microwave-safe mixing bowl. Pour in water or chicken broth. Cover bowl, leaving room for steam to escape.

4 Microwave on high 5 minutes. Stir, being careful not to burn yourself from the steam (use oven mitts and open the lid away from you).

5 Microwave again until the parsnips and potatoes are soft and very tender when pierced with a fork, about 5 to 6 minutes. The mixture should be soft enough to mash.

6 While the parsnip mixture cooks, peel, core, and coarsely cut the apples into chunks about $^1/_2$ to $^3/_4$ inch in size.

7 Melt butter in nonstick pan. Stir in the apples and ground cardamom. Cook on medium heat until soft and lightly browned in spots, about 10 minutes, stirring occasionally.

8 Add salt and pepper to the parsnip mixture.

9 Mash the parsnip mixture with a potato masher until soft and mashed together. (An ideal kid task!) If the mixture doesn't mash easily, microwave again on high until easily mashed.

10 Mash in the apples and milk. If the mixture seems dry, add more milk. The mixture doesn't have to be completely smooth — a little texture enhances the dish.

11 Serve the dish warm, reheating (covered) in the microwave if necessary.

Vary It! This recipe tastes great with milk of any kind (lowfat or regular), but for the occasional special celebration, adding just two tablespoons of real cream elevates the flavors — and still keeps the average serving below 30 percent calories from fat.

✔ Don't process this recipe or any mashed potato recipe in a food processor — you'll end up with an unpleasant, gooey mass. It's best to mash by hand.

✔ Be flexible with this recipe: the proportions are general. More or less parsnip, potato, or apple won't hurt it at all. Vary the proportions to suit your tastes.

Minted Mini-Carrots

Even the youngest chef can quickly prepare this dish, which cooks handy pre-trimmed baby carrots with honey and dried mint in the microwave. If parents cut the lemon in half, kids don't need to use a knife.

Prep time:	5 minutes (or less)
Cook time:	7 minutes
Yield:	4 servings

Do this first:

✔ Squeeze 2 tablespoons of fresh lemon juice from one lemon

Ingredients and steps:

1 pound trimmed baby carrots
1 tablespoon honey
3 tablespoons water
2 tablespoons fresh lemon juice
$^1/_2$ teaspoon dried mint flakes

1 Place all ingredients in microwave-safe baking dish, about 11 x 7 inches or equivalent. Stir to combine and leave in a single layer.

2 Cover dish tightly with a lid set slightly ajar to let steam escape or with microwave-safe plastic wrap. If using plastic wrap, poke with a fork several times for steam to escape and don't let the plastic rest on the carrots.

3 Microwave on high 5 minutes, stirring halfway through.

4 Let dish stand covered for 2 minutes before lifting lid. When handling the dish, be sure to use oven mitts and open the lid away from you to avoid steam burns. Test a carrot — it should be tender but still slightly crispy in the center. If too crunchy, re-cover the dish and heat for another minute or so. Serve warm or at room temperature as a side dish or snack.

TIP

When you have lemons, don't make lemonade — freeze 'em!

Bottled lemon juice just doesn't capture the flavor of fresh lemons. But you can have fresh tasting lemon juice all year round by freezing lemons whole — just pop 'em into the freezer and defrost in the microwave. Whole lemons and limes freeze beautifully for months — the skin suffers a bit, so they're not good for zesting, but the interior juice tastes as fresh as the day you froze them.

No fuss, no muss — Tender, Sweet Asparagus

Microwave steaming not only cooks quickly and neatly, it also retains more nutrients. Use this asparagus recipe as a model for steaming other vegetables in the microwave. (Cooking times for other vegetables vary, so check them every few minutes until they're done.) For best results, make sure the vegetables are of uniform size so they cook evenly. Asparagus gives off enough water during cooking that it doesn't need extra liquid to microwave-steam, but you should add a tablespoon or two of water to broccoli, carrots, and other dense vegetables. To microwave-steam asparagus, you need:

1 pound fresh asparagus
Dash salt

☼ Rinse the asparagus in the sink. to remove the tough stem sections, see the "Snapping asparagus" sidebar, later in this chapter.

☼ Place the asparagus in a rectangular glass (or other microwave-safe) baking dish.

☼ To cook, sprinkle a dash of salt on the asparagus. Cover the dish with a microwave-safe lid or plastic wrap, leaving one corner open to vent. Microwave on high for 2 to 3 minutes, depending on the thickness of the spears. Stir the asparagus and test for doneness — they should be crisply tender. Be careful not to overcook — better to undercook them than to cook them too long. If serving the asparagus cold, refrigerate until ready to use. Or, serve warm with olive oil or butter.

Orange-Scented Couscous

Prep time:	5 minutes
Cook and stand time:	7 minutes
Yield:	4 servings as a side dish

In this recipe, a hint of fresh citrus wakes up plain couscous, making it an elegantly fragrant side dish. *Couscous* (KOOS-koos) is actually a North African and Middle Eastern pasta that looks like a tiny grain. You can find instant couscous in the supermarket's rice or pasta aisles. Couscous is a busy person's dream food, because you can prepare it in minutes, it comforts and satisfies, and it can be used as a backdrop for more complex flavors, as suggested in the variations that follow this recipe. Kids old enough to grate the zest from an orange can be a big help with this recipe.

Ingredients and steps:

1 medium whole orange with peel, washed and dried
1 cup water, less 2 tablespoons
1 tablespoon extra virgin olive oil or butter
$1/2$ teaspoon salt
1 cup quick-cooking couscous
1 green onion, for garnish

1 Cover the finest grating side of a box grater with plastic wrap, extending the wrap below it to catch the zest, as shown in the "Say yes to zest!" sidebar in Chapter 11.

2 Grate the zest from all sides of the orange, making sure to get only the colored surface and none of the bitter white part below the surface.

3 When the orange is completely grated, scrape the zest from the plastic into a small mound; you should end up with about 1 teaspoon or more zest.

4 In a medium saucepan, combine water, olive oil or butter, and salt. Bring to a boil.

5 While the water is coming to a boil, cut the orange in half and squeeze out 2 tablespoons of juice. Set juice aside and reserve the remaining orange for garnish or another use.

6 When the water comes to a boil, remove the pan from the heat and stir in the orange juice and couscous until completely mixed.

7 Cover the pot and let stand for 5 minutes.

8 Stir in the reserved zest, fluffing with a fork or chopstick until the couscous grains are separated.

9 Cover until ready to serve, and fluff again right before serving.

10 Chop the green onion and sprinkle on top before serving.

Vary It! Substitute any other citrus fruit, such as lemon or lime, for the orange juice and zest. Use the couscous as a bed for sautéed, grilled, or stewed vegetables, making it into a meatless main course.

Peas and Shiitake Mushrooms

Prep time:	5 minutes (or less)
Cook time:	10 minutes
Yield:	4 to 6 servings

The rich, earthy taste of *shiitake* (shee-TAH-kay) mushrooms adds a deep layer of flavor to all kinds of dishes. This recipe takes these mushrooms beyond traditional Japanese meals and pairs them with a very French combination — peas and lettuce. Look for fresh shiitake mushrooms in the produce section of many markets, or substitute any other flavorful mushroom.

Ingredients and steps:

> 8 ounces (about 2 cups) frozen peas
> 1 green onion
> 3 ounces fresh shiitake mushrooms (about 11 medium or $2^1/_2$ cups sliced)
> 3 medium Romaine lettuce leaves
> 1 tablespoon butter or margarine
> Salt and pepper

1 In a microwave-safe bowl, cook the peas in 1 teaspoon water, covered, for 3 minutes on high. (Leave the cover slightly vented so that steam can escape.) Stir. Cook another 2 minutes or until just cooked through.

2 While the peas cook, finely chop the green onion.

3 Slice the mushroom caps into strips, cutting off the stems and discarding.

4 Slice the lettuce into thin strips or chiffonade, as shown in Chapter 11. Cut the leaves in half first, down the center rib, to make them more manageable. Stack the lettuce leaves and roll tightly to form a cigar shape. Cut across the leaves to make thin shreds, about $^1/_8$-inch wide.

5 Melt the butter in a skillet over medium heat. Sauté the green onion until soft, about $^1/_2$ minute.

6 Stir in the mushrooms and sauté on medium-high until soft, about $2^1/_2$ minutes.

7 Stir in the peas, discarding any excess liquid.

8 Stir in the lettuce and cook just until lettuce begins to wilt but is still a bit crisp, less than 1 minute. Season to taste with salt and pepper and serve warm.

Vary It! Shiitake mushrooms are flavorful, but can be pricey. You can substitute any mushroom — portabellas, oyster mushrooms, and other wild mushrooms are especially tasty.

Serving Suggestion: To make a satisfying meal, serve these flavorful peas with delicate shreds of Succulent Chinese Chicken (see Chapter 18), and Garlic Wonton Crisps (discussed later in this chapter). It's perfect as a light supper or lunch, especially in warm weather.

Perfectly Nice Rice

Prep time:	5 minutes
Cook time:	15 minutes, plus 5 to 10 minutes standing time
Yield:	3 cups cooked rice

Rice feeds more people in the world than any other grain. But just as beauty is in the eye of the beholder, the concept of what makes rice "perfect" varies from culture to culture. Many Japanese prefer medium-grained rice; its starchy stickiness is best for eating with chopsticks or rolling into sushi. East Indians steam aged, long grain rice, called *basmati* (bahs-MAH-tee) into loose, fluffy grains. Italians grow plump *Arborio* (ar BOH-ree-oh) rice for their creamy risotto dishes. Many Americans cook rice in butter and salt, a treatment that puzzles most Asians who value the balance that unseasoned steamed rice lends to a meal.

White rice, from which the husk, bran, and germ of the grain has been removed, contains fewer nutrients but is often preferred for its milder flavor. Nutritious brown rice, with its nutty taste and chewy texture, is the entire grain with only the husk removed. Wild rice isn't rice at all, but rather an aquatic grass.

Many cultures rinse the outer starch away from rice before cooking to get light, fluffy, separate grains. In the United States, however, white rice is sprayed with added nutrients, so some people avoid rinsing rice before cooking, even though unrinsed rice turns out sticky. Because rinsing is a matter of taste and preference, this recipe includes methods for cooking white rice, rinsed and unrinsed, as well as for cooking the more nutritious brown rice varieties. (For instant rice, or Converted or parboiled rice, which are specially treated, follow the package instructions.)

To prevent boiling over, the rice and water should never exceed $1/3$ the depth of the pot. If water starts to dribble over the side, lift the lid (using an oven mitt) and let the steam escape. Replace the lid and continue cooking.

Ingredients and steps:

> 1 cup long grain white rice
> $1^3/_4$ to 2 cups water

1 Place the rice in a heavy-bottomed saucepan. Add 2 cups water to the unrinsed rice. For rinsed rice, add $1^3/_4$ cups water after rinsing and draining (see instructions after this recipe).

2 Using the smaller burner of the stove, bring the water and rice to a boil on high heat.

3 Reduce the heat to very low. Cover and cook until the water is completely absorbed and deep holes appear in the surface, about 15 minutes. Time may vary though, depending on the pan used.

4 Turn off the heat. Stir the rice with a chopstick (or fork handle) to loosen the grains. Cover and let steam 5 to 10 minutes before serving. Rice will stay hot for as long as 30 minutes.

✔ If you're rinsing the rice before cooking, place a colander or sieve in the sink to catch any loose grains as you pour the rice water out. Place the rice in the pot and fill it with water. Swirl the rice with your hand to loosen the starch. Hold back the grains with one hand and pour out most of the water over the colander. Repeat until the water runs fairly clear, about four to six times. Pour out as much water as possible. If any rice falls into the colander, return it to the pot. Add $1^{3}/_{4}$ cups water and proceed to cook as indicated in this recipe.

✔ For perfect rice every time, an electric rice cooker keeps the rice hot, reheats rice, and never boils over. Even unrinsed rice turns out light and fluffy, because much of the starch collects beneath a special insert, away from the rice.

Vary It! To cook brown rice, use $2^{1}/_{2}$ cups water or stock for 1 cup of long grain brown rice; use 2 cups water for short grain brown rice. Cook 45 minutes, or until the water is absorbed and the grains are tender. For added flavor, cook rice in broth or cook it with finely chopped raw veggies, such as carrot, celery, or broccoli, or cooked beans.

 Tuscan Braised Green Beans and Tomatoes

Prep time:	5 minutes
Cook time:	20 minutes
Yield:	4 servings as a side dish; 6 servings as a topping for pasta or couscous

Super-fresh, thin green beans cook best when they're steamed until crisply tender. Larger, older, tougher green beans improve by slow cooking until they're soft, but not mushy. This simple but classic Italian dish braises green beans in a sauce of fresh tomatoes and basil. Serve it as a side dish or top it on couscous or pasta for a meatless main meal in minutes.

Kids can practice their chopping skills with the easier tasks of cutting the green beans into 1¹/₂-inch lengths and coarsely chopping the tomatoes. Younger children can rinse and trim the beans by hand.

Ingredients and steps:

³/₄ pound green beans
¹/₂ medium onion
1 clove garlic
3 large Roma tomatoes or one can (14.5-ounces) chopped tomatoes with juice
1 tablespoon olive oil
¹/₄ teaspoon salt
Freshly ground black pepper to taste
¹/₄ cup fresh basil, or 1 tablespoon dried

1 Trim the stem end of the green beans. Cut the beans into 1¹/₂-inch lengths and set aside.

2 Peel the onion and garlic. Dice the onion and finely chop the garlic.

3 Coarsely chop the tomatoes.

4 Sauté the onion and garlic in olive oil in a skillet until soft.

5 Add beans, tomatoes, salt, pepper, and enough water to come half-way up the depth of the bean mixture.

6 Cover and simmer until tender, about 15 to 20 minutes, stirring occasionally.

7 Remove the lid, stir in the basil (fresh or dried) and simmer uncovered until sauce thickens, about 3 minutes.

Vary It! Stretch this dish and add flavor with a diced potato, microwaved until almost tender. Stir in the diced potato at the beginning, when starting to cook the beans. You can also use different herbs, like tarragon or herbes de Provence.

Simple Stir-Fried Asparagus

Prep time:	5 minutes
Cook time:	5 minutes
Yield:	4 servings

Start kids stir-frying with this simple Korean dish.
The chopping and stir-frying are minimal, and the sweet taste and crunchy texture please young palates. Unlike other types of Asian stir-fry, this recipe lacks the traditional chopped garlic, ginger, and sugar, and focuses instead on the crisp, clean

taste of the asparagus. To enhance the natural sugars in the dish, use the type of sesame oil found in the Asian products aisle — it's dark and aromatic because it's made from toasted sesame seeds. Hulled from actual pine cones, crunchy pine nuts can be found in health food, gourmet, Asian, Middle Eastern, Latin, and Italian markets. For an exceptional combination, balance the flavors of this dish with the contrast of plain steamed rice — see the Perfectly Nice Rice recipe in this chapter.

Do this first:

✔ Toast the pine nuts. Heat a dry skillet or wok on medium. Add 3 tablespoons pine nuts and cook, shaking the pan or stirring every 30 seconds to keep them from burning. The nuts will take about $2^1/_2$ minutes to cook. Be careful: nuts cook quickly and can go from toasty brown to burned in seconds. To save time in the future, toast large quantities of pine nuts and freeze them. (Larger quantities will take longer to cook.)

Ingredients and steps:

3 tablespoons toasted pine nuts
$1^1/_4$ pounds fresh asparagus
1 tablespoon sesame oil
$^1/_4$ cup low-salt chicken broth
1 tablespoon soy sauce

1 Coarsely chop the pine nuts and set aside. Or, place the nuts in a plastic bag and crush with the bottom of a jar.

2 Snap or cut off the woody section of the asparagus. See the "Snapping asparagus" sidebar, later in this chapter.

3 Cut the tender stalks on the diagonal into 1-inch lengths.

4 Heat the sesame oil in a medium skillet or wok. Add the asparagus and stir-fry over high heat for 1 to 2 minutes.

5 Add the broth and soy sauce and then cover and simmer on low until crisply tender, about 3 to 5 minutes, depending on the size of the asparagus.

6 Spoon the asparagus onto a platter. Continue cooking the sauce, uncovered, until it's reduced to about 2 tablespoons.

7 Pour the sauce over the asparagus. Serve the dish topped with the toasted pine nuts. Serve hot or at room temperature.

 Cooking times vary depending on the size of the asparagus. Pencil-thin asparagus needs barely any cooking time, while thicker asparagus takes longer. Don't overcook — the asparagus should be tender but still crisp when you bite into it.

Snapping asparagus

Snapping asparagus isn't an endangered species — it's a simple method for removing the tough, woody section from an asparagus spear, an especially fun task for very young children — although adults seem to get a kick out of it too.

To snap the woody end off an asparagus spear, hold the spear with both hands. Place one hand on the thick, stem end and the other about halfway down the stalk. Bend the stalk. The spear snaps in two where the woody, tough section begins. However, the inner part of the woody section is actually quite tender. Instead of snapping, you can also peel the fibrous outer section away with a vegetable peeler, leaving the tender area exposed.

Use the snapped ends and trimmings to make soup by freezing them in a resealable bag. After you accumulate several cupfuls, simmer them in chicken broth or water, and then strain to make a delicious soup base. Rice cooked in the asparagus broth tastes subtly sweet and wonderful.

Best-of-the-Dressed Salads

Did you know that people have been eating salads for centuries? Both before and after a meal, the Romans served lettuce sprinkled with *sal*, or salt, which is how the word *salad* evolved. Soldiers received a valuable salt allowance, known as a salarium, from which our word *salary* derives.

Every child can assist in salad making, from young ones who rinse and tear lettuce leaves, to older kids who slice vegetables, shred cheese, and cook pasta or grill chicken as hearty salad additions. The tart and tangy flavorings of salads like the ones in this section can add that perfect counterpoint to a meal — in flavor and in texture. Some of these recipes work even better as main course salads, either for lunch, brunch, or supper. For more salad dressing recipes to top a leafy green or chopped vegetable salad, see Chapter 20.

For best salad results, avoid drowning salads in dressings, and follow these tips:

    ✔ To keep a salad crisp before dressing it, place a damp paper towel on top and refrigerate as long as one hour.

- Potato, rice, pasta, and other grain salads absorb dressings best when warm (the opposite of leafy greens). For maximum flavor, dress them while warm, then chill. After chilling, taste these salads — you may need to refresh the flavors by adding more acid, like lemon juice or vinegar, and more salt.

- Young children can toss salads with less mess if you place the ingredients in a plastic bag. Seal and let the little ones gently shake.

- To keep salad dressing from sliding off lettuce, dry the leaves well. Use a salad spinner (shown in Chapter 3) or roll them in a dish towel and gently shake or pat them dry.

- Romaine lettuce has more nutrients than other varieties of lettuce; iceberg lettuce has the least. In general, dark green leaves are more nutritious.

- Break out of the lettuce rut by trying spinach, escarole, endive, watercress, arugula, and other greens in salads and sandwiches.

15-Minute Potato Salad

Prep and cook time:	15 minutes
Chill time:	30 minutes or more, if desired
Yield:	8 servings

Whip up a superb potato salad in minutes using a microwave oven. Older kids can cut the vegetables and cook the potatoes in the microwave, making this recipe entirely by themselves, while younger children can help by mixing.

The Grainy Mustard Sauce in Chapter 20 makes about $1^1/_2$ cups — but you only need $^1/_2$ cup for this recipe. You can make the sauce in advance or while the potatoes in this recipe cook (the sauce takes only 5 minutes to make). When you make the sauce, reserve $^1/_2$ cup for this recipe and refrigerate the remainder for another use. Look for seasoned rice vinegar next to regular rice vinegar in the Asian foods aisle.

Ingredients and steps:

1 pound red potatoes (about 3 to 4 medium)
$^1/_4$ cup seasoned rice vinegar
$^1/_4$ teaspoon salt
$^1/_2$ cup Grainy Mustard Sauce (see Chapter 20)
2 stalks celery
2 green onions
Freshly ground pepper

1 Cut the potatoes in half to keep them from rolling. Placing the cut side down, cut across the potatoes to make slices about $^1/_4$-inch thick.

2 Toss potatoes with seasoned rice vinegar and salt in microwave safe baking dish.

3 Cover with a microwave-safe lid or plastic wrap, leaving one corner slightly open for steam to escape. Microwave potatoes on high until tender when pierced with a fork, but not mushy, about 8 minutes, stirring halfway through.

4 While the potatoes cook, chop the celery and green onions. If you need to make the Grainy Mustard Sauce, do it now.

5 Toss hot potatoes with ½ cup of the Grainy Mustard Sauce, reserving any extra sauce for another use.

6 Stir in the celery, green onions, and pepper to taste. You can serve the salad now, but chilling for 30 minutes allows the flavors to blend. If desired, garnish with chopped celery leaves.

 Open the microwaved potato container with care to avoid steam burns. Point the lid away from you as you open it and wear oven mitts.

 # *Napa Chicken Salad*

Prep time:	15 to 20 minutes
Yield:	4 servings as a light meal, or 6 servings as a sandwich filling.

For best results, make this exceptional salad using the recipe for Succulent Chinese Chicken in Chapter 18. The moist, flavorful meat needs little mayonnaise, which is often used excessively in other salads to replace the moisture in dried-out chicken meat. Cook the Succulent Chinese Chicken one day and then morph it into this salad later in the week.

Do this first:

✔ Using clean fingers, shred enough Succulent Chinese Chicken meat to make 3 cups (or use other cooked chicken meat); young children are especially handy at shredding.

✔ Toast, skin, and coarsely crush enough hazelnuts to make ½ cup. (See Chapter 17 for information on toasting and skinning hazelnuts.)

✔ Stack about six napa cabbage leaves, or enough to make 3 packed cups when shredded. Cut across the leaves to make thin shreds. If the shreds are too long, cut them in half. (See the "Napa cabbage: Nifty and thrifty" sidebar, in this chapter.)

Ingredients and steps:

3 cups shredded, cooked chicken (about 3 breast halves)
3 tablespoons rice vinegar
3 green onions
3 tablespoons mayonnaise
3 cups packed shredded napa cabbage leaves (about 6 medium leaves)
$1/2$ cup toasted, coarsely crushed hazelnuts
Salt and freshly ground black pepper to taste

1 Place the chicken in a mixing bowl. Mix the vinegar into the chicken until absorbed.

2 Trim and diagonally slice green onions about $1/4$-inch wide. Add to the bowl.

3 Mix in the mayonnaise, napa cabbage, hazelnuts, salt, and freshly ground pepper to taste.

4 Taste to correct the seasonings. Add salt, vinegar, or mayonnaise as needed.

 # Spinach-Mango Technicolor Salad

Prep time:	5 minutes
Yield:	4 servings as a side dish

A no-flame, no-fire recipe

Fancy flower arrangements can't compete with the colors in this salad. The bright orange mango, green spinach, and red onion dazzle the eyes even before hitting the palate, and they're as rich in nutrients as they are in hue. Layer the ingredients in a large shallow bowl to show off their vibrant colors, and toss just before serving.

Do this first:

✔ If using non-washed spinach, rinse well and remove the stems. Dry before using.

✔ Peel and cut 1 small red onion in half across the diameter. Thinly slice into half-rings and cut the slices in half to form quarter-rings.

✔ Peel the skin from $1/2$ mango. Slice the flesh into bite-size pieces or wedges.

Ingredients and steps:

$^1/_4$ of a 10-ounce bag trimmed, pre-washed spinach (2.5 ounces), or equivalent fresh spinach

$^1/_2$ small red onion, thinly sliced into quarter-rings

$^1/_2$ mango, peeled and cut into bite-size wedges

$^1/_4$ teaspoon dried basil

2 tablespoons extra virgin olive oil

2 teaspoons cider vinegar

$^1/_8$ teaspoon salt or to taste

Freshly ground black pepper to taste

1 Place the spinach in a large salad bowl. Layer the red onions on top of the spinach. Mound the mango pieces on top in the center.

2 Crush the basil between your fingers and sprinkle on top of the salad. (At this point, you can cover and refrigerate the salad for up to 2 hours before serving.)

3 To dress the salad, top with the olive oil, cider vinegar, salt, and pepper. Toss the mixture well before serving.

Napa cabbage: Nifty and thrifty

For a nutritious kid-friendly vegetable, pick up a head of napa cabbage — its mild flavor appeals to more sensitive palates and doesn't give off a strong odor when heated. Found in most supermarkets, napa cabbage (or Chinese cabbage), comes in tight barrel-shaped heads and loose-headed varieties, both with crinkly, pale-green leaves and thick white ribs. Napa cabbage cooks quickly, can last two weeks in the crisper, and its small head is so compact that it may weigh as much as three pounds. It's an excellent source of vitamins C and A, fiber, potassium, and folic acid, and contains small amounts of calcium and iron. While much of it is indeed grown in Napa, California, the name is thought to derive from the Japanese word *nappa*, meaning *greens*. Slice it thinly for salads, soups, and stir-fry, and for Napa Chicken Salad and Hearty Wonton Soup. One large leaf shredded makes about 1 cup, tightly packed.

Surf's Up Seafood Salad

Prep time:	25 minutes, including making the dressing
Chill time:	2 hours
Yield:	6 servings (side dish) 4 servings (main course)

Frozen shrimp and peas retain their flavor and texture in salads better than most foods and make great time-savers — keep them on hand for emergency meals. Young children enjoy the seashells of this mildly-sweet, but sophisticated, pasta salad, which uses the Cool-as-a-Cucumber Dressing found in Chapter 20. Older kids can easily make this salad and dressing on their own with a parent's supervision.

Do this first:

✔ Peel and cook $^3/_4$ pound shrimp or use pre-peeled, cooked shrimp (defrost in the microwave, if frozen).

✔ Defrost $^1/_2$ cup frozen peas in a microwave until just thawed.

Ingredients and steps:

$^1/_2$ pound seashell pasta or similar pasta of choice
2 teaspoons salt
1 cup Cool-as-a-Cucumber Dressing (see Chapter 20)
$^3/_4$ pound peeled, cooked shrimp
$^1/_2$ cup frozen peas, cooked and cooled

1 Bring a large pot of water (about 4 quarts) to a boil. Add the salt.

2 When the water returns to a full boil, stir in the pasta. Boil until pasta is al dente, or tender but with a slight resistance when bitten, about 8 minutes.

3 While the water starts to boil and as the pasta cooks, make the Cool-as-a-Cucumber Dressing.

4 When the pasta is cooked, drain it in a colander in the sink. Don't rinse.

5 Toss the still-warm pasta with 1 cup of dressing, reserving the rest for another use (such as Grilled Velvet Chicken in Chapter 18). Stir in the shrimp and peas.

6 Refrigerate 2 hours or until well chilled. If the pasta seems dry, stir in some of the reserved dressing and adjust the seasonings as needed. To refresh the flavors, add a splash of rice vinegar just before serving. Serve chilled.

Vary It! Add cooked crab meat to the salad. Increase the vegetables by adding more peas or chopped bell pepper, carrot, celery, or radishes. If you have extra cucumber, dice it for garnish.

Yogurt-Waldorf Salad

Prep time:	20 minutes
Chill time:	20 minutes
Yield:	6 to 8 servings

A no-flame, no-fire recipe

This is a healthier variation of the famous Waldorf Salad, created in the 1890s at New York's Waldorf-Astoria Hotel. Made entirely without any type of cooking heat, it can be made by kids old enough to handle knives safely. (It does require advance preparation of the toasted hazelnuts, but you can make a batch ahead of time, as described in Chapter 17, and stash some in the freezer.) Serve this crunchy salad as an after-school snack, lunch, or side dish on a bed of lettuce. Kids love the cinnamon taste, and while I think it's perfect the way it is, you can always add a spoonful of honey for a sweeter touch.

Do this first:

✔ Toast and crush enough hazelnuts to make 1 cup, as shown in Chapter 17.

Ingredients and steps:

> 2 medium Granny Smith apples
> $^1/_2$ cup plain yogurt
> 1 cup chopped, toasted hazelnuts, or chopped walnuts
> 2 stalks celery
> $^1/_2$ pound red seedless grapes
> $^1/_2$ teaspoon cinnamon

1 Core and coarsely chop the apples into bite-size bits, about $^1/_2$ inch dice or smaller. Place in a medium mixing bowl.

2 Stir in the yogurt and hazelnuts.

3 Thinly slice the celery stalks, chopping up the leaves, and add the stalks and leaves to the bowl.

4 Slice the grapes in half. Add to the bowl.

5 Add the cinnamon and mix all ingredients well. You can serve it at this point, but chilling for 20 minutes blends the flavors better. This salad tastes best within 2 days of making; if it gets dry, add more yogurt.

Vary It! Raisins (being dried grapes) make lovely substitutes for fresh grapes, but add an extra spoonful of yogurt if you use raisins. Hazelnuts add a special, unique flavor to this salad, but you can also substitute walnuts or other favorite nut.

Meal Morphing: To meal-morph the main ingredients into a differently seasoned sandwich, prepare 1¹/₂ times the amounts of apple, yogurt, and hazelnuts in the recipe. At the end of Step 2 above, reserve ¹/₃ of the mixture and use it in the Hazelnut-Apple-Cheese Pockets in Chapter 17, starting with Step 2 of that recipe.

Soup, Soup, Beautiful Soup!

Cold for summer and hot for winter, the soups in this section make a complete meal with just some crackers, rolls, or cookie-cutter croutons. Add a side salad for extra greens and to balance the flavors of the meal.

4-Way Potato Soup

Prep time:	20 minutes
Cook and blend time:	25 minutes
Yield:	8 cups

Four, four, four soups in one! From a single basic recipe, you can turn this Basic Potato Soup into several hot or cold variations, each unique in taste, temperature, and texture. The core recipe comes together in 30 minutes and freezes conveniently, to adapt into a new soup at a later date. Rich and satisfying as they are, these soups are amazingly low in fat — they taste creamy but there's not a speck of cream in them. Leave the potato peels on: they add nutrients, enrich the flavor, and save on all that peeling time. (Be sure to wash the potatoes well.) Make these soups with a blender, handheld blender, or food processor.

Kids old enough to handle a knife can chop the vegetables. Younger children can open cans, measure ingredients, press the blender or processor buttons, and stir. Kids can also help prepare a green salad, toast, or hot rolls to round out any of these soups.

Basic Hot Potato Soup ingredients and steps:

    1 pound onions (2 large or 3 average)
    2 stalks celery
    1 tablespoon butter
    1¹/₂ pounds unpeeled potatoes (4 to 5 medium)
    2 cans (14.5 ounces each) low-salt chicken broth (or vegetable broth)
    ¹/₄ teaspoon white pepper, or to taste
    ¹/₂ teaspoon salt, or to taste
    Optional garnishes

1 Chop the onions and celery.

2 Place the butter in a large pot and melt over medium heat.

3 When the butter is melted, stir the onions and celery into the pot.

4 Increase the heat to medium-high. Cook the vegetables, stirring occasionally, until the onions become soft, about 7 minutes.

5 While the mixture cooks, coarsely chop the potatoes into 1-inch chunks.

6 When the onions are soft and translucent, stir in the potatoes, chicken broth, and pepper. Bring to a boil.

7 Cover the pot. Reduce the heat and simmer, stirring occasionally, until the potatoes are tender and can be easily pierced with a fork, about 12 to 15 minutes.

8 *Caution:* The soup is hot — only parents should proceed with this step: Puree the soup, ladling it into a blender or food processor (you may need to puree it in batches); or puree it in the pot with a handheld blender. *Note:* If you're making the Kielbasa-Vegetable Soup, don't puree completely — leave some chunks for texture and reserve 3 cups of this mixture and continue to puree the remaining soup.

9 Serve the soup hot. At this point, the soup tastes mild and comforting. It's not strongly flavored, but you can jazz it up with one of the garnishes or variations described below. Serve it with bread and salad for a balanced meal.

Garnishes suitable for Hot Potato Soup include nutmeg (just a dash), shredded cheddar cheese, chopped parsley or other fresh herb, crushed dried herbs like thyme or savory, and diced tomatoes or sun dried tomatoes.

This recipe makes about 8 cups. Freeze or refrigerate 3 cups for each of the variations below, which, when their ingredients are added, make about 4 cups or more per variation.

Vary It! Use 3 cups of the Basic Hot Potato Soup to make the following:

✔ **Cold Cucumber Vichyssoise:** Vichyssoise (VIH-shee-swahs) is a classic French cold soup made from potatoes and sour cream. The cucumber in this version lightens both the flavor and the texture. To make it, peel, seed, and chop 1 medium cucumber. Puree $1/2$ cup nonfat yogurt with the cucumber and 3 cups of Basic Hot Potato Soup. Chill. Garnish with chopped chives or green onions and a dollop of yogurt.

✔ **Cold or Hot Broccoli Soup (or Asparagus Soup):** Steam fresh or frozen broccoli until tender (from 10 ounces to 1 pound). Puree with 3 cups of Basic Hot Potato Soup. Add salt and fresh cracked pepper to taste. If serving hot, add a touch of nutmeg or grated cheddar cheese. If serving cold, stir in a dollop of yogurt or sour cream. For Asparagus Soup, substitute asparagus for the broccoli and proceed with the same steps.

✔ **Kielbasa-Vegetable Soup:** This soup has a pleasant, rustic texture if you leave some chunks in the Basic Hot Potato Soup, but a smoothly pureed base is fine too. Dice $1/2$ pound lowfat kielbasa or smoked sausage (such as a variety made with turkey). Set aside 2 cups mixed vegetables, such as diced zucchini, yellow squash, celery, shredded cabbage, corn kernels, cooked beans, carrots, sliced mushrooms, or other vegetables. Heat 2 teaspoons butter or canola oil in a medium saucepan, on high. Brown the kielbasa, vegetables and $1/2$ teaspoon of dried thyme, caraway seeds, or dried savory. Stir in 3 cups of Basic Potato Soup and add more chicken broth or water if the mixture is too thick. Season with salt and pepper to taste. Serve hot with hearty rolls.

Crock Pot Pizza Soup

Prep time:	15 minutes
Cook time:	4 hours in a slow cooker
Yield:	4 to 6 servings

Jean of San Antonio, Texas, has a passion — and a definite knack — for crock pot cooking. I adapted this dish from Jean's personal collection of recipes, ones frequently requested by her fellow teachers and busy parents. I have to admit I was skeptical when I first read it (thinking this dish may be too much like "kid-food" because it's so simple), but I'm pleased to report that it tastes great! a really satisfying soup for adults, young kids, and teenagers alike. This recipe makes seasoning a snap by using "Italian style" or "Italian recipe" canned stewed tomatoes, and canned fresh tomatoes packed with basil, garlic, and oregano — some of the quality time-savers available in cans today. A crock pot slow cooks this dish in just a few hours, but the variation at the end of the recipe gives instructions for stovetop cooking. (Flip to Chapter 14 for tips on using a crock pot.) Round out this meal with a simple salad and some breadsticks or focaccia (see Chapter 17).

Do this first:

✔ Slice enough mushrooms to make 3 ounces (about 1 cup), or use convenient pre-sliced mushrooms (you need half of a 6-ounce container). White button mushrooms, crimini, or portabella mushrooms all work well. Keep the mushrooms refrigerated until they're called for in the recipe.

✔ Grate enough Parmesan or mozzarella cheese to make $1/2$ cup; refrigerate until ready to serve.

Ingredients and steps:

3 links of turkey Italian-style sausage (about ^{2}/$_3$ pound)
1 teaspoon olive oil
1 medium onion
1 small green bell pepper
1 can (14.5 ounces) stewed tomatoes, Italian style
1 can (14.5 ounces) fresh diced tomatoes, Italian style
1 can (14.5 ounces) beef broth, or 2 cups fresh
1 cup sliced mushrooms (about 3 ounces)
1 teaspoon fresh oregano leaves (optional)
^{1}/$_2$ cup grated Parmesan or mozzarella cheese, or as desired

1 Remove the sausage from its casings.

2 Heat the olive oil in a non-stick skillet on medium-high heat. Add the turkey sausage, breaking it up with a wooden spoon.

3 While the sausage cooks, peel and chop the onion.

4 Chop the bell pepper into 1-inch chunks, discarding the seeds, membranes, and stem. Set aside.

5 When the sausage is half-cooked and breaks up easily into pecan-size chunks, stir in the onion. Cook, stirring occasionally, until the sausage is browned and the onion soft and cooked through.

6 Pour the mixture into a 3^1/$_2$ to 5 quart slow cooker.

7 Stir in the cans of stewed and diced tomatoes, beef broth, and the bell pepper.

8 Cook on low about 3^1/$_2$ to 4 hours, or until the bell pepper is just cooked through. Stir in the mushrooms and fresh oregano (if using) and cook another 30 minutes. (It doesn't hurt to cook the soup longer, but the longer bell pepper cooks, the softer it becomes.)

9 Serve in bowls, passing the grated cheese on the side.

Vary It! To cook on the stovetop, follow Steps 1 through 5 and combine the ingredients in Steps 6 and 7 in a heavy-bottomed pot instead of a slow cooker. Cover and simmer on low for about 45 minutes, stirring occasionally, or until the flavors come together. Stir in the ingredients in Step 8 and simmer another 10 minutes, or until the mushrooms soften. Serve as in Step 9.

Vary It! Instead of Italian sausage, add ^{1}/$_2$ pound lowfat pepperoni or smoked sausage directly to the crock pot, without precooking.

Hearty Wonton Soup

Prep time:	20 minutes
Cook time:	5 minutes
Yield:	4 hearty servings

The fresh chicken broth and cooked chicken in this soup are left over from the Succulent Chinese Chicken recipe in Chapter 18. If you don't have enough broth left over, supplement this soup with canned low-salt chicken broth. You can use canned broth for the whole amount, but the flavor just won't be the same. As another example of meal morphing — in which a leftover dish is reincarnated into something totally new and exciting — this soup makes you feel healthy just smelling it. It's hearty without being heavy and is as enjoyable in the summer as it is in winter.

Do this first:

✔ Make Succulent Chinese Chicken (see Chapter 18) one or two days before making this soup. Reserve and refrigerate the broth and at least 1 chicken breast half, or enough meat to make 1 cup, shredded. Remove any fat that has solidified on the top of the broth and discard.

✔ Shred enough cooked chicken meat to make 1 cup. Tear the pieces apart with clean fingers.

✔ This recipe calls for two green onions, each chopped differently. For the wontons, finely chop 1 green onion into small bits. For the soup, slice 1 green onion on the diagonal, into about $1/4$-inch-wide pieces.

✔ Shred enough napa cabbage to make 3 cups packed (about 4 medium leaves). For more on this vegetable, visit the "Napa cabbage: Nifty and thrifty" sidebar in this chapter.

Ingredients and steps:

For wontons:
  1 cup (about $1/8$ pound) ground turkey, chicken, or pork
  1 green onion, finely chopped
  1 teaspoon soy sauce
  1 teaspoon dry sherry
  $1/8$ teaspoon white pepper
  20 wonton skins
  1 small dish of water

For soup:
4 cups chicken broth (from Succulent Chinese Chicken)
3 cups packed shredded napa cabbage
$^1/_2$ teaspoon sesame oil
1 cup shredded cooked chicken meat
1 green onion, sliced on the diagonal
1 tablespoon toasted sesame seeds (see Chapter 17)

To make the wontons:

1 While you're filling the wontons, bring a large pot of water to a boil. Set out 4 large soup bowls.

2 Make the wonton filling: Mix the ground meat, finely chopped green onion, soy sauce, sherry, and pepper together to form a smooth paste.

3 Separate and place several wonton skins on a cutting board or sheet of waxed paper. Using 2 teaspoons or a teaspoon and a melon baller, scoop about 1 teaspoon of filling onto the center of each skin.

4 Dab your clean finger in water, then run it around 2 adjoining edges of each wonton skin to dampen. Do this to all the skins that you've set out.

5 Fold the wonton skins over to form triangles (see Figure 19-2). Press the edges firmly all the way around to seal. If edges don't seal shut, add more water. Set filled wontons aside (don't let them touch or they'll stick together). Repeat with remaining wonton skins until all are made.

6 Gently lower all the wontons with a slotted spoon into the boiling water, dropping them in successively one by one, so that they don't stick together. Boil until the meat is cooked and the wontons float; about 4 to 5 minutes.

7 Remove with a slotted spoon and distribute equally in the soup bowls (5 wontons per bowl), or drain in a colander.

To make the soup:

8 While the wontons cook, heat the chicken broth until boiling.

9 Stir in the cabbage and sesame oil. Cook for 1 minute, until the cabbage softens.

10 Ladle the soup evenly into the bowls. Garnish each bowl with equal amounts of chicken, green onions, and sesame seed. Serve hot.

Vary It! Add your favorite vegetables to the soup, like mushrooms, carrots, celery. For the wontons, replace $^1/_4$ cup meat with $^1/_4$ cup finely chopped vegetable. For egg-drop soup, rapidly stir one beaten egg into the hot broth — the egg cooks almost instantly into fine strands.

> Feathery light and crisp, seasoned wontons skins make easy meal accompaniments or crunchy lowfat snacks. Little ones especially enjoy scooping up peas and carrots into wonton cups, which are baked in a muffin tin.

Garlic Wonton Crisps and Cups: To make the cups, spray wonton skins on one side with nonstick spray. Dust with granulated garlic and salt. For flat wonton crisps, cook on a baking sheet in single layer at 400° for 4 to 5 minutes, until crisp, but not burned. Place single wonton skins in muffin cups and bake at 400° for 5 to 7 minutes. Cold wonton skins (not room temperature) work best for the cups, because the corners stand up better when baking.

Figure 19-2: Seal wonton skins with water, pressing firmly.

Wontons

Separate wonton skins and place on a cutting board. Scoop about 1 teaspoon of filling onto the center of each skin.

bullseye!

Dab your clean finger in water and run it around 2 adjoining edges to dampen.

Fold the skins over to form triangles.

Press the edges firmly all the way around to seal.

☆ Set the finished wontons aside. DON'T let them touch or they will stick together!

Watermelon Gazpacho

Prep time:	25 minutes
Chill time:	1 hour
Yield:	7 cups

In Andalusia, Spain's largest region, citizens refresh themselves by sipping on *gazpacho* (gahz-PAH-choh). Originally a cold soup of bread, olive oil, vinegar, water, and garlic, gazpacho dates back to Roman influence in the 17th Century. Later, field workers needing a modest lunch and instant relief from the fiery heat added tomatoes and peppers —arrivals from the New World — transforming it into today's classic red gazpacho. Many variations have evolved, including a white gazpacho made from almonds and melons. I selected the ultimate symbol of American summer, watermelon (which actually hails from Africa), to blend with colorful sweet peppers, tart green apple, tangy vinegar, and other ingredients for this unique mouthwatering heat antidote, rich in vitamins and virtually fat-free.

A food processor (or blender) makes fast work of this refreshing cold summer soup. (Remember that only parents should handle the blades of chopping appliances, but young kids can push the buttons and older kids can prechop the produce.) Keep a big bowl in the fridge for an instant snack or light lunch. (Because fresh foods vary in taste and beacuse chilling makes flavors less pronounced, be sure to always taste the soup before serving and adjust the vinegar and salt. The final soup should be a perfect blend of sweet and tart.)

Ingredients and steps:

$^1/_2$ red bell pepper
$^1/_2$ green bell pepper
$^1/_2$ yellow bell pepper (or more red or green pepper)
$^1/_2$ small red onion, peeled
4 green onions
$^1/_2$ bunch fresh cilantro (or parsley)
1 Granny Smith apple
$^1/_2$ small seedless watermelon, about 3 pounds
3 tablespoons cider vinegar
2 tablespoons balsamic vinegar
1 tablespoon extra virgin olive oil
1 teaspoon salt

1 Trim and cut the red, green, and yellow peppers and the red onion into large chunks, about 1 inch in size.

2 Trim the green onions and chop into 1-inch lengths.

3 Cut cilantro into 1-inch lengths.

4 Core the apple and cut into 1-inch chunks.

5 Place the peppers, red onion, green onions, and cilantro into the work bowl of a food processor. Pulse to coarsely chop them into small bits, but don't puree. Pour the mixture into a large bowl.

6 Process the apple into small bits and add it to the vegetables.

7 Scrape or cut out the watermelon flesh. Process in batches until pureed, emptying each batch into the bowl of vegetables.

8 Stir in the cider vinegar, balsamic vinegar, olive oil, and salt. Taste to correct the seasonings. Chill 1 hour before serving. (Start with well-chilled ingredients to cut the soup's chilling time in half.)

Vary It! For a spicier gazpacho, stir in 1 or 2 finely chopped jalapeño peppers or Tabasco sauce to taste. For a thicker gazpacho, soak 4 pieces sourdough bread (crusts removed) in water; squeeze the water out, process into fine bits, and add to the soup.

Chapter 20

Snacks, Sauces, Dressings, and Dips

In This Chapter

▶ Creating kid-friendly snacks without flame or fire

▶ Dipping into savory sauces

▶ Making dressings and salsas from fresh fruits and veggies

What did the mayonnaise say to the refrigerator?
Close the door, I'm dressing.

Munching, crunching, and between-meal treats help fuel growing bodies — and keep hungry parents from getting cranky. But what can you fix fast that's not fast-food? All age-groups can make these deliciously nutritious snacks for after-school, mid-morning, or for an emergency energy boost. Whether you call them sauces, dips, or dressings, these lively recipes have multiple uses, from perking up salads to topping pastas.

Snacks, Dippers, and Spreads

Take your taste buds around the world with these multi-cultural snacks. Look up each country on the globe to see where families like yours may be enjoying the very same treats.

Jamaican Sunshine Salsa

Prep time:	5 minutes
Yield:	3 cups

A no-flame, no-fire recipe

Savor the flavor of Jamaica, where allspice grows in abundance and seasons everything from the island's namesake dish, Jamaican jerk chicken, to desserts. While allspice sounds like a spice blend, it's actually an evergreen berry that naturally tastes like a mix of cinnamon, cloves, and nutmeg. European colonists named it allspice, but it's also known as *pimiento* (Spanish for "pepper") because it resembles black peppercorns. Allspice shines like the Jamaican sun in this simple salsa, a kid-friendly recipe that requires only simple chopping and mixing. Many of these ingredients are soft enough so that children who are ready to begin practicing their knife skills can cut and chop. For kids too young to work with knives, parents can chop and kids can mix.

Do this first:

- Peel, seed, and chop enough cucumber to make $1/2$ cup. (A melon baller makes quick work of seeding cucumbers.)

- Peel, seed, and chop the mango.

- Remove the outer papery skin from the red onion.

- Chop enough of red onion, red bell pepper, and green pepper to make $1/2$ cup of each. (These amounts are approximate — add more or less as you wish.)

Ingredients and steps:

1 peeled, seeded, and chopped ripe mango
$1/2$ cup peeled, seeded, and chopped cucumber
$1/2$ cup chopped red onion
$1/2$ cup chopped red bell pepper
$1/2$ cup chopped green pepper
1 teaspoon ground allspice
2 limes

1 Combine the chopped mango, cucumber, red onion, red and green peppers, and allspice in a small bowl.

2 Cut the limes in half and squeeze the juice into the mixture.

3 Stir to combine and serve as a fresh salsa with chips, or on cooked chicken, fish, or vegetables.

Vary It! Use papaya instead of mango. Add 1 tablespoon of chopped Asian-style pickled ginger for a livelier flavor, as described in the "Pretty-in-pink pickled ginger" sidebar, further on in this chapter. For a spicier salsa, add Tabasco or hot sauce.

Pretty-in-pink pickled ginger

Japanese or Chinese pickled ginger, which is more delicate than fresh ginger, brightens a dish with its crisp, clean, mild bite that's slightly sweet. Rice vinegar turns the paper-thin slices of fresh ginger a lovely pale pink. Chop pickled ginger into a fruit salad or salsa to sharpen the flavors. To cleanse the palate after fish or a spicy dish, skewer pineapple, fresh mint, and pickled ginger together and eat in one bite. Look for pickled ginger in the refrigerated section where wonton wrappers are sold or in Asian markets.

Faster-than-5 Black Bean Salsa

Prep time:	5 minutes
Yield:	2 cups

A no-flame, no fire recipe

Seasoned canned beans come to the rescue when fresh ingredients are hard to come by — or even when they're not. Serve this flavorful, mildly zesty salsa with nachos, chips, or on Mexican Fiesta Tacos (in Chapter 18). It takes less than five minutes to make, and kids can nimbly dish it up as a no-flame, no-fire after-school snack.

Ingredients and steps:

> 1 can (15 ounces) seasoned black beans, such as Ranch Style or other brand
> 2 green onions
> 1 lime
> $^1/_2$ teaspoon ground cumin
> $^1/_4$ to $^1/_2$ teaspoon dried oregano, crushed
> $^1/_2$ teaspoon red or green Tabasco sauce, or to taste

1 Pour the beans into a bowl.

2 Trim and chop the green onions, and add to the bowl.

3 Cut the lime in half and squeeze in the juice.

4 Stir in the cumin, oregano, and Tabasco. Taste and adjust the seasonings, as desired. If you have the time, allow 15 to 30 minutes for the flavors to blend. Serve at room temperature as a salsa.

Vary It! You can add other chopped fresh vegetables, such as red, yellow or green peppers, fresh tomatoes, jícama, jalapeño, cucumber, or red onion. To make an instant bean dip, mash the beans with 2 or 3 tablespoons sour cream before adding the vegetables.

Yo Quiero Taco Shells

Prep time: 5 minutes

Cook time: 12 to 15 minutes

Yield: 6 taco shells

Light because they're baked, not fried, these unusual taco shells look more like four-legged starfish, blooming flowers, or fanciful bowls than traditional shells do. You shape them by using an inverted muffin tin, gently nestling a softened tortilla in-between the muffin cups. The tortillas bake into an X-shape that looks like a four-pointed star, with a cup-like indentation in the center to hold the taco ingredients, surrounded by four points that stick out like handles. Make them in batches and reheat just before serving.

Also, unlike deep-fried shells that can splatter hot oil on tender skin, these baked shells are much safer for kids to make. Young children and school-age kids can moisten the tortillas, coat them with nonstick spray, sprinkle spices on them, and fit them in the muffin tin. Parents and older children can use oven mitts to move the pans in and out of the oven.

Ingredients and steps:

> 6 corn tortillas (6-inch diameter works best)
> Nonstick vegetable spray

1 Place a rack in the center of the oven. Heat oven to 375°.

2 While the oven is heating, soften the tortillas, according to the "Softening tortillas — without cracking up" sidebar, later in this chapter.

3 Place a standard-sized muffin tin (one that makes 12 muffins) upside down on the counter. Note that the 12 muffin cups point upward, with their bottoms raised up, leaving six vacant areas between them.

4 When the softened tortillas are cool enough to handle, lightly coat one side of each tortilla with nonstick vegetable spray.

5 Place a softened corn tortilla over one of the vacant areas of the muffin tin, coated side facing up. Gently poke the center down with your clean fingers, folding up the edges between the muffin cups as shown in Figure 20-1, forming an X.

6 Bake the tortillas for 15 to 20 minutes, until they reach desired crispness. (I prefer mine slightly chewy, so I remove them after 15 minutes, but cook them longer if you like them fully crisp). Serve hot.

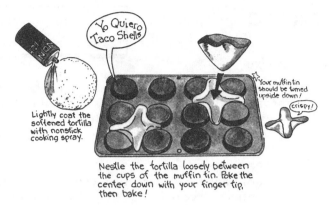

Figure 20-1:
Bake
tortillas on
an upside-
down muffin
tin to make
crispy
shells.

▸ When you have two tortillas in vacant areas next to each other, both of them will have edges that need to fold up into the same space, between the cups, as shown in Figure 20-1. Adjust them so that the folded edges lie next to each other, each pointing in the opposite direction, instead of being jammed up.

▸ You can also make these in advance and reheat for 3 to 5 minutes at 375° just before serving.

▸ To use as taco shells, fill the shells with your favorite taco fixings, or try the Mexican Fiesta Taco mix in Chapter 18.

Vary It! For a tastier shell, sprinkle on a pinch of ground cumin, chili powder, granulated garlic, salt, or other favorite spices before baking.

Softening tortillas — without cracking up

Unless they're very fresh, tortillas can crack and break when rolling into wraps or burritos. To soften corn or flour tortillas and to heat them, rub each tortilla on one side lightly with water. Using microwave-safe plates, place from 1 to 5 tortillas on a plate and cover with an inverted plate, resting slightly ajar so that steam can escape. Microwave on high for 1 to 2 minutes. Let the tortillas steam for a minute or so before lifting up the plate. (Be sure to use pot holders or oven mitts — the plates can get hot.) To cook more evenly, move the middle tortillas to the top and bottom of the stack, and microwave again another few seconds until the tortillas are soft and pliable. Serve them in the plates to keep the tortillas hot.

Tahini Sauce

A no-flame, no-fire recipe

Tahini, a thick, rich paste of ground sesame seeds, appears as a kitchen staple throughout the Middle East. Available in health-food stores and Middle Eastern markets, tahini (ta-HEE-nee) resembles natural peanut butter in that the oil often separates and rises to the top of the jar. Mix it up with a chopstick or fork before using.

Blend tahini paste with yogurt, garlic, and lemon juice to make this tart and tangy Tahini Sauce, served in countries from Greece to Iran as a dip, marinade, or dressing on salads, vegetables, and grilled meats.

Do this first:

- Squeeze enough lemon juice from 1 lemon to make 2 tablespoons
- If the tahini paste has separated in the jar, stir until blended before measuring.
- Peel 1 clove of garlic.

Ingredients and steps:

1 clove garlic, peeled
2 tablespoons fresh lemon juice
2 tablespoons tahini paste
$^1/_4$ cup plain yogurt
$^1/_8$ teaspoon salt

1a To make by machine: Place all ingredients in the work bowl of a handheld blender or mini-chopper and process until the garlic is chopped and all ingredients well blended.

1b To make by hand: Crush and finely mince garlic. Place in mixing bowl with lemon juice, tahini paste, yogurt, and salt; stir with a fork until well blended.

Vary It! This is a powerful flavor mixture — if the taste of the Tahini Sauce is too strong, thin the sauce down by adding yogurt or water to taste. Drizzle Tahini Sauce on cooked broccoli or zucchini instead of butter, or on lettuce and tomatoes as a salad dressing. But when making the Hummus recipe that follows, don't dilute the Tahini Sauce — the other ingredients in Hummus tone down the flavor.

Hummus

A no-flame, no-fire recipe

Prep time:	5 minutes
Yield:	2 cups

Hummus, one of the most famous and popular dishes of the Middle East, combines Tahini Sauce with mashed chickpeas. Serve hummus (HUM-muhs) on pita bread or celery sticks, or as a topping on the Grilled Meatless Mushroom Burgers in Chapter 18.

Ingredients and steps:

> 1 can (15 ounces) chickpeas (also known as garbanzo beans), rinsed and drained, or 1¹/₂ cups fresh, cooked chickpeas
> ¹/₂ cup Tahini Sauce (see previous recipe)
> ¹/₄ teaspoon ground cumin
> ¹/₄ teaspoon paprika
> ¹/₄ teaspoon salt
> Olive oil and paprika for garnish (optional)

Place all ingredients except the olive oil and paprika garnish in a mixing bowl. Mash to a chunky paste using a potato masher or fork. If desired, drizzle a spoonful of olive oil on top and dust with paprika before serving.

 Serve Yummy Hummies — hummus on raw vegetables or pita bread — as a nutritious after-school snack. Hummus also travels well in a thermal container with celery and carrot sticks, as a tasty lunch alternative.

Saturday Night Date Shake

Prep time:	5 minutes (or less)
Yield:	1 shake

A no-flame, no-fire recipe

Dates grow high in the palm trees of hot, dry deserts. The Middle East, Africa, and California produce these sweet, succulent fruits in abundance. Some of the best varieties are the Medjool and Barhi types, available at whole foods markets and specialty stores — their rich, buttery flavor surpasses the average dates sold in supermarkets and they are worth seeking out.

Loopy for labneh: Making yogurt cheese

Known across the Eastern Mediterranean as *labneh* (LAHB-neh), yogurt cheese makes a thick, rich, and refreshing lowfat substitute for cream cheese and sour cream. You can top it on toast with fruit preserves; spread it on sandwiches, crackers, or veggie sticks; or shape it into balls and roll in seasonings for a bite-size snack. Labneh thickens salad dressings with a pleasant tang and creamy texture (try the yogurt cheese variation of Home-on-the-Ranch Dressing in this chapter).

Remarkably easy for anyone to make, labneh is simply yogurt that is drained until thick. The liquid that drains out is called *whey,* the same part of the milk that separates out from the curds in other types of cheese making. You can save the whey and use it in bread recipes or add it to soups for a lemon-like tartness.

Be sure to use yogurt that has no gelatin in it (read the label to see if it does). If you're unsure, scoop out a spoonful from the container. If the hole starts to fill with liquid within 10 minutes, then the yogurt can be made into yogurt cheese.

To make 1¼ cups of yogurt cheese, all you need is:

☺ A bowl to catch the drained whey

☺ A colander or sieve to hold the yogurt as it drains

☺ Some cheesecloth or a large coffee filter to place in the colander or sieve

☺ 1 quart yogurt (regular, lowfat or nonfat yogurt)

Line a colander or sieve with 2 layers of cheesecloth or place a coffee filter in a sieve. Place the colander or sieve over a large bowl, as shown in the following figure. Dump the yogurt into the lined colander or sieve. Cover and refrigerate overnight, preferably for 24 hours. The liquid whey collects in the bowl; reserve it for another use or discard. Scrape the thickened yogurt into a container. It keeps 4 to 5 days refrigerated, covered.

Labneh

Making Yogurt Cheese

Buy pre-chopped dates, or chop your own from whole pitted ones. A blender or food processor works fine, but if you're chopping by hand, sprinkle a bit of powdered sugar on the date bits to keep them from sticking together.

This super-refreshing recipe takes only a few whirls in the blender and voilà! — you have a cold, frothy snack to refresh everyone from Saturday night party-goers to after-school athletes. For a post-practice pick-me-up, make it in batches for the whole team. You'll be an instant hit.

Ingredients and steps:

$1/3$ cup chopped dates
$1/2$ to $3/4$ cup milk (lowfat or according to preference)
$1/2$ pint vanilla frozen yogurt (1 cup)

1 Place the dates in the blender and blend until more finely chopped.

2 Add the milk and blend until mixed.

3 Blend in the frozen yogurt until frothy.

4 Pour into a tall, chilled glass and serve immediately. Don't be concerned if some small bits of dates remain — enjoy these tasty, chewy morsels with a spoon.

 Besides their high natural sugar content, dates are rich in potassium, a mineral particularly important for active athletes to balance the body's fluids. In fact, while bananas lead dates in vitamins C and A, dates have about twice as much potassium, three times as much iron, twice as much protein, and six times as much calcium as bananas. Snack on them whole, stuff them with almonds, or spread them with cream cheese for an instant, high-energy snack.

 # Lassi, Come Home!

A no-flame, no-fire recipe

Prep time:	5 minutes (or less)
Yield:	2 cups

Families in India combat the torrid, tropical heat by whipping up pitchers of ice-cold lassi (LAH-see), India's answer to our Western smoothie. These yogurt-blended drinks may be sweet with fruit juice or savory with spices, and may be as medicinal in their intent (depending on the herbs and spices used) as they are for pure refreshment. This recipe makes 2 cups, but if you visit an Indian home, don't be surprised to be served an entire jug of lassi just for yourself — in India's triple-digit temperatures, you'll eagerly welcome this generous gesture of cool — and cooling — hospitality.

Ingredients and steps:

    1 cup yogurt
    ³/₄ cup fresh or 1 can (5.5 ounces) pineapple chunks
    Juice from ¹/₂ lime, or to taste
    2 teaspoons honey or sugar, or to taste
    5 or 6 ice cubes

1 Place all ingredients in a blender. Blend until mixed. (If using canned pineapple, add some or part of the juice in the can, to taste.)

2 Serve immediately or chill until ready to drink.

Vary It! This recipe uses pineapple, but experiment with your own favorite fruits and flavorings. Indians may sweeten this drink with sugar, fruit, or fruit juice, and enhance the taste with cardamom, nutmeg, mint, or rose water, among others. For a savory lassi, blend in chiles, ginger, cumin, salt, or garlic. Use the Cool-as-a-Cucumber Dressing in this chapter as the basis of a refreshing non-fruit lassi, thinning it as desired with more yogurt or ice.

Dressings for Salads, Marinades, and Dunks

Got five minutes? Go beyond salads with these light, but vibrant, dressings — each can be made in minutes. Dunk crisp vegetable sticks in them, or marinate their flavor into boneless chicken breasts and shish-kebabs.

Home-on-the-Ranch Dressing

| **Prep time:** 5 minutes |
| **Yield:** 1³/₄ cups |

A no-flame, no-fire recipe

Most picky eaters will happily munch away on fresh vegetables — if accompanied by ranch dressing, either in a salad or as a dip. This healthy, home-made version tastes fresh, whips together almost instantly, and, unlike most bottled dressings, contains no preservatives or additives.

Youngsters old enough to chop can make this recipe by themselves, either by hand or with a mini-chopper or handheld blender. For little children, seal the ingredients in a screw-top jar and let the little ones shake, rattle, and pour.

Do this first:

✔ Using a mini-chopper, handheld blender, or knife, chop enough parsley to make 2 tablespoons.

✔ Trim and mince 1 green onion.

✔ Peel and mince 1 clove of garlic.

Ingredients and steps:

2 tablespoons chopped parsley
1 green onion, minced
1 clove garlic, peeled and minced
1 cup buttermilk
$\frac{1}{2}$ cup plain yogurt
2 tablespoons mayonnaise
1 teaspoon white or cider vinegar
$\frac{3}{4}$ teaspoon fresh ground black pepper
$\frac{1}{4}$ teaspoon salt

Combine all ingredients in the work bowl of a mini-chopper or handheld blender, or seal in a screw-top jar. Shake vigorously to mix. Dressing stays fresh, covered and chilled, for 1 week. Mix well again before using.

Vary It! For a thicker, tangier dressing, replace the yogurt with yogurt cheese. The "Loopy for labneh: Making yogurt cheese" sidebar in this chapter explains how easy yogurt cheese is to make.

If chopping with a machine, process the parsley first, then drop in the green onion (cut into 1-inch lengths), and the garlic clove. Add the remaining ingredients, and process until mixed.

Cool-as-a-Cucumber Dressing

Prep time:	5 minutes
Yield:	2 cups

A no-flame, no-fire recipe

This refreshingly light blender dressing, spiked with just a hint of sweetness, makes twice as much as needed for the Surf's Up Seafood Salad in Chapter 19, but it has so many other uses that it'll never go to waste. Use it to marinate the Grilled Velvet Chicken in Chapter 18. Serve it with vegetable sticks as a dip. Blend it with ice to make an Indian lassi, a yogurt-based drink perfect for hot weather (as explained in the Lassi, Come Home! recipe in this chapter). For other ways to use this versatile dressing, see the variations that follow the recipe.

Ingredients and steps:

$^1/_2$ pound cucumber (about $^1/_2$ large cucumber or 2 small)
2 green onions
$^1/_2$ cup nonfat or lowfat yogurt
$^1/_2$ cup reduced-fat cream cheese
3 tablespoons white distilled vinegar
2 to 3 tablespoons honey, to taste
$^1/_2$ teaspoon dried dill, crushed
$^1/_2$ teaspoon salt
$^1/_2$ teaspoon white pepper, or to taste

1 Peel, seed, and coarsely chop the cucumber into large chunks.

2 Trim and coarsely chop the green onions.

3 In a blender or food processor, process the cucumber, green onions, yogurt, cream cheese, vinegar, honey, dill, salt, and white pepper until pureed. The mixture will be light and airy, like the foam on an ocean wave. This dressing lasts four days in the refrigerator.

Vary It! For an Indian-inspired cold soup, mix 2 cups of the dressing with 1 cup of defatted chicken broth and serve chilled with fresh mint. For a healthy and refreshing summer drink and after-school snack, blend with ice. Pour it on grilled fish as a sauce, or serve instead of tartar sauce. Coarsely chop the vegetables, replace the dill with cilantro and add chopped chiles and tomatoes for a salsa. Toss it with melon balls for a fruit salad or as a dressing for a green salad.

Kiwi Vinaigrette

A no-flame, no-fire recipe

Prep time:	5 minutes
Yield:	¹/₂ cup

Cool, tangy, and slightly sweet, this bright green, naturally nonfat dressing makes an excellent dip for vegetables, chips, fruit, and for tossing on salad greens. Add ingredients in the order listed for easier measuring and mixing.

In this no-flame, no-fire recipe, younger children can safely peel the kiwi and cucumber with a vegetable peeler and measure ingredients. Children old enough to use a knife and work a mini-chopper can make this recipe by themselves, with parental supervision.

Do this first:

- Peel, seed, and coarsely chop enough cucumber to make ¹/₂ cup.
- Peel and coarsely chop 1 kiwi.

Ingredients and steps:

   ¹/₄ cup rice vinegar
   ¹/₄ teaspoon salt
   ¹/₂ teaspoon vanilla extract
   2 tablespoons pickled ginger
   2 teaspoons honey
   ¹/₂ cup peeled, seeded, and coarsely chopped cucumber
   1 kiwi, peeled and coarsely chopped
   Fresh ground pepper to taste

1 In the bowl of a mini-chopper or handheld blender, process the rice vinegar, salt, vanilla extract, pickled ginger, and honey.

2 Add and process the cucumber pieces into a mixture of liquid and small bits.

3 Add and process the kiwi pieces until just chopped — overprocessing crushes the seeds and darkens the mixture.

4 Add fresh cracked pepper to taste. Spoon on mild greens, fresh fruit, or as a sauce for grilled chicken, pork, or fish.

Vary It! Turn this dressing into a lively summer salsa by adding a spoonful or two each of chopped cucumber, tomatoes, and green onion, and chopped fresh chiles, to taste.

Cold and Warm Sauces

From crispy fish to oven-baked lasagna, these savory sauces make simple foods sparkle.

Grainy Mustard Sauce

Prep time:	5 minutes
Yield:	Makes about 1$^1/_2$ cups

A no-flame, no-fire recipe

You can make this zesty, all-purpose sauce with smooth mustard, but the coarse seeds in whole-grain mustard add texture and contrast. This sauce zips up the flavors of poached salmon, broiled or poached chicken, grilled meats, sliced tomatoes, celery sticks, and salad greens. Use $^1/_2$ cup to make the 15-Minute Potato Salad in Chapter 19.

Because this sauce requires no special equipment, appliances, or heat, kids old enough to handle measuring spoons and cups can make this sauce with just parental supervision. If parents cut the lemon in half, kids won't need knives, either.

Do this first:

✔ Squeeze 2 tablespoons fresh lemon juice from one lemon.

Ingredients and steps:

$^1/_2$ cup lowfat yogurt
$^1/_2$ cup mayonnaise, regular or lowfat
4 tablespoons coarse-ground Maille or Dijon mustard
2 tablespoons fresh lemon juice
2 teaspoons prepared horseradish (optional)
$^1/_8$ teaspoon salt, or to taste

1 In a small bowl, stir together all of the ingredients until they're blended.

2 Cover and chill until ready to use. It keeps in the refrigerator for up to 5 days.

Tangy Tartar Sauce

A no-flame, no-fire recipe

Prep time:	5 minutes
Chill time:	15 minutes
Yield:	1 cup

Like most things homemade, this bright and tangy tartar sauce beats any sauce from a jar, and kids can make it in minutes. Serve it with oven-fried Crunchy Fish Kisses in Chapter 18.

Do this first:

✔ Mince enough onion to make 2 tablespoons.

✔ Mince enough parsley to make 1 tablespoon.

✔ Squeeze 1 tablespoon fresh lemon juice from one lemon.

✔ If not using pickle relish, chop enough sweet pickles to make ¹/₃ cup.

Ingredients and steps:

¹/₃ cup sweet pickle relish, or chopped sweet pickles
¹/₃ cup regular or lowfat mayonnaise
2 tablespoons minced onion
1 tablespoon minced parsley
1 tablespoon lemon juice
1 teaspoon Dijon mustard
¹/₂ teaspoon prepared horseradish (optional)
¹/₈ teaspoon paprika

1 Mix all ingredients together.

2 Cover and refrigerate for 15 minutes before use to let the flavors blend.

3 Serve with your favorite fish, or as a sauce for fresh vegetables.

Vary It! Tartar sauce comes in two varieties: tart or sweet, depending on the type of pickle you use. If you prefer a less sweet version, use chopped dill pickle, or for variety, divide the basic sauce into two bowls and stir one of each type of pickle into each bowl. For extra zing, add chopped capers.

Chimichurri Sauce

Prep time:	5 minutes
Yield:	1¹/₃ cups

A no-flame, no-fire recipe

This sauce has rhythm! Make this parsley-laden Argentine sauce lickety-split using a handheld blender or mini-chopper (or a food processor or blender). Add a few minutes to the preparation time if you chop the ingredients by hand. This sauce is the traditional accompaniment to grilled steaks and sausages, but I find this pleasantly sharp sauce accents any meat, seafood, or chicken. Drizzle it on grilled vegetables for extra zing. Young kids can rinse and dry the parsley, push the buttons on the mini-chopper, and squeeze out the lemon juice.

Do this first:

✔ Rinse and squeeze-dry one bunch of parsley.

✔ Squeeze 2 tablespoons fresh lemon juice from one lemon.

Ingredients and steps:

8 cloves garlic
1 bunch parsley, rinsed and dried
²/₃ cup olive oil
4 tablespoons sherry wine vinegar (or red wine vinegar)
2 tablespoons fresh lemon juice (or more vinegar)
1 teaspoon salt
¹/₂ teaspoon freshly ground black pepper, or to taste

1 Peel the garlic. Chop the garlic in the work bowl of a handheld blender or mini-chopper.

2 Cut across parsley bunch to remove stems. Place parsley leaves in work bowl.

3 Add olive oil, vinegar, lemon juice, salt, and pepper on top of parsley, to weigh the parsley down for easier chopping. Cover work bowl with lid and pulse until mixed and finely chopped, but not totally pureed. Serve at room temperature.

Vary It! Replace half the parsley with fresh cilantro or mint. Stir a spoonful or two of the sauce into yogurt and make it into a dip. Use leftover (or fresh) Chimichurri Sauce as an excellent marinade for grilled chicken breasts and vegetables.

✔ The strength of this sauce depends on the amount of parsley you use, the size of the garlic clove, and the intensity of the olive oil and vinegar. Taste and adjust the seasonings as you prefer.

✔ Parsley has great flavor and is rich in vitamins A and C, so don't just use it as a garnish!

Young children can help measure and add the ingredients to the work bowl or blender, and they can push the buttons, but parents should always be the ones to handle the blades.

 ## Twice-as-Red Tomato Sauce

Prep time:	15 minutes, plus occasional stirring
Cook time:	40 minutes
Yield:	1 quart

This brilliant, crimson-colored sauce gets its color from red peppers and tomatoes, which together make it naturally sweet and flavorful but not at all spicy. Parents love it because it contains no oil or fat, and it's loaded with vitamins C and A. The pureed onion can't be seen or chewed, so that even onion-phobic kids can enjoy it. Use it on pastas, casseroles, and in Lazy, Crazy Lasagna (see Chapter 18).

Young chefs can practice their knife skills with this recipe. Because the sauce is pureed, the vegetables can be coarsely chopped, and it doesn't matter if they're not completely uniform in size. This is a simple recipe, but it does require some experience working with blenders or handheld blenders.

Ingredients and steps:

2 large red bell peppers, about 14 ounces
3 large cloves garlic
1 medium onion
$\frac{1}{2}$ cup chicken broth or vegetable broth
1 can (28 ounces) peeled, chopped tomatoes in juice

1 Remove the core and membrane from the peppers and discard.

2 Peel and trim the garlic and onion.

3 Coarsely chop the peppers, garlic, and onion.

4 Combine the peppers, garlic, onions, chicken broth, and tomatoes with their juice in a large pot or saucepan on high heat. (*Tip:* Deep sides keep the sauce from splattering.) Cover the sauce and bring to a boil.

5 Remove the cover, lower the heat and simmer, uncovered, stirring occasionally, until the vegetables are soft, about 25 minutes. Remove from heat and allow to cool slightly.

6 Blend the sauce until smoothly pureed. If using a handheld blender, insert the blending end directly into the sauce, as described in Chapter 14. If using a tabletop blender, blend the sauce in batches to prevent over-filling the blending container.

7 When all of the sauce is evenly pureed, boil uncovered, about 12 minutes, until reduced to about 4 cups ($^2/_3$ of the original amount). Taste the sauce — the flavors should be concentrated, not watery. Serve on pasta or in the Lazy, Crazy Lasagna recipe in Chapter 18. The sauce may be refrigerated until cold, and then frozen for later use.

When blending hot sauces, be careful not to burn yourself from the sauce or its steam. Let the sauce cool slightly first. Hold a folded kitchen towel securely on the blender lid to protect your hands from any heat and to keep the lid in place. Flip to Chapter 14 for more tips on working with blenders.

For easy cleanup, use a wire mesh splatter guard (shown in Chapter 3) to keep the sauce from splattering.

Chapter 21

Holiday Celebrations and Desserts

In This Chapter

▶ Creating festive holiday food gifts

▶ Making easy Mother's Day and Father's Day meals

▶ Whipping up Halloween, Valentine's Day, and birthday treats

What did the mama ghost tell the baby ghost when he ate too fast? Stop goblin your food!

Certain times of the year call for special indulgences. Parents love receiving gifts of food hand-made by their own kids, and a special Mom Day or Dad Day meal is better than any store-bought gift. Holiday recipes, like Spider Web Brownies and Cobblers for Gobblers, are so kid-friendly that even young preschoolers can join in on the fun. This chapter's fresh fruit desserts sparkle with cinnamon, nutmeg, and citrus, making festive and flavorful treats for every season and for every celebration, including the best one of all — your birthday!

Remember that the uncooked bacteria in raw meats, poultry, fish, and eggs can be harmful, so cook foods thoroughly before eating them. Use hot, soapy water to clean hands, cutting boards, knives, and counters to avoid cross-contamination. Follow the safety tips described in Chapter 8.

Neater beaters

When using an electric mixer, stop splatters from redecorating your kitchen by using a paper plate or a length of wax paper. Hold the plate or wax paper over the holes of the mixer and pop in the beater attachments. Drape the edges of the paper over the bowl while beating, and your counters and cabinets won't need cleaning.

Year-Round and Seasonal Treats

Make the mouth-watering desserts in this section with the best ingredients of all — Mother Nature's fresh fruits and sweet spices.

Carrot 'n' Spice Cupcakes

Prep time:	30 minutes, plus cupcake cooling time
Cook time:	25 minutes
Yield:	12 cupcakes

Moist and sweet from fresh carrots and applesauce, these cream cheese-frosted cupcakes include raisins, walnuts, cinnamon, and spice — a little bit of everything nice (including vitamins A and C!).

Do this first:

✔ Grate enough carrots to make 1²/₃ cups (about 3 large carrots).

✔ If the brown sugar is hard, soften it by microwaving on high until soft, checking it every 30 seconds.

✔ Separate the egg whites from the yolks. Reserve the yolks for another use.

Ingredients and steps:

Cupcakes:

    1¹/₄ cups all-purpose flour
    1¹/₂ teaspoons baking powder
    1 teaspoon ground cinnamon
    ¹/₂ teaspoon ground ginger
    ¹/₂ teaspoon baking soda
    ¹/₄ teaspoon ground nutmeg
    ¹/₈ teaspoon ground cloves
    ¹/₈ teaspoon salt
    ²/₃ cup brown sugar, packed
    2 tablespoons butter
    3 egg whites
    ¹/₃ cup unsweetened applesauce
    1 teaspoon vanilla extract
    1²/₃ cups grated carrots (about 3 large)
    ¹/₃ cup raisins, preferably golden raisins
    ¹/₂ cup chopped walnuts

    Cream Cheese Icing (see following recipe)

1 Heat oven to 350°. Line muffin tin with cupcake liners.

2 Combine the flour, baking powder, cinnamon, ginger, baking soda, nutmeg, cloves, and salt in a medium-sized mixing bowl.

3 Using an electric mixer, blend the brown sugar and butter together until creamy.

4 Beat in the egg whites, applesauce, and vanilla until blended.

5 Beat in the flour mixture, scraping the bowl down as needed. Stop beating when the ingredients are just combined.

6 Using a spatula, stir in the carrots, raisins, and walnuts until just mixed.

7 Pour the batter into the muffin cups, filling them about ³/₄ full.

8 Bake 25 to 30 minutes or until a toothpick inserted in the center comes out clean.

9 Cool the cupcakes on a rack.

10 Frost tops with Cream Cheese Icing.

Cream Cheese Icing

4 ounces regular or lowfat cream cheese, softened
2 tablespoons confectioners' sugar
1 teaspoon grated lemon zest (from 1 lemon — see Chapter 12 for tips on grating lemon zest)
2 tablespoons walnut pieces for garnish (optional)

1 Place the cream cheese, confectioners' sugar, and lemon zest in a mixing bowl.

2 Using a spatula, mash the ingredients together until well mixed and creamy.

3 Spread icing on cupcake tops.

4 Garnish with walnut pieces, if desired.

Icings that include dairy products must be refrigerated. Store cupcakes with cream cheese icing in the refrigerator; unfrosted cupcakes can be stored at room temperature.

Cobblers for Gobblers

Prep time:	25 minutes
Cook time:	30 to 35 minutes
Yield:	6 to 8 servings

This cobbler is easier than pie! A cobbler showcases the best fruit of any season under a layer of quick-to-fix biscuit dough. With a parent standing by, school-age children can make most or all of this recipe themselves — and how proud young chefs will be when you share this at your Thanksgiving table! To use different fruits, check out the variation ideas at the end of this recipe.

Ingredients and steps:

$1^1/_2$ pounds (about 3 large) Granny Smith or other tart green apples
3 cups (about a 12-ounce bag) fresh or frozen cranberries
$^1/_2$ cup sugar
$^1/_4$ cup all-purpose flour
1 teaspoon ground cinnamon
$^1/_2$ teaspoon ground nutmeg
Cobbler Dough (see following recipe)

1 To catch any drips from the cobbler, place a foil-lined baking sheet on a lower rack and arrange a rack in the middle of the oven above it.

2 Heat oven to 375°.

3 Lightly grease an 8- x 8-inch or 9- x 9-inch baking dish with nonstick spray or butter.

4 Core and chop apples into $^3/_4$-inch size pieces. (Peel only if desired — peeling isn't necessary. Wash apples well if not peeling.)

5 In a large mixing bowl, toss apples with cranberries, sugar, flour, cinnamon, and nutmeg. Let mixture sit 15 minutes.

6 Prepare the Cobbler Dough (see the following recipe).

7 When the filling has stood for 15 minutes, pour it into the prepared pan.

8 Drop the cobbler dough by spoonfuls on top, leaving space between the spoonfuls.

9 Bake 30 to 35 minutes, or until the fruit can be seen bubbling at the sides. Let cool slightly before serving.

Cobbler Dough

1 cup all-purpose flour
$^1/_3$ cup sugar
$1^1/_2$ teaspoons baking powder
$^1/_4$ teaspoon salt

$^1/_2$ stick (4 tablespoons) cold butter

$^1/_2$ cup buttermilk or milk, plus extra for browning

$^1/_2$ teaspoon vanilla extract

1 Mix the flour, sugar, baking powder, and salt together in a large mixing bowl.

2 Cut the butter into small pieces, about $^1/_2$-inch in size.

3 Add the butter to the flour mixture. Use a pastry blender (shown in Chapter 3) to cut and break up the butter into the flour mixture, until the pieces fall between the size of coarse breadcrumbs and small peas. If you don't have a pastry blender, use a dinner fork to break up the butter into the flour, but don't mash the mixture to a paste — it should stay crumbly. You can also rub the butter into the flour until the mixture resembles oatmeal.

4 Stir in buttermilk and vanilla and mix with a fork until the dough is moist and just comes together.

5 Top desired fruit fillings with cobbler dough and bake according to the recipe instructions. If desired, drizzle a spoonful or two of milk on top for browning.

Vary It! Cobblers can be made with almost any fruit. To adapt this cobbler, substitute 7 to 8 cups of fruit for the cranberries and apples. Play around with other spices, too, including ground ginger, cardamom, allspice, cloves, and pumpkin-pie spice blend. Keep the amount of flour the same, but you may want to adjust the sugar depending on the sweetness of the fruit, or you may wish to use brown sugar for a more pronounced flavor. In the summer, make peach and brown sugar cobbler, blueberry and lime juice cobbler, or a mixed berry cobbler. In spring, try rhubarb and strawberries. Winter cobblers can be made from a mix of canned and dried fruits, such as canned pears and dried blueberries. Go wild!

Tropical Berry Ambrosia

Prep time:	15 minutes
Cook time:	1 hour
Yield:	4 servings

A no-flame, no-fire recipe

According to Greek and Roman mythology, ambrosia — the food of the gods — was thought to give the gift of immortality. Here on earth, mere mortals create ambrosia from tangy oranges, sweet coconut, and other luscious fresh fruits. Rich in vitamin C and antioxidants, this brightly colored fruit salad tastes truly divine.

Any child old enough to peel and cut an orange can make this Tropical Berry Ambrosia as a dessert for the whole family. The salad keeps for several days in the refrigerator and can easily be made in larger quantities for entertaining at Easter, July 4th, and other holidays.

Do this first:

- Rinse the berries in a colander (in the sink) just before using. Remove any green leaves. Pat berries dry on paper towels.

- Peel 2 oranges by either cutting the skin off with a knife or by peeling it with your hands. Be sure to cut off any of the excess bitter white part (the *pith*) that lies below the skin.

Ingredients and steps:

2 pints fresh strawberries, rinsed and dried
6 to 8 ounces fresh blueberries, rinsed and dried
2 medium oranges, peeled
$3/4$ cup sweetened shredded coconut
1 lime

1 Slice the orange across into $1/4$-inch-wide slices, removing any seeds. (The slices should look like wheels with spokes.) Cut the lime in half. Cut the strawberries in quarters or bite-size pieces.

2 Place half the orange slices in the bottom of the serving bowl. Add a layer of coconut, then half the strawberries, another layer of coconut, half the blueberries and another layer of coconut. Squeeze half the lime over the top. Repeat the layers with the remaining ingredients, finishing the top layer with another squeeze of lime.

3 Cover and refrigerate for at least one hour. About 30 minutes before serving, stir the salad to mix the ingredients. Serve chilled. ***Tip:*** For a lovely presentation, bring the Tropical Berry Ambrosia to the table before mixing, so all can appreciate the colorful layers.

Vary It! The essential ingredients in Tropical Berry Ambrosia are oranges and coconut, but you can add any other combination of fruits. Pick whatever is fresh and in season — nectarines, blackberries, pineapple, and any kind of melon work well. If desired, garnish with fresh chopped mint leaves for a refreshing taste, or sprinkle some chopped toasted hazelnuts or almonds on top for extra crunch and flavor.

Don't wash berries until you're ready to use them — they start to mold in storage. Refrigerate fresh, unwashed berries layered between paper towels in an airtight container for two to five days.

Watermelon Ice

A no-flame, no-fire recipe

Prep time:	10 minutes before freezing, 10 minutes after freezing
Freeze time:	2 hours
Yield:	5 cups

Cool off your summer barbecues with a scoop of these icy watermelon crystals. This recipe is a great way to use up half of a small, seedless watermelon, like the remaining half of the one used in Watermelon Gazpacho (see Chapter 19). Parents and older kids can work the food processor in this recipe, and young children have plenty to do by scooping the melon flesh and scraping the ice crystals — the biggest tasks of this whole recipe!

Do this first:

✔ Cut a 6-pound seedless watermelon into two equal pieces and use ¹/₂ for this recipe, reserving the other half for another use.

Ingredients and steps:

> 1 lemon
> ¹/₂ of a small, seedless watermelon (about 3 pounds)
> 4 tablespoons confectioners' sugar (also called powdered sugar)

1 Cut the lemon in half. Squeeze the lemon juice from each half into the work bowl of a food processor (fitted with the metal blade). To keep the seeds from falling in, squeeze the lemons over a sieve.

2 Cut or scrape the melon flesh into chunks, discarding the rind.

3 Place the melon chunks in the work bowl.

4 Add the confectioners' sugar.

5 Cover the work bowl with the lid and process until the mixture is pureed.

6 Pour the mixture into a large, resealable freezer bag. Seal, pushing out as much air as possible, and place the bag flat in the freezer.

7 To serve, scrape the frozen mixture with a metal spoon, scooping the crystals into small bowls. If the mixture is too hard to scrape, microwave the sealed bag on high for about 30 seconds, or until crystals scrape easily.

> ✔ To hasten the freezing process, place the bag on a metal tray or pan (metal conducts cold more efficiently than air). Also, the mixture freezes faster in a flat, thin layer than in a thick layer.

    ✔ Every half hour or so, squish the bag to move the frozen crystals around. Kids make great squishers.

    ✔ To keep the scraped crystals from melting, place the bowls in the freezer until they're all filled and ready to serve. You may want to chill the bowls in advance.

Vary It! This basic recipe is just the beginning of refreshing variations like the following:

✔ Flavored garnishes add extra sparkle. Top the servings with fresh chopped mint leaves, or use dried mint leaves finely crushed between your fingers or in your palm. Or, sprinkle a dash of dried ground ginger (also called *powdered ginger*) on top.

✔ Substitute orange juice for the lemon juice, adjusting the sugar to taste.

✔ Before freezing, puree the watermelon mixture with a pint of rinsed raspberries or strawberries, adjusting the lemon juice and sugar to taste.

✔ Instead of scraping the mixture, freeze it in ice cube trays and add the cubes to fresh lemonade or other fruit drinks.

Irma's Spiced Nuts-to-You!

Prep time:	5 minutes
Cook time:	45 minutes, plus one day to season
Yield:	4 cups pecans

Irma Way, my mother-in-law, shares her recipe for these addictive pecans. Kids can wrap up these delicacies in fanciful containers, airtight tins, and colorful plastic wrap before giving them to a favorite parent, teacher, uncle, or aunt. Don't forget to include a ribbon, bow, and personal, handwritten greeting. Or, keep them around in a resealable bag for handy snacking and for sprinkling on salads.

Do this first:

✔ Separate one egg. Keep the white for this recipe and reserve the yolk for another use.

Ingredients and steps:

    1 egg white
    $^1/_2$ cup sugar
    1 teaspoon cinnamon
    $^1/_2$ teaspoon salt
    1 pound shelled pecan halves (about 4 cups)

1 Heat oven to 225°. Line a baking sheet with foil for easy cleanup.

2 Using an electric beater or wire whisk, beat the egg white until it forms a stiff peak when the beater or whisk is lifted up through it.

3 Lightly beat in sugar, cinnamon, and salt until just mixed.

4 Stir in pecans to coat.

5 Spread pecans in single layer on baking sheet.

6 Bake until pecans are dry to the touch, about 45 minutes. (It's okay if some pecans stick together.) Let the pecans dry on a baking sheet at room temperature for one day.

7 Store in an air-tight container; pecans will keep 3 to 4 weeks.

Except for using the oven, most kids can proudly prepare these nuts by themselves. Depending on their age, younger kids may need help with beating the egg white.

Lacy Angels with Dirty Faces

Prep time:	5 minutes
Cook time:	40 to 60 minutes
Yield:	8 dozen

Hold these cookies up to the light to see through them, like an angel's lace. The spices in these cookies give them a freckled or "dirty" look. For pale cookies, omit the spices — they'll taste just as good but different, more like rich butter cookies. Make the cookies in about 40 minutes using two baking sheets, or allow 60 minutes if using one baking sheet.

Do this first:

✔ Allow 1 stick of butter to soften by leaving it at room temperature for 30 minutes. You can also microwave it on low until it's soft, but not melted, checking every 3 minutes.

✔ Set up a mixer, either a stand-mixer with a mixing paddle and bowl or a hand mixer with beaters and a mixing bowl.

✔ If you're using one baking sheet, set the oven rack in center of oven. If you're using two baking sheets at the same time, evenly space two racks in the oven — one in the top third and the other in the bottom third of the oven.

Ingredients and steps:

1 stick unsalted butter (^{1}/$_2$ cup), softened
1 cup granulated sugar
1 egg
1 teaspoon vanilla extract
1^1/$_4$ cups quick oats ("1-minute oats")
^{1}/$_4$ cup all-purpose flour
^{1}/$_2$ teaspoon salt
1^1/$_2$ teaspoons baking powder
1^1/$_2$ teaspoons ground cinnamon
1^1/$_2$ teaspoons ground ginger
1 teaspoon ground cloves
1 tablespoon (approximately) confectioners' sugar for dusting (optional)

1 Heat oven to 325°.

2 Line one or two baking sheets with foil. Lightly coat with nonstick spray.

3 In mixing bowl, beat softened butter and granulated sugar until blended into a rough paste.

4 Beat in egg and vanilla until smooth.

5 Add oats, flour, salt, baking powder, cinnamon, ginger, and cloves. Beat just until the mixture combines evenly, stopping to scrape down the beaters and bowl with a spatula, as needed.

6 Drop dough by ^{1}/$_2$ teaspoons about 2 inches apart on the baking sheet(s). (See the "Dough-Droppin'" sidebar in this chapter for tips on getting the best results.) A 15- x 10- x 1-inch pan holds 15 cookies (3 columns of 5 cookies each).

7 Bake until the cookies flatten out, the edges are brown, and the centers no longer look doughy or raw, about 10 minutes. If baking two sheets at the same time, one may take longer to cook.

8 Remove cookies from oven and let cool, then lift off with fingers. They should be about 2 inches in diameter. If the cookies stick in the center, cook the next sheet of them a little longer.

9 Coat the foil-lined baking sheet(s) with nonstick spray again between each batch and continue baking cookies until the dough is used up.

10 Optional: To give the cookies a frosted, holiday look, hold a small sieve with a spoonful or two of confectioners' sugar over the cookies and gently tap once or twice, until they're lightly dusted in white.

Bake a single sheet of cookies first, let them cool, and then remove them to see if you're cooking them long enough. Of course, this also requires tasting them. (Any volunteers?)

Dough-droppin'

For best results, drop cookies should be uniform in shape and size, so that they cook evenly and so that large drops don't melt into the small ones. To accurately measure ¹/₂ teaspoon of cookie dough, use a melon baller, which is covered in Chapter 3. A 1-inch diameter melon baller holds ¹/₂ teaspoon exactly. Fill the melon baller with dough, level it with a small rubber spatula or teaspoon and spoon the dough onto the cookie sheet with the tip of the spatula or teaspoon. To measure 1 whole teaspoon of cookie dough, use a 1¹/₂-inch melon baller.

Spider Web Brownies

Prep time:	10 minutes
Cook time:	25 to 30 minutes
Yield:	16 brownies

Little goblin hands can stir up these devilishly-easy brownies anytime of year — in one pot — but piping a spider web on top transforms them into special Halloween treats. The trick is to squeeze melted peanut butter chips (or white chocolate chips) through a tiny hole in a resealable bag, as shown in the Easy, Squeezy Decorative Piping recipe. Add a few nuts, red hot candies, or other beasties in the web to enhance the eerie, but cheery, effect.

Stephanie Zonis, the "I Love Chocolate" columnist at the Global Gourmet Web site, created this recipe using nonfat liquid egg substitute (the type that comes in a little carton). The brownies are good warm or cold, but they only cut neatly when completely cooled. Cool before decorating, as well.

Do this first:

✔ You need ¹/₂ cup unsweetened cocoa powder for this recipe. If the cocoa powder is lumpy, sift before measuring, as described in the "Sifting for smoothness" sidebar.

Ingredients and steps:

   ¹/₂ cup (1 stick) unsalted butter
   1¹/₂ cups sugar
   ¹/₂ cup unsweetened cocoa powder (if lumpy, sift before measuring)

1 teaspoon vanilla extract
Pinch salt
$^1/_2$ cup liquid egg substitute
$^2/_3$ cup flour
$^1/_4$ cup peanut butter chips or white chocolate chips (For spider web decoration)

1 Heat oven to 350°. Position rack in center of oven.

2 Line an 8-inch square pan with aluminum foil, shiny side up (for easy clean up), and lightly coat with nonstick spray.

3 In a heavy-bottomed, 2-quart pot, melt the butter over very low heat, stirring occasionally. When the butter is melted, remove from heat.

4 Add sugar, cocoa powder, vanilla, and salt. With a large spoon, stir well (the mixture will look like wet sand at this point).

5 Stir in the egg substitute until well-mixed. Add flour; stirring only until combined.

6 Turn into prepared pan and spread evenly.

7 Bake 25-30 minutes, or until cake tester or toothpick inserted in center emerges with only a few moist crumbs clinging to it. Don't overbake.

8 Set pan on rack to cool. Cool completely before cutting or decorating. Store in an airtight container.

9 To create a spider web decoration, follow the Easy, Squeezy Decorative Piping recipe.

Easy, Squeezy Decorative Piping

To decorate Spider Web Brownies and other desserts, all you need is a saucepan, a small, heat-proof bowl, a plastic resealable bag, and scissors. You can use any kind of chocolate chips, but in this example, I use my favorite web-making material, Reese's peanut butter chips:

1 Fill a saucepan with 1 inch of water.

2 Set a heat-proof bowl over the saucepan, so that it rests on the rim of the pan. Pour $^1/_4$ cup peanut butter chips (or white chocolate chips) into the bowl. (You can use a double-boiler instead of saucepan and bowl if you have one.)

3 Turn the heat to medium-low. The heat from the water slowly melts the chips. Stir the chips until they're just melted and smooth.

4 Spoon the melted chips into a small, plastic, resealable bag. Snack size bags are perfect for this amount, but small sandwich bags work well too.

5 Seal the bag and push the melted chips into one of the bottom corners.

6 Carefully snip just the very tip of that corner — no more than $^1/_8$th inch across.

7 Gently squeeze the melted chips through the hole, piping a spider web design, as shown in Figure 21-1.

Figure 21-1:
Pipe melted peanut butter chips to make a spider web or other design.

Pipe several straight lines in a spoke fashion first and then pipe curves in between each straight line, radiating out in sequence from the center spoke to the edges.

Vary It! Use this same technique to pipe icings on cookies or cakes, and to decorate savory snacks with mayonnaise or softened cream cheese. Vary the size of the piping by cutting a larger hole, or poking the tip with a pin to make extra-thin lines. Snip points in the hole to make star-shaped piping. Squeeze the bag to make festive designs, such as a mayonnaise squirt on a slice of tomato or cocktail bread, or some chocolate stars on a white cupcake. Try the following decorative ideas for other holidays:

Sifting for smoothness

If your cocoa powder (or flour or any other fine, powdery ingredient) is lumpy, sift the powder to remove lumps and make a smooth mixture. Keep your work area neat and contain accidental spills by placing a baking sheet on the counter. Set a dry measuring cup in one end of the baking sheet and spread a length of waxed paper (or clean typing paper) next to it. Pour the cocoa powder through a sieve over the waxed paper, gently shaking until the cocoa powder falls though. If the lumps are particularly stubborn, use a spoon to help push the powder through the sieve. Pour the sifted cocoa powder into a dry measuring cup, until you measure the amount called for in the recipe. As long as the excess cocoa powder is still clean, you can return it to its original container.

Sifting for Smoothness!

✔ Pipe names on gingerbread cookies and use as seating tags at Christmas.

✔ Pipe star-shaped centers into deviled eggs for Easter or the 4th of July.

✔ Decorate Jack-O-Lantern faces on pumpkin pies.

✔ Make birthday cookies using animal-shaped cookie cutters. Pipe chocolate spots on leopards and stripes on zebras.

✔ Write "Be Mine" and "I Love You" notes on heart-shaped Valentine's Day cookies.

Special Celebrations

Everyone has at least one special day to celebrate. Team up to make these menus especially festive for Mom, Dad, or the kids.

Quick holiday kids' projects

Holidays are for the kid in you. Here are some festive holiday projects:

☺ **Make an edible dreidel by skewering a marshmallow and chocolate kiss on a toothpick.** A *dreidel* is a traditional spinning top for Jewish children at Hanukkah. Decorate the sides of the dreidel with tubes of colored frosting or pipe designs by following the recipe for Easy, Squeezy Decorative Piping.

☺ **Bake cookie-cutter shaped gingerbread or sugar cookies as strung ornaments.** Before baking, insert a section of paper straw into the tops of the cookies, making a hole. After baking, decorate and thread the cookies on ribbons and hang them as ornaments.

☺ **Don't have time to bake a gingerbread house?** Decorating the house is the most fun, so spend your time on that. You can make the frame from a milk carton or two (a gallon and a quart, for example) and some cardboard. Spread all surfaces with vanilla frosting, top with graham crackers, or decorate with gumdrops, cookies, candy canes, sprinkles, and so on.

Mother's Day candlelight dinner

She may be your Mom, but she probably still has a romantic streak in her, cleverly disguised beneath diapers and dishwater since the day you were born. Pamper her with this elegant but easy, meal, a little of her favorite music, dim lights, and tall candles on the table. Or, if she prefers, serve this as an elegant lunch or brunch, with fresh flowers to accent and brighten the table.

Kids, ask Dad or another adult for permission to use the kitchen and for their supervision while you cook. Because this meal can be made mostly in advance, Dad and the kids can entertain Mom with a few spins on the dance floor before serving, and everyone — from the littlest to the biggest family member — can pitch in to show Mom just how special she is!

Mother's Day menu

Make Mom a special meal using the following recipes:

✔ Shrimp Cocktail — Class on a Glass (Chapter 18)

✔ Cold Poached Salmon (Chapter 18)

✔ Grainy Mustard Sauce (Chapter 20)

    ✔ Cold Asparagus Spears — see the "No fuss, no muss: Tender, Sweet Asparagus" sidebar (Chapter 19)

    ✔ Orange-Scented Couscous (Chapter 19)

    ✔ Tropical Berry Ambrosia (in this chapter)

Cooking countdown

Except for the couscous, which takes only ten minutes to make, this elegant meal can be prepared early in the day, or as much as a day in advance — even by kitchen novices. On Mother's Day, allow 30 minutes for finishing up the preparation and serving the meal. She'll be so impressed!

The day before (or 2 to 3 hours before serving):

    ✔ Poach the salmon.

    ✔ Steam the asparagus.

    ✔ Mix the Grainy Mustard Sauce.

    ✔ Prepare the shrimp and cocktail sauce.

    ✔ Prepare the Tropical Berry Ambrosia.

    ✔ Cover and chill all of the above until ready to serve.

On Mother's Day

With most of the foods cooked in advance, you only need to do these few tasks before announcing your Mother's Day meal:

    ✔ Set the table. See Chapter 15 for tips on table settings.

    ✔ Start preparing the couscous about 30 minutes before serving.

    ✔ Bring the foods out of the refrigerator to come to room temperature about 20 minutes before serving.

To serve the meal:

    ✔ Start with the Shrimp Cocktail as the appetizer. Set the small bowls of shrimp cocktail on saucers. If you have small forks, set those out, too. After the appetizer has been eaten, remove the bowls and saucers.

    ✔ For the main course, serve the salmon and asparagus with the Grainy Mustard Sauce on the side. Serve the couscous as a side dish. For a special touch, garnish the salmon with fresh chopped parsley and lemon wedges, and sprinkle finely chopped green onions over the couscous.

    ✔ After the main course is over, remove the plates and serve the Tropical Berry Ambrosia in small plates or bowls. Your Mother's Day menu is now complete!

Father's Day summer picnic

Grab dad's sunglasses and cap — it's time to treat him to a relaxing, refreshing, fun-in-the-sun picnic. Take him to a park, a lake, or even your own backyard — wherever you go, this palate-pleasing picnic will tell him that he's the world's best dad!

Kids, be sure to get Mom's or another adult's permission to use the kitchen and ask for their supervision while you cook. You'll also need a good ice chest and ice if you plan to take this meal on the road.

For food safety tips, flip to Chapter 8 — and remember that to keep foods safe, keep hot foods hot and cold foods cold.

Father's Day menu

You can prepare and refrigerate this entire picnic the day before, or make it earlier that day. You can grill the chicken in advance and serve it cold, or if you're going to a place with a barbecue, grill it on the spot.

- ✔ Watermelon Gazpacho (Chapter 19)
- ✔ Grilled Ruby-Red Grapefruit Chicken (Chapter 18)
- ✔ Faster-than-5 Black Bean Salsa (Chapter 20)
- ✔ Cool-as-a-Cucumber Dressing with mixed greens (Chapter 20)
- ✔ Veggie sticks and chips for dipping in the salsa and dressing
- ✔ Peach (or other fruit) Cobbler (see Cobblers For Gobblers recipe in this chapter)

Cooking countdown

To make your Dad's Day menu taste its best, follow these simple tips:

- ✔ If you're making the full menu that day, allow at least 3 hours to prepare it. You may find it easier, though, to prepare at least the Watermelon Gazpacho and Cool-as-a-Cucumber Dressing a day in advance.
- ✔ Marinate the chicken overnight for better flavor.
- ✔ If you're making the Watermelon Gazpacho that day, start with cold ingredients to cut the chilling time down — this refreshing soup tastes best when it's very cold!

> ✔ Pack the salad greens in a plastic bag and the dressing in a screw top jar. Dress the salad just before serving by pouring a small amount of dressing in the bag, sealing the bag, and tossing the dressing until mixed.
>
> ✔ The cobbler tastes best if prepared that day. Or, if you make it the day before, cover with wax paper and foil, and chill until ready to serve.

A very merry birthday bash

Birthdays come but once a year — and everyone is entitled to go a little wild on their birthday! Kids deserve to pick out and even help make their own special treat. But parents should still try to offset all of that sugary ice cream and cake with some type of balanced meal, before the kids' little metabolisms have them bouncing off ceilings, windows, and walls.

Few children object to celebrating with pizza — especially if you include a dessert pizza! Start with a traditional savory pizza, letting kids add their own toppings, and then surprise the gang with a cookie-like pizza made of crunchy oatmeal, raspberries, and white chocolate chips.

For individual savory pizzas, prepare batches of Pizza-Pizza: Double-Dough (see Chapter 17). Make it a day in advance or a few weeks before and freeze. Set out a buffet of assorted toppings, so that kids can customize their own pizzas. To speed things along, shape and partially bake the crusts a day in advance (at 350° for about 5 minutes, or until slightly firm), and refrigerate. Then the kids can top and finish baking off the pizzas, cooking them at 450° for 5 to 10 minutes, or until the crusts brown. Parents of younger children should man the oven instead of the kids, and be sure to have plenty of oven mitts and potholders available for older kids.

Other than pizza, hamburgers, and hot dogs, what else do kids enjoy that isn't solid sugar? Most kids find pasta tasty, and a tray of Lazy, Crazy Lasagna (see Chapter 18) serves a crowd easily. Pasta shapes can also be big hits, especially wagon wheels, corkscrews, and seashells. Specialty food stores sell pastas in all sorts of fanciful shapes, like sailboats, cars, stars, carrots, and Christmas trees.

Birthday Cookie-Pizza

Prep time:	20 minutes
Cook time:	45 minutes

This variation on traditional, fruit-filled bar cookies looks more like a real pizza if you spread the top with a layer of sour cream and decorate it with fruity pizza fixings — fresh raspberries and blueberries, dried cranberries, or toasted coconut flakes. Young kids can help make it by measuring ingredients, cutting the butter into the flour, and decorating the surface, letting parents and older kids take the pan in and out of the oven.

Ingredients and steps:

$1^1/_4$ cups all purpose flour, preferably unbleached
$1^1/_4$ cups quick-cooking or old fashioned oats
$^1/_4$ cup granulated sugar
$^1/_4$ cup packed brown sugar
$^1/_2$ teaspoon baking powder
$^1/_8$ teaspoon salt
$^3/_4$ cup ($1^1/_2$ sticks) butter, well chilled
$^3/_4$ cup raspberry all-fruit spread (or preserves)
$^2/_3$ cup white chocolate chip pieces

1 Heat oven to 375°.

2 Tear off a length of foil about 18 inches long. Press the middle of the foil into an 8-inch round (or similarly sized) pan, covering the bottom and sides, and leave a few inches of foil overhanging at each end. (You use the overhanging foil ends later to easily lift the dessert pizza out of the pan after it has cooled.)

3 In a large bowl, stir together the flour, oats, sugar, brown sugar, baking powder, and salt.

4 Cut the cold butter into pieces, about $^1/_2$-inch-sized cubes.

5 Add the butter to the flour mixture. Use a pastry blender (shown in Chapter 3) to break up the butter into the flour mixture, until the pieces look like small peas. If you don't have a pastry blender, use a dinner fork to break up the butter into the flour, but don't mash the mixture to a paste — it should stay crumbly.

6 Reserve — $^3/_4$ cup of the flour mixture and set aside.

7 Press the remaining flour mixture into the bottom of the pan, shaping the edges a bit higher than the center, as if shaping a pizza.

8 Bake 10 minutes.

9 Being careful not to burn yourself on the pan, spread the raspberry all-fruit spread over the partially baked crust, but don't spread it all the way to the edge of the pan — leave a $^1/_4$ inch border or crust showing around the edge.

10 Sprinkle the white chocolate chips on top, leaving a $1/4$-inch border of raspberry spread showing.

11 Sprinkle the reserved flour mixture on top, this time leaving a $1/4$-inch border of white chocolate chips showing.

12 Bake until golden brown, about 35 to 40 minutes. Cool completely.

13 Using the overhanging foil ends, gently lift the cookie pizza out of the pan. Cut into wedges and serve with ice cream or frozen yogurt.

Vary It! After the cookie has cooled, you can make it look even more like a pizza by spreading $1/2$ cup reduced-fat sour cream over the top, allowing a border of raspberry spread to show through. Dot the surface with fresh or dried berries, sliced fruit, or toasted coconut. Cut into thin wedges and serve.

Part V
The Part of Tens

In this part . . .

1f you and your kids want to start cooking but aren't sure where to begin, flip through this part.

Here, you find the basic tools that your child will use most often. For kids ready and eager to jump into cooking, these chapters also identify recipes suitable for kids to prepare (with a parent's permission and supervision), whether they're in preschool, middle school, or high school.

Chapter 22

Ten Items for Your Kid's Cookware Kit

In This Chapter

▶ Giving kids their own kitchen equipment

▶ Providing a suitable space for kids to store their tools

Why did the lemon go to the doctor? Because it wasn't peeling well.

Give your young chef a set of simple cooking tools that's his or hers alone — and set aside a place to store them. Kids develop more pride in their cooking, take on kitchen and cleaning responsibility, and are more eager to cook when they have their own set of tools.

Kids' Tools and Pint-Size Equipment

You'll want to include these cookware essentials, shown in Figure 22-1, in your kid's cooking kit. You can find out more about them in Chapter 3.

- Measuring spoon set
- Measuring cups: one for dry ingredients and one for liquids
- Wooden spoon
- Apron or large T-shirt
- Potholders and/or oven mitts
- Small knife (plastic, paring, or as appropriate for your child)
- Vegetable peeler
- Safety scissors
- Rubber spatula
- Small cutting board

Figure 22-1:
Young chefs
cook best
with their
own
personal set
of tools.

A Place for Everything . . .

. . . and everything in it's place.

Young chefs need a permanent place for all these great tools, one that's easily accessible to the child and not stuck away in a closet, piled under stacks of linens or other things. For example, you can store your child's cookware in places like these:

✔ A large, lower kitchen drawer

✔ A portable tool kit

✔ A cardboard file box, known as a *banker's box*

✔ A plastic storage box, with handles and lid

Assemble the items first, adding any other equipment that you want your child to have (like the tools shown in Chapter 3). Then, choose a container with ample room, so that items aren't cramped and difficult to find.

Chapter 23

Ten "No-Flame, No-Fire" Recipes for Preschoolers

What do you get when you put three ducks in a box? A box of quackers.

Parents, cast yourselves as kitchen assistants and let your young chefs proudly command the kitchen with these simple, no-cook recipes. Little hands can easily make sauces, dips, and snacks — joyfully mixing, measuring, stirring, and whirring — while you assist by chopping and coaching along the way. And, as many parents have seen, kids are more likely to eat the meals and foods that they help create.

Little Dipper Recipes

Very young children are natural little dippers — they get a kick out of dipping veggie sticks, pretzels, lunchmeats — and especially their fingers — into sauces and dressings. Instead of using fat-laden bottled dressings and dips, let youngsters whip up their own healthier, home-made treats with these recipes:

✔ **Home-on-the-Ranch Dressing (Chapter 20):** Parents tell me that their kids eat anything — as long as it's dipped in ranch dressing. Parents can chop veggie sticks for dipping while the kids shake up this tasty treat.

✔ **Kiwi Vinaigrette (Chapter 20):** This tangy, no-fat dressing, rich in Vitamin C, is made with fresh kiwifruit and cucumber, and is sweetened with a kiss of honey. Serve it as dressing, dip, or salsa.

✓ **Cool-as-a-Cucumber Dressing (Chapter 20):** Let your little ones make a big batch of this multi-purpose sauce — it's refreshing as a dip, salad dressing, or marinade for Velvet Grilled Chicken (Chapter 18), and it's the basis of Surf's Up Seafood Salad (Chapter 19). Youngsters can easily peel and seed the cucumbers and do other major tasks, while parents take charge of the blender and chopping.

Five-A-Day Fixings

Kids can increase their own levels of fruits and vegetables in their diets with these seriously delicious — and nutritious! — sandwiches and snacks:

✓ **Hazelnut-Apple-Cheese Pockets (Chapter 17):** Pack your kid's lunchbox with a complete food pyramid: Kids can get their apple-a-day along with nutritious nuts and calcium-rich cheese and yogurt, packed as a spread in pita pocket bread. If you don't have hazelnuts, use pecans or almonds instead.

✓ **Tropical Berry Ambrosia (Chapter 21):** Kids love to color — watch them enjoy layering the strawberries, blueberries, and oranges in this summery salad, flecked with coconut snowflakes.

✓ **Lassi, Come Home! (Chapter 20):** Kids get the benefits of yogurt and fruit in this refreshing, tasty drink from India. It's not as thick as a smoothie and is light enough to be a perfect snack — one that won't interfere with lunch or dinner appetites.

✓ **Spinach-Mango Technicolor Salad (Chapter 19):** Rinse that spinach and tear it up! Tango with mango and then let's sup! Go team!

✓ **Green Eggs and Hamwiches (Chapter 17):** Parents need to hard-cook the eggs first, but after that, little hands can do the rest! Mashed avocado, full of nutrients, makes the eggs green.

✓ **Hummus Sauce on pita triangles (Chapter 20):** Parents love this Middle Eastern spread because it's full of nutrients. Youngsters love it 'cause it tastes great! Use it as a sandwich spread, or as a dip for chips and veggies.

✓ **Faster-Than-5 Black Bean Salsa (Chapter 20):** Vamanos niños! Let's go kids! — make this sassy salsa in less than 5 minutes for tortillas, tacos, or as a dip with chips! And it has almost no chopping involved — olé!

Chapter 24

Ten "I-Can-Do-It-Myself!" Snacks for Preteens

. . . .

In This Chapter

▶ Letting kids make their own snacks

▶ Taking cooking beyond cookies

▶ Giving kids nutritious recipes for sweets and treats

. . . .

What do cats call mice on skateboards? Meals on Wheels.

With just a parent's supervision, school-age kids can whip up their own after-school snacks, breakfast breads, and sweet treats. These recipes focus on building more nutritious fruits and vegetables into your fast-growing kids' diets. Help them see how many food groups they're getting in each recipe by using the Food Guide Pyramid in Chapter 4.

Snacks on the Sweet Side

Sweets aren't bad for you — as long as they're balanced in the overall diet and eaten in moderation. Pack a slice of these breads as a mid-morning snack, or serve the really sweet treats as special desserts. A glass of low-fat milk or slice of cheese adds calcium.

✔ **Gone Bananas Bread (Chapter 17):** The secret ingredient to this nutty bread is tart, dried cranberries. Preteens can make this moist, molasses-enriched bread for breakfast or snacks, and little brothers or sisters can assist the chef by mashing the bananas.

✔ **Happy, Dappy, Flappy Jacks (Chapter 17):** Who says that flapjacks are just for breakfast? Kids can cook up a batch of silver-dollar size pancakes, made with fruit and buttermilk, and freeze them in resealable bags for individual snacks. Or, keep a pitcher of batter handy in the fridge and pour just what you want when you want it.

✔ **Cobblers for Gobblers (Chapter 21):** A cranberry-apple cobbler for Thanksgiving is just the first step in fruit-baked desserts for kids to make. Children can create this incredibly delicious, but oh-so-simple, recipe in the fall, and improvise with their own flavors and fruits in summer and spring.

✔ **Spider Web Brownies (Chapter 21):** Need a chocolate fix? Invite your son or daughter into the kitchen for this one-pot recipe that takes just 10 minutes to mix. The kids can decorate it with a Halloween spider web (instructions included) or enjoy it straight from the oven.

✔ **Carrot 'n' Spice Cupcakes (Chapter 21):** Carrots make this cake better tasting and better for you than cake from a box. Children can practice their grating, mixing, and baking skills with this easy-to-fix recipe. Kids can make it for birthdays, too!

✔ **Irma's Spiced Nuts-to-You! (Chapter 21):** Sugar and spice and all things nice — that's what these pecans are made of! Children can bake them in batches as their personal holiday gifts for Grandma 'n' Grandpa — if their parents don't eat them all first!

Snacks on the Savory Side

Kids need to know how to make more than just cookies or cupcakes. These wholesome dishes show kids they can create recipes that can be served with real meals or as healthful snacks.

✔ **Frijole Fun-dido (Chapter 18):** Sit down with your kids and roll up this warm bean, cheese, and vegetable dip in soft, steamy tortillas. Enjoy it together as a balanced snack, a lunch, or a light supper.

✔ **15-Minute Potato Salad (Chapter 19):** Using a microwave, kids can make a really flavorful potato salad in just 15 minutes. They'll be awfully proud when you tell the others at the picnic who made it — and so will you!

✔ **Yogurt-Waldorf Salad (Chapter 19):** Apples, grapes, toasted nuts, and crisp celery mingle with tangy yogurt and a touch of cinnamon in this simple, five-step recipe. The whole family will love it — and kids don't need a stove or oven to make it.

✔ **Jamaican Sunshine Salsa (Chapter 20):** This recipe avoids fresh chiles, so kids won't hurt their skin or eyes with stinging chile oils. It does pack a perky punch though — brilliant with bright mango, pickled ginger, sweet red pepper, and seasoned with savory allspice. It's sweet, tart, and mild enough for even young, tender taste buds.

Chapter 25

Ten Favorite Recipes for Teens

> *Why did the student eat his homework?*
> *The teacher told him it was a piece of cake.*

*J*unior high and high school students are typically very image and body conscious — and today's kids are more health-savvy than ever. Soon, they'll be moving away from home, off to college or jobs. Don't let them cut the apron strings without first giving them a solid foundation in making tasty, balanced meals all by themselves. With a solid recipe repertoire, they'll never be forced to survive on fast-food or costly takeout. Awesome!

Having Your Pizza — and Eating It Too!

Teenagers need food — constantly! Adolescent eating machines can break out of the fast food habit but still enjoy their favorite meals — including pizza, burgers, and fries — with these nutritious but flavor-packed recipes.

✔ **Capture the Flag Pizza (Chapter 18):** Quite possibly the world's favorite food, pizza is one recipe everyone should know how to make! Teenagers can discover how great a homemade pizza — even one that's not dripping in oil or pepperoni — can taste.

✔ **Yo Quiero Taco Shells (Chapter 20) and Mexican Fiesta Taco Mix (Chapter 18):** Teenagers take to terrific tacos in hasty, tasty time. After pizza, Mexican food deserves top billing as a family favorite. Scoop up seasoned taco filling, savory with corn and other vegetables, in crispy taco shells — baked using a muffin tin!

- **Grilled Meatless Mushroom Burgers (Chapter 18):** Burgers, the national food of America, don't have to glisten with fat to taste great. These giant mushroom burgers are lean and meaty tasting — without the meat. Young folks will be delightedly surprised at how great these burgers taste — grilled like a regular hamburger. Way cool!

- **Everyday Oven Fries (Chapter 19):** What's a burger without fries? Kids (and parents) devour these crispy oven-fried potatoes almost before they come out of the oven. The secret? Thin slices, high heat, and just a tad bit of oil for flavor. Great taste and no guilt — enjoy them every day!

- **Saturday Night Date Shake (Chapter 20):** After-school athletes and active teens need extra potassium and liquids. Refuel the whole team with this cold, frothy treat made from frozen yogurt, buttery sweet dates, and low-fat milk. It's a natural dessert that's rich in potassium, iron, calcium, and other nutrients. What'll they cheer? Yum!

Main Courses and Side Dishes

By the time kids are old enough to drive, they should be able to cook a complete meal for themselves. These recipes are simple enough for even younger teenagers to make, and busy parents can appreciate being treated to a well-made, tasty meal that's balanced and nutritious.

- **Tortelloni Toss (Chapter 18):** No one complains about this one-pot, 20-minute meal that uses plump, stuffed tortelloni (the big brothers of little tortellini). It's also a great starter recipe for any kid learning to cook, because it's so simple, yet satisfying — a real treat to eat!

- **2-Bucket Batch of Oven-Fried Chicken (Chapter 18):** Kids will say "Tastes like Shake 'n' Bake — and I helped!" Actually, this crispy, seasoned skinless chicken tastes better, and teens can do more than help — they can make it themselves for the whole hungry gang. They'll eat it all up! No frying, no mess, no skin — no guilt!

- **Lazy, Crazy Lasagna (Chapter 18):** Teenagers may say that they're too busy to cook — but they can save time with this lasagna by not cooking the noodles first. An extra ladle of naturally fat-free sauce is enough to cook the noodles as they bake. And it tastes terrific.

- **Surf's Up Seafood Salad (Chapter 19):** Be cool as a cucumber with this pasta and shrimp salad, laced with a creamy cucumber dressing and bright green peas. Take it to the beach, the boat, the patio, or leave a bowl in the fridge for an instant snack.

- **Crock Pot Pizza Soup (Chapter 19):** A hearty soup for pizza lovers! This super-easy crock pot soup has all the flavor of pizza — but it takes only 15 minutes of hands-on preparation and almost no chopping. Serve it with pizza breadsticks (see Chapter 17).

Appendix
Additional Resources

• •

What did the hungry computer eat? Chips — one byte at a time.

For more information on cooking — especially with kids — try the following:

- ✔ Start by logging onto `www.cookingwithkids.com` on the Internet. Web sites come and go every day, but at this site, I've compiled recipes and tips on safety, meal planning, and other information — updated to keep you current.

- ✔ Log onto the Global Gourmet, at `www.globalgourmet.com`. The Global Gourmet brings you the world on a plate, with daily recipes, cultural tidbits, and cooking tips. America Online members can use keyword **GG** to get there.

- ✔ Mollie Katzen (the award-winning author who wrote the foreword to this book) presents a wealth of delicious and nutritious recipes to boost your fruit, grain, and vegetable intake, along with advice for vegetarian diets, time-saving tips, and excerpts from her books (including her award-winning children's cookbook, *Pretend Soup and Other Real Recipes*) at `www.molliekatzen.com`.

- ✔ The Vegetarian Resource Group (VRG) is a non-profit organization dedicated to educating the public on vegetarianism. They publish the *Vegetarian Journal,* cookbooks, pamphlets, and article reprints. Contact them at (410) 366-VEGE, or at `www.vrg.org`.

- ✔ Connie Evers (the registered dietitian profiled in Chapter 2) publishes *How to Teach Nutrition to Kids* and the accompanying Leader/Activity Guide, written for teachers and homeschoolers. It's available at (800) 291-6098 in the U.S. or at (503) 524-9318 in other countires. For families interested in healthier eating, her Nutrition for Children Web site is located at `www.nutritionforkids.com`, where you can also subscribe to her free e-mail newsletter, *Feeding Kids: News & Views on Child Nutrition*.

- ✔ To find a farmers' market in your area, log onto `www.ams.usda.gov/farmersmarkets/`, published by the U.S. Department of Agriculture. Type in your city and the nearest markets in your area appear, with dates and times of operation.

✔ To find cooking school teachers and community colleges that offer kids' cooking classes, ask a local cookware store (some even schedule their own cooking sessions). If you have trouble finding classes in your area, the International Association of Culinary Professionals (IACP) has members who offer classes for kids and adults. Call them at (800) 928-IACP in the U.S., or (502) 581-9786, or e-mail them at iacp@hqtrs.com. The Shaw Guides to Cooking Schools, at bookstores or online at www.shawguides.com, also lists cooking schools.

✔ The American Institute of Wine and Food (AIWF) sponsors Days of Taste, a nationwide program that takes kids from the classroom to chefs' kitchens and farmers' markets. For more information, phone (800) 274-2493 or (415) 255-3000, or e-mail aiwfmember@aol.com.

✔ Ask local chapters of the 4-H Club, the Girl and Boy Scouts, and local church groups whether they offer programs for kids and cooking.

✔ Visit your public library, museums, and bookstores for books, videos, and CD-ROMs devoted to food, cooking, and world cultures.

✔ Television cooking programs air regularly on public broadcasting stations and such cable channels as the Food Network, Discovery Channel, The Learning Channel, and others. Check out www.globalgourmet.com for a listing of local airtimes.

✔ Many catalogs specialize in kitchen tools and ingredients, some at discount prices, including:

- A Cook's Wares sells cookware and supplies at reasonable prices. Call (800) 915-9788 (in the U.S.) or (724) 846-9490, or visit their Web site at www.cookswares.com.

- The Baker's Catalog sells equipment and ingredients for home bakers. Call (800) 827-6836 (U.S. only) or (802) 649-3881, or visit their Web site at www.kingarthurflour.com.

- Chef's Catalog sells cookware and small appliances. Call (800) 338-3232 (U.S.), or visit their Web site at www.chefscatalog.com or on America Online at keyword **CHEFS**.

- Kitchen Glamor sells affordable cookware. Call (800) 641-1252 in the U.S.

- Penzeys Spices imports spices and seasonings from around the world and sells them in small and bulk quantities at reasonable prices. Call (414) 679-7207 or visit them at www.penzeys.com.

- Professional Cutlery Direct, PCD, sells knives, cookware, and chef's clothing at sizable discounts. They're especially knowledgeable and helpful about cutlery. Call (800) 859-6994 in the U.S. or visit their Web site at www.cutlery.com.

- Sur La Table sells cookware and small appliances in their stores and in their catalog. Call (800) 243-0852 in the U.S.

- Williams Sonoma sells premium cookware in their stores and catalog. Call (800) 541-2233 in the U.S.

Index

Playing games is really fun...
The Dummies Way™!

Pressman®
©1998 Pressman Toy Corporation, New York, NY 10010

Crosswords For Dummies™ Game
You don't have to know how to spell to have a great time. Place a word strip on the board so that it overlaps another word or creates a new one. Special squares add to the fun. The first player to use up all their word strips wins!
For 2 to 4 players.

Trivia For Dummies™ Game
You're guaranteed to have an answer every time! Each player gets 10 cards that contain the answer to every question. Act quickly and be the first player to throw down the correct answer and move closer to the finish line!
For 3 or 4 players.

Charades For Dummies™ Game
Act out one-word charades: when other players guess them, they move ahead. The special cards keep the game full of surprises. The first player around the board wins.
For 3 or 4 players.

...For Dummies and The Dummies Way are trademarks or registered trademarks of IDG Books Worldwide, Inc.

Discover *Dummies*™ Online!

The *Dummies* Web Site is your fun and friendly online resource for the latest information about *...For Dummies®* books on all your favorite topics. From cars to computers, wine to Windows, and investing to the Internet, we've got a shelf full of *...For Dummies* books waiting for you!

Ten Fun and Useful Things You Can Do at www.dummies.com

1. Register this book and win!
2. Find and buy the *...For Dummies* books you want online.
3. Get ten great *Dummies Tips*™ every week.
4. Chat with your favorite *...For Dummies* authors.
5. Subscribe free to *The Dummies Dispatch*™ newsletter.
6. Enter our sweepstakes and win cool stuff.
7. Send a free cartoon postcard to a friend.
8. Download free software.
9. Sample a book before you buy.
10. Talk to us. Make comments, ask questions, and get answers!

Jump online to these ten fun and useful things at **http://www.dummies.com/10useful**

For other technology titles from IDG Books Worldwide, go to
www.idgbooks.com

Not online yet? It's easy to get started with *The Internet For Dummies®*, 5th Edition, or *Dummies 101®: The Internet For Windows® 98*, available at local retailers everywhere.

Find other *...For Dummies* books on these topics:
Business • Careers • Databases • Food & Beverages • Games • Gardening • Graphics • Hardware
Health & Fitness • Internet and the World Wide Web • Networking • Office Suites
Operating Systems • Personal Finance • Pets • Programming • Recreation • Sports
Spreadsheets • Teacher Resources • Test Prep • Word Processing

IDG BOOKS WORLDWIDE BOOK REGISTRATION

We want to hear from you!

Register This Book and Win!

Visit **http://my2cents.dummies.com** to register this book and tell us how you liked it!

- ✔ Get entered in our monthly prize giveaway.

- ✔ Give us feedback about this book — tell us what you like best, what you like least, or maybe what you'd like to ask the author and us to change!

- ✔ Let us know any other ...*For Dummies*® topics that interest you.

Your feedback helps us determine what books to publish, tells us what coverage to add as we revise our books, and lets us know whether we're meeting your needs as a ...*For Dummies* reader. You're our most valuable resource, and what you have to say is important to us!

Not on the Web yet? It's easy to get started with *Dummies 101*®: *The Internet For Windows*® *98* or *The Internet For Dummies*®, 5th Edition, at local retailers everywhere.

Or let us know what you think by sending us a letter at the following address:

...*For Dummies* Book Registration
Dummies Press
7260 Shadeland Station, Suite 100
Indianapolis, IN 46256-3945
Fax 317-596-5498

BESTSELLING
BOOK SERIES